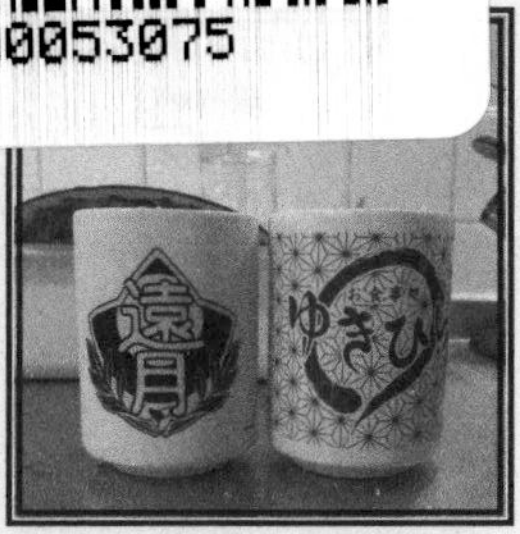
遠月
ゆきひ

Yuto Tsukuda

Bit by bit, I've finally acquired a taste for coffee, so someday, I want to become an adult who can brew a proper cup of both tea and coffee.

Shun Saeki

I've yet to catch this little guy sleeping, so my wife snapped this picture for me of him napping.

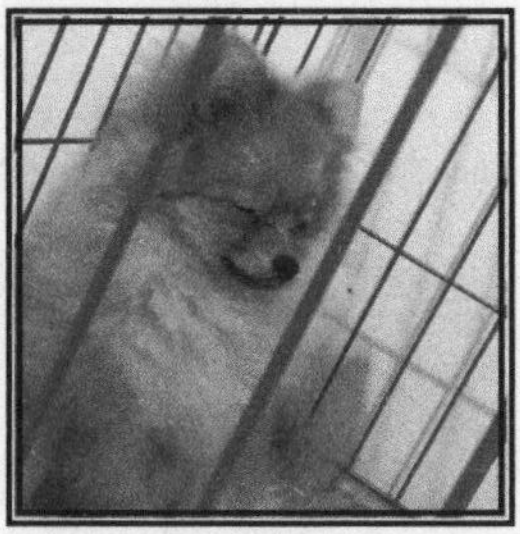

About the authors

Yuto Tsukuda won the 34th Jump Juniketsu Newcomers' Manga Award for his one-shot story *Kiba ni Naru*. He made his *Weekly Shonen Jump* debut in 2010 with the series *Shonen Shikku*. His follow-up series, *Food Wars!: Shokugeki no Soma*, is his first English-language release.

Shun Saeki made his *Jump NEXT!* debut in 2011 with the one-shot story *Kimi to Watashi no Renai Soudan*. *Food Wars!: Shokugeki no Soma* is his first *Shonen Jump* series.

Food Wars!
SHOKUGEKI NO SOMA

Volume 23
Shonen Jump Advanced Manga Edition
Story by Yuto Tsukuda, Art by Shun Saeki
Contributor Yuki Morisaki

Translation: Adrienne Beck
Touch-Up Art & Lettering: James Gaubatz, Mara Coman
Design: Alice Lewis
Editor: Jennifer LeBlanc

Printed in the U.S.A.

Published by VIZ Media, LLC
P.O. Box 77010
San Francisco, CA 94107

10 9 8 7 6 5 4 3 2 1
First printing, April 2018

www.viz.com

Food Wars!

SHOKUGEKI NO SOMA

WILDERNESS PIONEER

Original Creator:
Yuto Tsukuda

Artist:
Shun Saeki

Contributor:
Yuki Morisaki

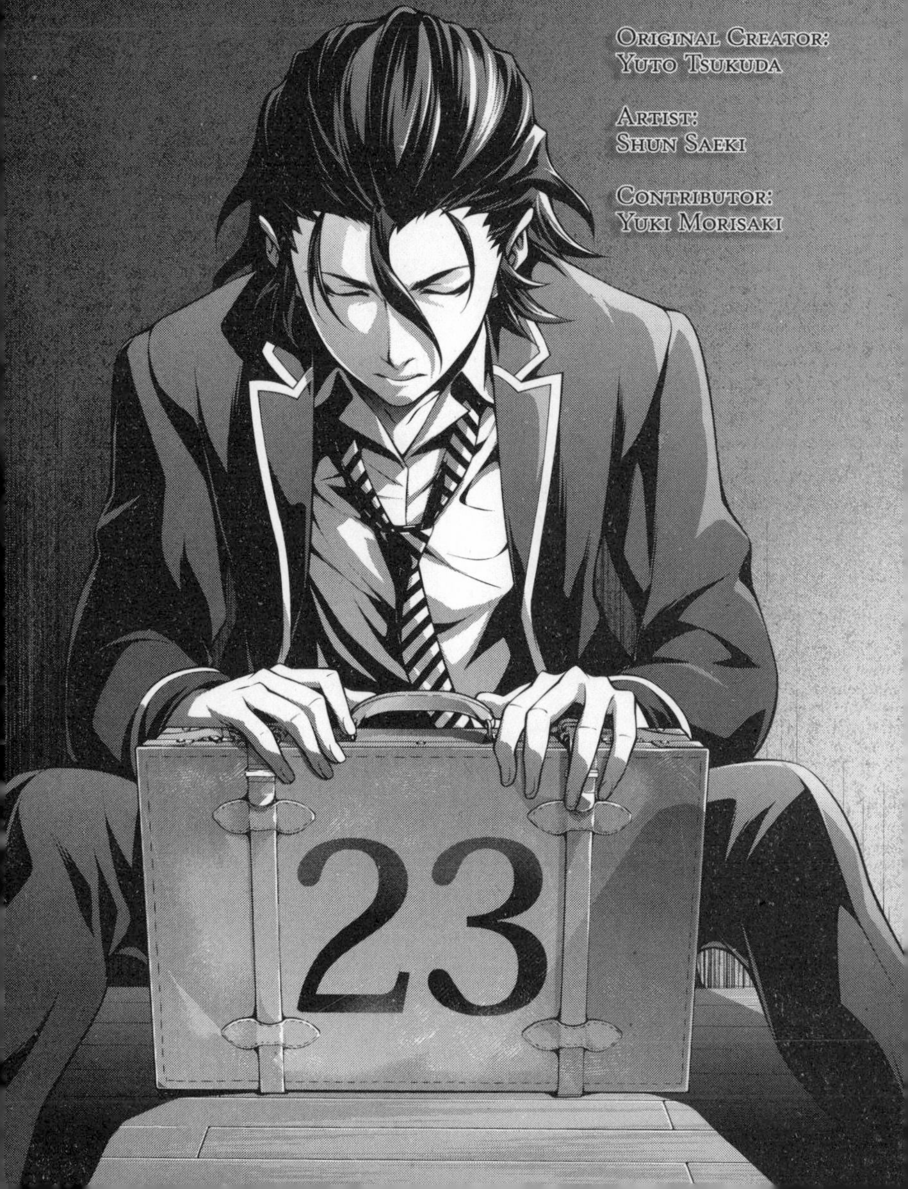

23

CHARACTERS

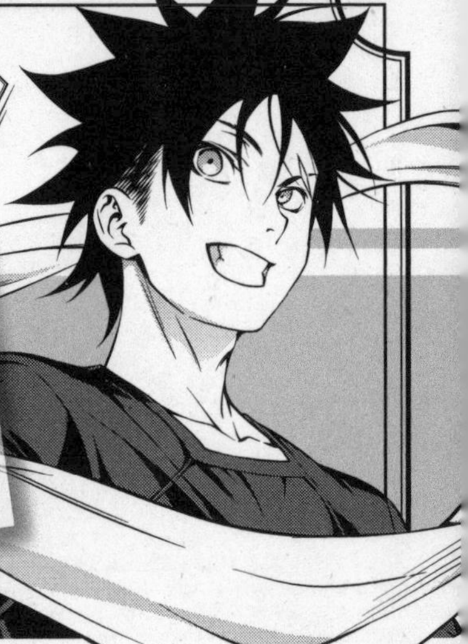

SOMA YUKIHIRA First Year High School

Helping out at his family's restaurant since he was little, Soma trained as a chef with the goal of someday surpassing his father. Out of junior high, he's suddenly sent off to culinary school. He's skilled, but sometimes invents questionable new recipes.

Shokugeki no SOMA

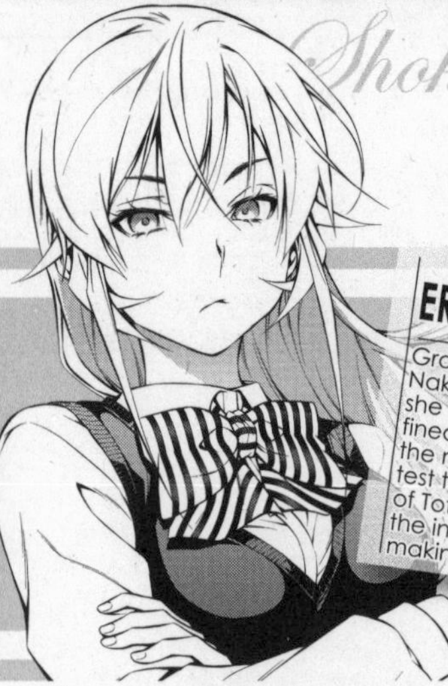

ERINA NAKIRI First Year High School

Granddaughter of Senzaemon Nakiri, dean of the Totsuki Institute, she has a sense of taste so refined, famous restaurants across the nation come to her to taste test their dishes. She is a member of Totsuki's Council of Ten Masters, the institute's highest decision-making student body.

STORY

Soma grew up helping to cook at his family's restaurant, Yukihira. But one day his father enrolls him in Japan's premier culinary school, the Totsuki Institute. Having met other students as skilled as he is and with similar goals, Soma has grown a little as a chef.

During stage three of the advancement exams, Soma faces off against new Council of Ten ninth seat Akira Hayama in a bear-meat shokugeki. Hayama, who only agreed to join Central as a way to save the Shiomi Seminar, makes Southern-fried bear, earning rave reviews from the three judges. Burning with a desire for payback over his loss in the Fall Classic, Soma pours everything he has into his dish, a bear menchi-katsu hamburger steak. Will he emerge the victor? And what of the other resistance members' battles with the council?

Shokugeki no SOMA

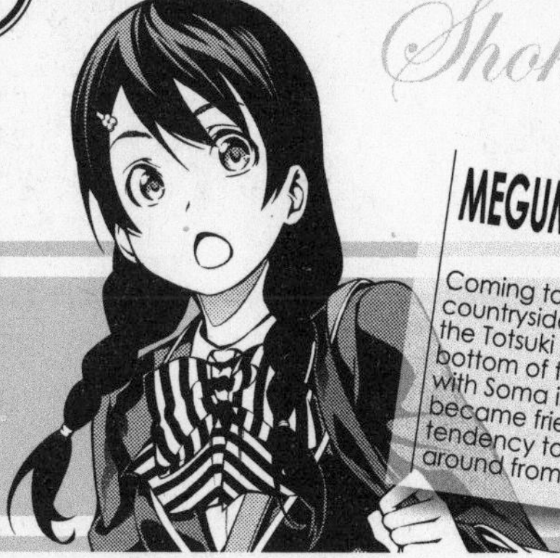

MEGUMI TADOKORO First Year High School

Coming to the big city from the countryside, Megumi made it into the Totsuki Institute at the very bottom of the rankings. Partnered with Soma in their first class, the two became friends. However, he has a tendency to inadvertently yank her around from time to time.

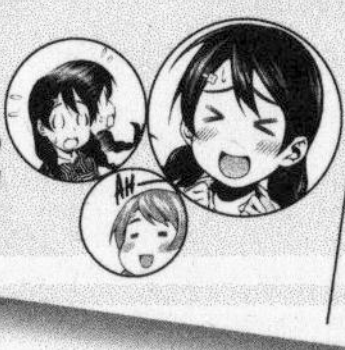
AH

ALICE NAKIRI First Year High School

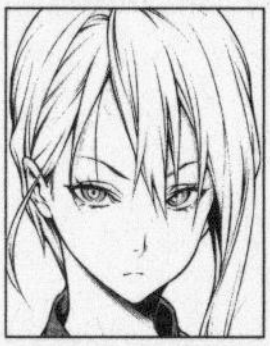

Erina's cousin, she has spent much of her life overseas with her parents learning cooking from a scientific perspective through molecular gastronomy.

RYO KUROKIBA First Year High School

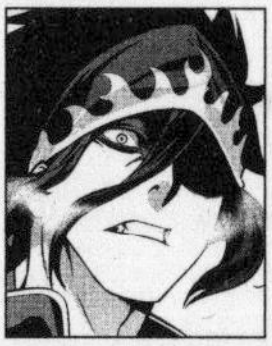

Alice's aide, he specializes in powerful, savory seafood dishes. His personality changes drastically when he puts on his bandanna.

TAKUMI ALDINI First Year High School

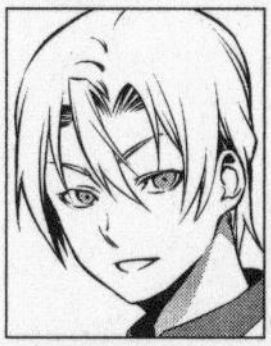

Working at his family's trattoria in Italy from a young age, he transferred into the Totsuki Institute in junior high. Isami is his younger twin brother.

AKIRA HAYAMA First Year High School

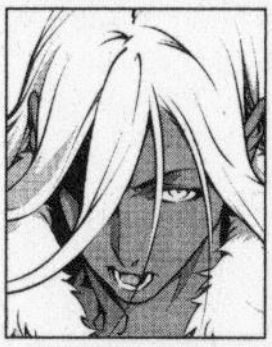

With his inhumanly sharp sense of smell, he's a master of manipulating fragrance. After joining Central, he was given the ninth seat on the Council of Ten...

RINDO KOBAYASHI Third Year High School

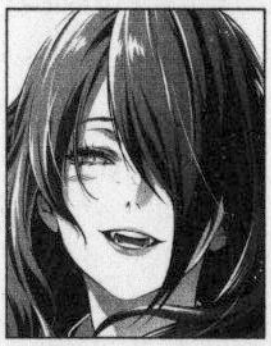

The current second seat on Totsuki's Council of Ten, Rindo is friendly, sociable and easygoing. Having met Soma during the Moon Festival, she finds him intriguing.

AZAMI NAKIRI

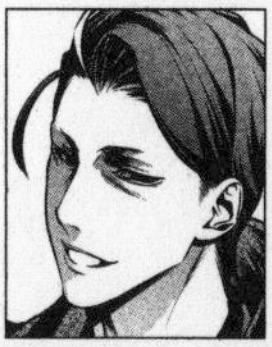

Erina's father, he convinced over half the Council of Ten to back him in staging a coup to take control of the institute, forcing former dean Senzaemon Nakiri into retirement.

Food Wars!
SHOKUGEKI NO SOMA

23

Table of Contents

191 PASSIONATE BATTLE'S END
IF ALL YOU DO IS STARE AT YOUR OWN PLATES ALL DAY LONG...
...THE ONLY THING THAT WILL LOOK BACK AT YOU IS YOUR OWN UNCHANGING REFLECTION.

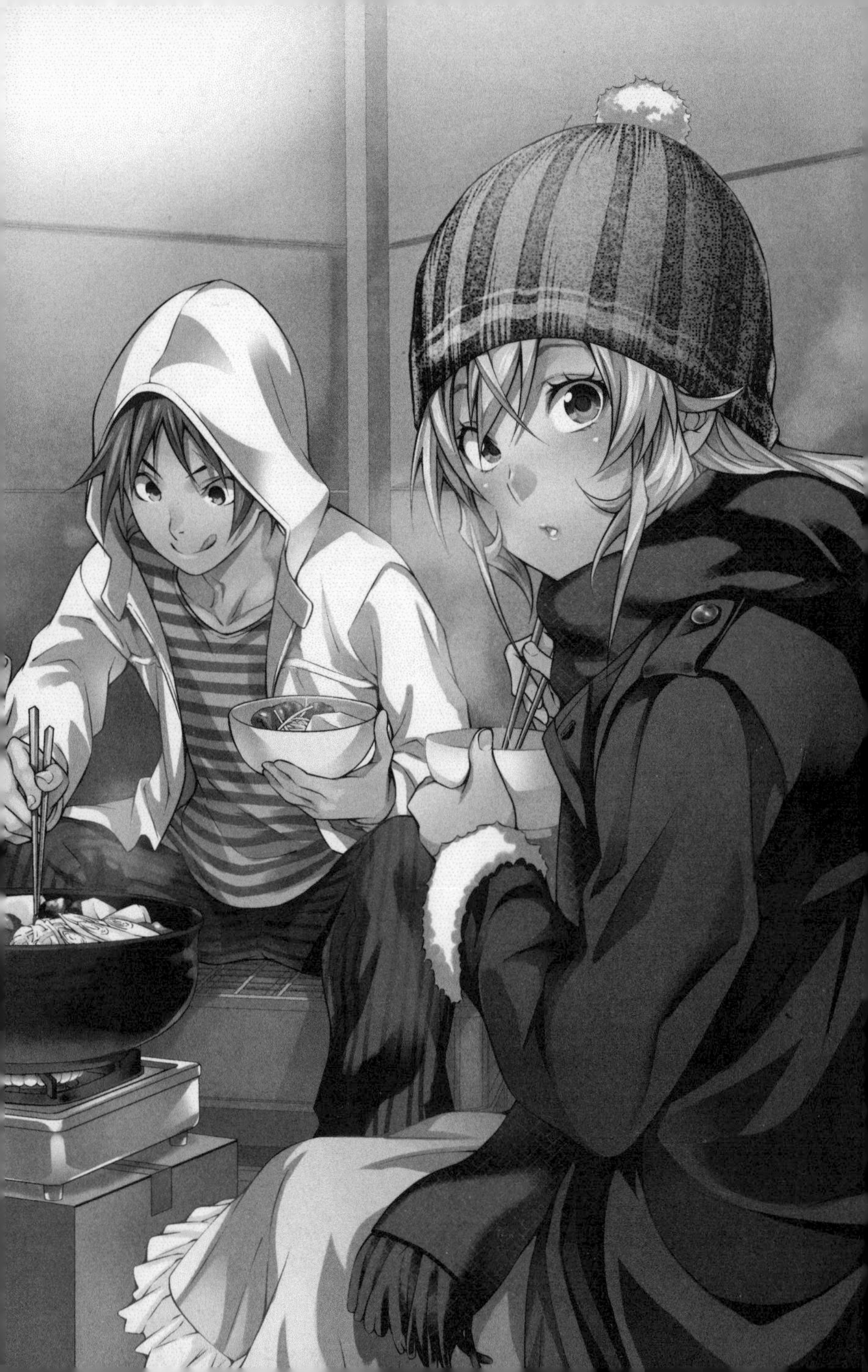

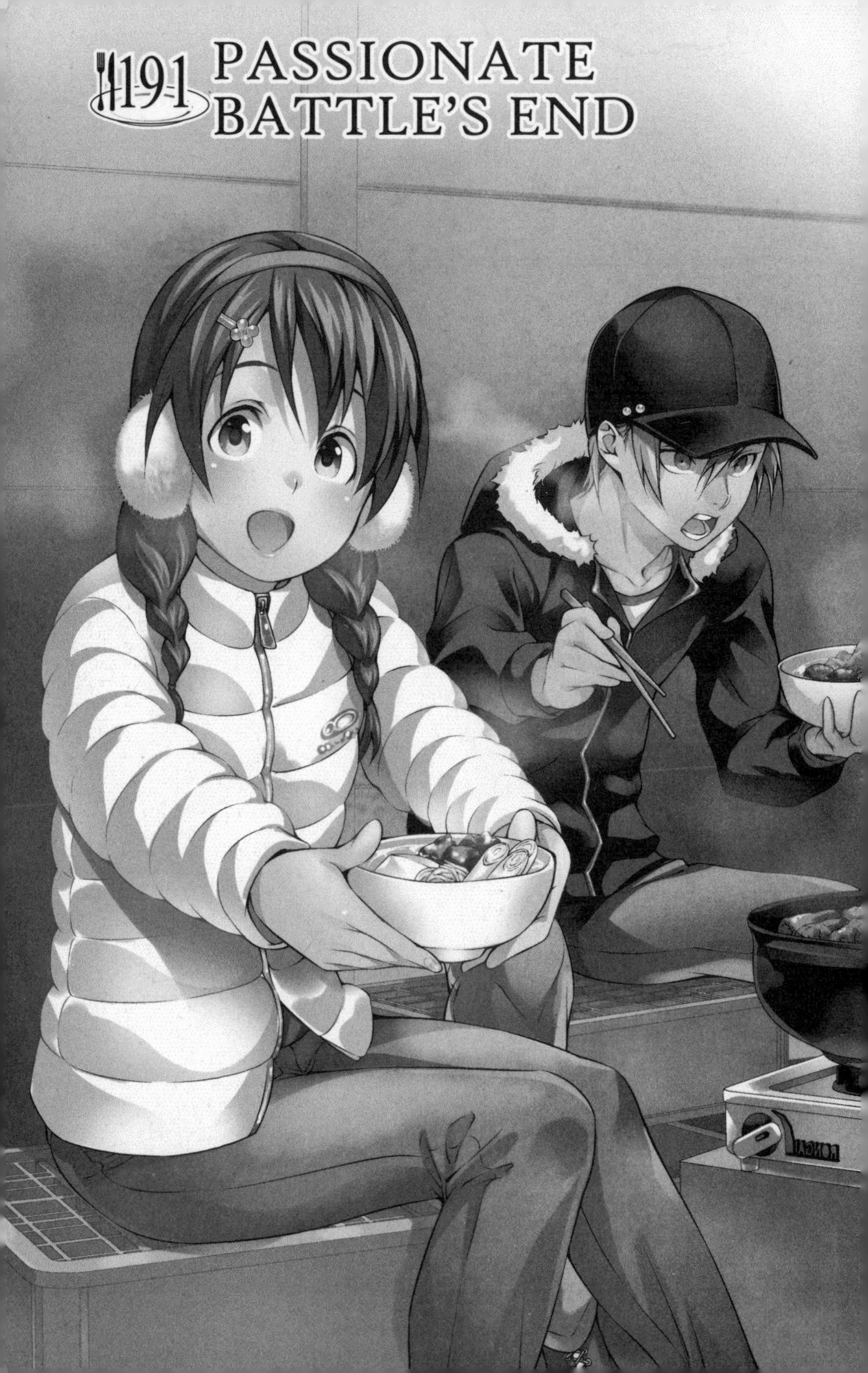
191
PASSIONATE
BATTLE'S END

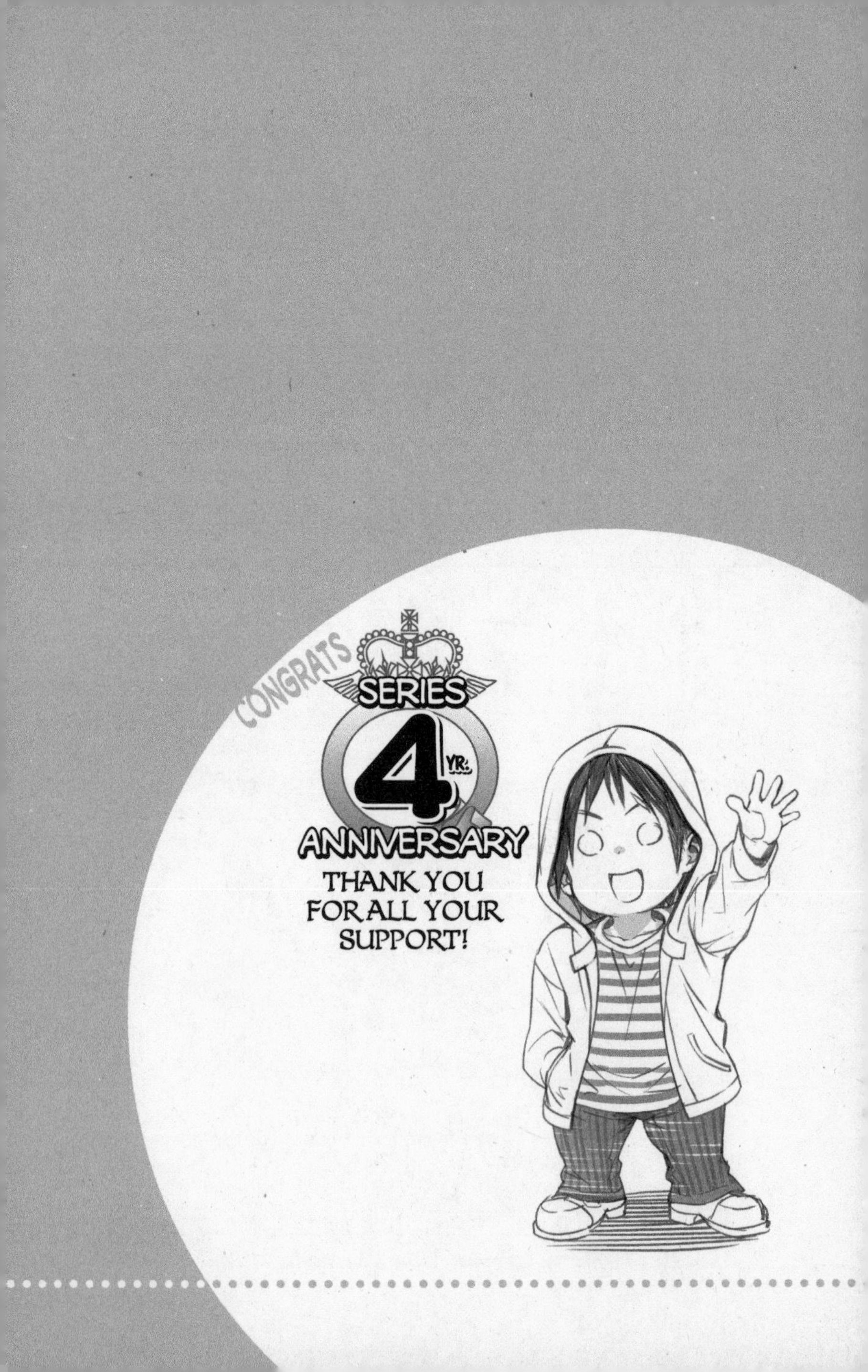
CONGRATS
SERIES
4 YR.
ANNIVERSARY
THANK YOU
FOR ALL YOUR
SUPPORT!

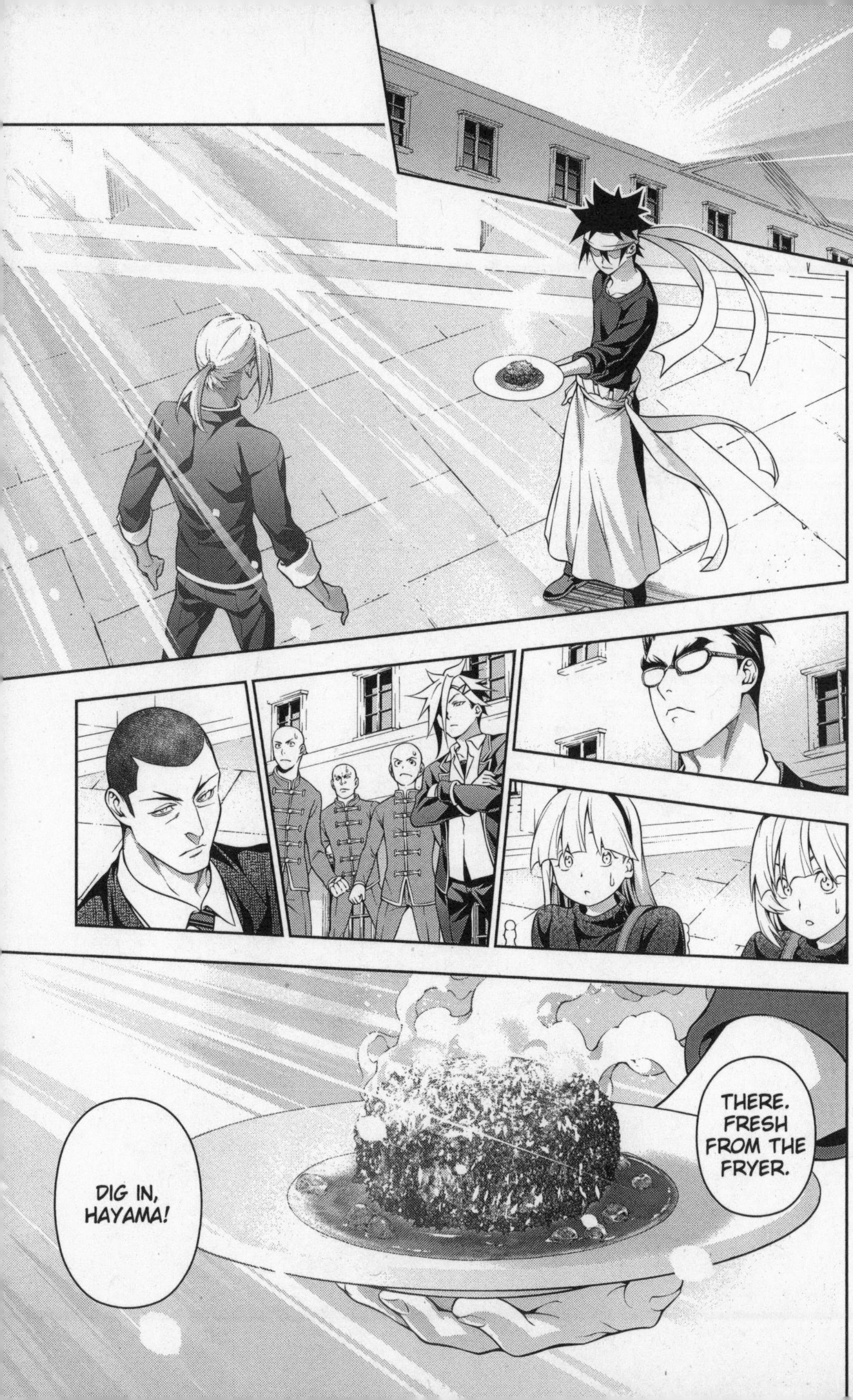
THERE. FRESH FROM THE FRYER.
DIG IN, HAYAMA!

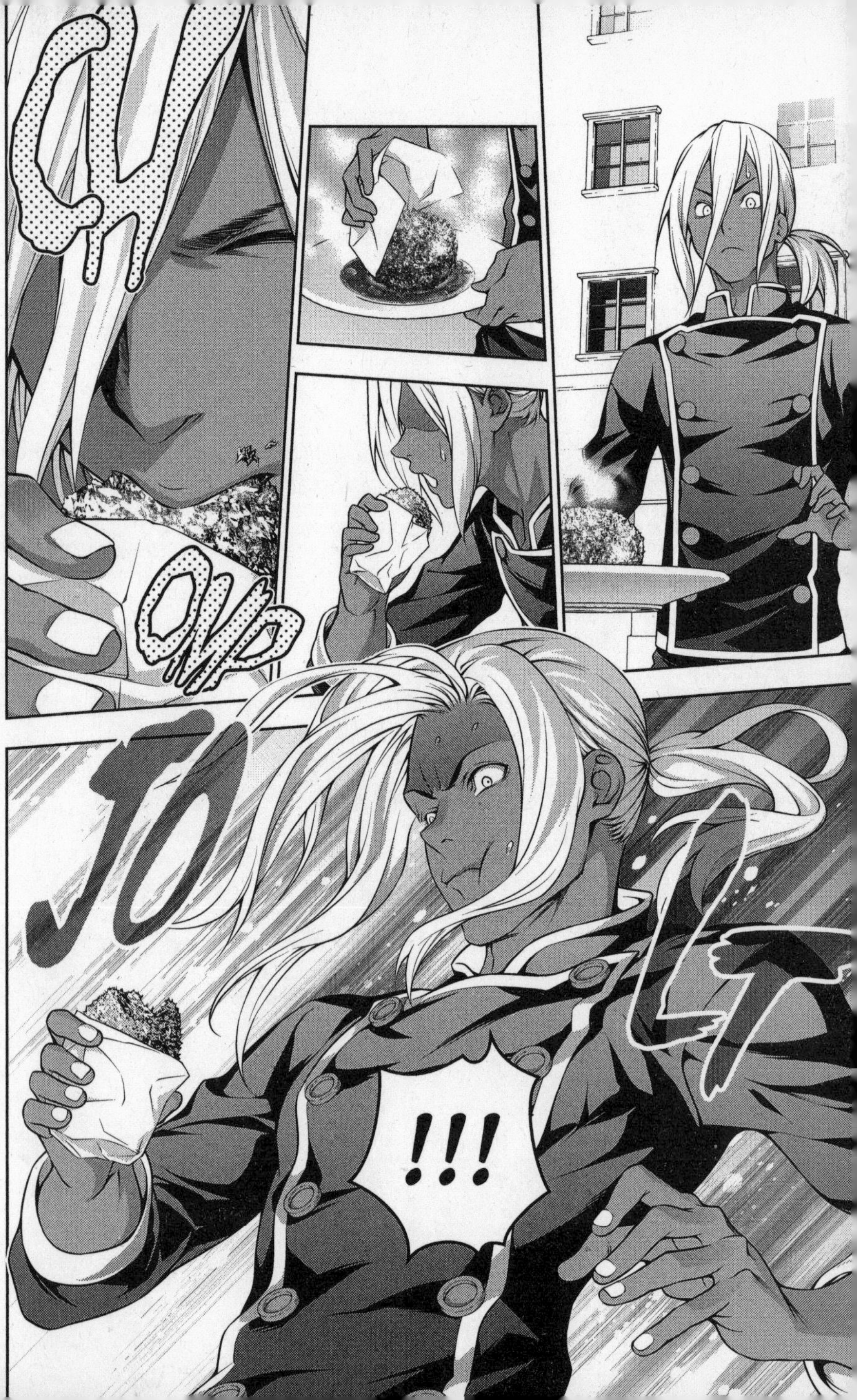
CHOMP
JOLT
!!!

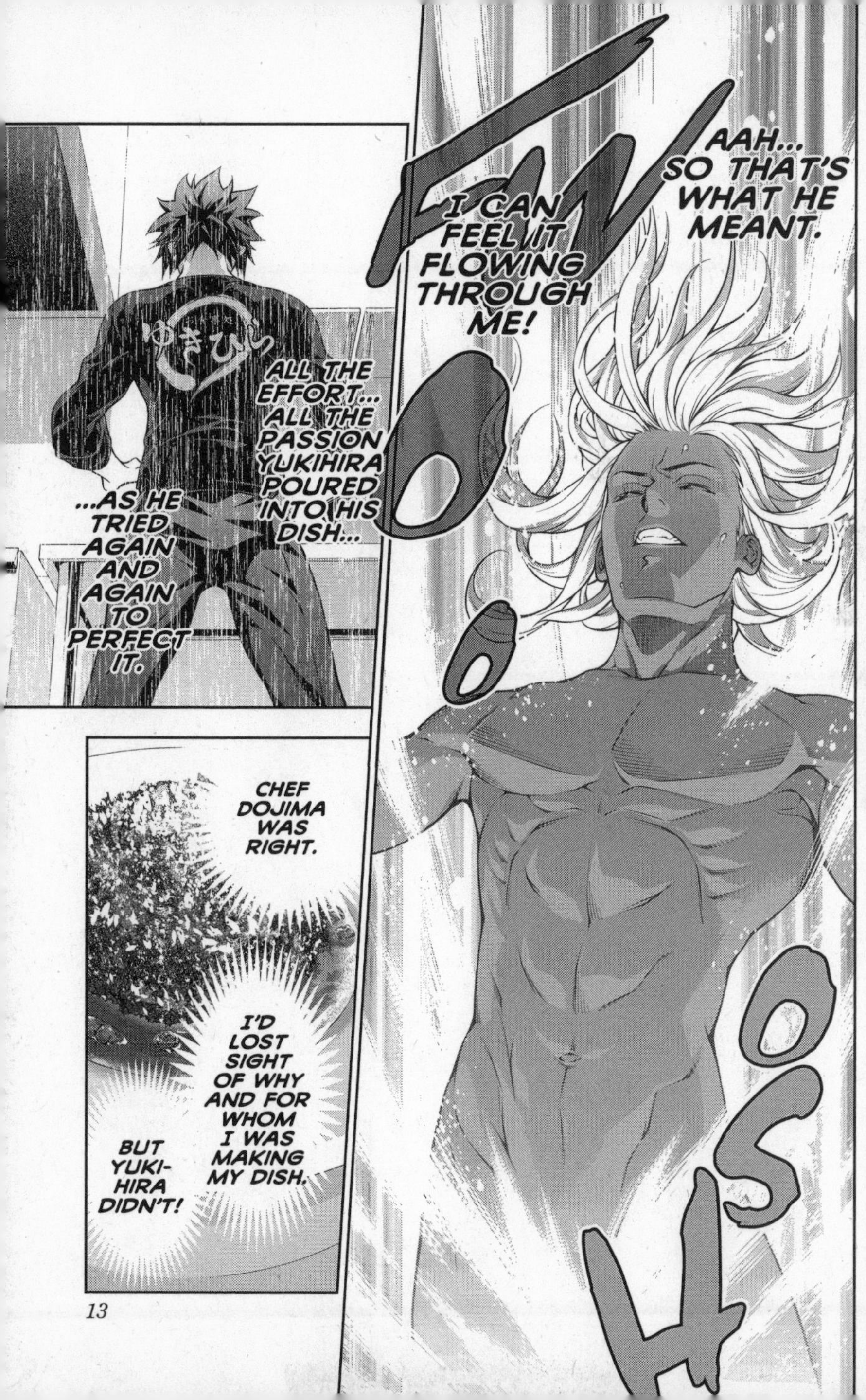
AAH... SO THAT'S WHAT HE MEANT.
I CAN FEEL IT FLOWING THROUGH ME!
ALL THE EFFORT... ALL THE PASSION YUKIHIRA POURED INTO HIS DISH...
...AS HE TRIED AGAIN AND AGAIN TO PERFECT IT.
CHEF DOJIMA WAS RIGHT.
I'D LOST SIGHT OF WHY AND FOR WHOM I WAS MAKING MY DISH.
BUT YUKI-HIRA DIDN'T!

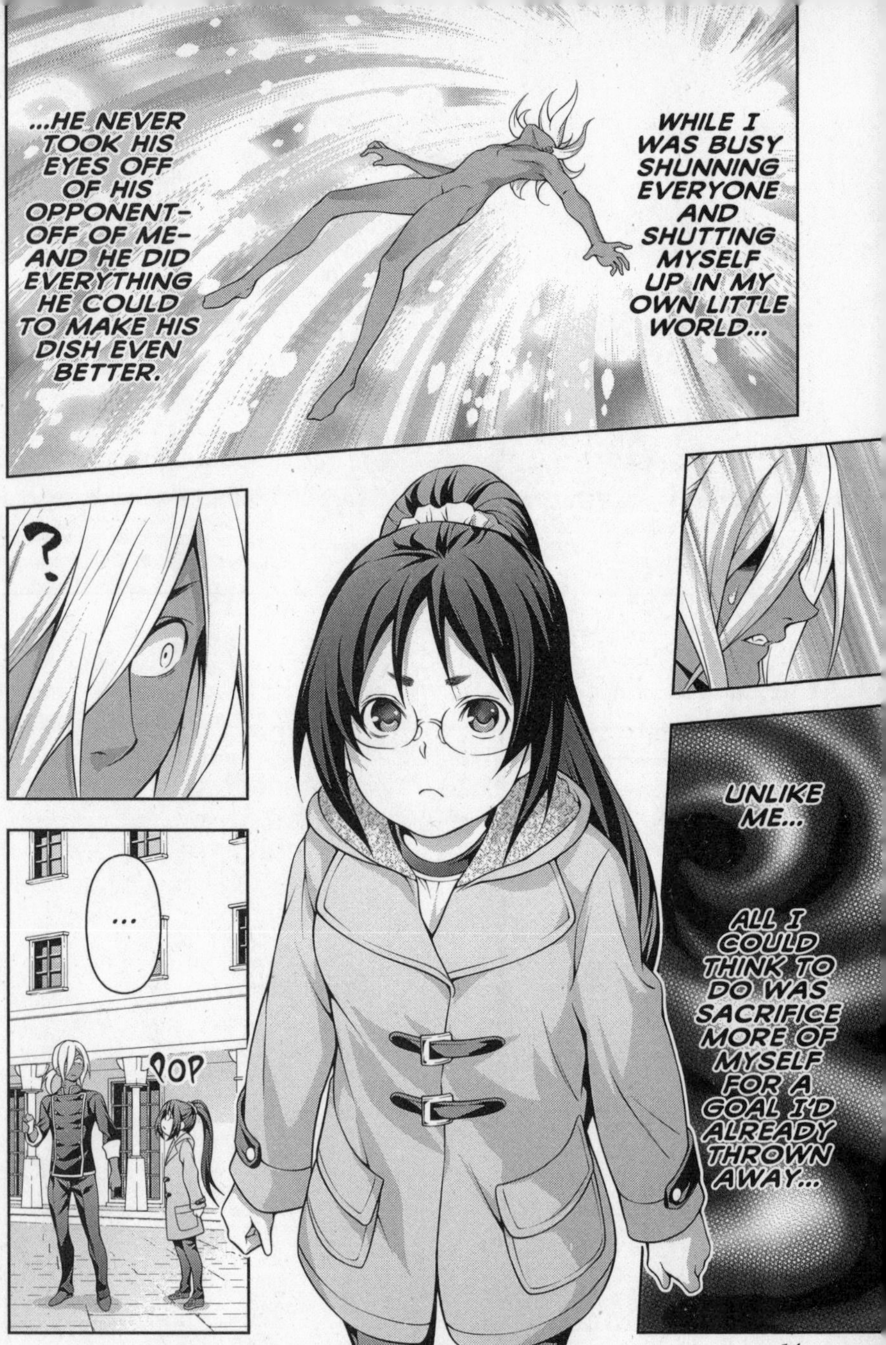
WHILE I WAS BUSY SHUNNING EVERYONE AND SHUTTING MYSELF UP IN MY OWN LITTLE WORLD...
...HE NEVER TOOK HIS EYES OFF OF HIS OPPONENT- OFF OF ME- AND HE DID EVERYTHING HE COULD TO MAKE HIS DISH EVEN BETTER.
UNLIKE ME...
ALL I COULD THINK TO DO WAS SACRIFICE MORE OF MYSELF FOR A GOAL I'D ALREADY THROWN AWAY...
?
...
POP

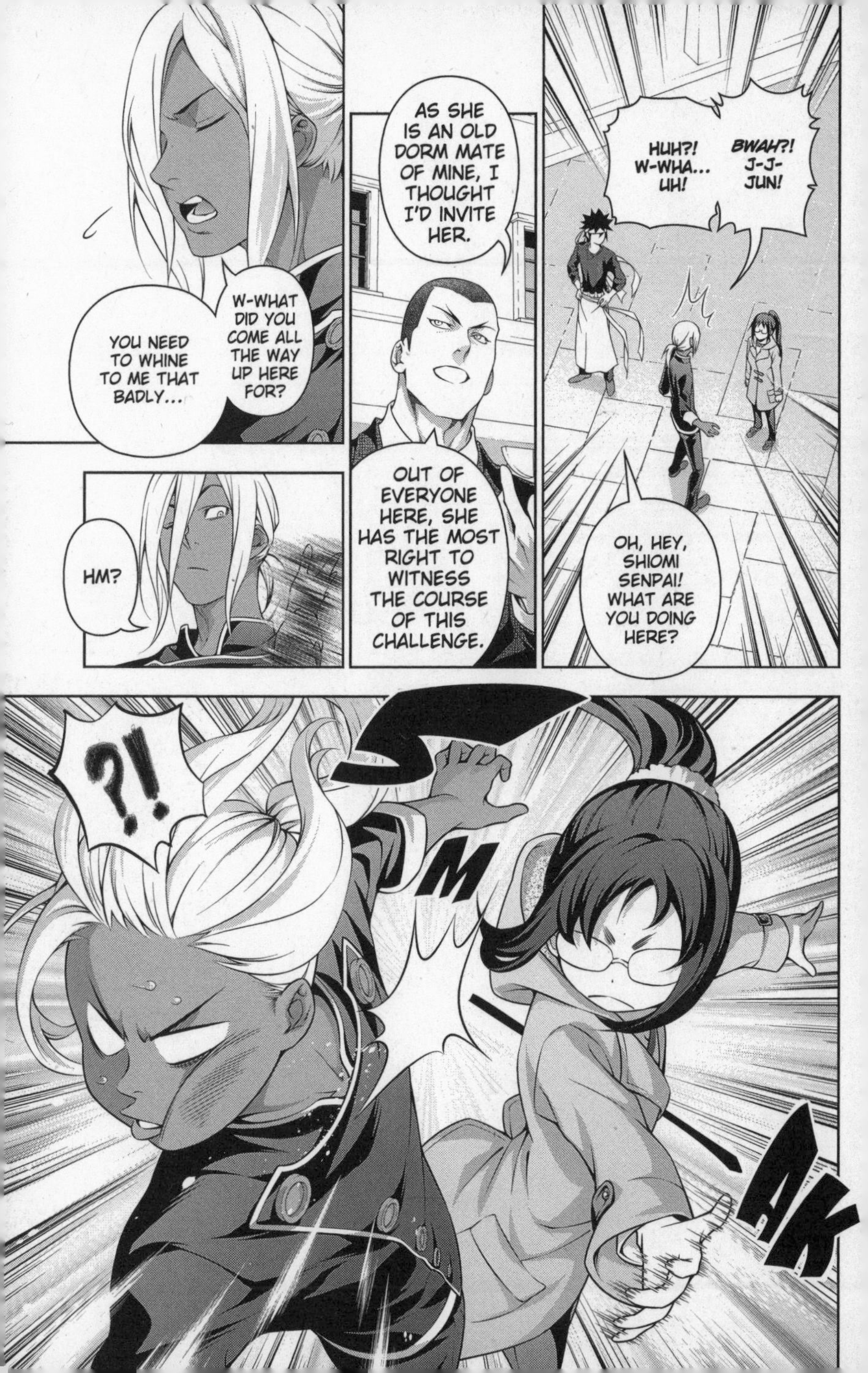
BWAH?! J-J-JUN!
HUH?! W-WHA... UH!
OH, HEY, SHIOMI SENPAI! WHAT ARE YOU DOING HERE?
AS SHE IS AN OLD DORM MATE OF MINE, I THOUGHT I'D INVITE HER.
OUT OF EVERYONE HERE, SHE HAS THE MOST RIGHT TO WITNESS THE COURSE OF THIS CHALLENGE.
W-WHAT DID YOU COME ALL THE WAY UP HERE FOR?
YOU NEED TO WHINE TO ME THAT BADLY...
HM?
?!
M
AK

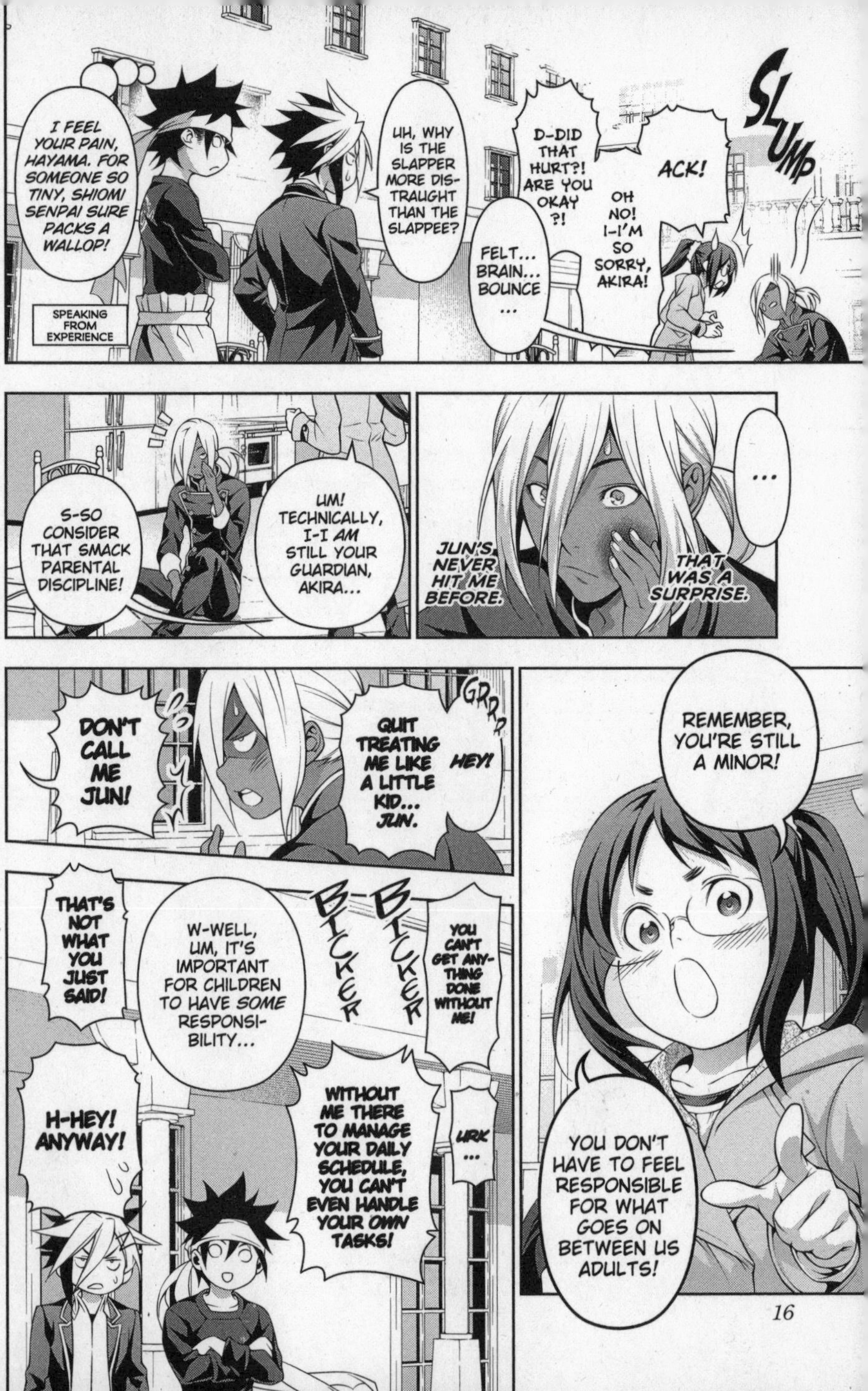
SLUMP
ACK!
OH NO! I-I'M SO SORRY, AKIRA!
D-DID THAT HURT?! ARE YOU OKAY ?!
FELT... BRAIN... BOUNCE ...
UH, WHY IS THE SLAPPER MORE DIS-TRAUGHT THAN THE SLAPPEE?
I FEEL YOUR PAIN, HAYAMA. FOR SOMEONE SO TINY, SHIOMI SENPAI SURE PACKS A WALLOP!
SPEAKING FROM EXPERIENCE
...
THAT WAS A SURPRISE.
JUN'S NEVER HIT ME BEFORE.
UM! TECHNICALLY, I-I AM STILL YOUR GUARDIAN, AKIRA...
S-SO CONSIDER THAT SMACK PARENTAL DISCIPLINE!
REMEMBER, YOU'RE STILL A MINOR!
YOU DON'T HAVE TO FEEL RESPONSIBLE FOR WHAT GOES ON BETWEEN US ADULTS!
GRRR
HEY!
QUIT TREATING ME LIKE A LITTLE KID... JUN.
DON'T CALL ME JUN!
YOU CAN'T GET ANY-THING DONE WITHOUT ME!
BICKER
BICKER
W-WELL, UM, IT'S IMPORTANT FOR CHILDREN TO HAVE SOME RESPONSI-BILITY...
THAT'S NOT WHAT YOU JUST SAID!
URK ...
WITHOUT ME THERE TO MANAGE YOUR DAILY SCHEDULE, YOU CAN'T EVEN HANDLE YOUR OWN TASKS!
H-HEY! ANYWAY!

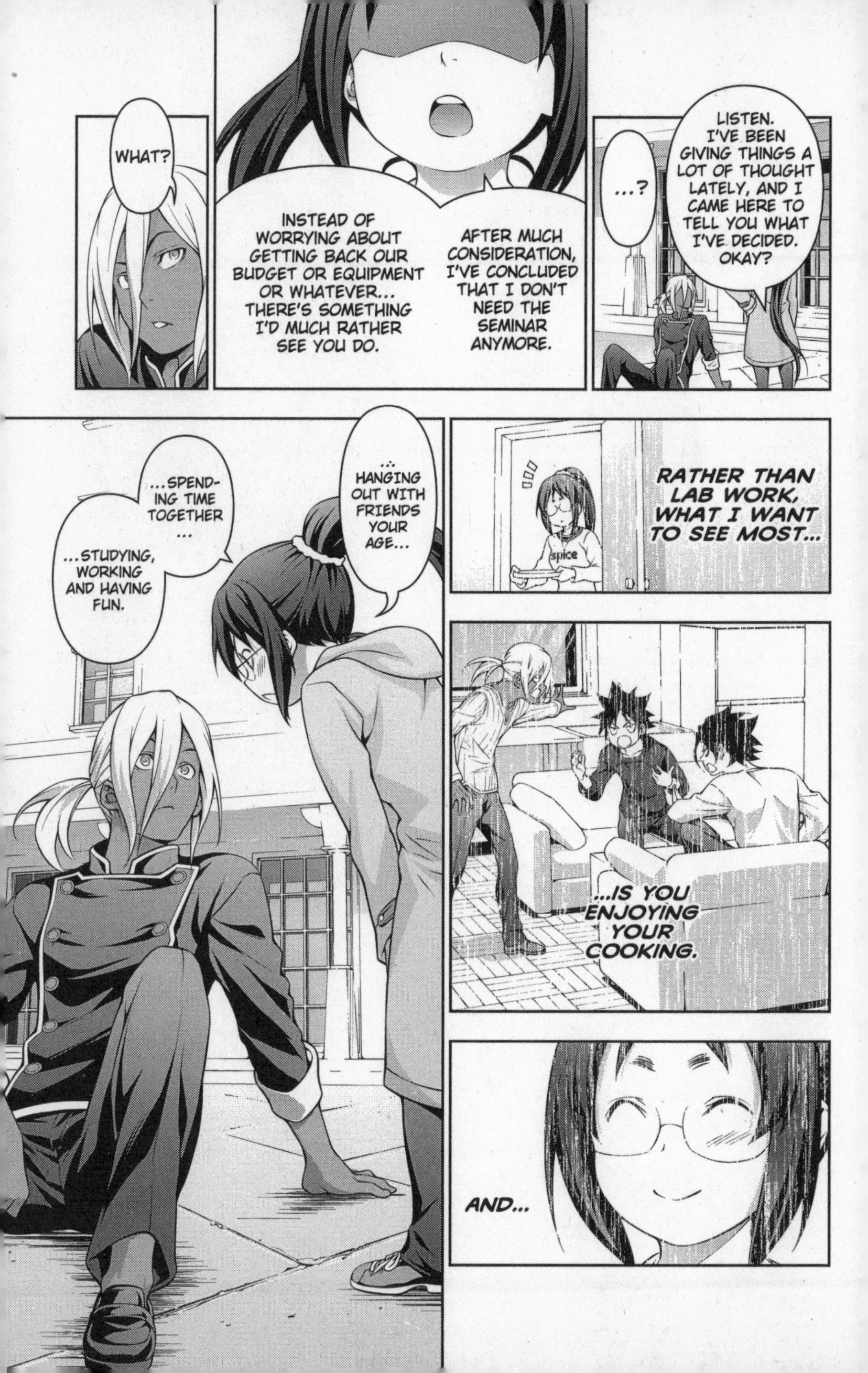
LISTEN. I'VE BEEN GIVING THINGS A LOT OF THOUGHT LATELY, AND I CAME HERE TO TELL YOU WHAT I'VE DECIDED. OKAY?
...?
AFTER MUCH CONSIDERATION, I'VE CONCLUDED THAT I DON'T NEED THE SEMINAR ANYMORE.
INSTEAD OF WORRYING ABOUT GETTING BACK OUR BUDGET OR EQUIPMENT OR WHATEVER... THERE'S SOMETHING I'D MUCH RATHER SEE YOU DO.
WHAT?
RATHER THAN LAB WORK, WHAT I WANT TO SEE MOST...
spice
...IS YOU ENJOYING YOUR COOKING.
AND...
... HANGING OUT WITH FRIENDS YOUR AGE...
...SPENDING TIME TOGETHER...
...STUDYING, WORKING AND HAVING FUN.

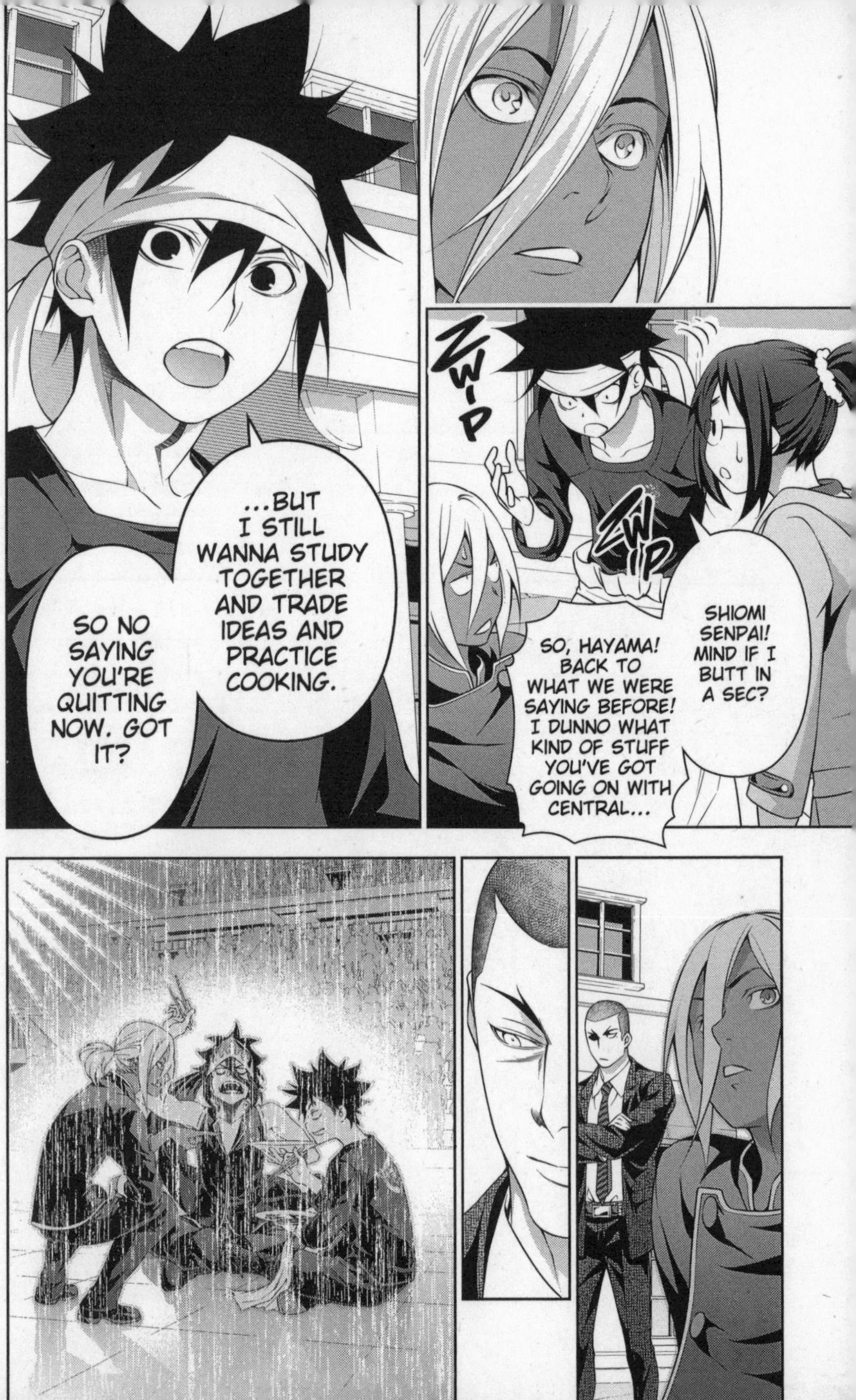
ZWIP
SHIOMI SENPAI! MIND IF I BUTT IN A SEC?
ZWIP
SO, HAYAMA! BACK TO WHAT WE WERE SAYING BEFORE! I DUNNO WHAT KIND OF STUFF YOU'VE GOT GOING ON WITH CENTRAL...
...BUT I STILL WANNA STUDY TOGETHER AND TRADE IDEAS AND PRACTICE COOKING.
SO NO SAYING YOU'RE QUITTING NOW. GOT IT?

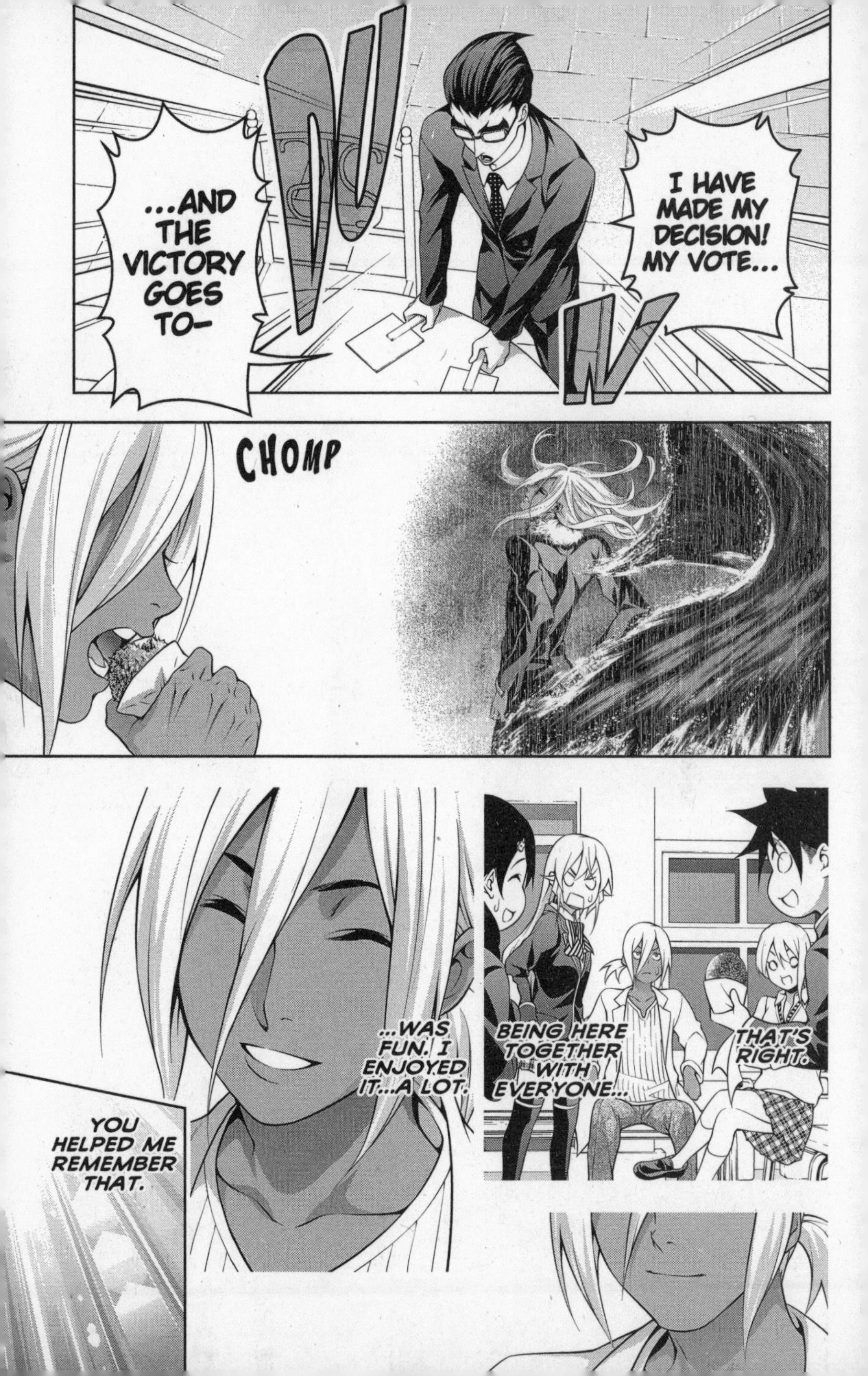
I HAVE MADE MY DECISION! MY VOTE...
...AND THE VICTORY GOES TO-
CHOMP
THAT'S RIGHT.
BEING HERE TOGETHER WITH EVERYONE...
...WAS FUN. I ENJOYED IT...A LOT.
YOU HELPED ME REMEMBER THAT.

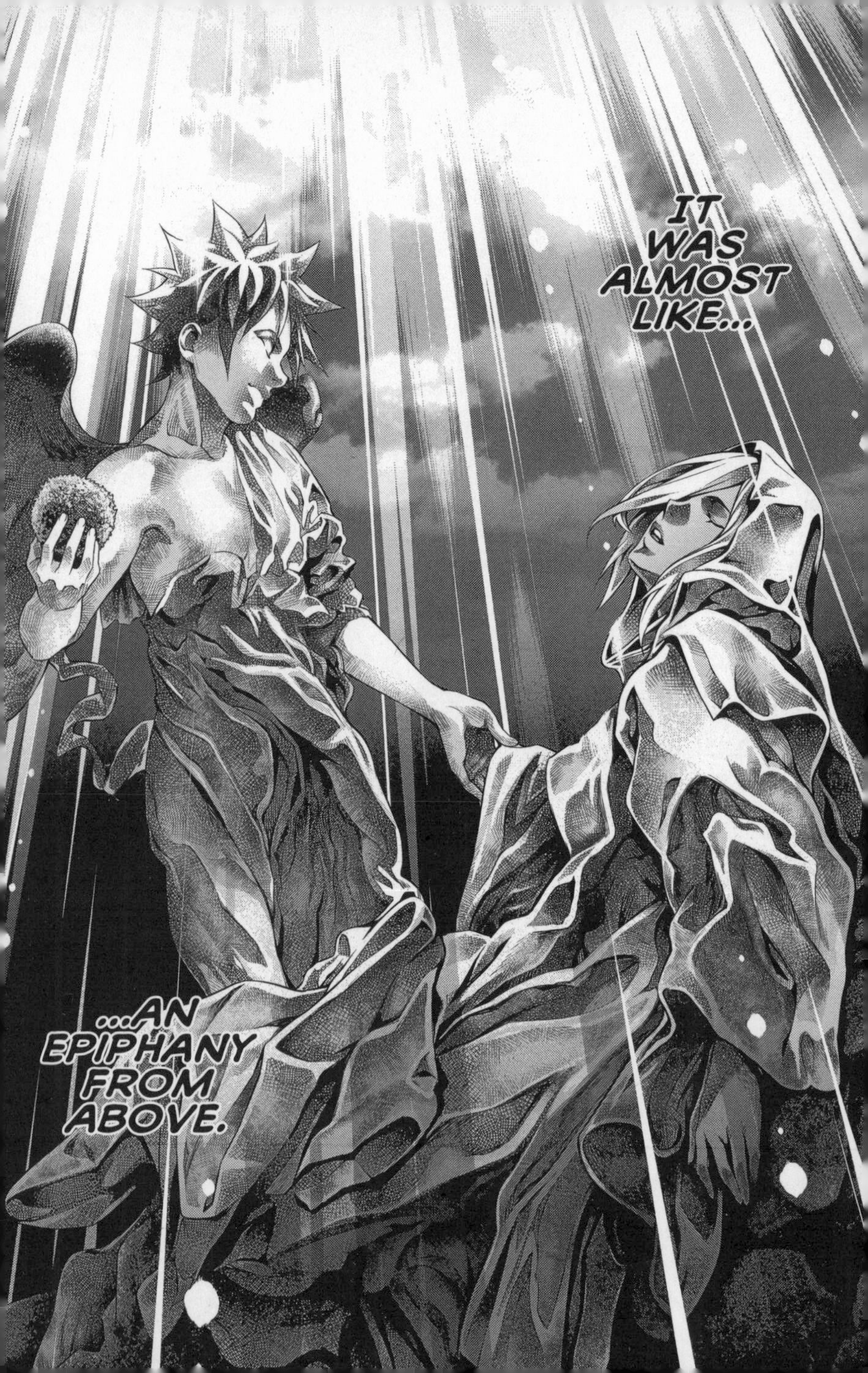
IT WAS ALMOST LIKE...
...AN EPIPHANY FROM ABOVE.

A BLOCK RANKINGS
1st	AKIRA HAYAMA	9
2nd	SOMA YUKIHIRA	9
2nd	RYO KUROKIBA	9
4th	ZENJI MARUI	88
4th	SHUN IBUSAKI	88

FINALLY.

BDMP

BDMP

FINALLY!

WNAAAA

Winner
Akira
Hayama

CLENCH

FINALLY!

QUIVER

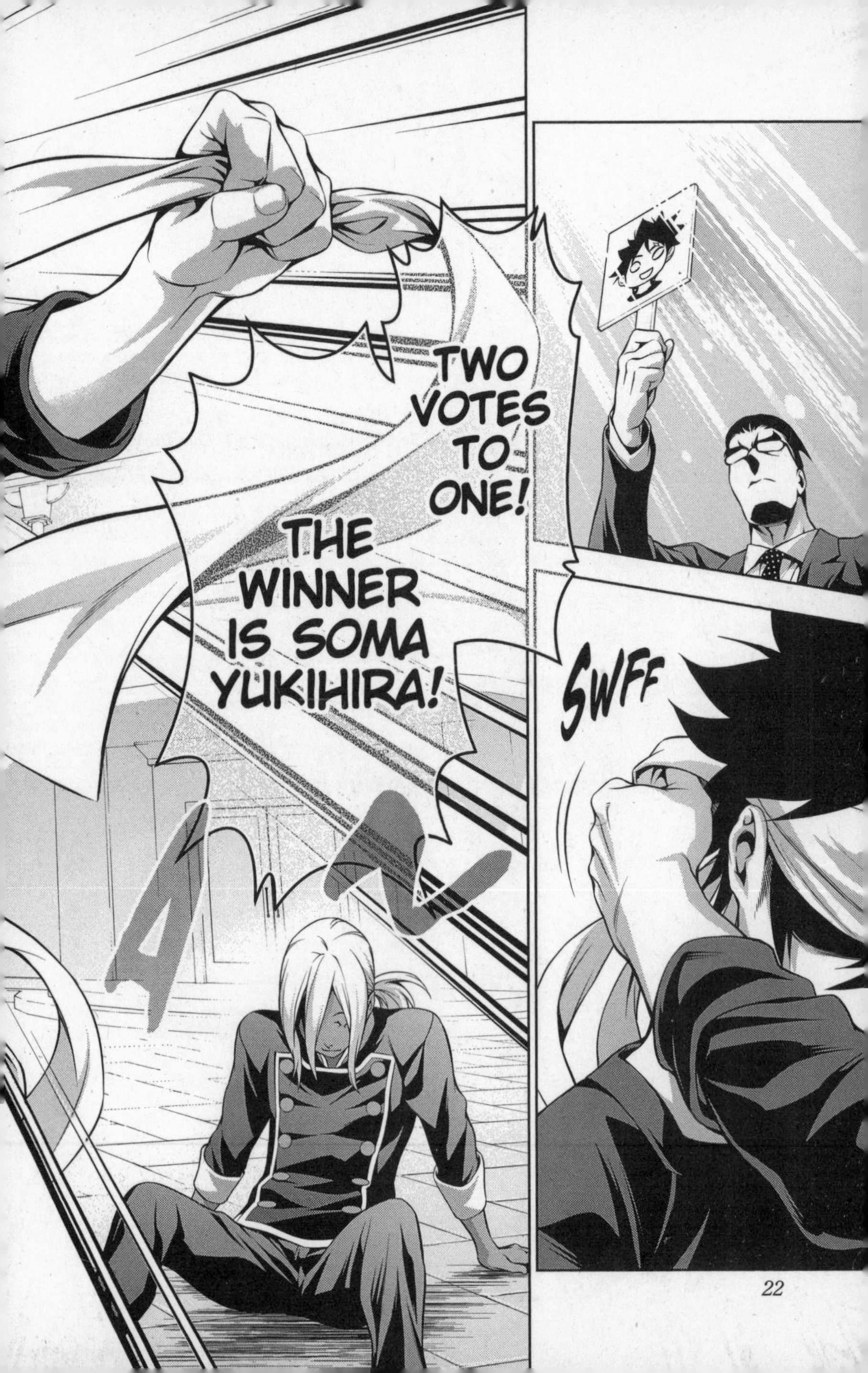
TWO VOTES TO ONE!
THE WINNER IS SOMA YUKIHIRA!
SWFF

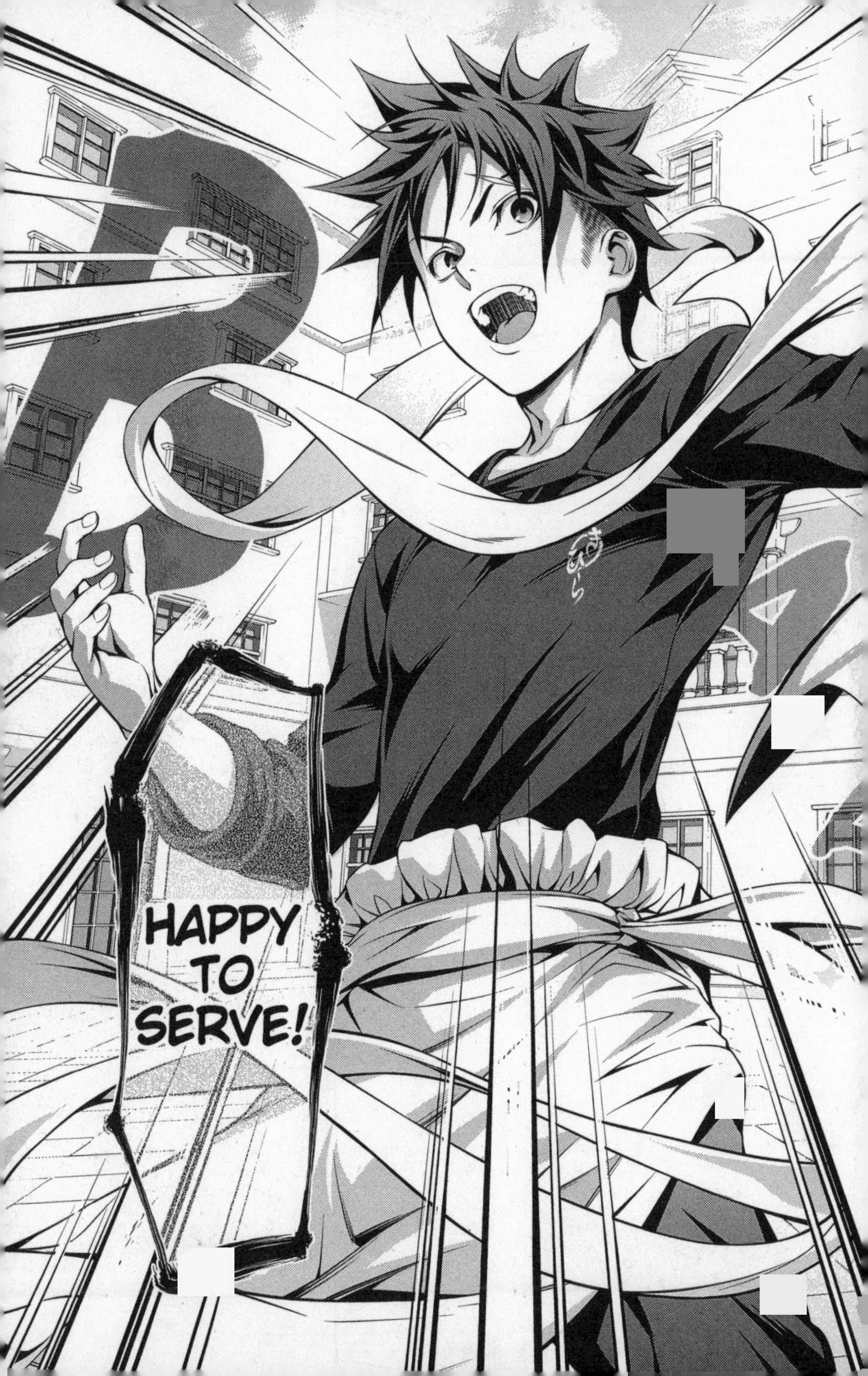
HAPPY TO SERVE!

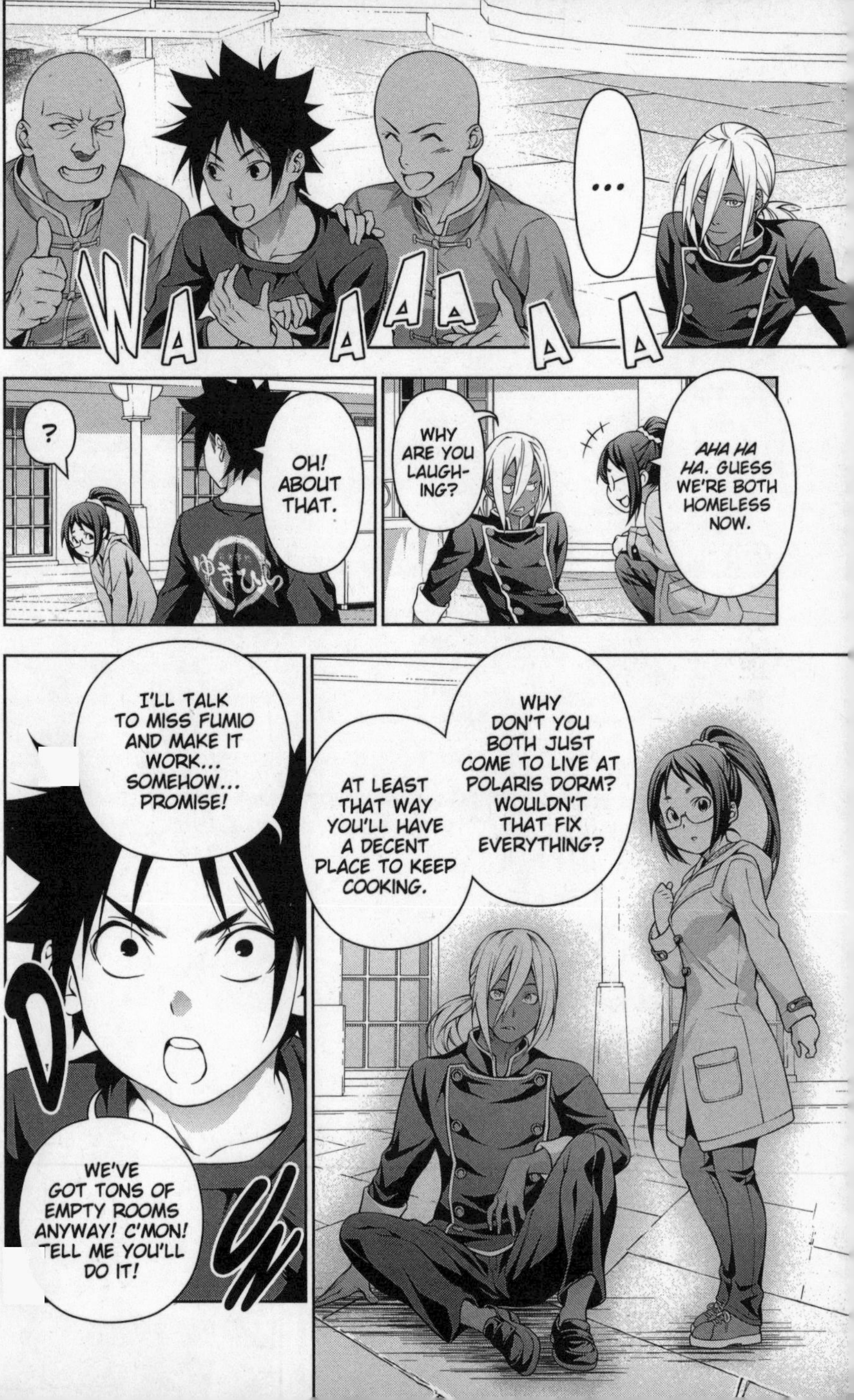
...
WAAAAAAA
AHA HA HA. GUESS WE'RE BOTH HOMELESS NOW.
WHY ARE YOU LAUGHING?
OH! ABOUT THAT.
?
WHY DON'T YOU BOTH JUST COME TO LIVE AT POLARIS DORM? WOULDN'T THAT FIX EVERYTHING?
AT LEAST THAT WAY YOU'LL HAVE A DECENT PLACE TO KEEP COOKING.
I'LL TALK TO MISS FUMIO AND MAKE IT WORK... SOMEHOW... PROMISE!
WE'VE GOT TONS OF EMPTY ROOMS ANYWAY! C'MON! TELL ME YOU'LL DO IT!

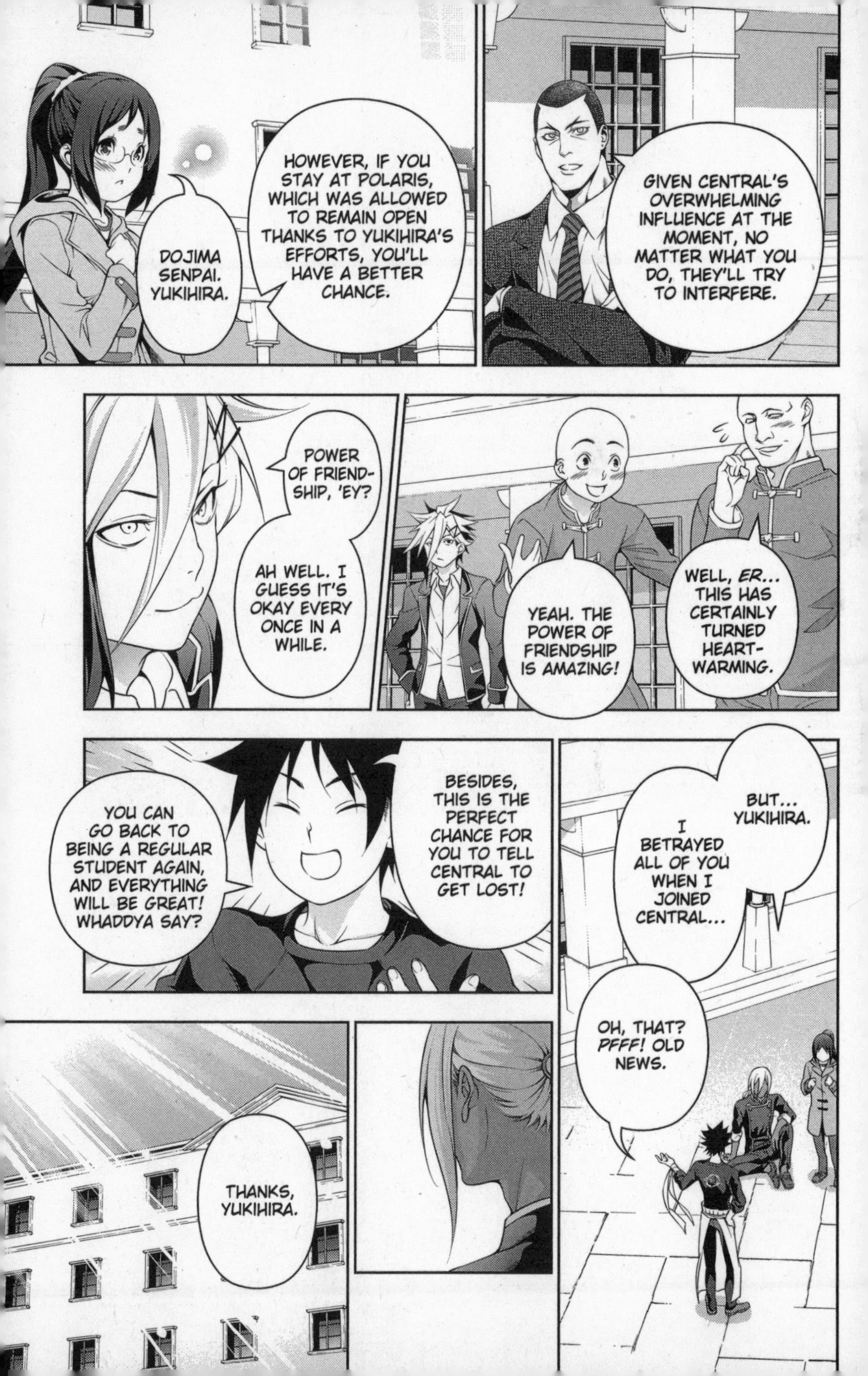
GIVEN CENTRAL'S OVERWHELMING INFLUENCE AT THE MOMENT, NO MATTER WHAT YOU DO, THEY'LL TRY TO INTERFERE.
HOWEVER, IF YOU STAY AT POLARIS, WHICH WAS ALLOWED TO REMAIN OPEN THANKS TO YUKIHIRA'S EFFORTS, YOU'LL HAVE A BETTER CHANCE.
DOJIMA SENPAI. YUKIHIRA.
WELL, *ER*... THIS HAS CERTAINLY TURNED HEART-WARMING.
YEAH. THE POWER OF FRIENDSHIP IS AMAZING!
POWER OF FRIEND-SHIP, 'EY?
AH WELL. I GUESS IT'S OKAY EVERY ONCE IN A WHILE.
BUT... YUKIHIRA.
I BETRAYED ALL OF YOU WHEN I JOINED CENTRAL...
OH, THAT? *PFFF!* OLD NEWS.
BESIDES, THIS IS THE PERFECT CHANCE FOR YOU TO TELL CENTRAL TO GET LOST!
YOU CAN GO BACK TO BEING A REGULAR STUDENT AGAIN, AND EVERYTHING WILL BE GREAT! WHADDYA SAY?
THANKS, YUKIHIRA.

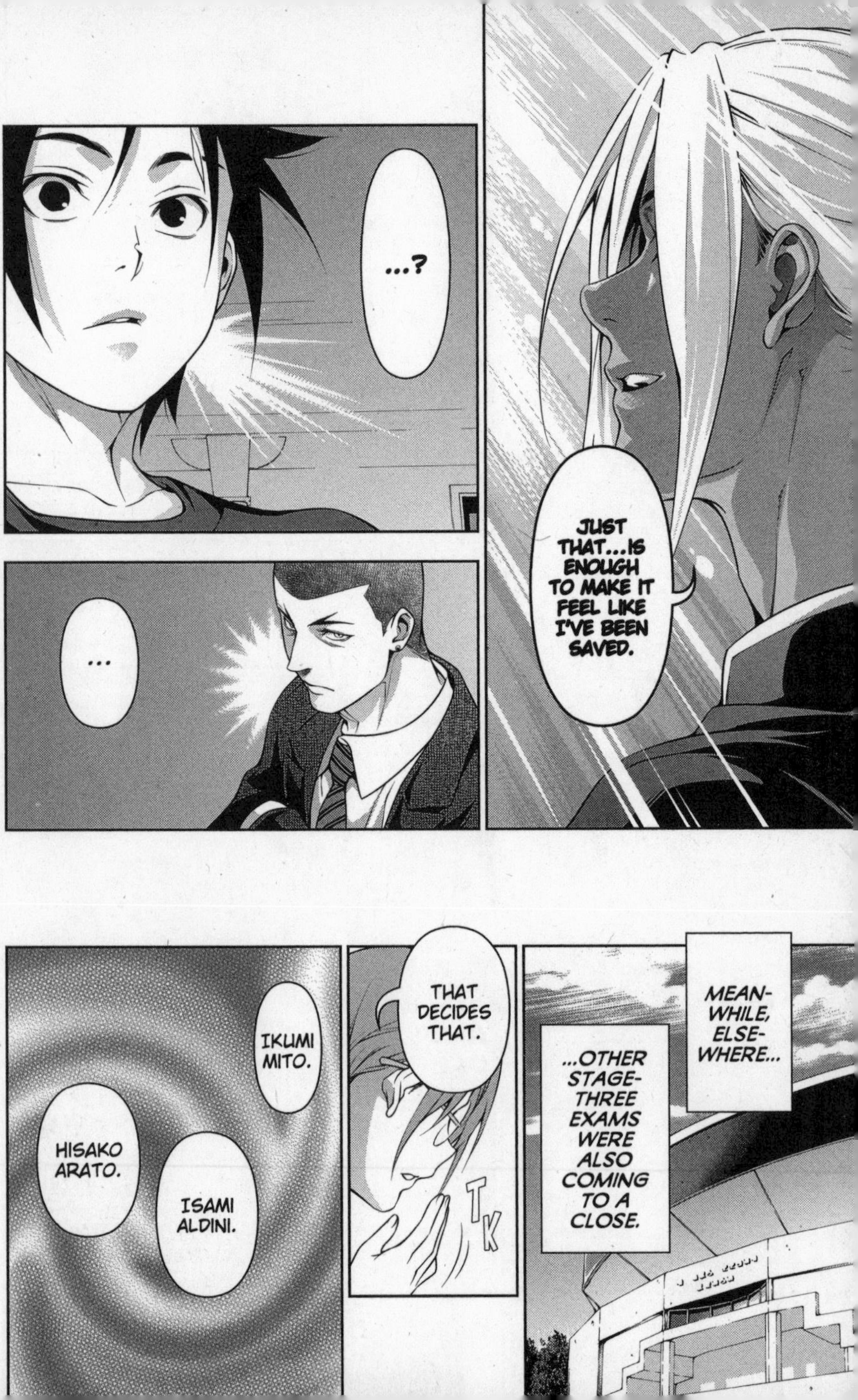
JUST THAT...IS ENOUGH TO MAKE IT FEEL LIKE I'VE BEEN SAVED.
...?
...
MEAN-WHILE, ELSE-WHERE...
...OTHER STAGE-THREE EXAMS WERE ALSO COMING TO A CLOSE.
THAT DECIDES THAT.
TK
IKUMI MITO.
HISAKO ARATO.
ISAMI ALDINI.

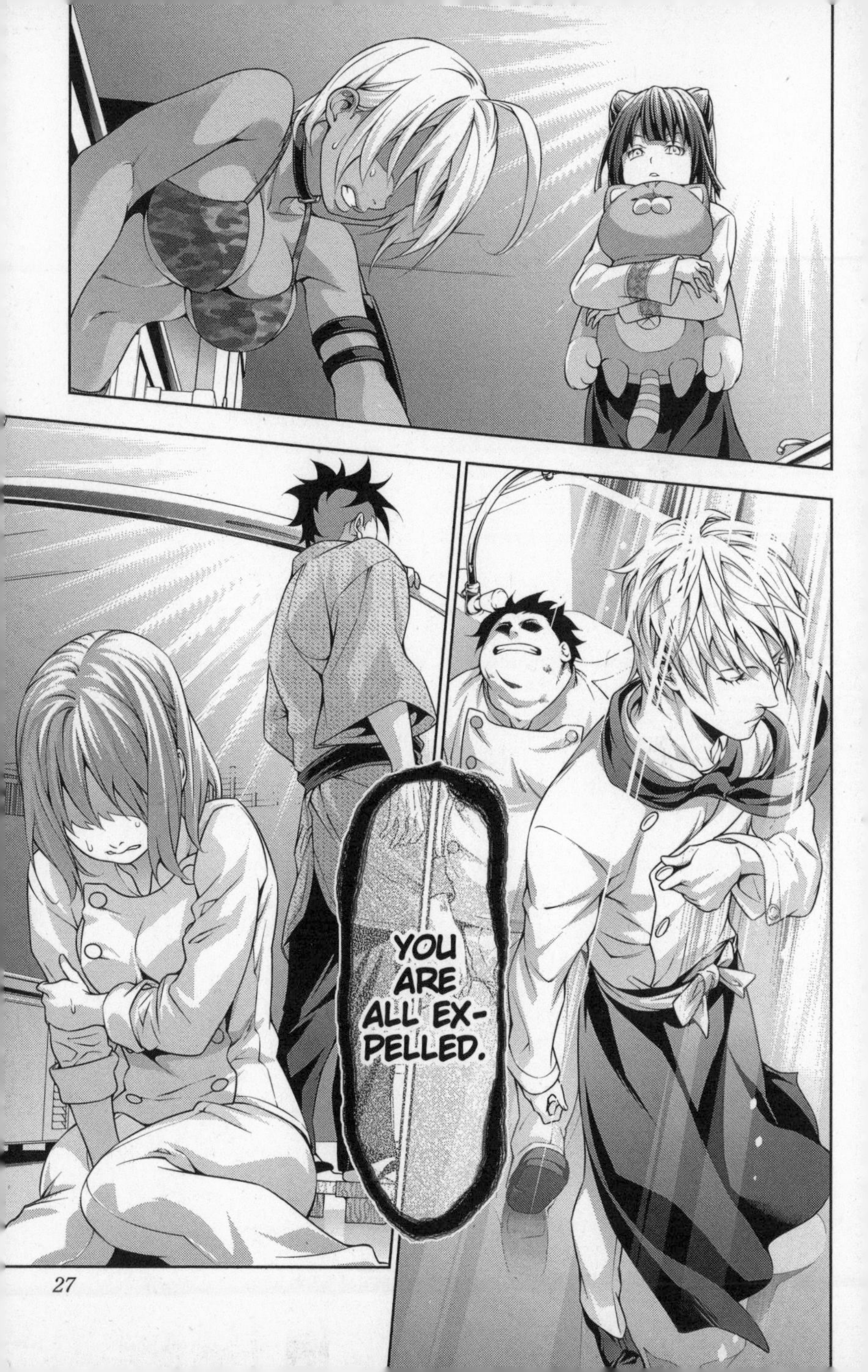
YOU ARE ALL EX-PELLED.

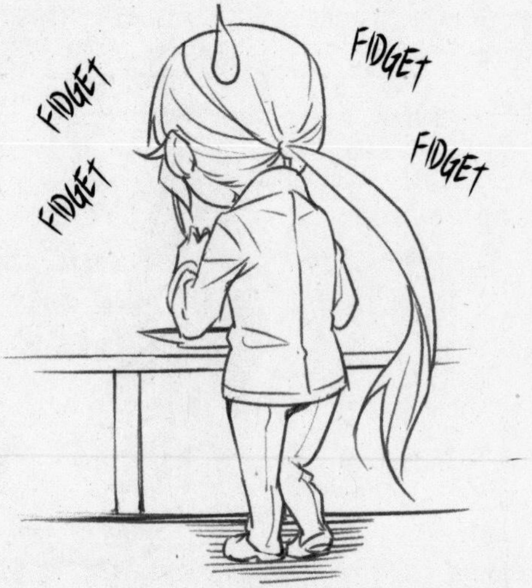
FIDGET
FIDGET
FIDGET
FIDGET

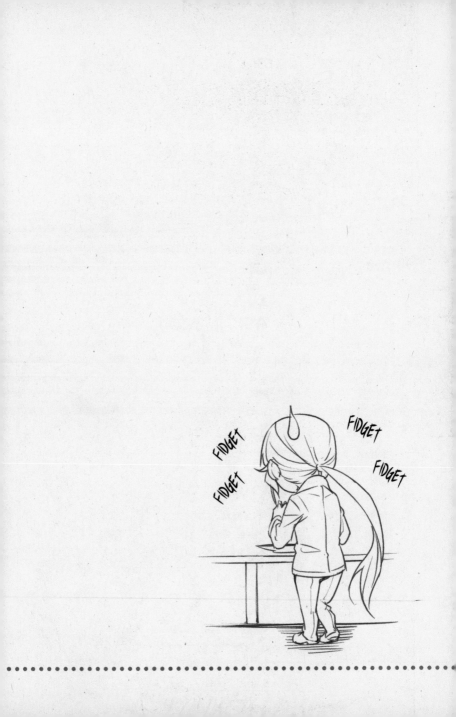

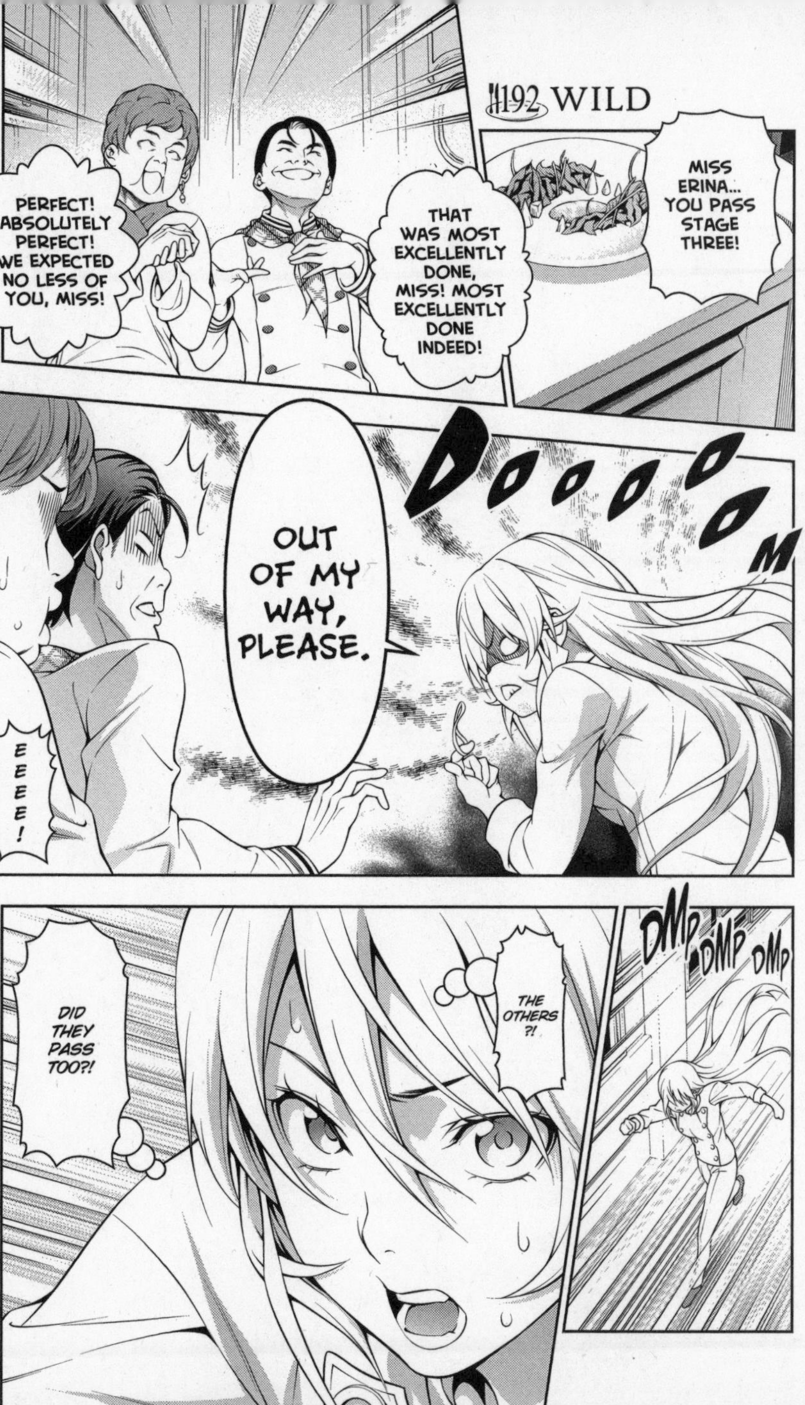
192 WILD
MISS ERINA... YOU PASS STAGE THREE!
THAT WAS MOST EXCELLENTLY DONE, MISS! MOST EXCELLENTLY DONE INDEED!
PERFECT! ABSOLUTELY PERFECT! WE EXPECTED NO LESS OF YOU, MISS!
DOOOOOM
OUT OF MY WAY, PLEASE.
EEEE!
DMP DMP DMP
THE OTHERS?!
DID THEY PASS TOO?!

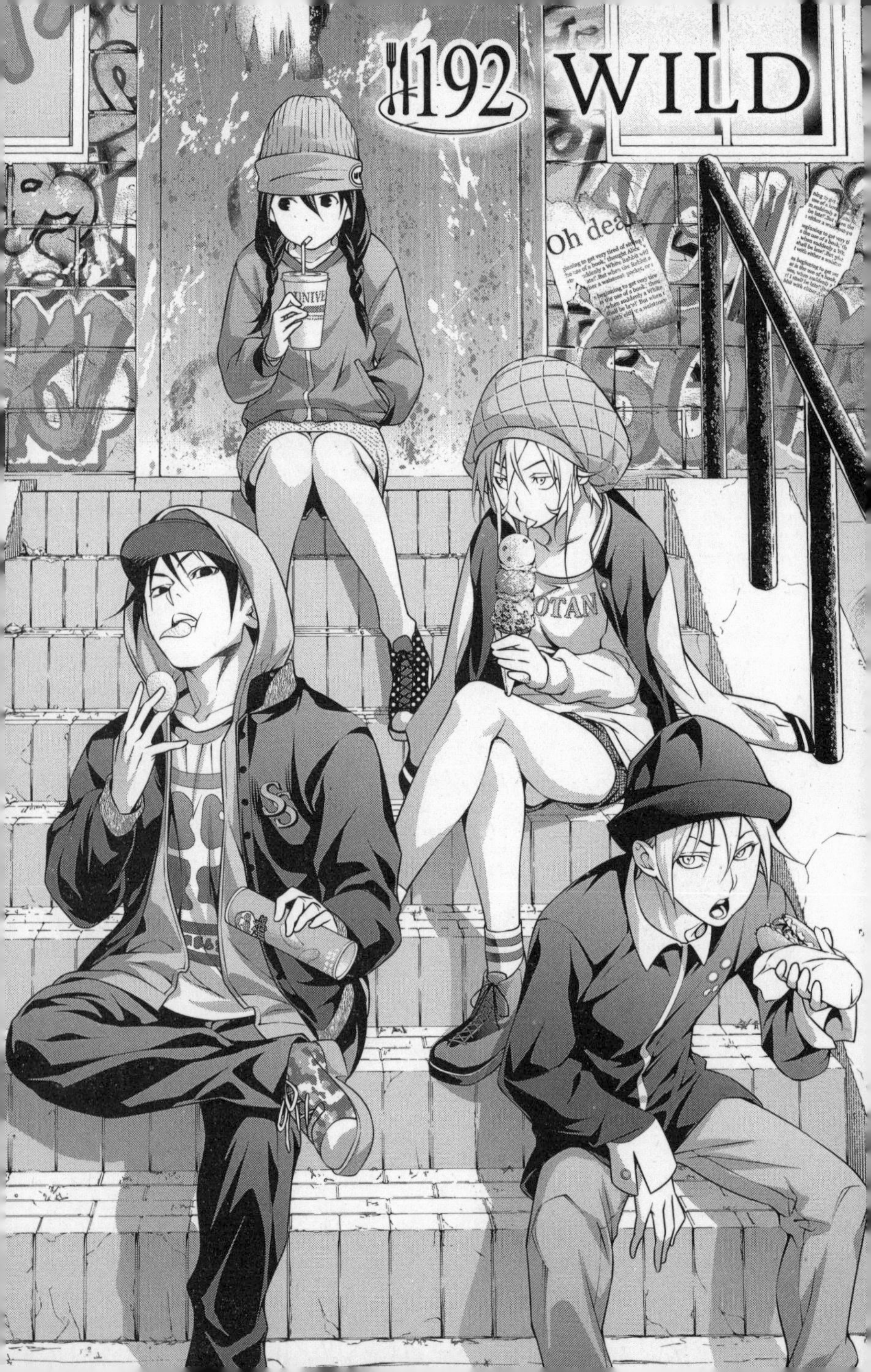
192
WILD
Oh dea
UNIVE
OTAN

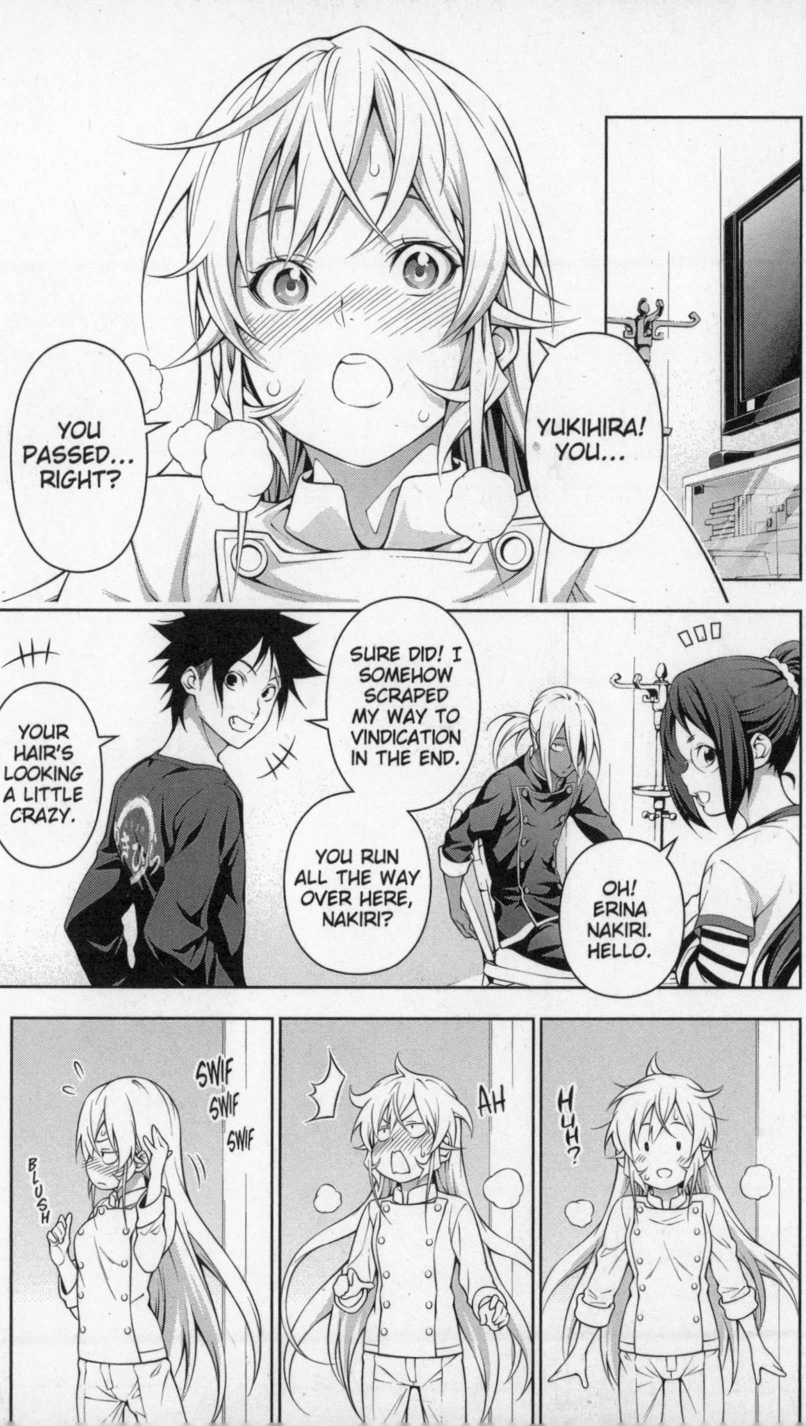
YUKIHIRA! YOU...
YOU PASSED... RIGHT?
OH! ERINA NAKIRI. HELLO.
SURE DID! I SOMEHOW SCRAPED MY WAY TO VINDICATION IN THE END.
YOU RUN ALL THE WAY OVER HERE, NAKIRI?
YOUR HAIR'S LOOKING A LITTLE CRAZY.
HUH?
AH
SWIF SWIF SWIF
BLUSH

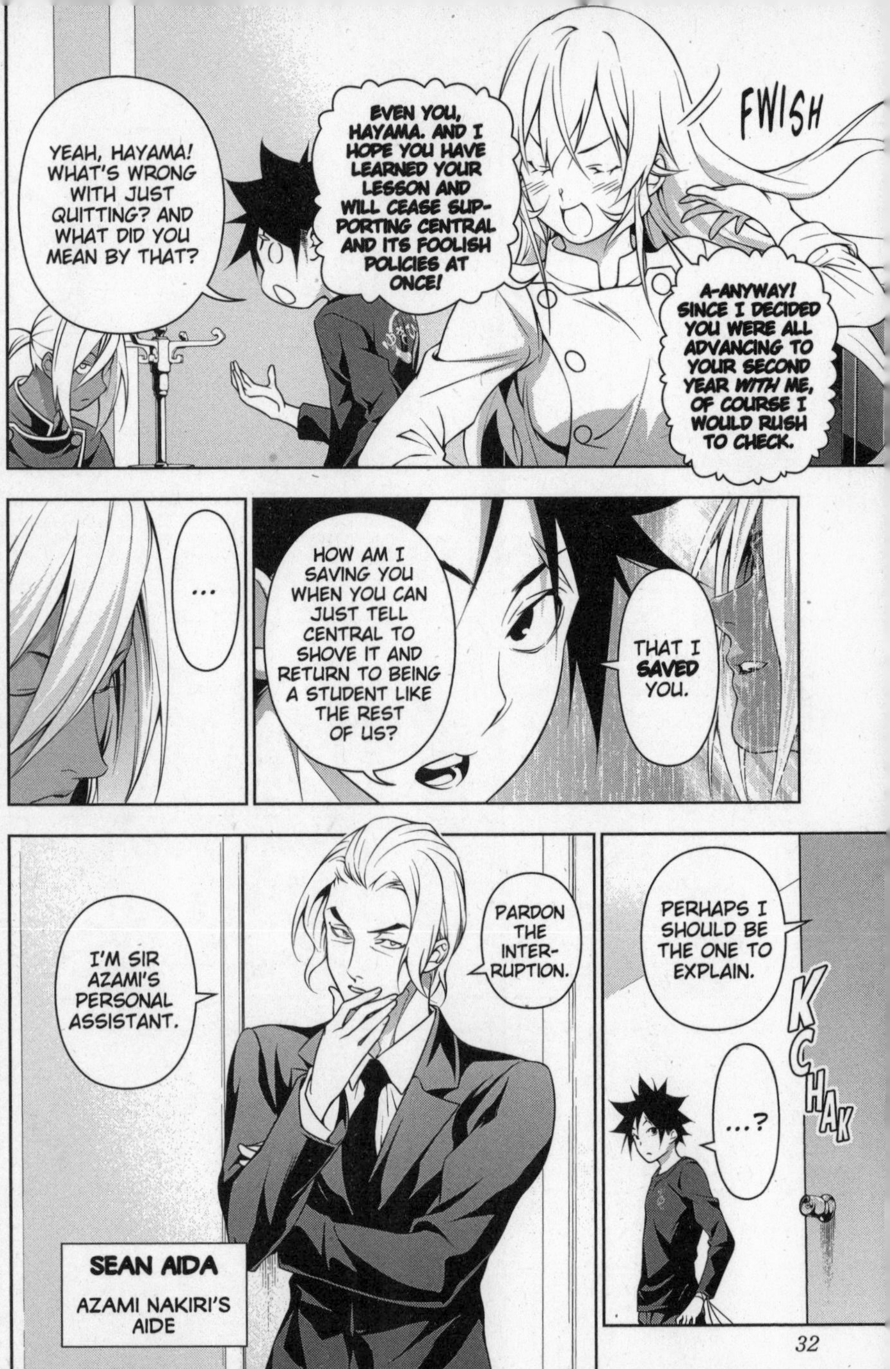
FWISH
EVEN YOU, HAYAMA. AND I HOPE YOU HAVE LEARNED YOUR LESSON AND WILL CEASE SUPPORTING CENTRAL AND ITS FOOLISH POLICIES AT ONCE!
A-ANYWAY! SINCE I DECIDED YOU WERE ALL ADVANCING TO YOUR SECOND YEAR *WITH ME*, OF COURSE I WOULD RUSH TO CHECK.
YEAH, HAYAMA! WHAT'S WRONG WITH JUST QUITTING? AND WHAT DID YOU MEAN BY THAT?
THAT I SAVED YOU.
HOW AM I SAVING YOU WHEN YOU CAN JUST TELL CENTRAL TO SHOVE IT AND RETURN TO BEING A STUDENT LIKE THE REST OF US?
...
PERHAPS I SHOULD BE THE ONE TO EXPLAIN.
KCHAK
...?
PARDON THE INTERRUPTION.
I'M SIR AZAMI'S PERSONAL ASSISTANT.
SEAN AIDA
AZAMI NAKIRI'S AIDE

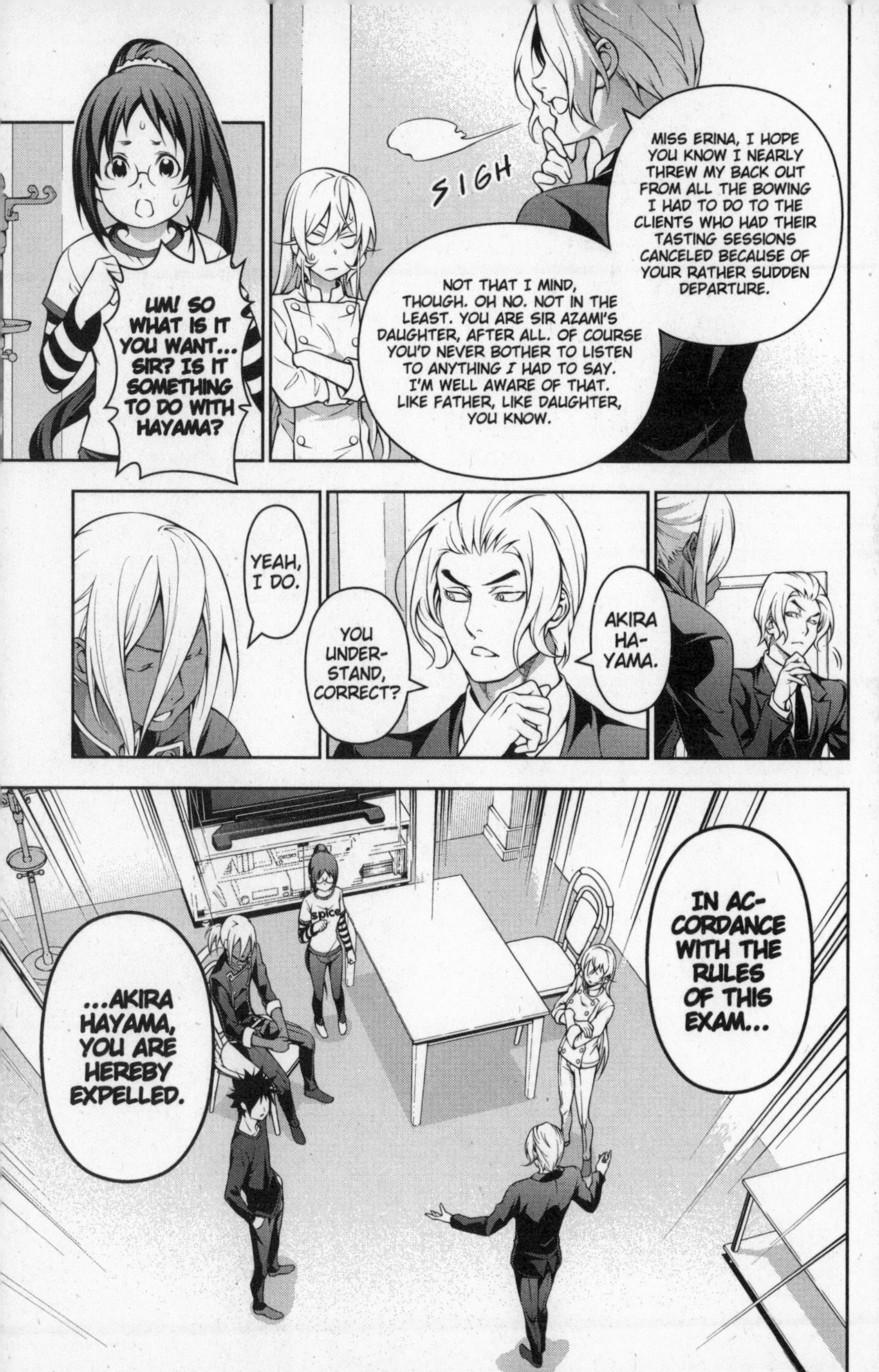
MISS ERINA, I HOPE YOU KNOW I NEARLY THREW MY BACK OUT FROM ALL THE BOWING I HAD TO DO TO THE CLIENTS WHO HAD THEIR TASTING SESSIONS CANCELED BECAUSE OF YOUR RATHER SUDDEN DEPARTURE.
SIGH
NOT THAT I MIND, THOUGH. OH NO. NOT IN THE LEAST. YOU ARE SIR AZAMI'S DAUGHTER, AFTER ALL. OF COURSE YOU'D NEVER BOTHER TO LISTEN TO ANYTHING *I* HAD TO SAY. I'M WELL AWARE OF THAT. LIKE FATHER, LIKE DAUGHTER, YOU KNOW.
UM! SO WHAT IS IT YOU WANT... SIR? IS IT SOMETHING TO DO WITH HAYAMA?
AKIRA HAYAMA.
YOU UNDERSTAND, CORRECT?
YEAH, I DO.
spice
IN ACCORDANCE WITH THE RULES OF THIS EXAM...
...AKIRA HAYAMA, YOU ARE HEREBY EXPELLED.

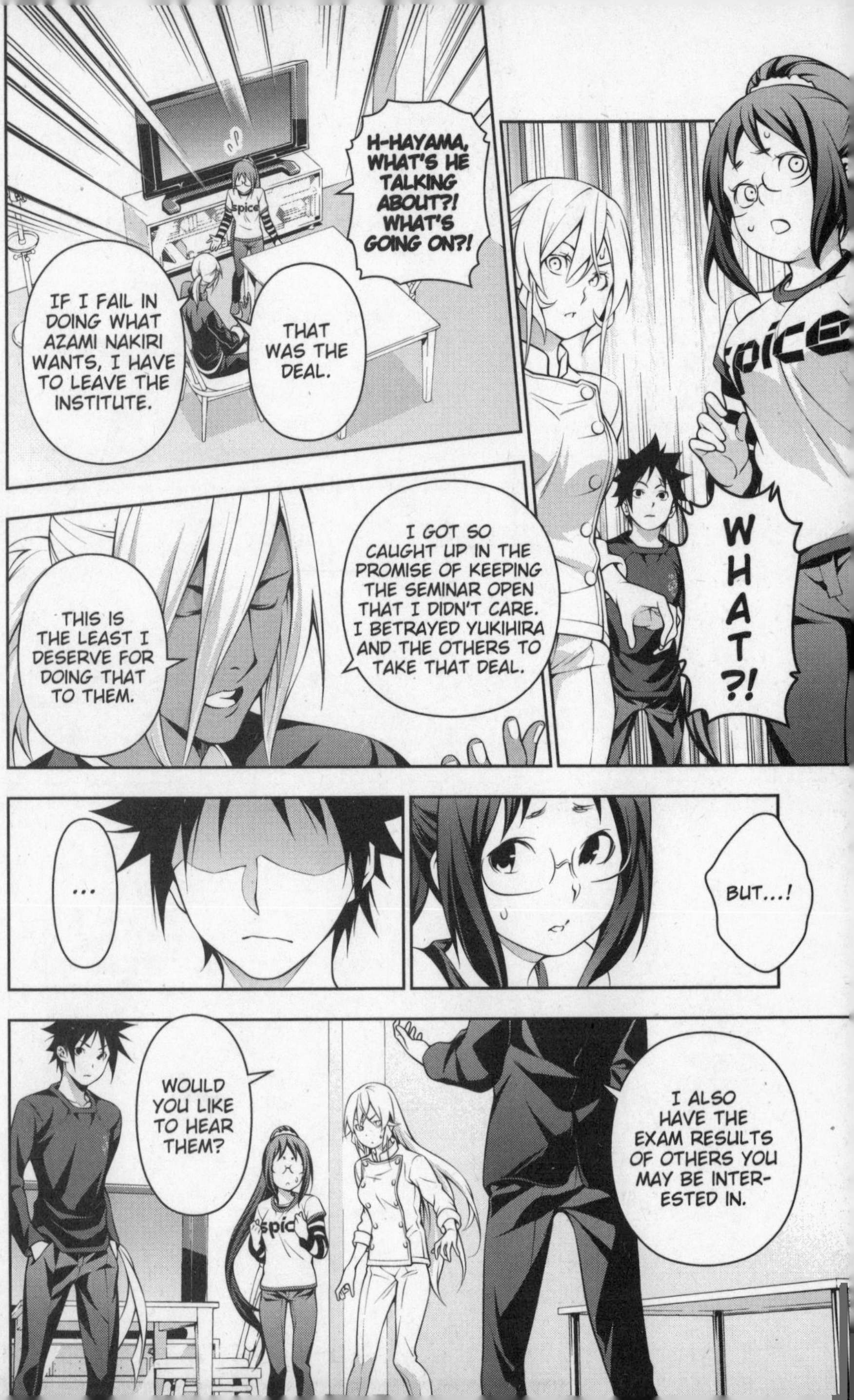
H-HAYAMA, WHAT'S HE TALKING ABOUT?! WHAT'S GOING ON?!
WHAT?!
IF I FAIL IN DOING WHAT AZAMI NAKIRI WANTS, I HAVE TO LEAVE THE INSTITUTE.
THAT WAS THE DEAL.
I GOT SO CAUGHT UP IN THE PROMISE OF KEEPING THE SEMINAR OPEN THAT I DIDN'T CARE. I BETRAYED YUKIHIRA AND THE OTHERS TO TAKE THAT DEAL.
THIS IS THE LEAST I DESERVE FOR DOING THAT TO THEM.
BUT...!
...
I ALSO HAVE THE EXAM RESULTS OF OTHERS YOU MAY BE INTER-ESTED IN.
WOULD YOU LIKE TO HEAR THEM?

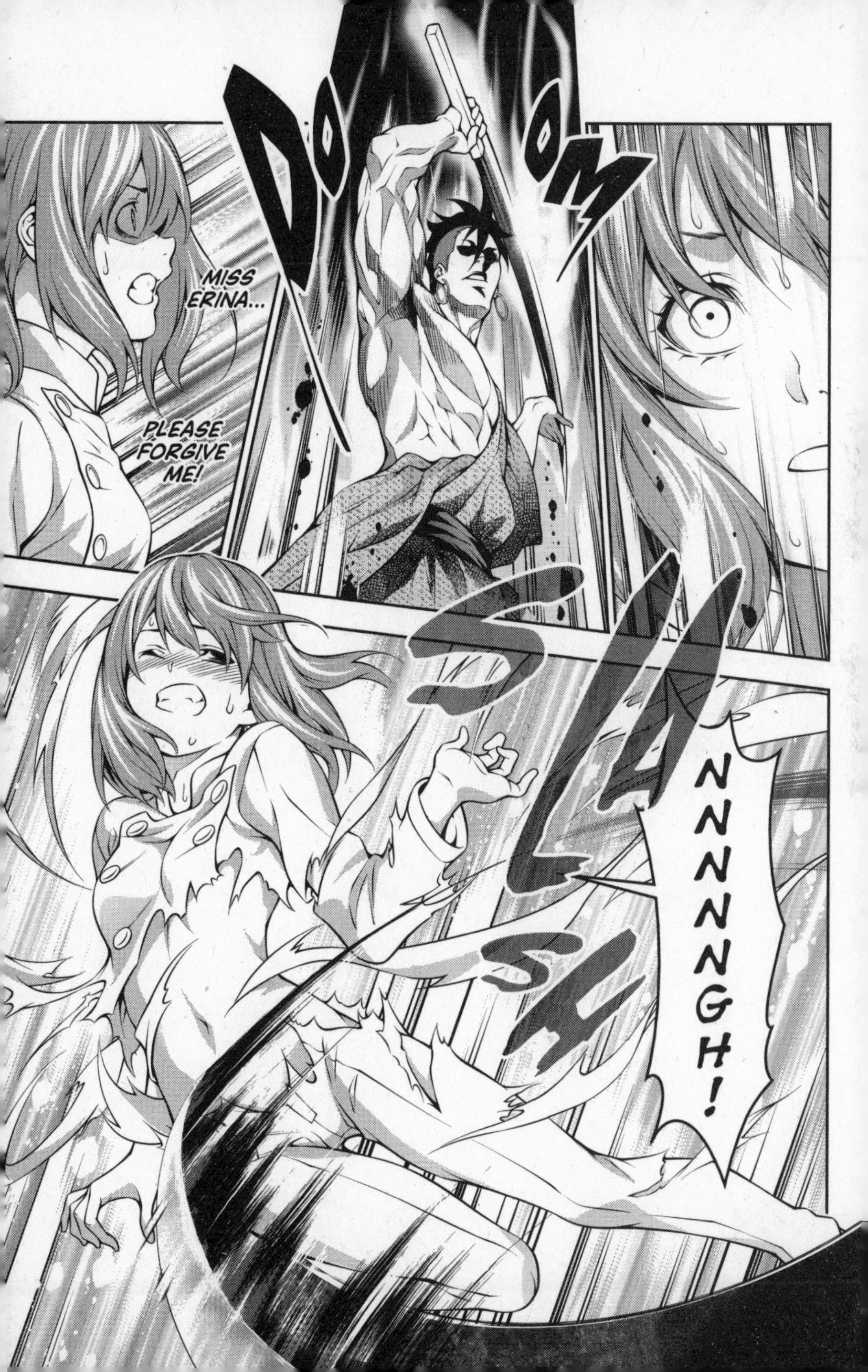

DOOM
MISS ERINA...
PLEASE FORGIVE ME!
SLASH
NNNNNGH!

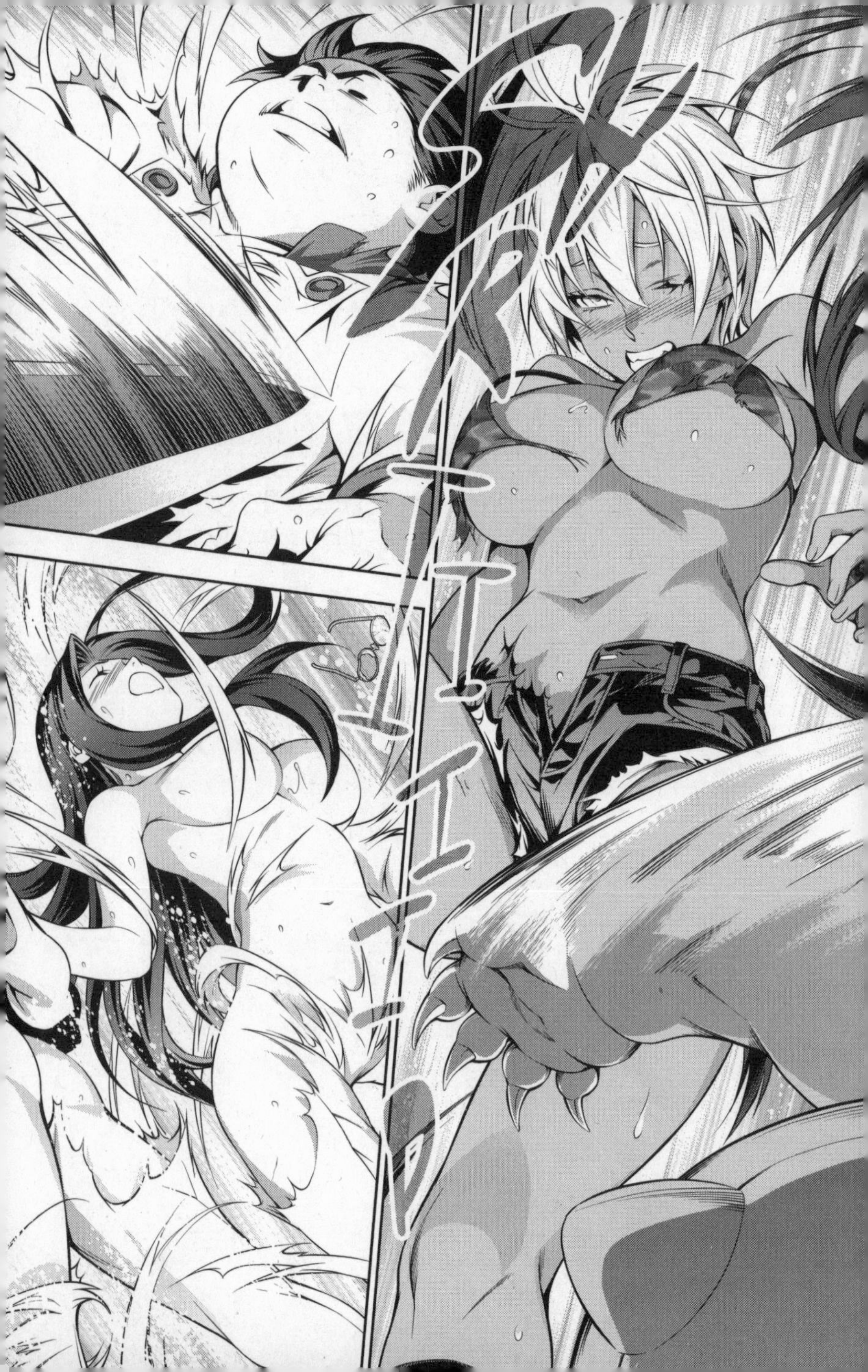

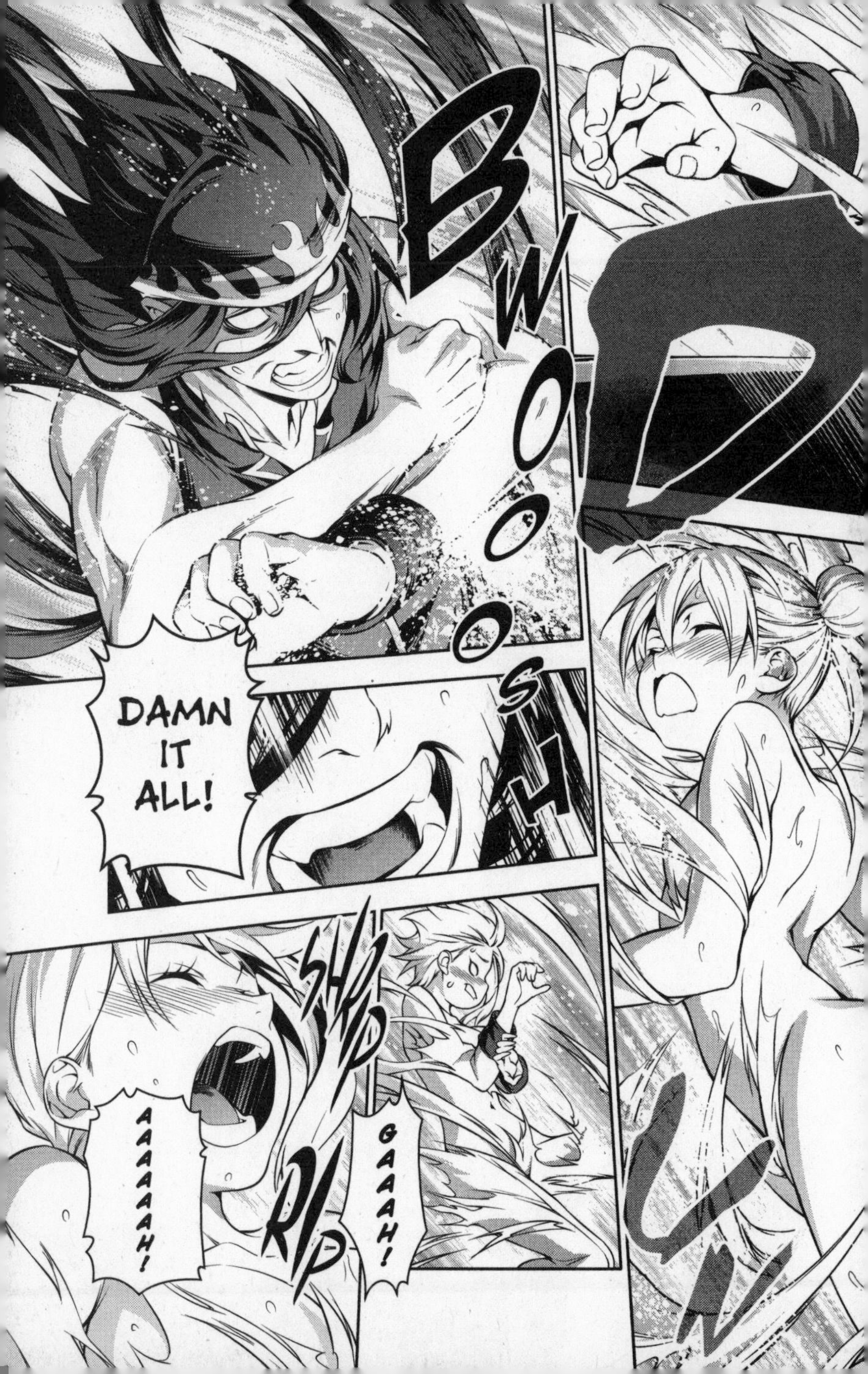
BWOOOOSH
DAMN IT ALL!
AAAAAAH!
GAAAH!
RIP

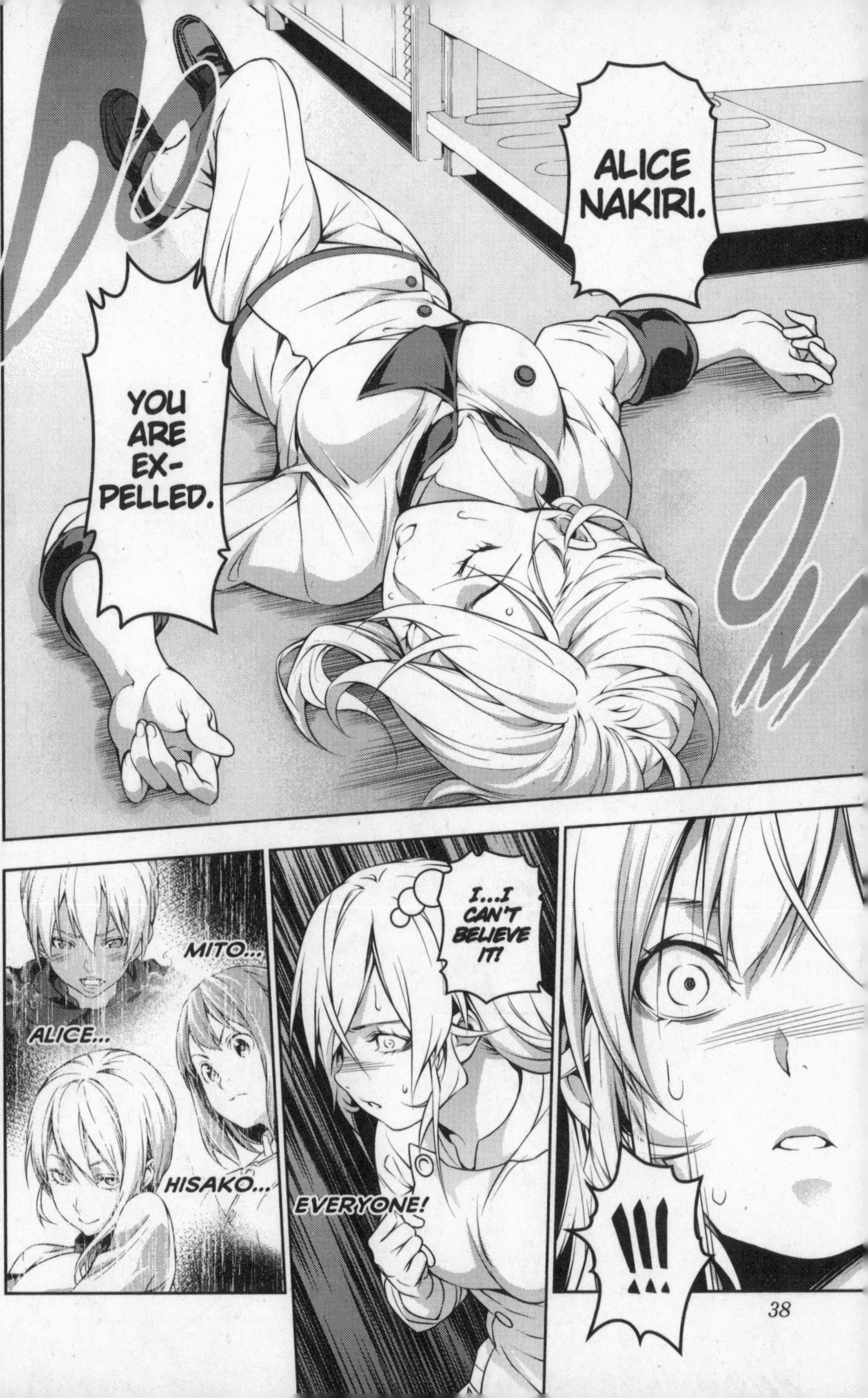
ALICE NAKIRI.
YOU ARE EX-PELLED.
!!!
I...I CAN'T BELIEVE IT!
EVERYONE!
MITO...
ALICE...
HISAKO...

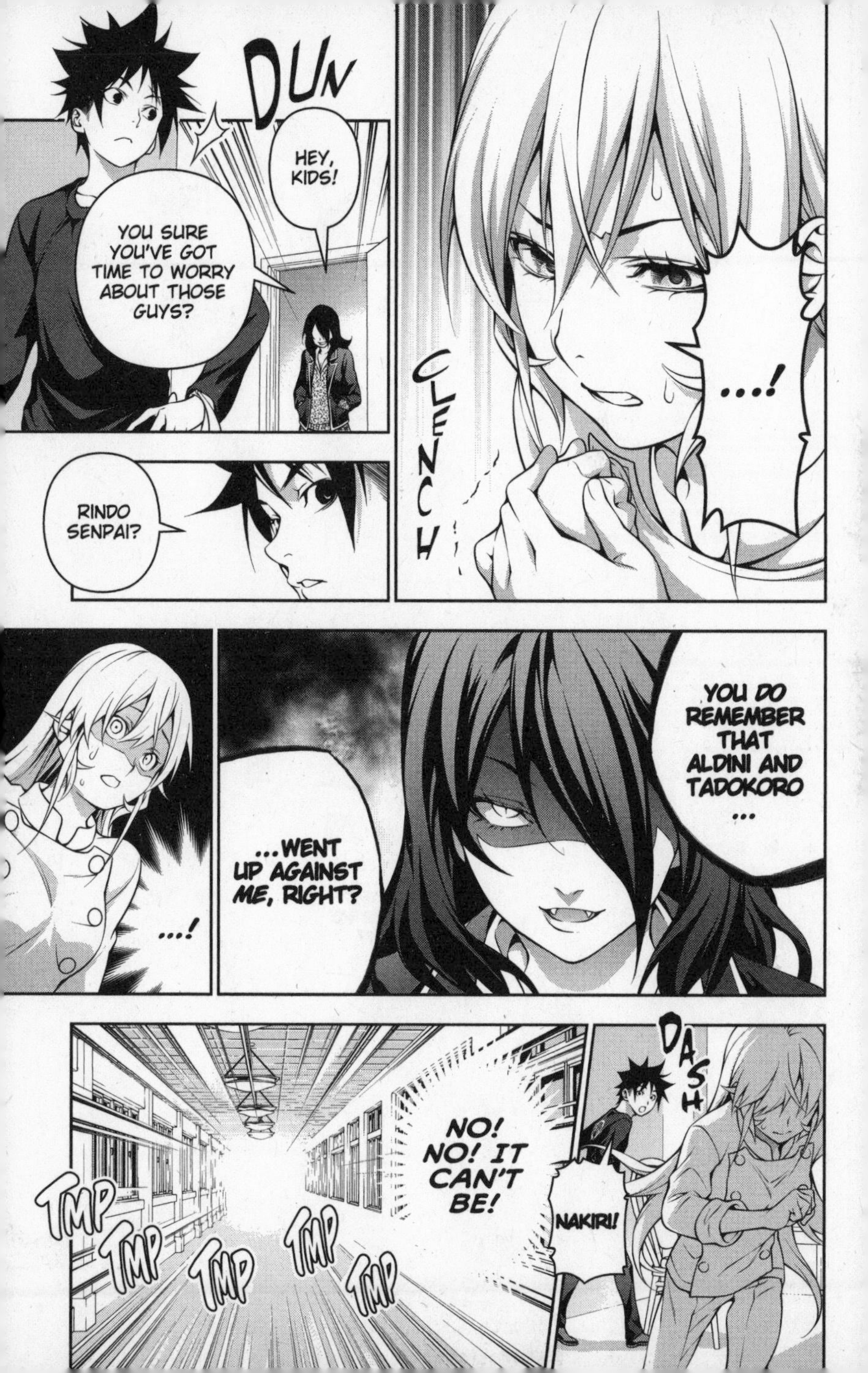
CLENCH
...!
DUN
HEY, KIDS!
YOU SURE YOU'VE GOT TIME TO WORRY ABOUT THOSE GUYS?
RINDO SENPAI?
YOU DO REMEMBER THAT ALDINI AND TADOKORO ...
...WENT UP AGAINST ME, RIGHT?
...!
DASH
NAKIRI!
NO! NO! IT CAN'T BE!
TMP TMP TMP TMP TMP

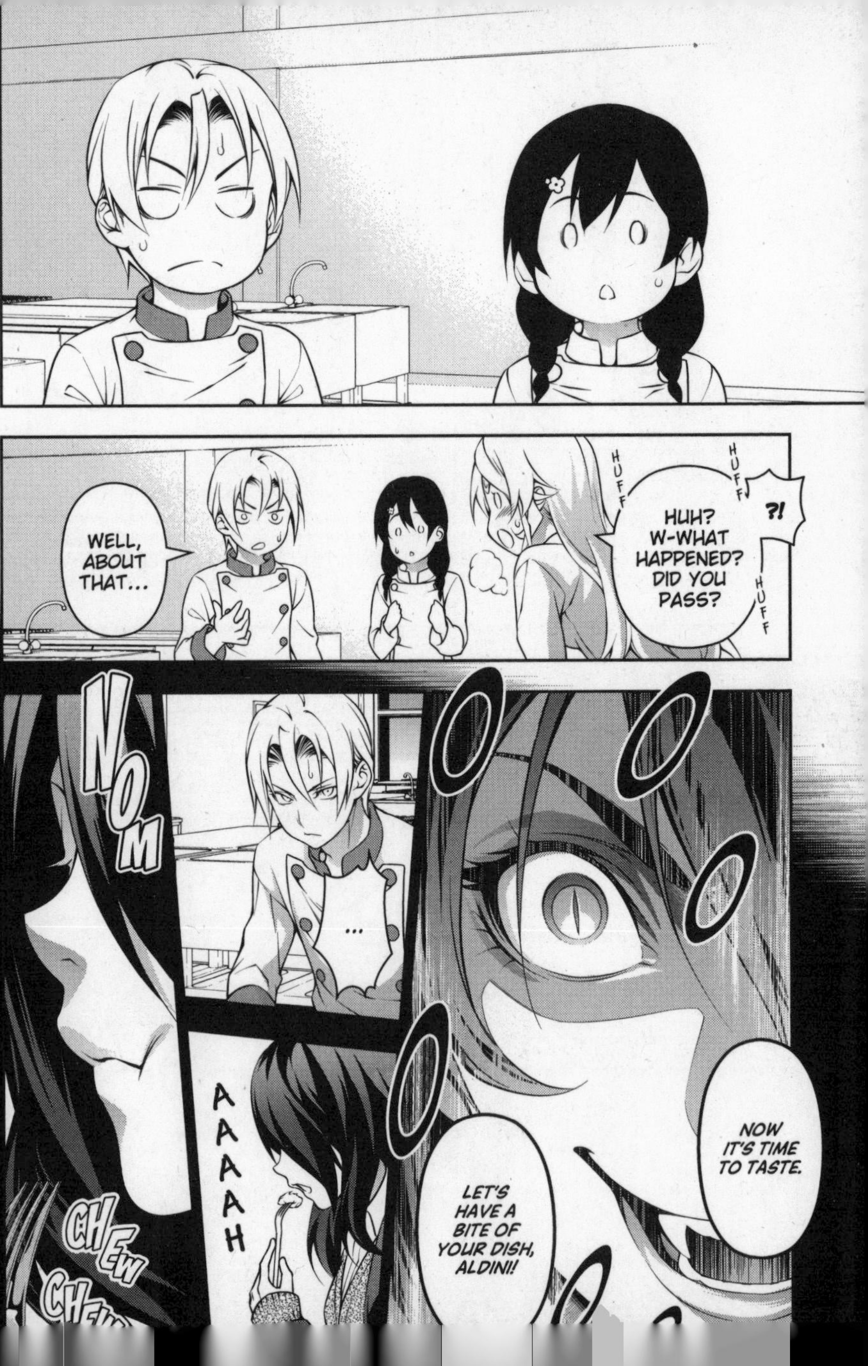
?!
HUFF HUFF HUFF
HUH? W-WHAT HAPPENED? DID YOU PASS?
WELL, ABOUT THAT...
NOW IT'S TIME TO TASTE.
LET'S HAVE A BITE OF YOUR DISH, ALDINI!
...
NOM
AAAAH
CHEW CHEW

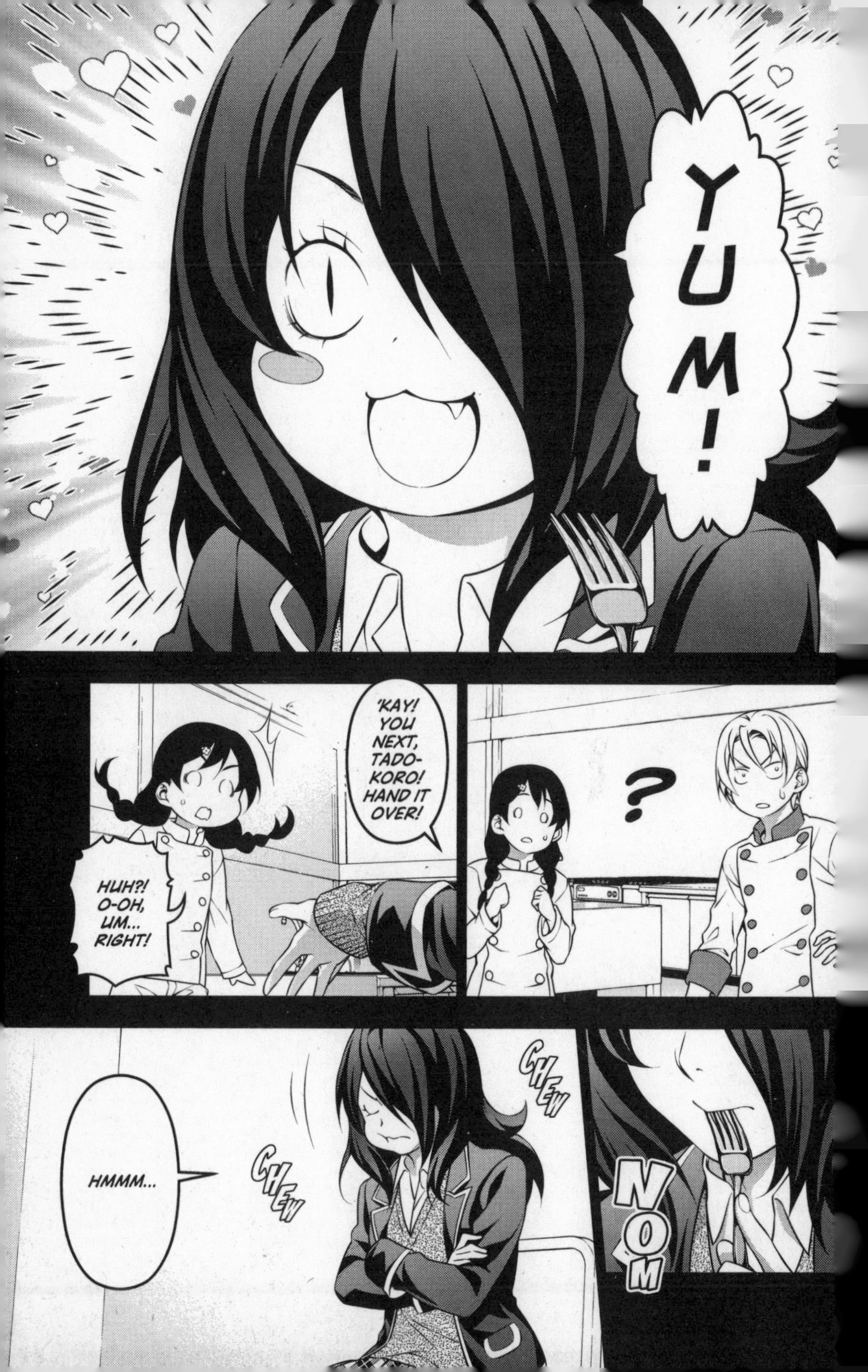
YUM!
?
'KAY! YOU NEXT, TADOKORO! HAND IT OVER!
HUH?! O-OH, UM... RIGHT!
NOM
CHEW
CHEW
HMMM...

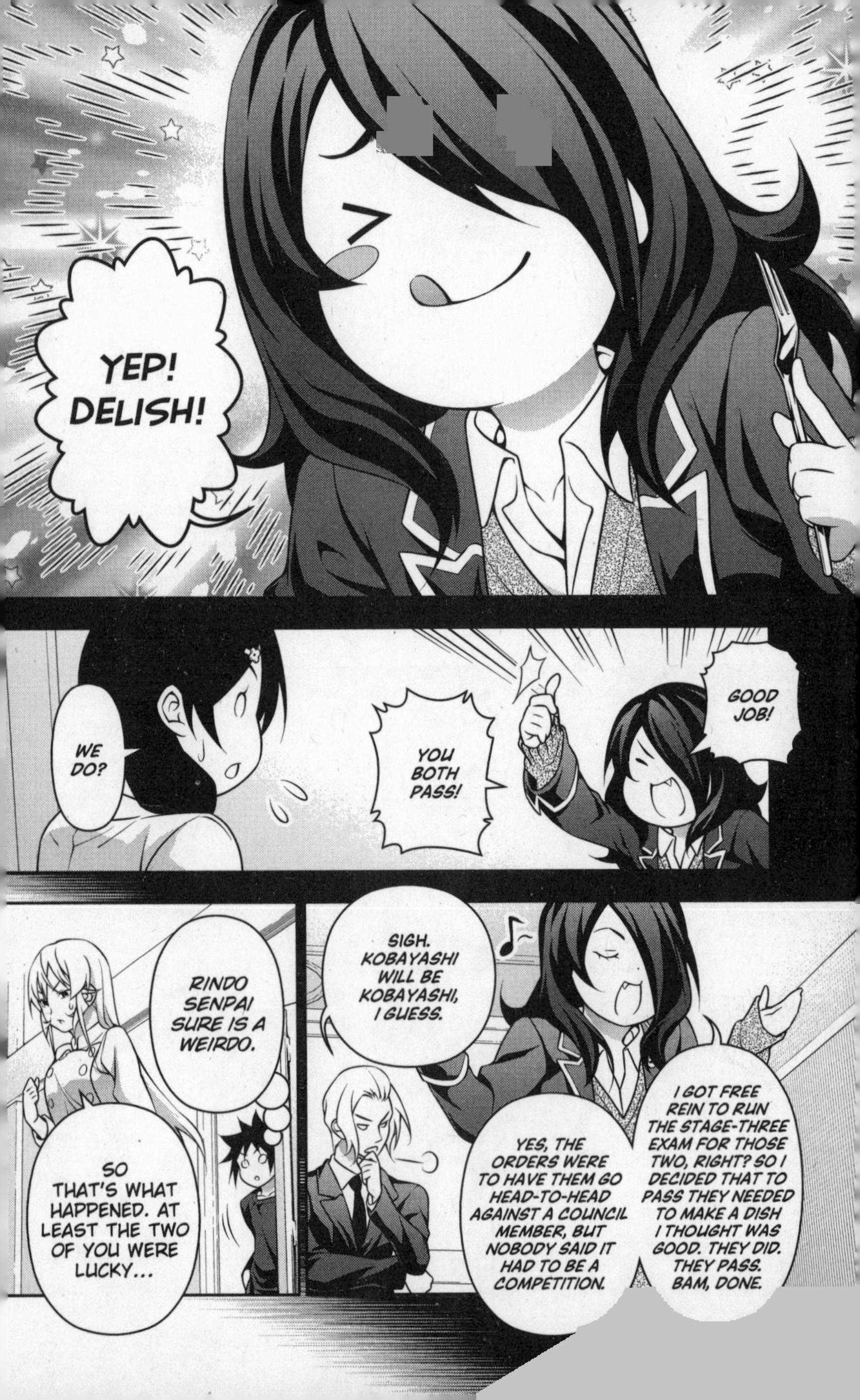
YEP! DELISH!
GOOD JOB!
YOU BOTH PASS!
WE DO?
I GOT FREE REIN TO RUN THE STAGE-THREE EXAM FOR THOSE TWO, RIGHT? SO I DECIDED THAT TO PASS THEY NEEDED TO MAKE A DISH I THOUGHT WAS GOOD. THEY DID. THEY PASS. BAM, DONE.
YES, THE ORDERS WERE TO HAVE THEM GO HEAD-TO-HEAD AGAINST A COUNCIL MEMBER, BUT NOBODY SAID IT HAD TO BE A COMPETITION.
SIGH. KOBAYASHI WILL BE KOBAYASHI, I GUESS.
RINDO SENPAI SURE IS A WEIRDO.
SO THAT'S WHAT HAPPENED. AT LEAST THE TWO OF YOU WERE LUCKY...

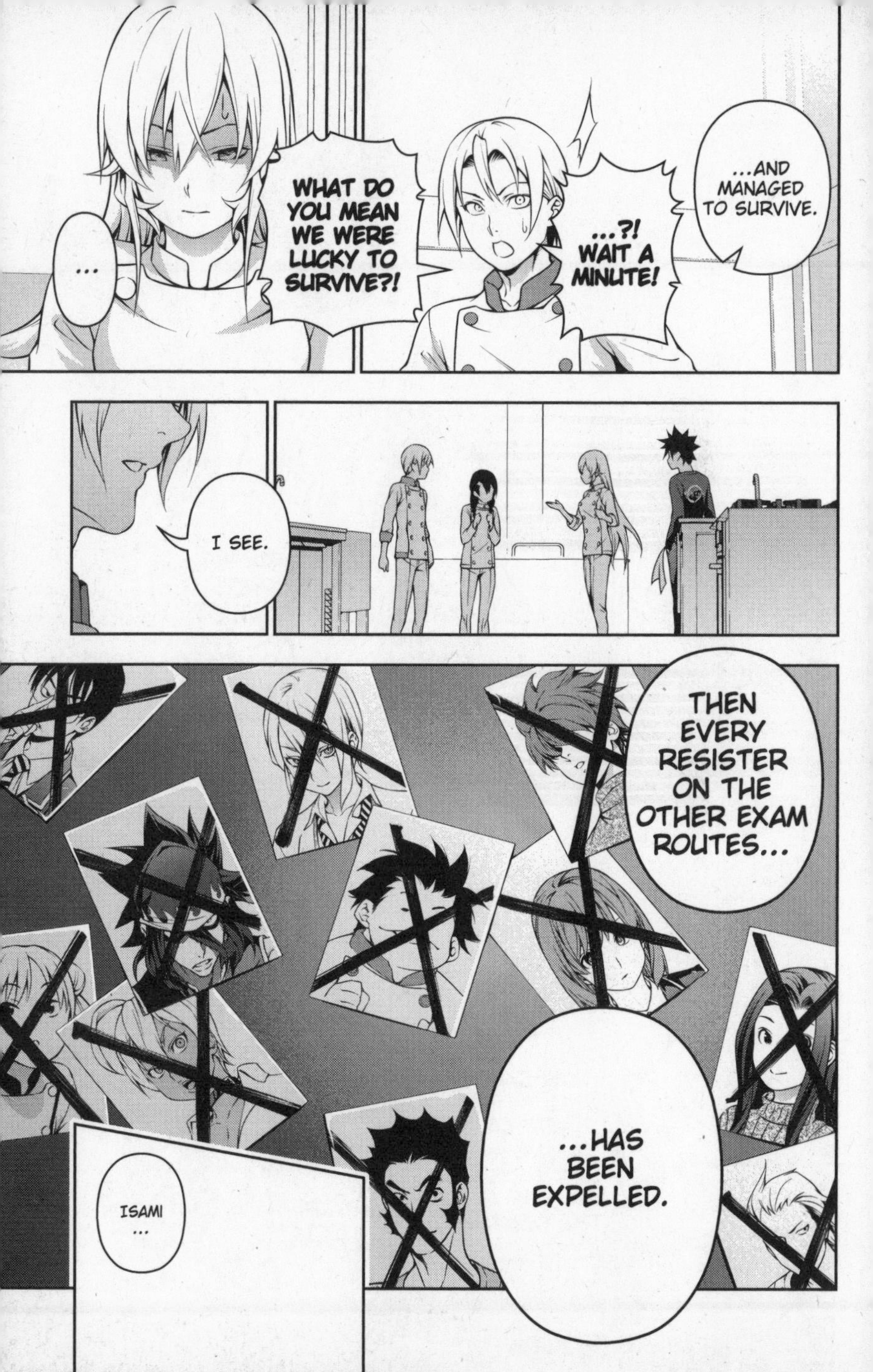
...AND MANAGED TO SURVIVE.
...?! WAIT A MINUTE!
WHAT DO YOU MEAN WE WERE LUCKY TO SURVIVE?!
...
I SEE.
THEN EVERY RESISTER ON THE OTHER EXAM ROUTES...
...HAS BEEN EXPELLED.
ISAMI ...

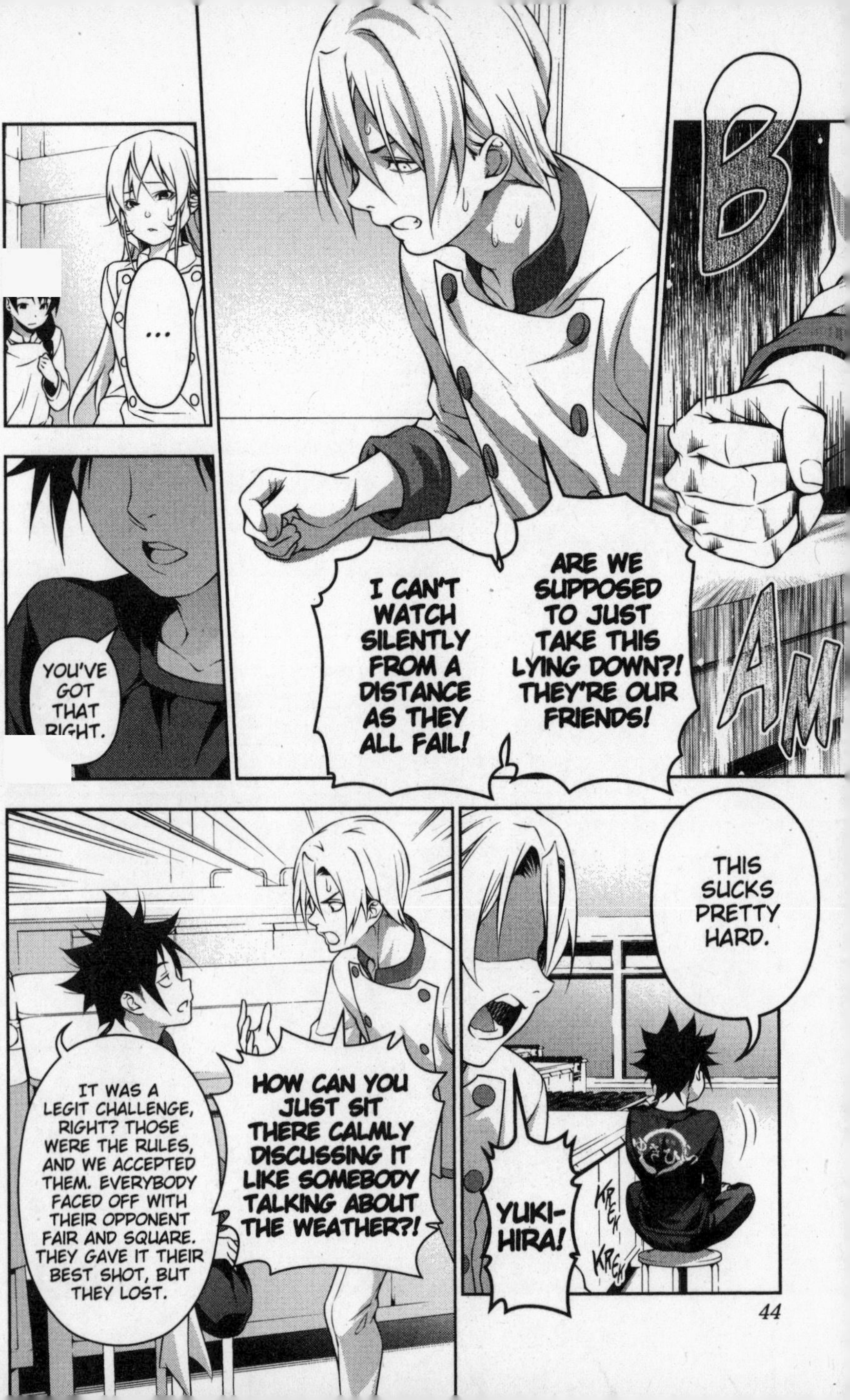
BAM
ARE WE SUPPOSED TO JUST TAKE THIS LYING DOWN?! THEY'RE OUR FRIENDS!
I CAN'T WATCH SILENTLY FROM A DISTANCE AS THEY ALL FAIL!
...
YOU'VE GOT THAT RIGHT.
THIS SUCKS PRETTY HARD.
YUKI-HIRA!
KREK
KREK
HOW CAN YOU JUST SIT THERE CALMLY DISCUSSING IT LIKE SOMEBODY TALKING ABOUT THE WEATHER?!
IT WAS A LEGIT CHALLENGE, RIGHT? THOSE WERE THE RULES, AND WE ACCEPTED THEM. EVERYBODY FACED OFF WITH THEIR OPPONENT FAIR AND SQUARE. THEY GAVE IT THEIR BEST SHOT, BUT THEY LOST.

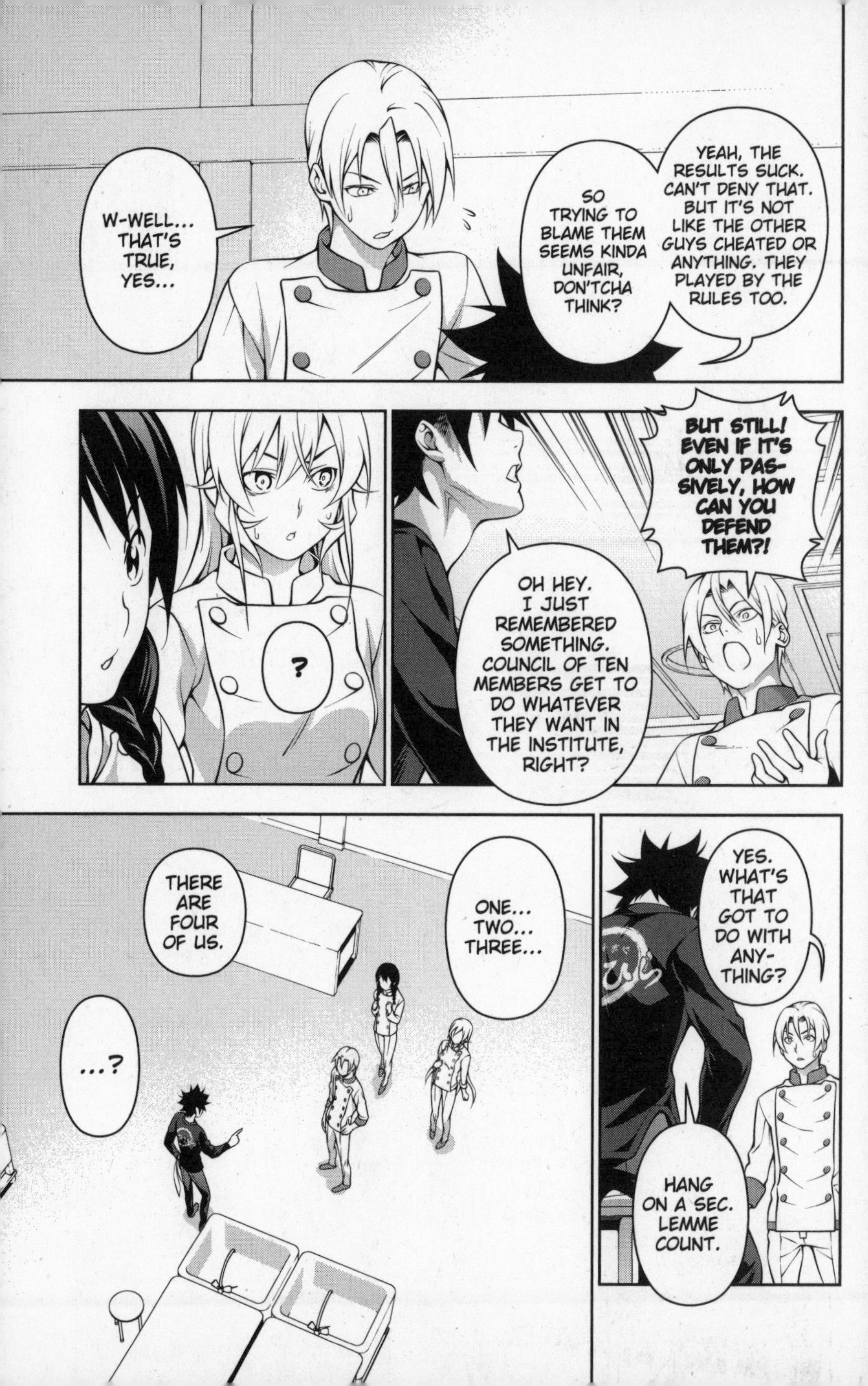
YEAH, THE RESULTS SUCK. CAN'T DENY THAT. BUT IT'S NOT LIKE THE OTHER GUYS CHEATED OR ANYTHING. THEY PLAYED BY THE RULES TOO.
SO TRYING TO BLAME THEM SEEMS KINDA UNFAIR, DON'TCHA THINK?
W-WELL... THAT'S TRUE, YES...
BUT STILL! EVEN IF IT'S ONLY PAS-SIVELY, HOW CAN YOU DEFEND THEM?!
OH HEY. I JUST REMEMBERED SOMETHING. COUNCIL OF TEN MEMBERS GET TO DO WHATEVER THEY WANT IN THE INSTITUTE, RIGHT?
?
YES. WHAT'S THAT GOT TO DO WITH ANY-THING?
HANG ON A SEC. LEMME COUNT.
ONE... TWO... THREE...
THERE ARE FOUR OF US.
...?

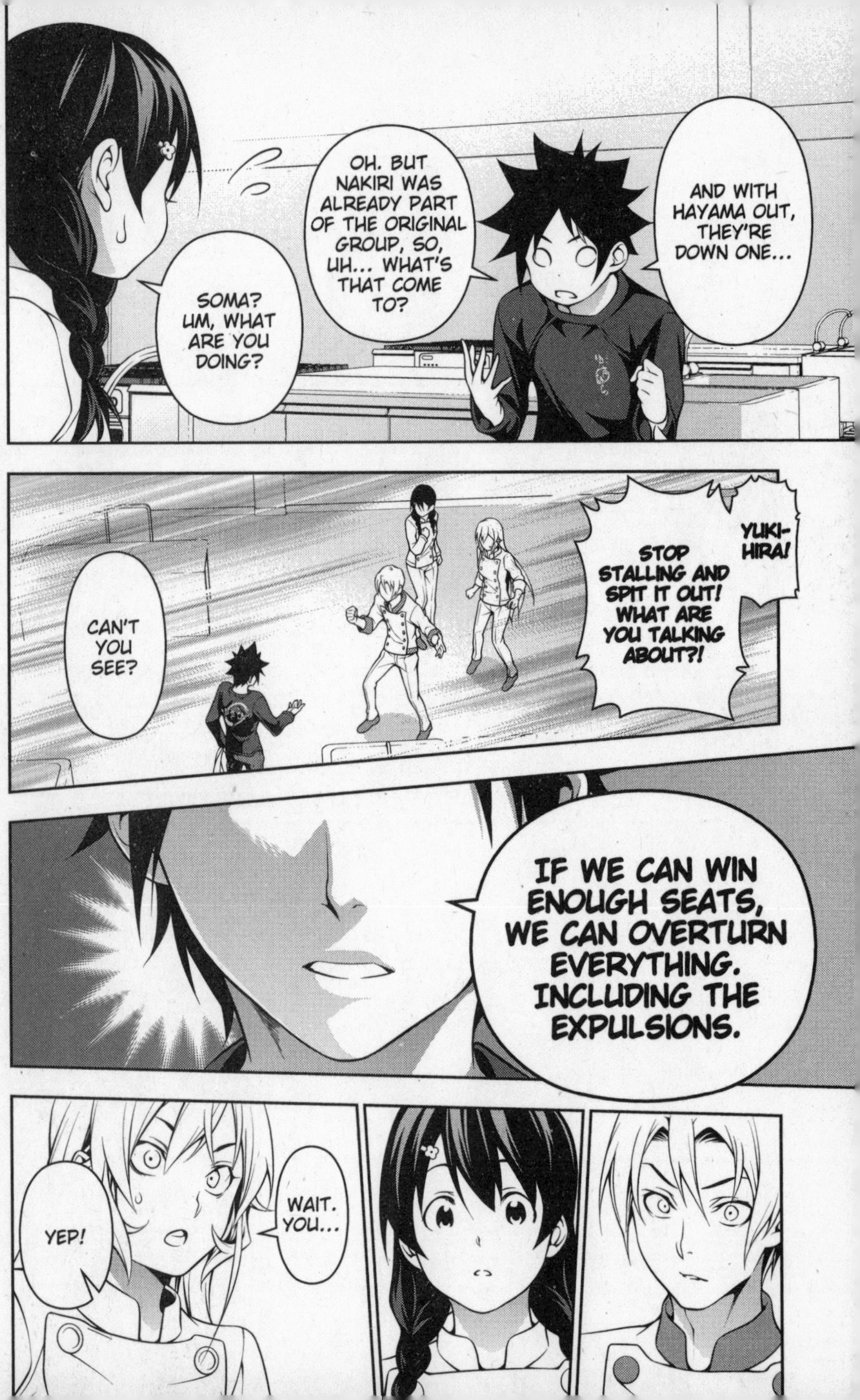
AND WITH HAYAMA OUT, THEY'RE DOWN ONE...
OH. BUT NAKIRI WAS ALREADY PART OF THE ORIGINAL GROUP, SO, UH... WHAT'S THAT COME TO?
SOMA? UM, WHAT ARE YOU DOING?
YUKI-HIRA!
STOP STALLING AND SPIT IT OUT! WHAT ARE YOU TALKING ABOUT?!
CAN'T YOU SEE?
IF WE CAN WIN ENOUGH SEATS, WE CAN OVERTURN EVERYTHING. INCLUDING THE EXPULSIONS.
WAIT. YOU...
YEP!

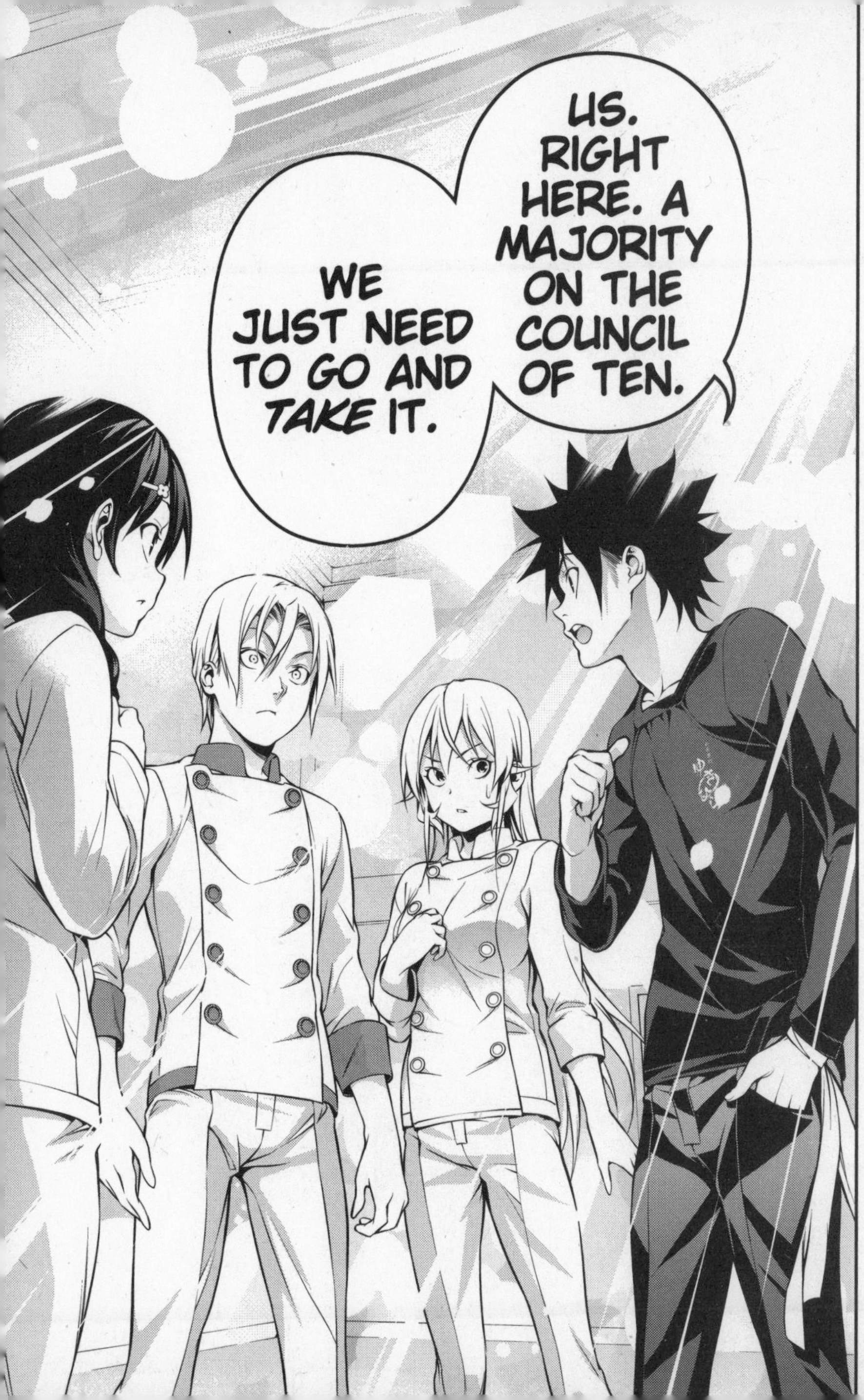
US. RIGHT HERE. A MAJORITY ON THE COUNCIL OF TEN.
WE JUST NEED TO GO AND *TAKE* IT.

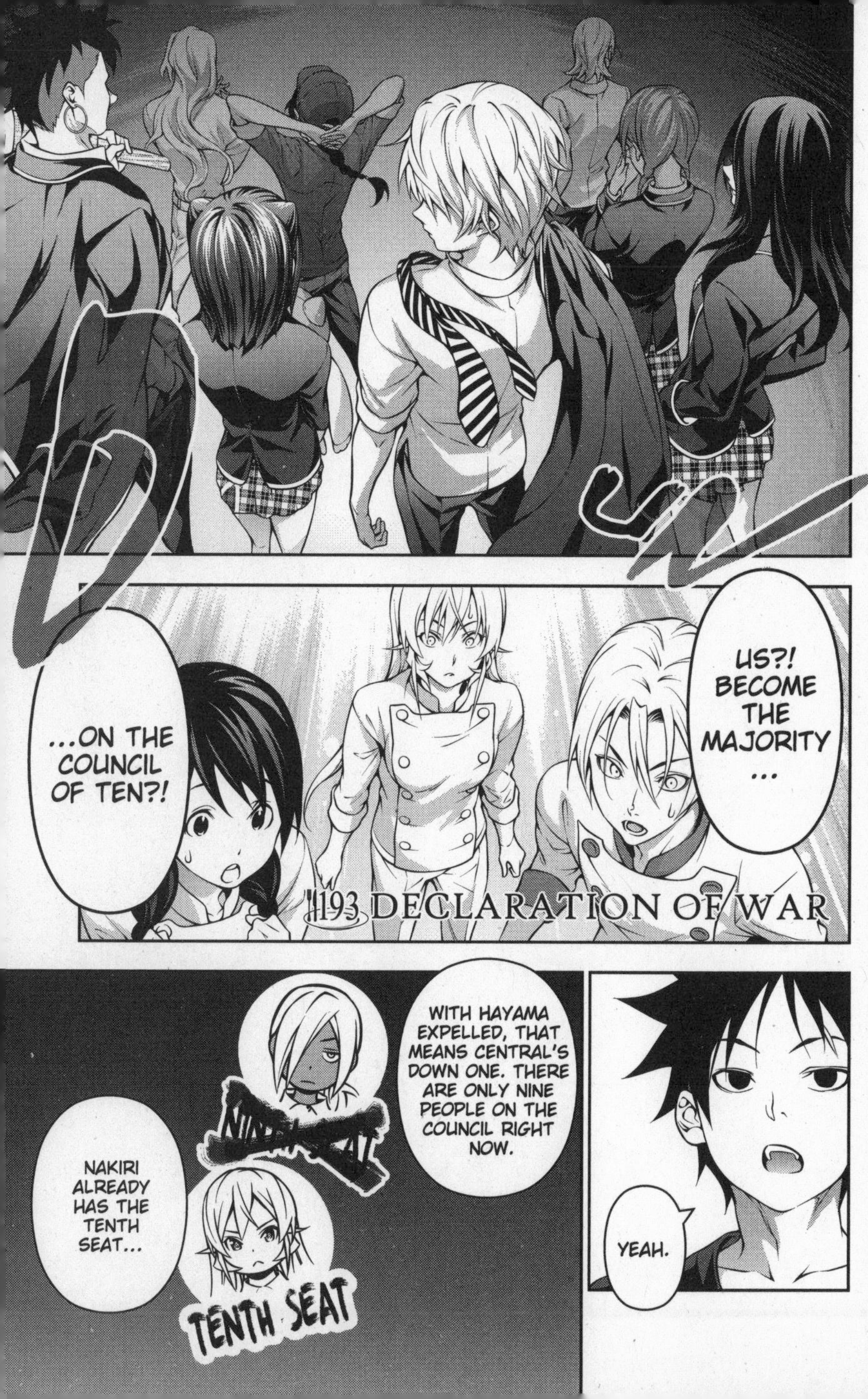
US?! BECOME THE MAJORITY ...
...ON THE COUNCIL OF TEN?!
193 DECLARATION OF WAR
YEAH.
WITH HAYAMA EXPELLED, THAT MEANS CENTRAL'S DOWN ONE. THERE ARE ONLY NINE PEOPLE ON THE COUNCIL RIGHT NOW.
NAKIRI ALREADY HAS THE TENTH SEAT...
TENTH SEAT

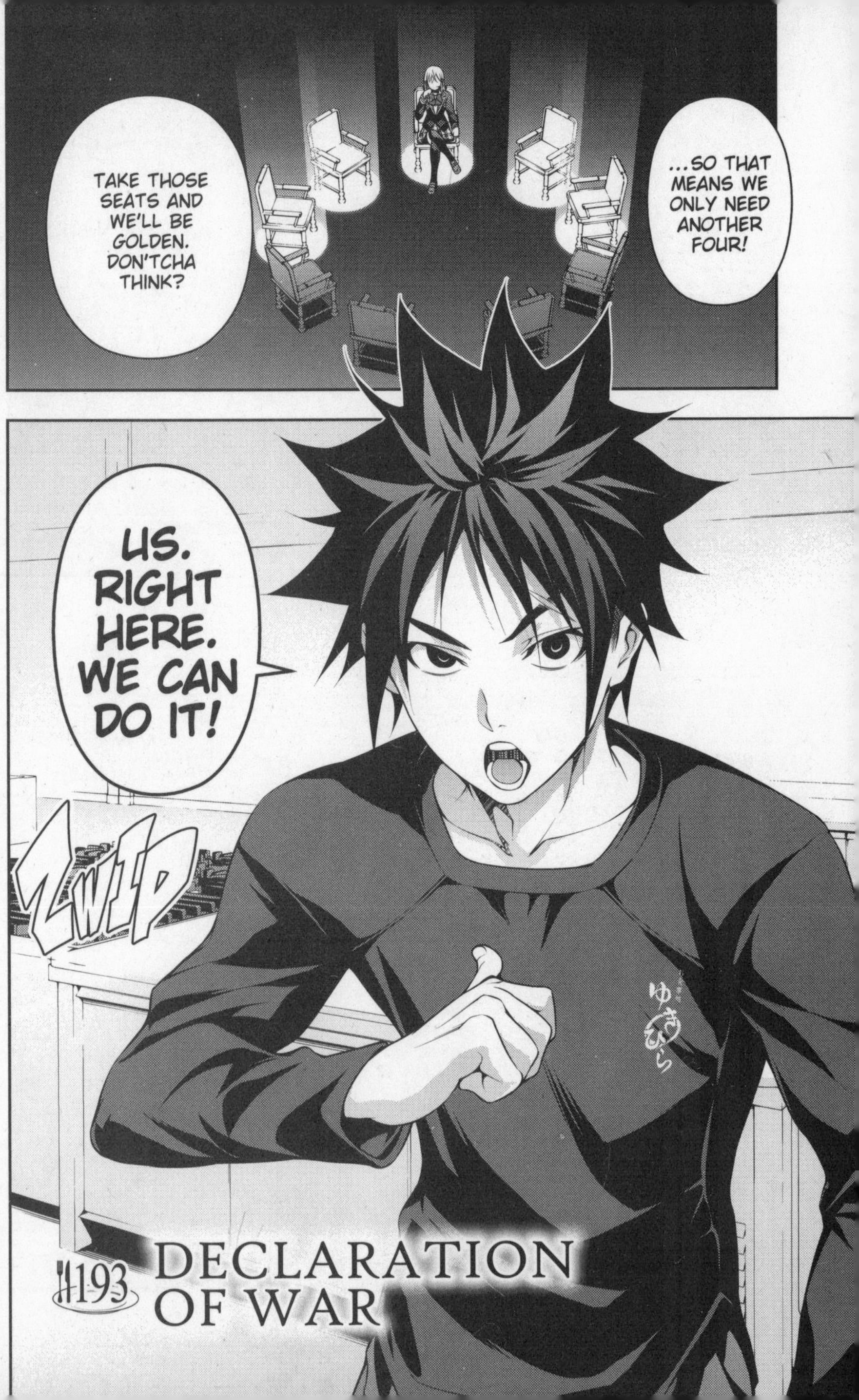
...SO THAT MEANS WE ONLY NEED ANOTHER FOUR!
TAKE THOSE SEATS AND WE'LL BE GOLDEN. DON'TCHA THINK?
US. RIGHT HERE. WE CAN DO IT!
ZWIP
193 DECLARATION OF WAR

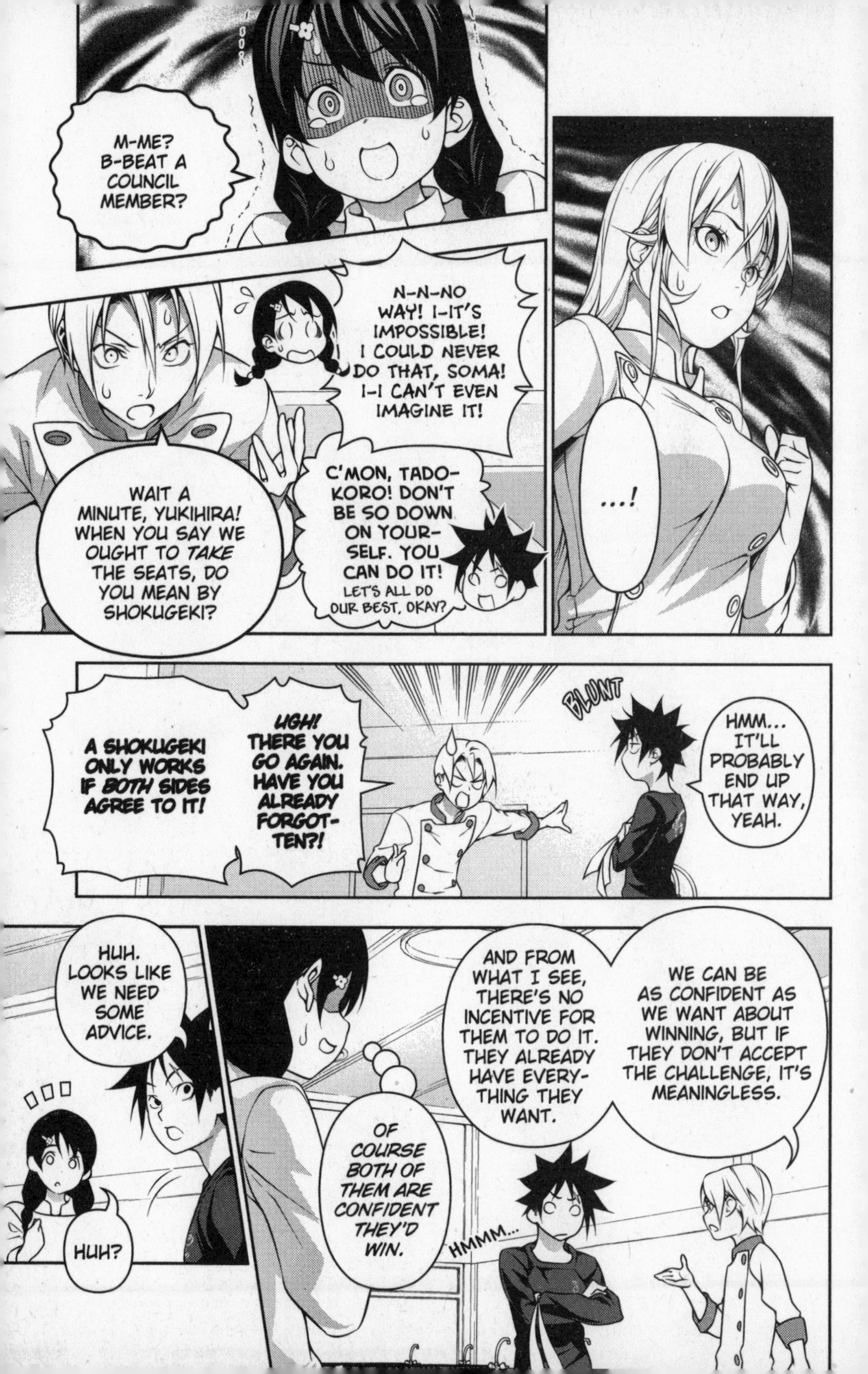

M-ME? B-BEAT A COUNCIL MEMBER?
...!
N-N-NO WAY! I-IT'S IMPOSSIBLE! I COULD NEVER DO THAT, SOMA! I-I CAN'T EVEN IMAGINE IT!
C'MON, TADO-KORO! DON'T BE SO DOWN ON YOUR-SELF. YOU CAN DO IT! LET'S ALL DO OUR BEST, OKAY?
WAIT A MINUTE, YUKIHIRA! WHEN YOU SAY WE OUGHT TO *TAKE* THE SEATS, DO YOU MEAN BY SHOKUGEKI?
HMM... IT'LL PROBABLY END UP THAT WAY, YEAH.
BLUNT
UGH! THERE YOU GO AGAIN. HAVE YOU ALREADY FORGOT-TEN?!
A SHOKUGEKI ONLY WORKS IF *BOTH* SIDES AGREE TO IT!
WE CAN BE AS CONFIDENT AS WE WANT ABOUT WINNING, BUT IF THEY DON'T ACCEPT THE CHALLENGE, IT'S MEANINGLESS.
AND FROM WHAT I SEE, THERE'S NO INCENTIVE FOR THEM TO DO IT. THEY ALREADY HAVE EVERY-THING THEY WANT.
OF COURSE BOTH OF THEM ARE CONFIDENT THEY'D WIN.
HMMM...
HUH. LOOKS LIKE WE NEED SOME ADVICE.
HUH?

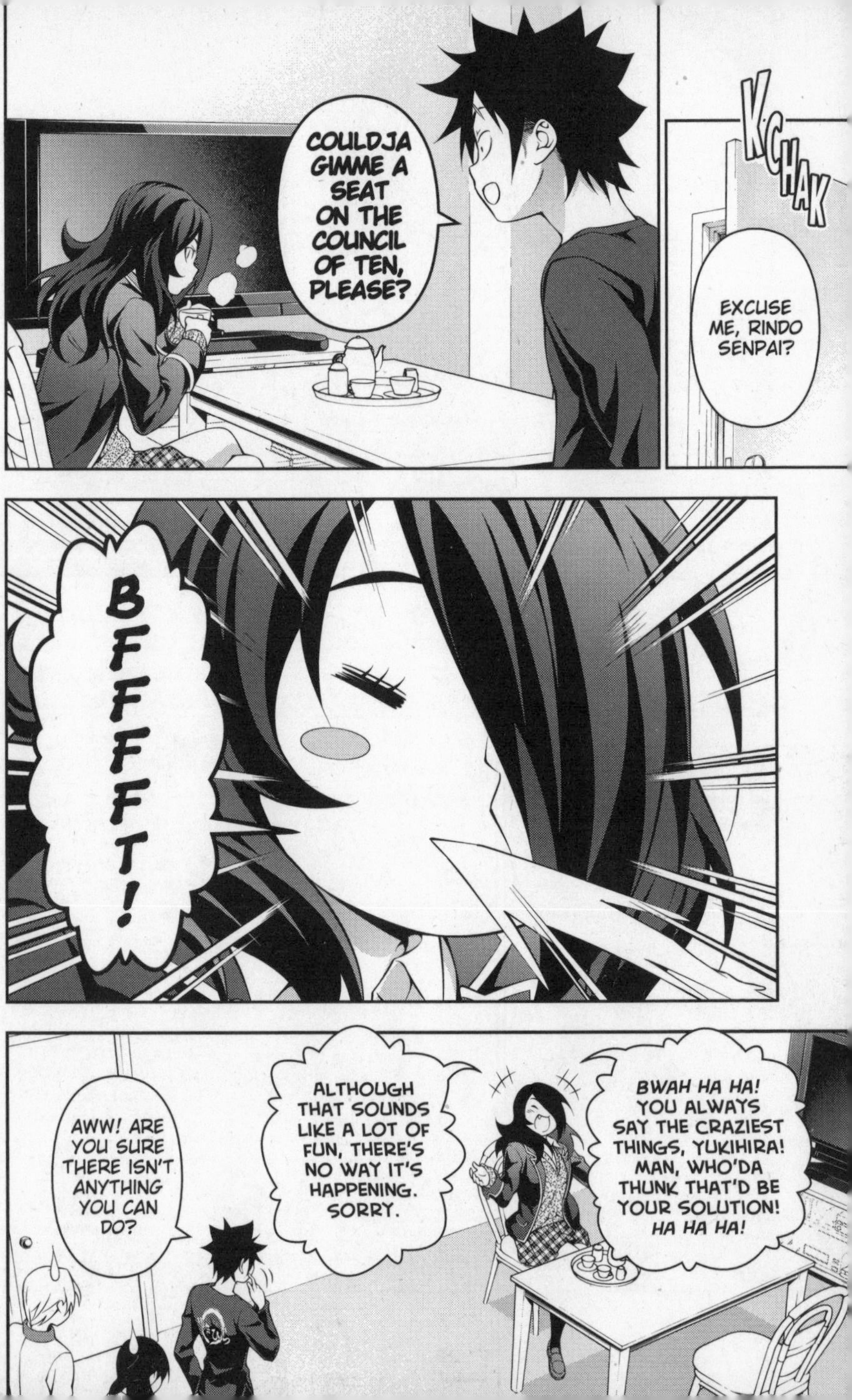

K-CHAK
EXCUSE ME, RINDO SENPAI?
COULDJA GIMME A SEAT ON THE COUNCIL OF TEN, PLEASE?
BFFFFT!
BWAH HA HA! YOU ALWAYS SAY THE CRAZIEST THINGS, YUKIHIRA! MAN, WHO'DA THUNK THAT'D BE YOUR SOLUTION! HA HA HA!
ALTHOUGH THAT SOUNDS LIKE A LOT OF FUN, THERE'S NO WAY IT'S HAPPENING. SORRY.
AWW! ARE YOU SURE THERE ISN'T ANYTHING YOU CAN DO?

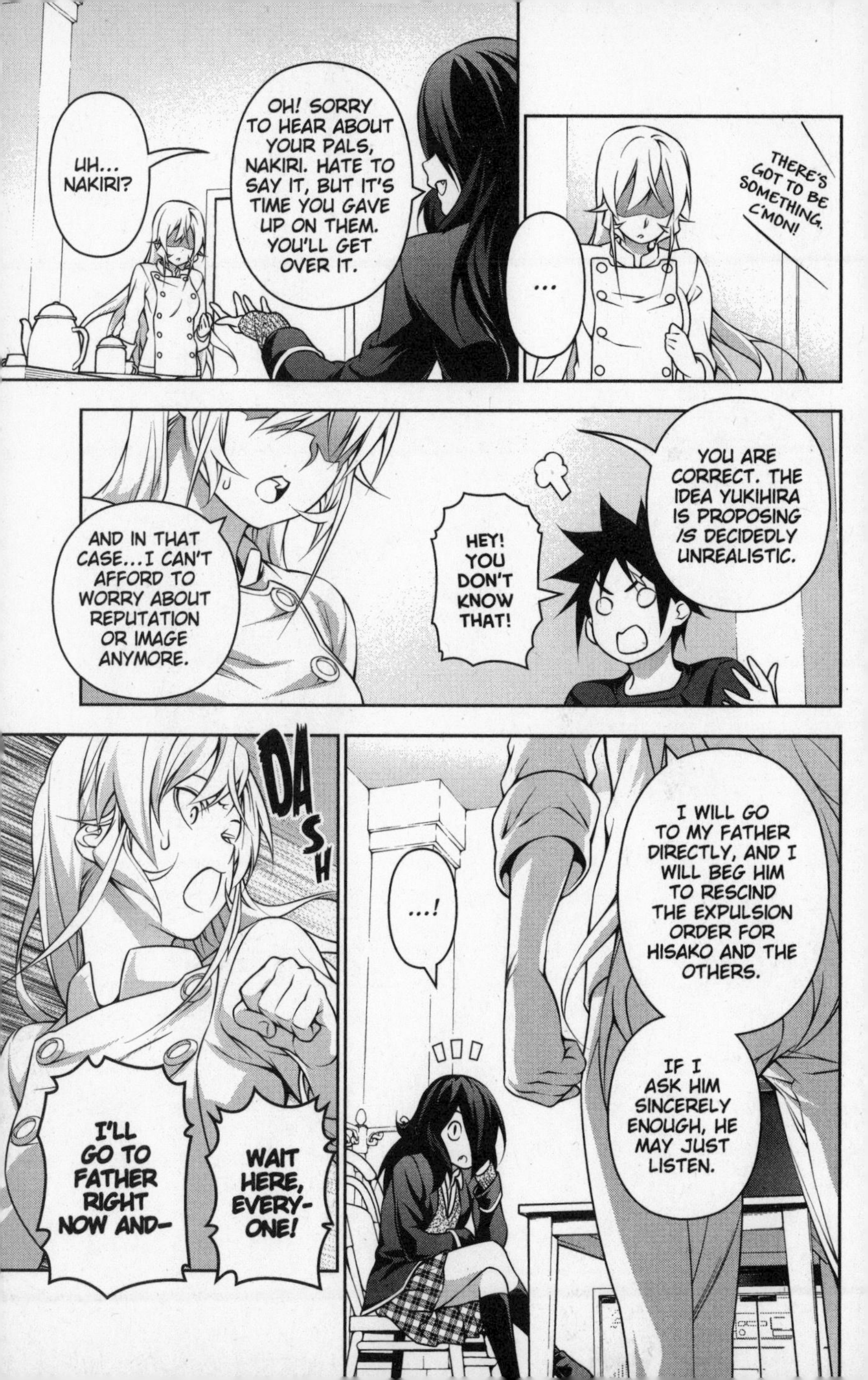
THERE'S GOT TO BE SOMETHING. C'MON!
...
OH! SORRY TO HEAR ABOUT YOUR PALS, NAKIRI. HATE TO SAY IT, BUT IT'S TIME YOU GAVE UP ON THEM. YOU'LL GET OVER IT.
UH... NAKIRI?
YOU ARE CORRECT. THE IDEA YUKIHIRA IS PROPOSING *IS* DECIDEDLY UNREALISTIC.
HEY! YOU DON'T KNOW THAT!
AND IN THAT CASE...I CAN'T AFFORD TO WORRY ABOUT REPUTATION OR IMAGE ANYMORE.
I WILL GO TO MY FATHER DIRECTLY, AND I WILL BEG HIM TO RESCIND THE EXPULSION ORDER FOR HISAKO AND THE OTHERS.
...!
IF I ASK HIM SINCERELY ENOUGH, HE MAY JUST LISTEN.
DASH
WAIT HERE, EVERYONE!
I'LL GO TO FATHER RIGHT NOW AND-

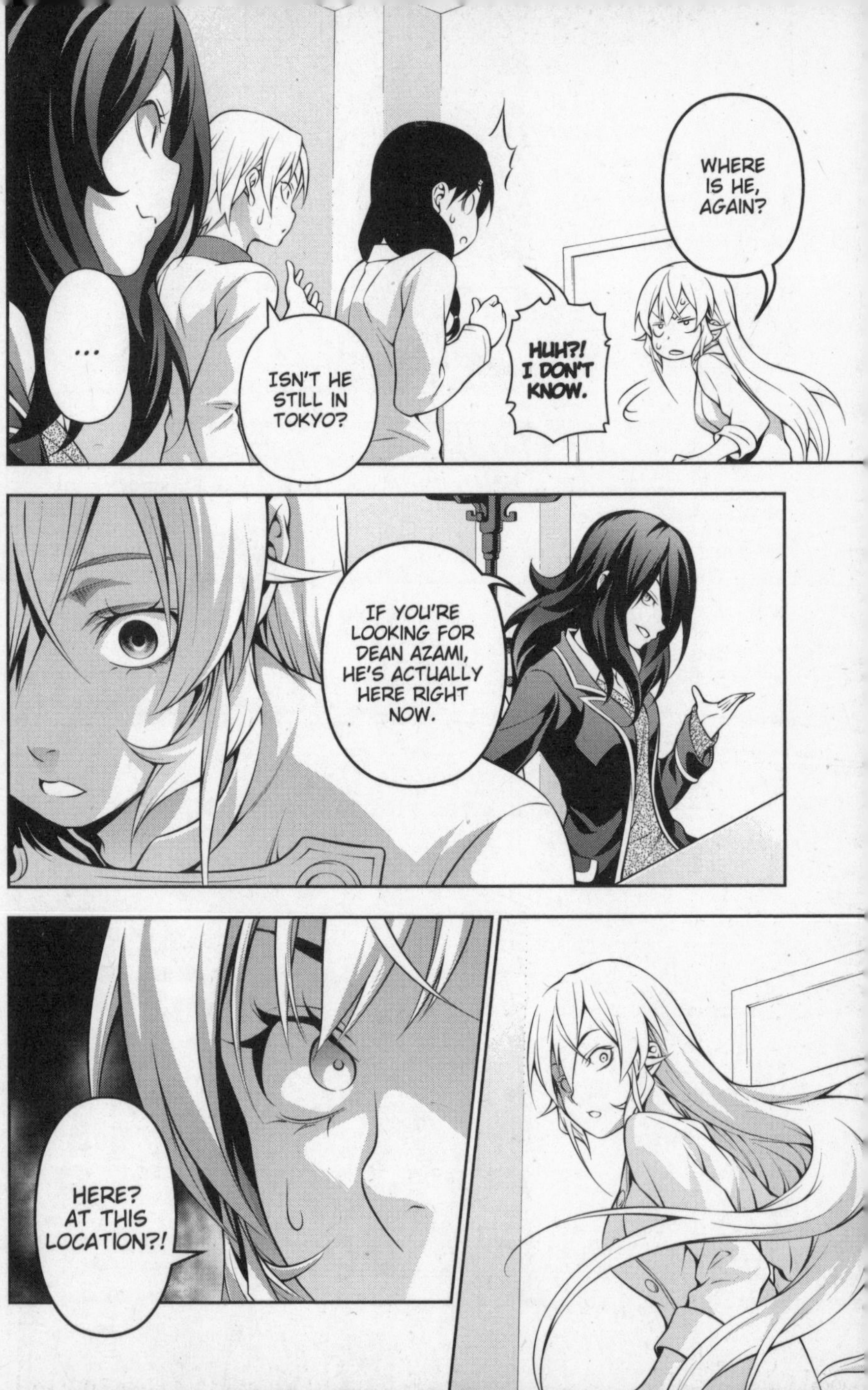
WHERE IS HE, AGAIN?
HUH?! I DON'T KNOW.
ISN'T HE STILL IN TOKYO?
...
IF YOU'RE LOOKING FOR DEAN AZAMI, HE'S ACTUALLY HERE RIGHT NOW.
HERE? AT THIS LOCATION?!

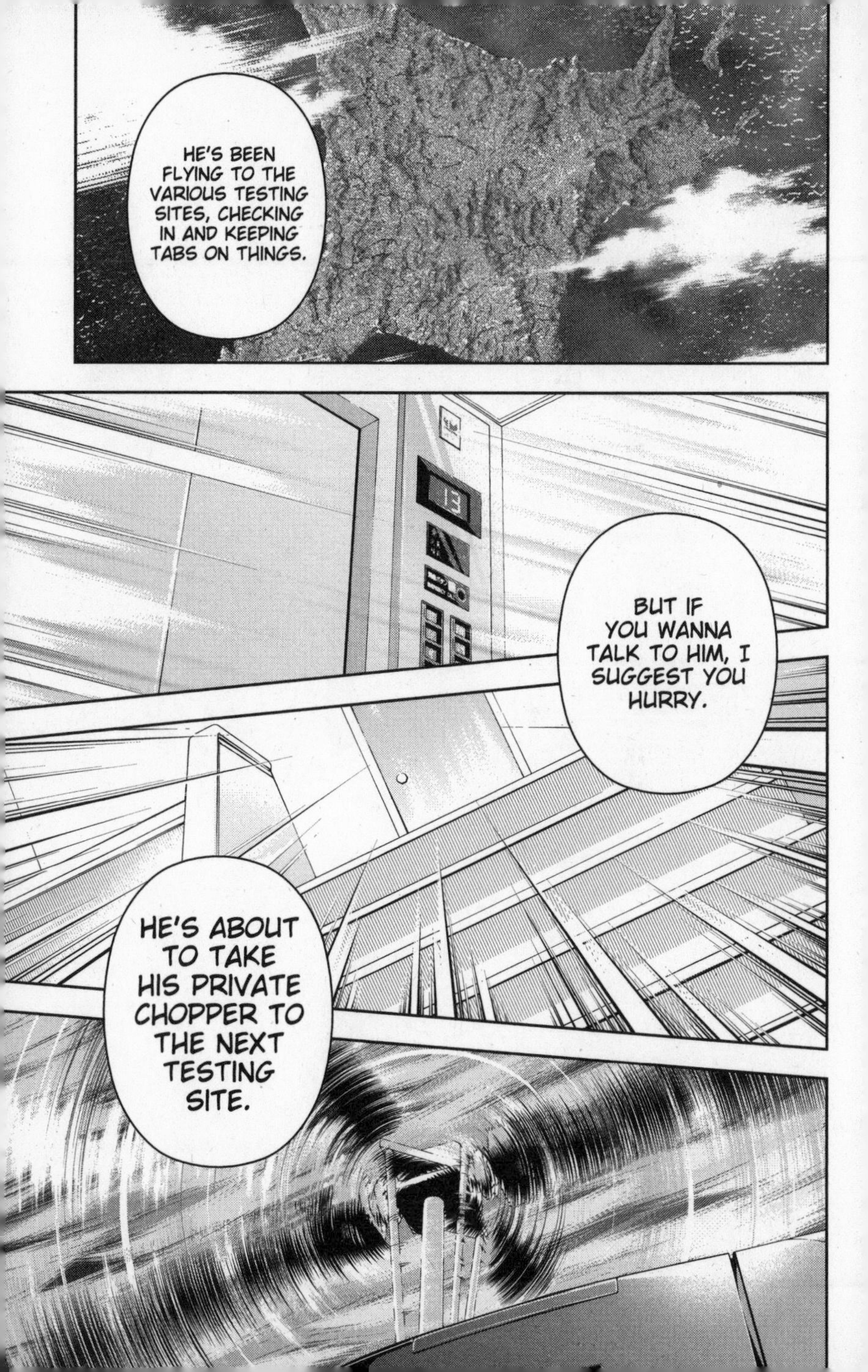
HE'S BEEN FLYING TO THE VARIOUS TESTING SITES, CHECKING IN AND KEEPING TABS ON THINGS.
BUT IF YOU WANNA TALK TO HIM, I SUGGEST YOU HURRY.
HE'S ABOUT TO TAKE HIS PRIVATE CHOPPER TO THE NEXT TESTING SITE.

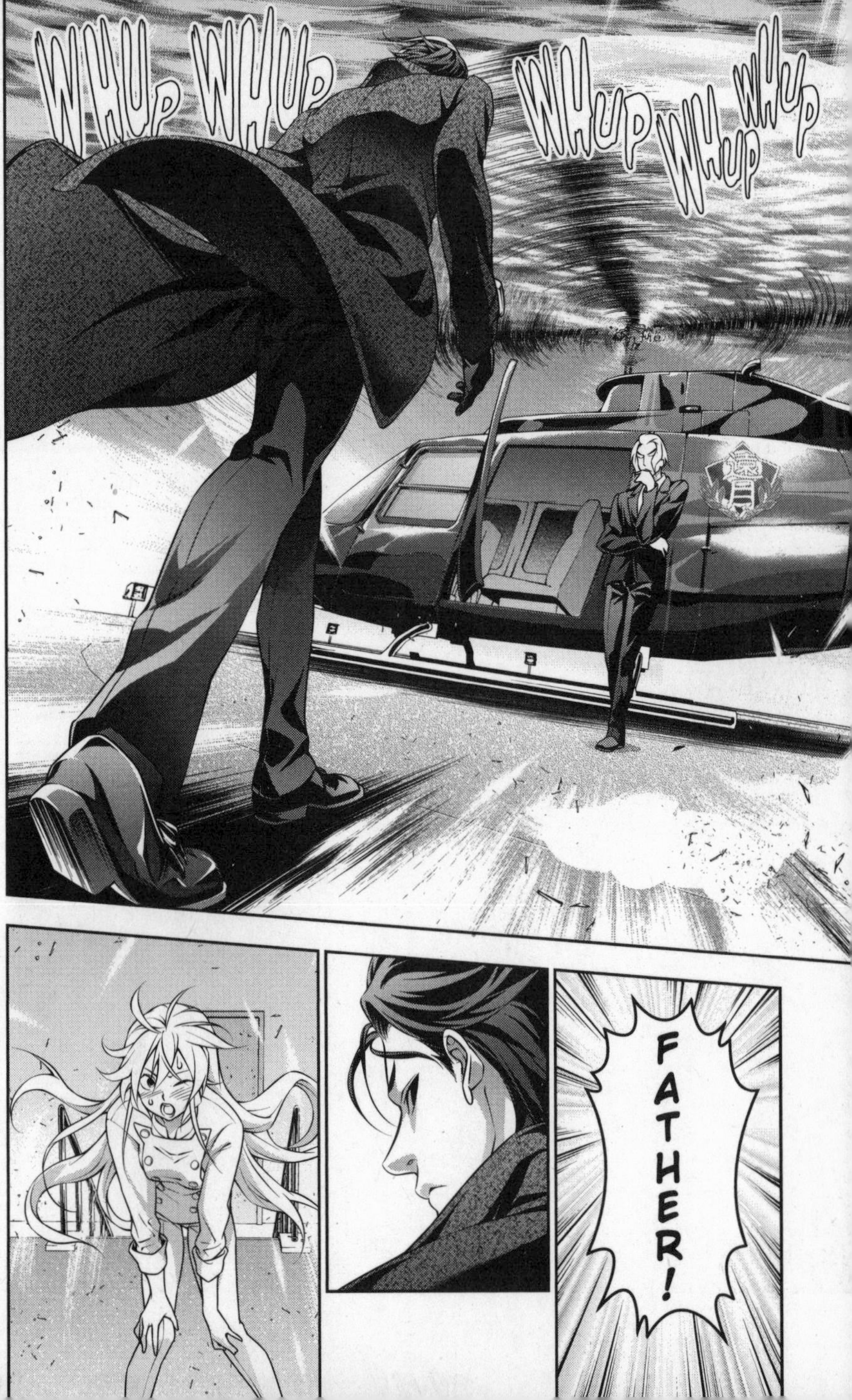
WHUP WHUP WHUP WHUP
WHUP WHUP
FATHER!

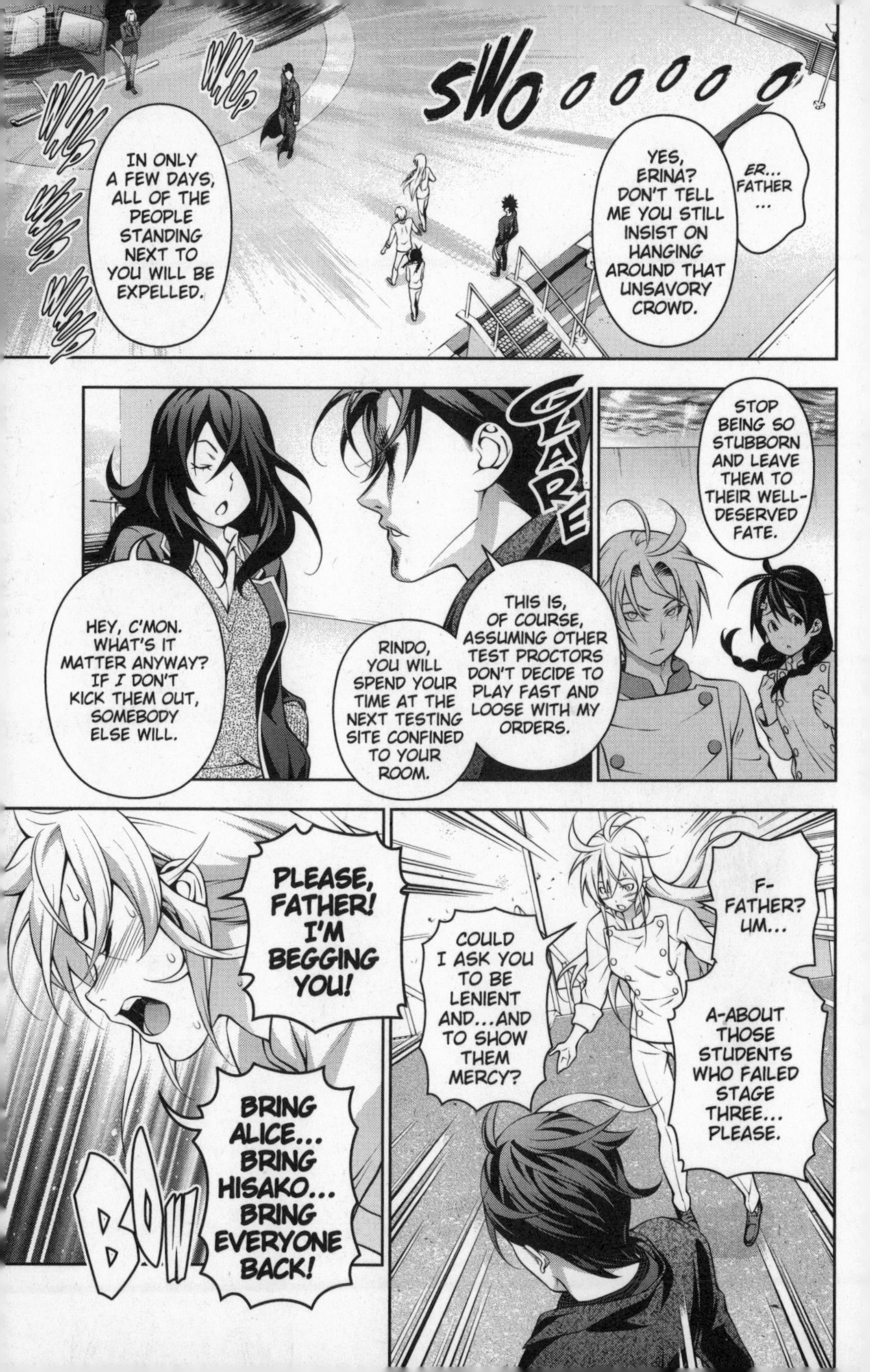
SWOOOOOOO
ER... FATHER...
YES, ERINA? DON'T TELL ME YOU STILL INSIST ON HANGING AROUND THAT UNSAVORY CROWD.
IN ONLY A FEW DAYS, ALL OF THE PEOPLE STANDING NEXT TO YOU WILL BE EXPELLED.
STOP BEING SO STUBBORN AND LEAVE THEM TO THEIR WELL-DESERVED FATE.
GLARE
RINDO, YOU WILL SPEND YOUR TIME AT THE NEXT TESTING SITE CONFINED TO YOUR ROOM.
THIS IS, OF COURSE, ASSUMING OTHER TEST PROCTORS DON'T DECIDE TO PLAY FAST AND LOOSE WITH MY ORDERS.
HEY, C'MON. WHAT'S IT MATTER ANYWAY? IF *I* DON'T KICK THEM OUT, SOMEBODY ELSE WILL.
F-FATHER? UM...
A-ABOUT THOSE STUDENTS WHO FAILED STAGE THREE... PLEASE.
COULD I ASK YOU TO BE LENIENT AND...AND TO SHOW THEM MERCY?
PLEASE, FATHER! I'M BEGGING YOU!
BRING ALICE... BRING HISAKO... BRING EVERYONE BACK!
BOW

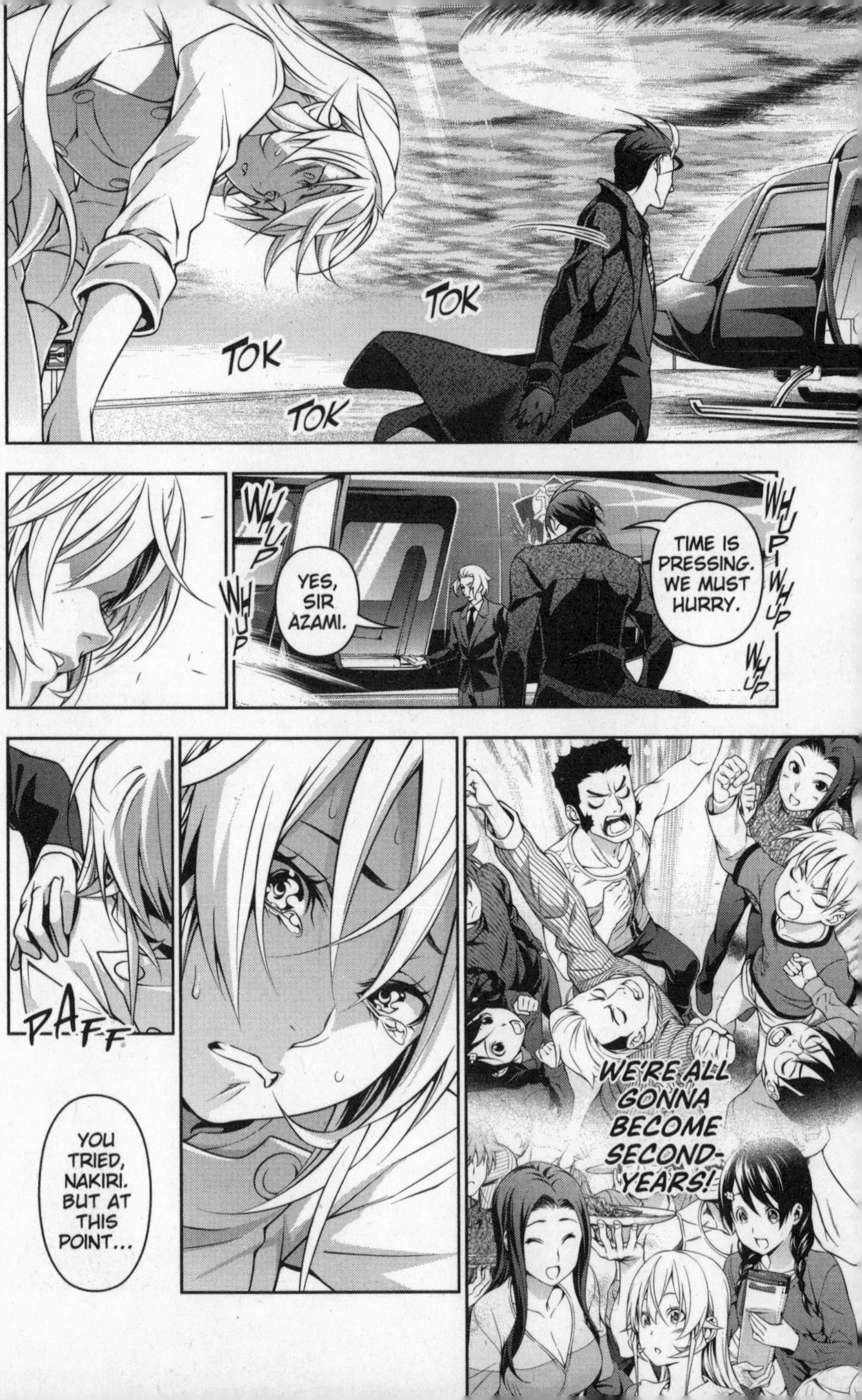
TOK
TOK
TOK
WHUP WHUP
WHUP
TIME IS PRESSING. WE MUST HURRY.
YES, SIR AZAMI.
WHUP
WHUP
WE'RE ALL GONNA BECOME SECOND-YEARS!
PAFF
YOU TRIED, NAKIRI. BUT AT THIS POINT...

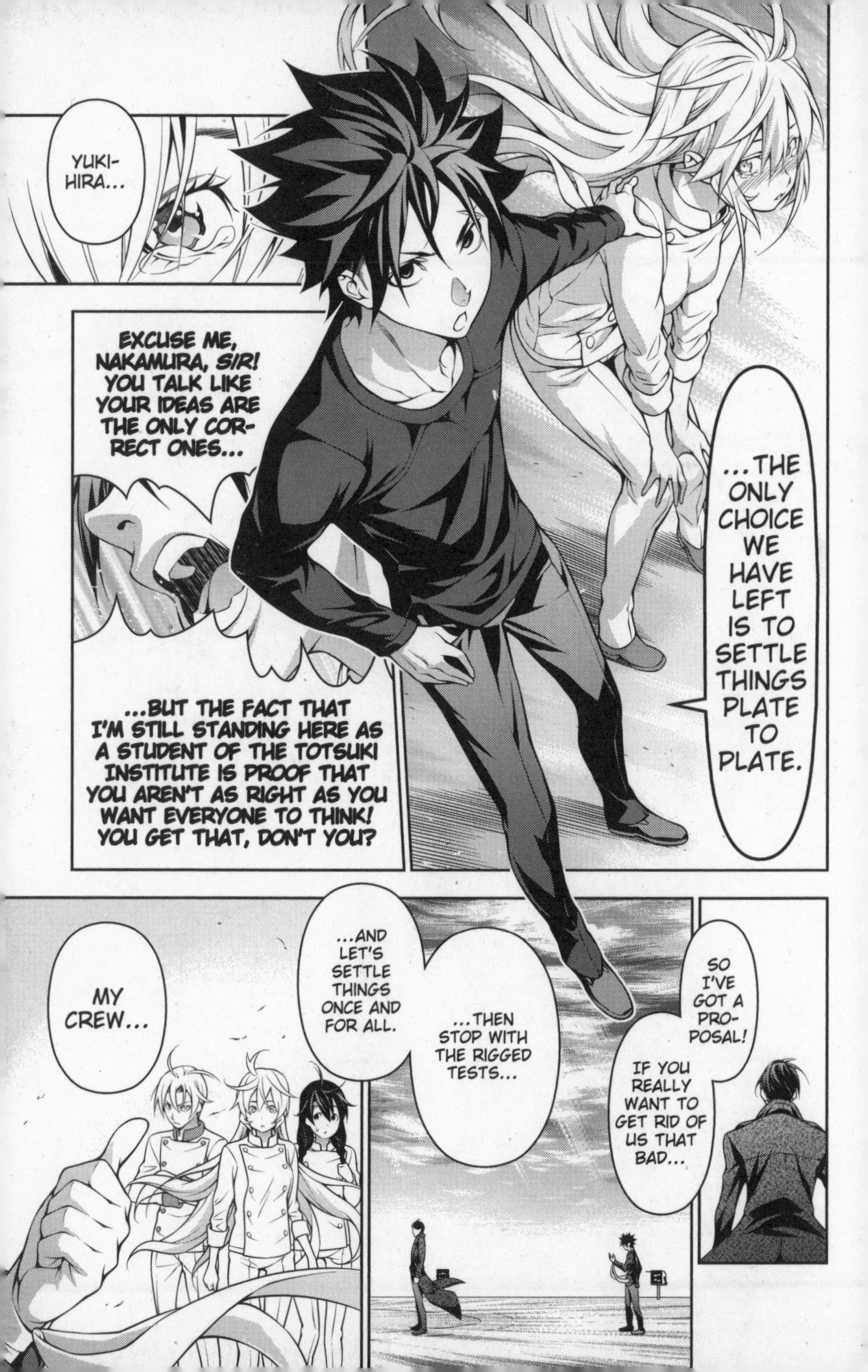
...THE ONLY CHOICE WE HAVE LEFT IS TO SETTLE THINGS PLATE TO PLATE.
YUKI-HIRA...
EXCUSE ME, NAKAMURA, *SIR!* YOU TALK LIKE YOUR IDEAS ARE THE ONLY COR-RECT ONES...
...BUT THE FACT THAT I'M STILL STANDING HERE AS A STUDENT OF THE TOTSUKI INSTITUTE IS PROOF THAT YOU AREN'T AS RIGHT AS YOU WANT EVERYONE TO THINK! YOU GET THAT, DON'T YOU?
SO I'VE GOT A PRO-POSAL!
IF YOU REALLY WANT TO GET RID OF US THAT BAD...
...THEN STOP WITH THE RIGGED TESTS...
...AND LET'S SETTLE THINGS ONCE AND FOR ALL.
MY CREW...

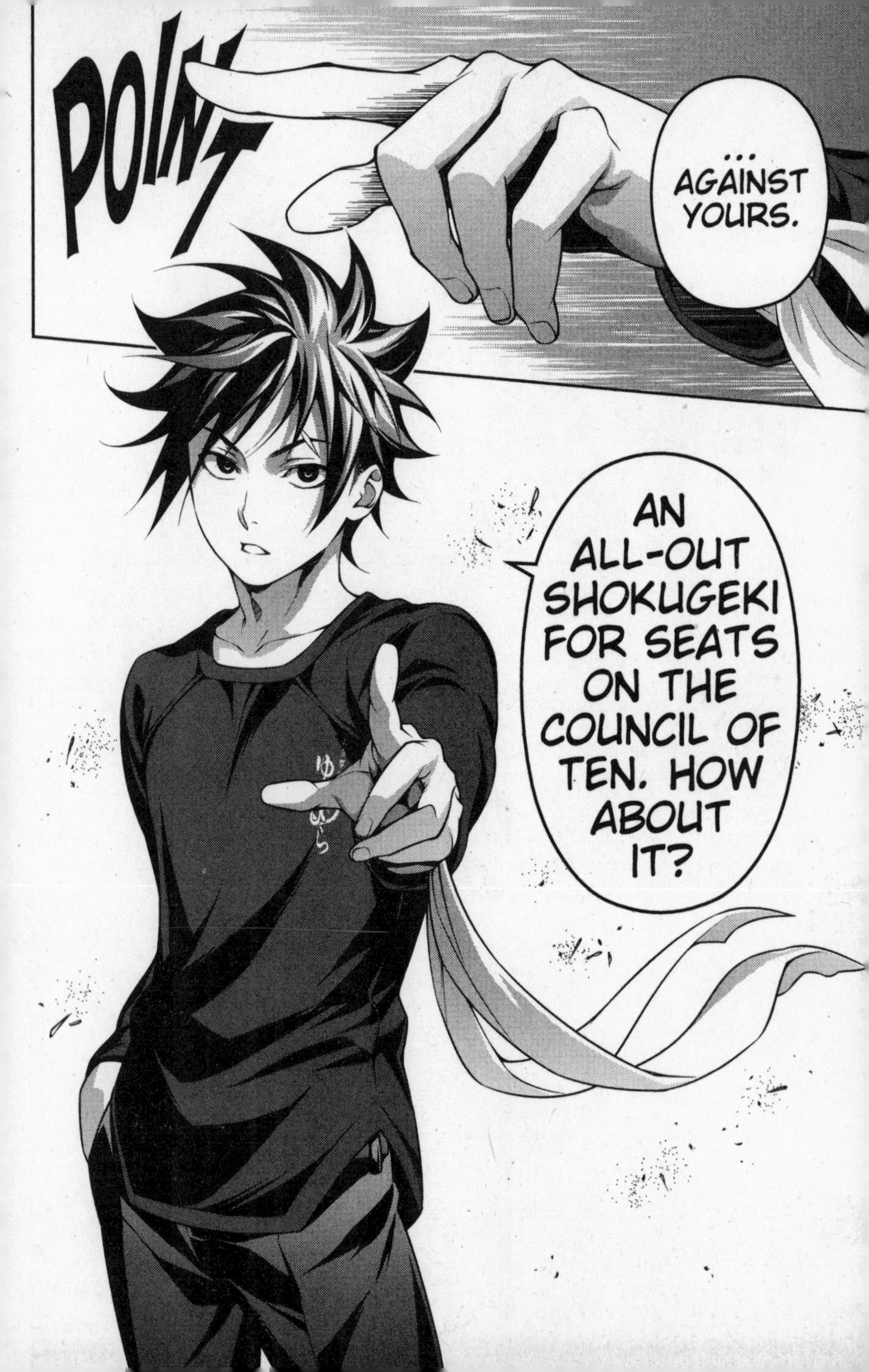
... AGAINST YOURS.
POINT
AN ALL-OUT SHOKUGEKI FOR SEATS ON THE COUNCIL OF TEN. HOW ABOUT IT?

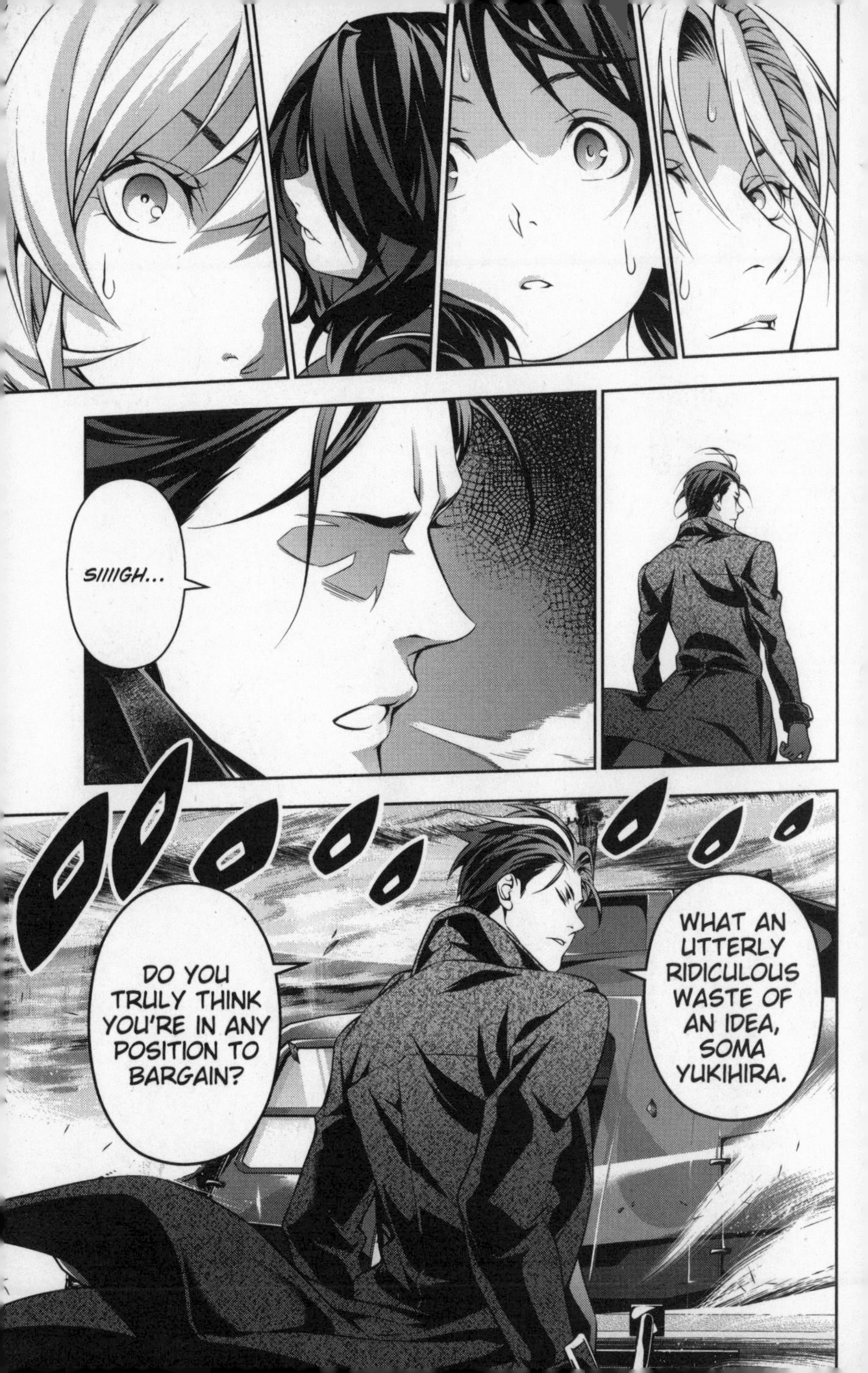
SIIIGH...
WHAT AN UTTERLY RIDICULOUS WASTE OF AN IDEA, SOMA YUKIHIRA.
DO YOU TRULY THINK YOU'RE IN ANY POSITION TO BARGAIN?

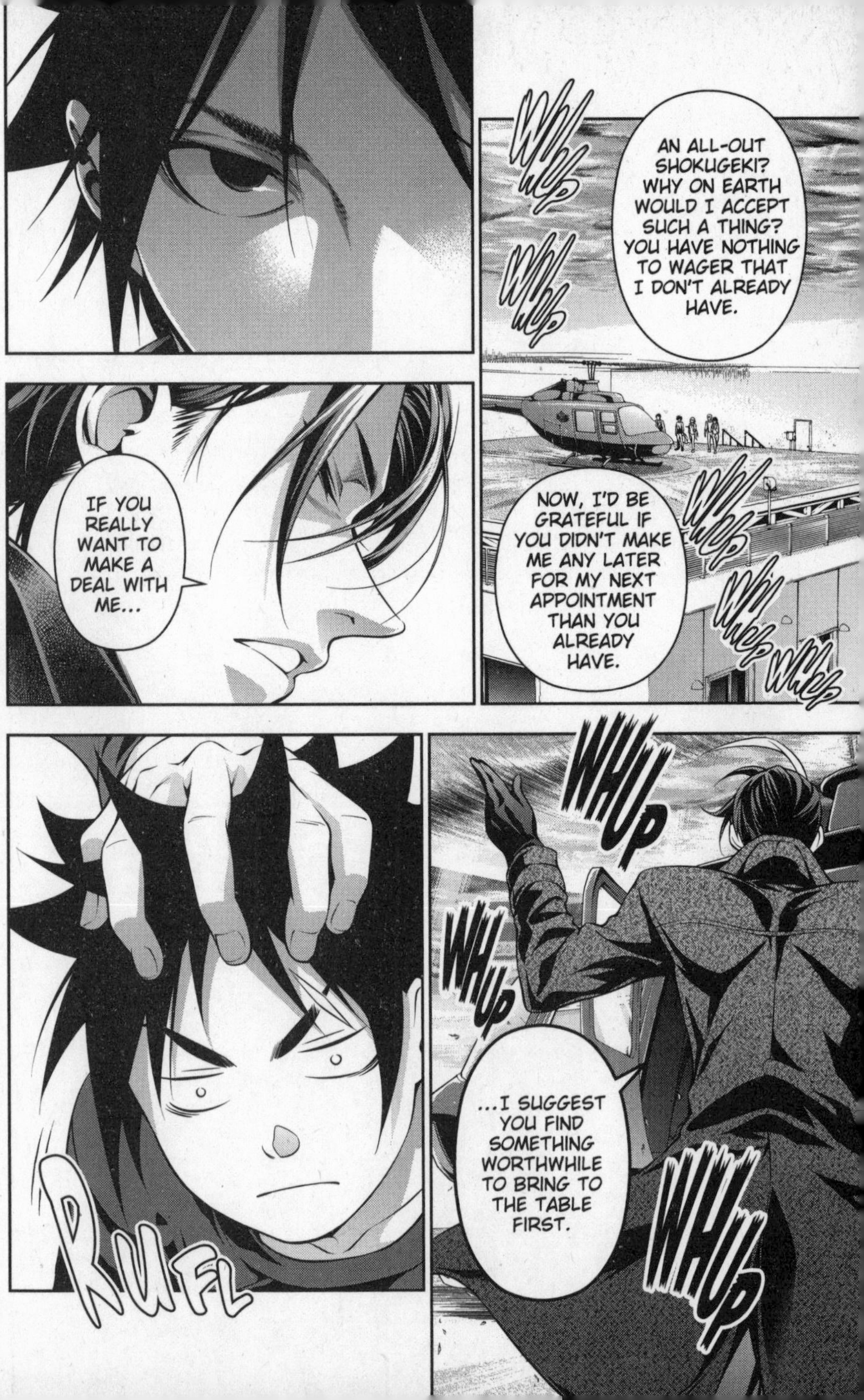
AN ALL-OUT SHOKUGEKI? WHY ON EARTH WOULD I ACCEPT SUCH A THING? YOU HAVE NOTHING TO WAGER THAT I DON'T ALREADY HAVE.
NOW, I'D BE GRATEFUL IF YOU DIDN'T MAKE ME ANY LATER FOR MY NEXT APPOINTMENT THAN YOU ALREADY HAVE.
IF YOU REALLY WANT TO MAKE A DEAL WITH ME...
WHUP
WHUP
...I SUGGEST YOU FIND SOMETHING WORTHWHILE TO BRING TO THE TABLE FIRST.
WHUP
RUFL

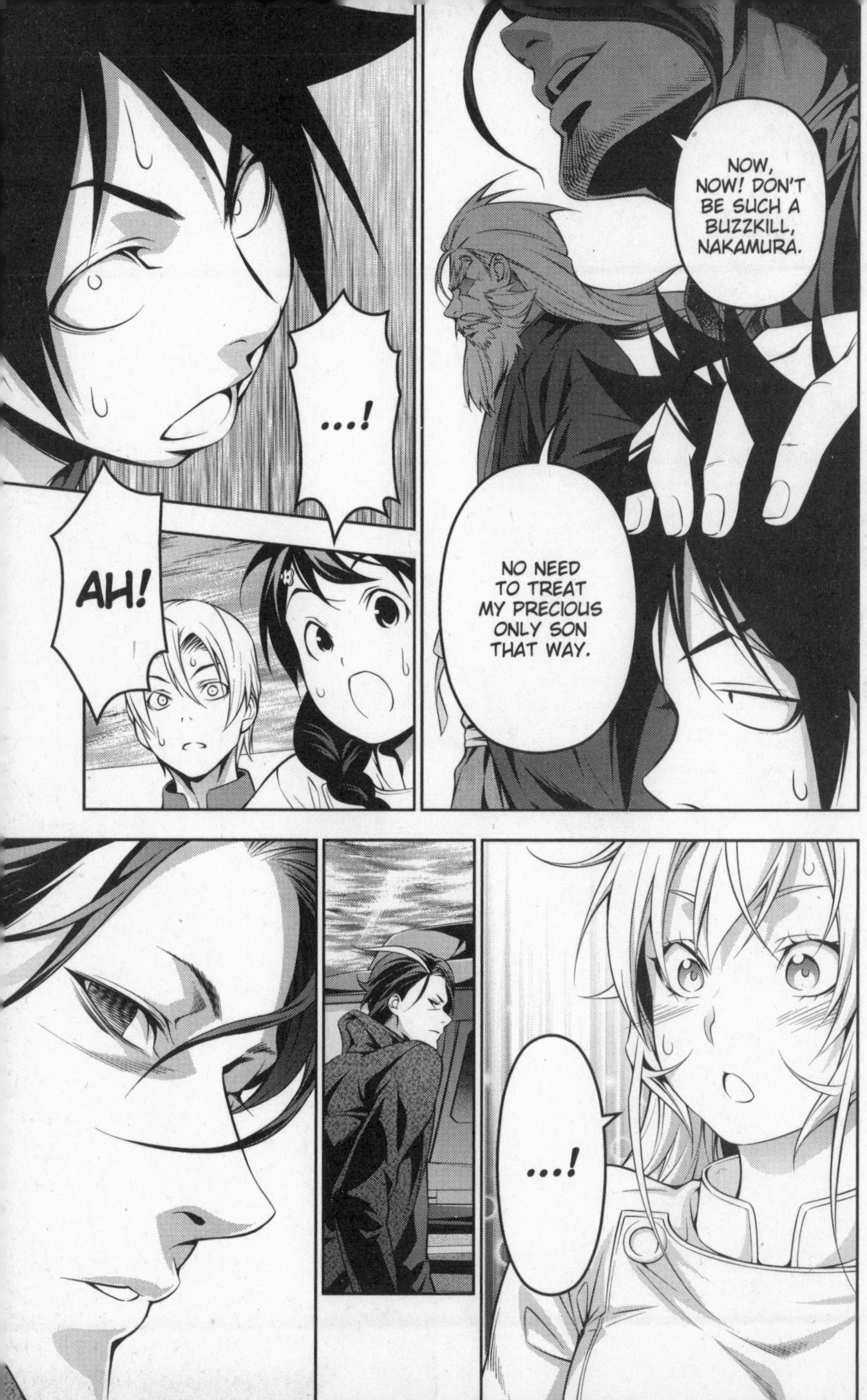
NOW, NOW! DON'T BE SUCH A BUZZKILL, NAKAMURA.
NO NEED TO TREAT MY PRECIOUS ONLY SON THAT WAY.
...!
AH!
...!

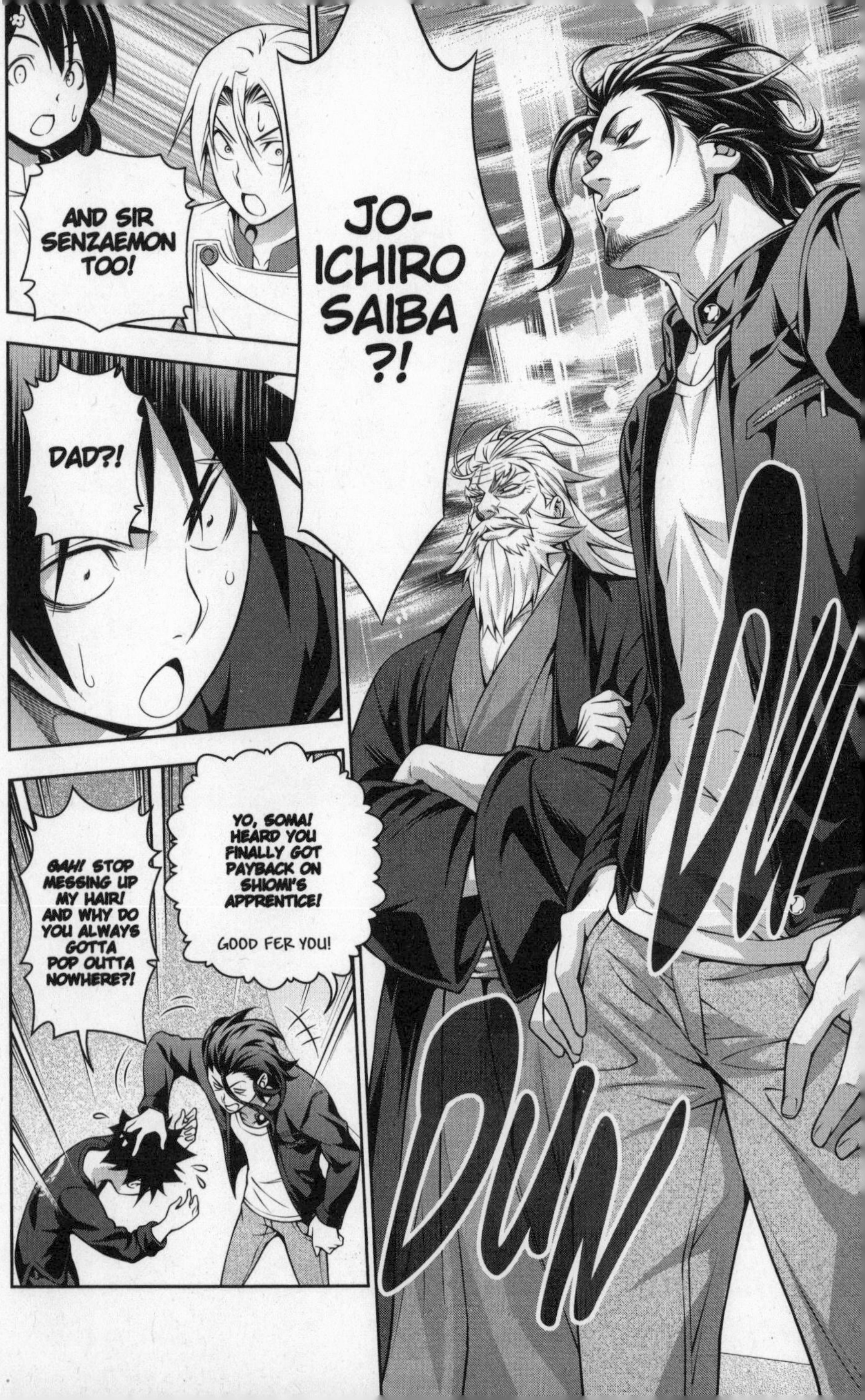
JO-ICHIRO SAIBA?!
DUN
DUN
AND SIR SENZAEMON TOO!
DAD?!
YO, SOMA! HEARD YOU FINALLY GOT PAYBACK ON SHIOMI'S APPRENTICE!
GOOD FER YOU!
GAH! STOP MESSING UP MY HAIR! AND WHY DO YOU ALWAYS GOTTA POP OUTTA NOWHERE?!

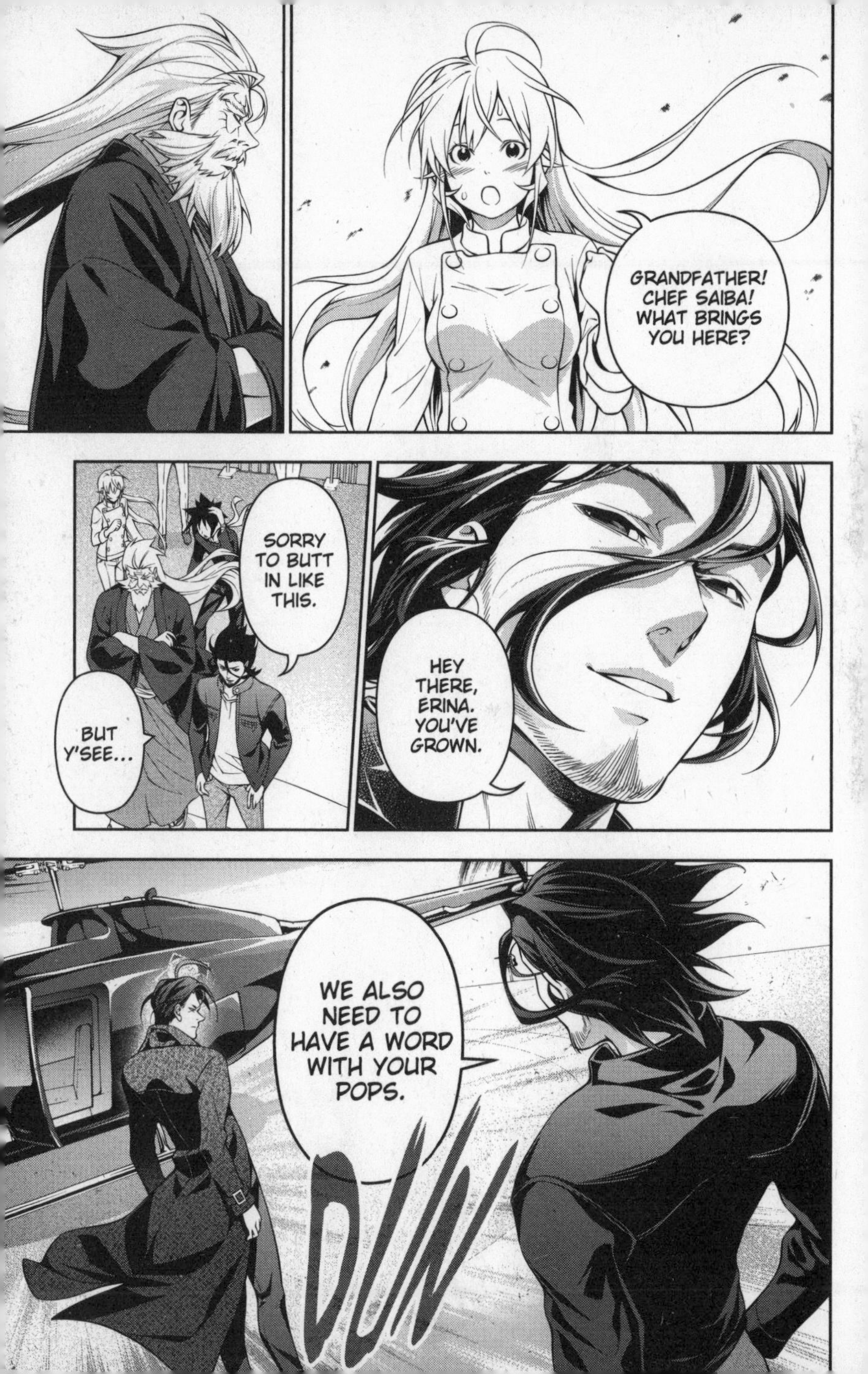
GRANDFATHER! CHEF SAIBA! WHAT BRINGS YOU HERE?
HEY THERE, ERINA. YOU'VE GROWN.
SORRY TO BUTT IN LIKE THIS.
BUT Y'SEE...
WE ALSO NEED TO HAVE A WORD WITH YOUR POPS.

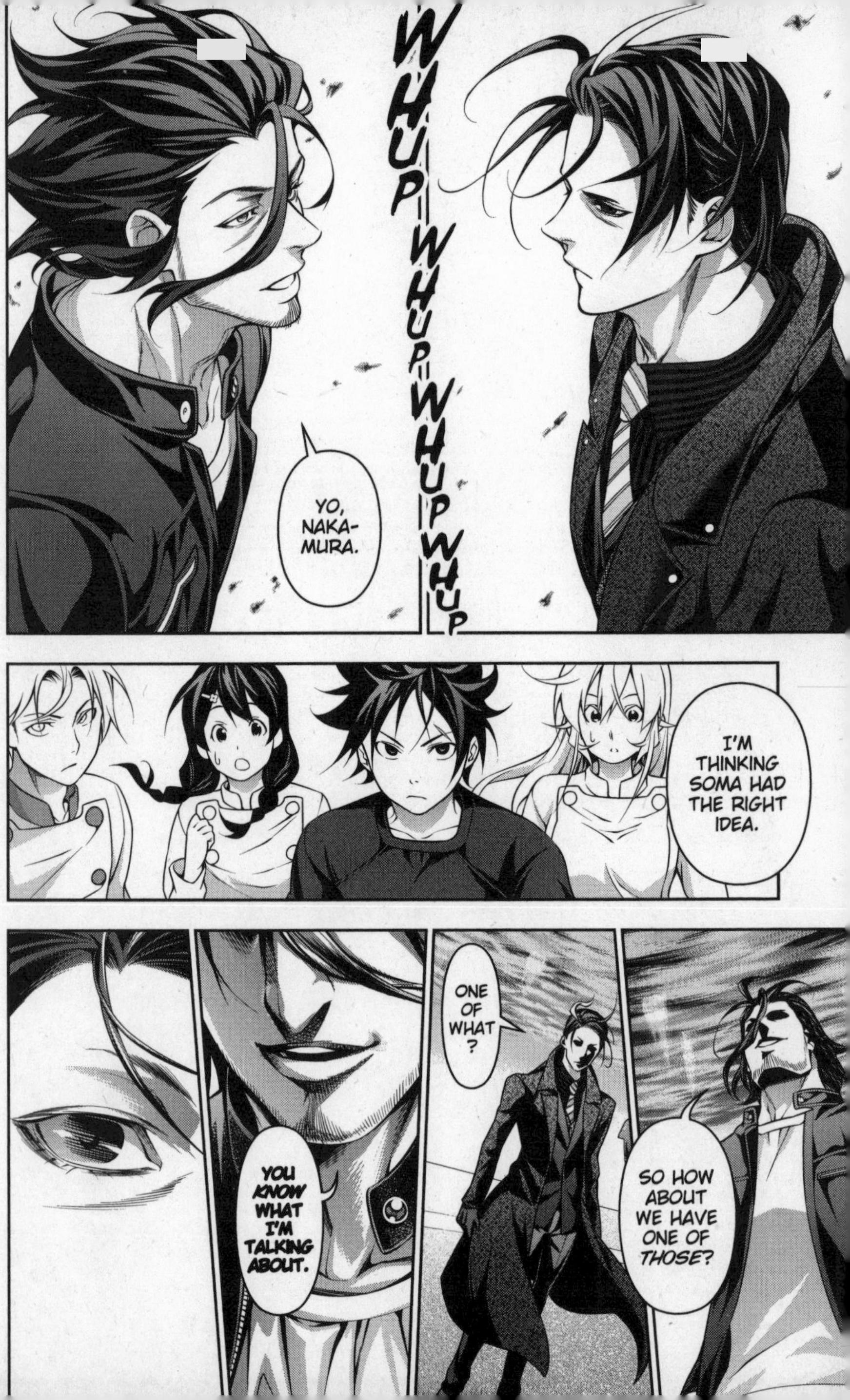
WHUP WHUP WHUP WHUP
YO, NAKAMURA.
I'M THINKING SOMA HAD THE RIGHT IDEA.
SO HOW ABOUT WE HAVE ONE OF THOSE?
ONE OF WHAT?
YOU KNOW WHAT I'M TALKING ABOUT.

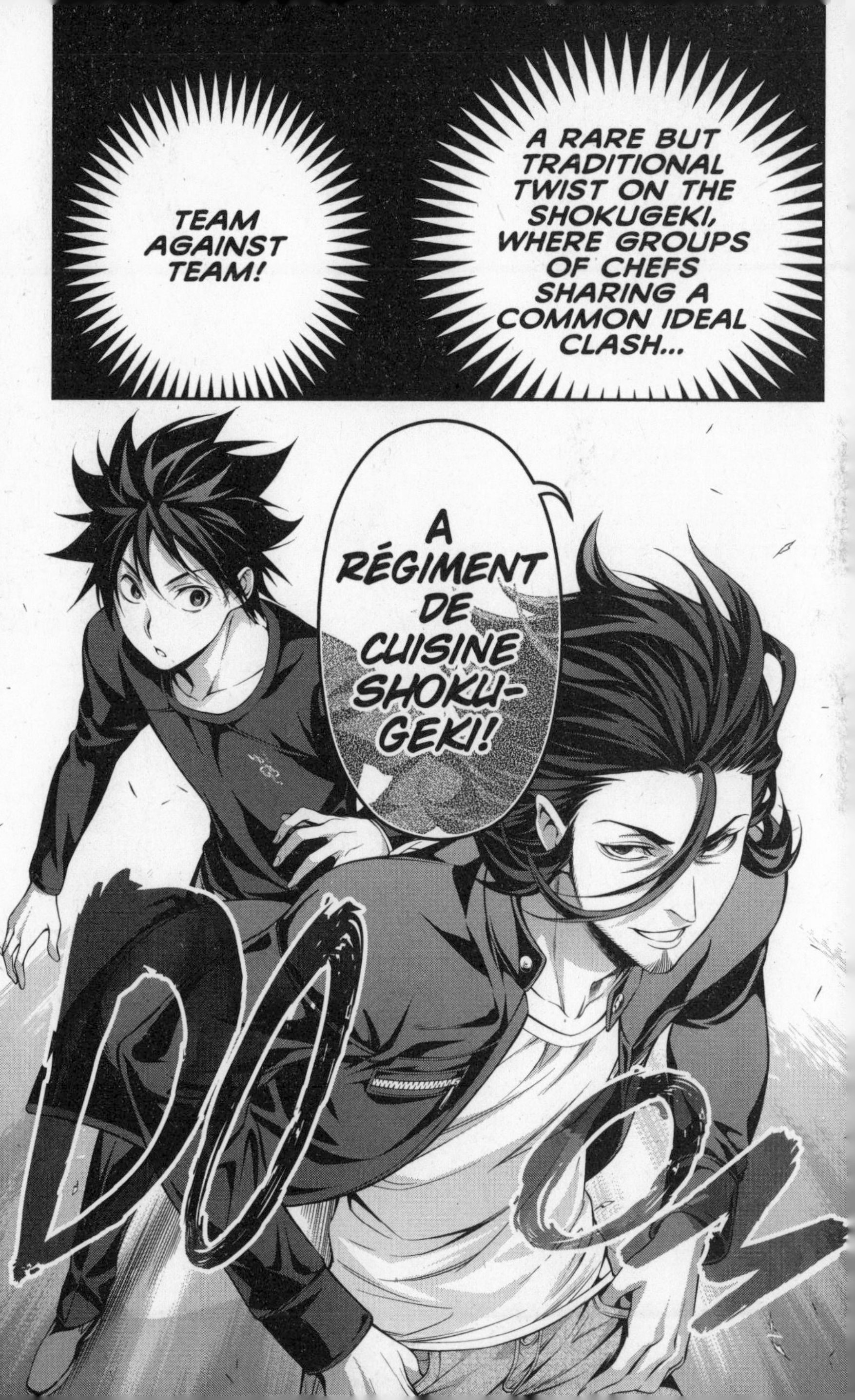
A RARE BUT TRADITIONAL TWIST ON THE SHOKUGEKI, WHERE GROUPS OF CHEFS SHARING A COMMON IDEAL CLASH...
TEAM AGAINST TEAM!
A RÉGIMENT DE CUISINE SHOKU-GEKI!
DOOM

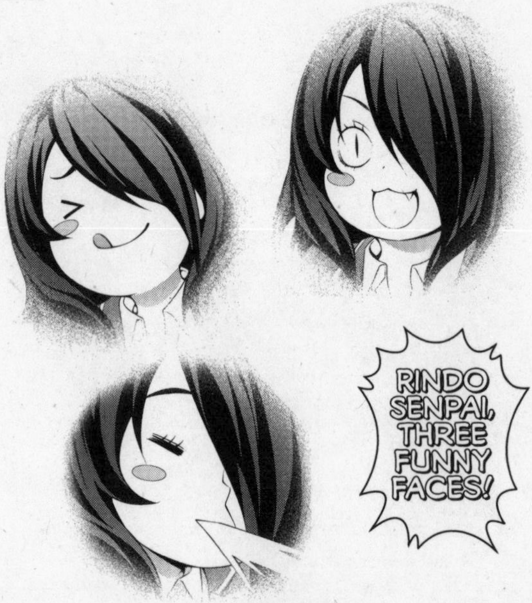
RINDO SENPAI, THREE FUNNY FACES!

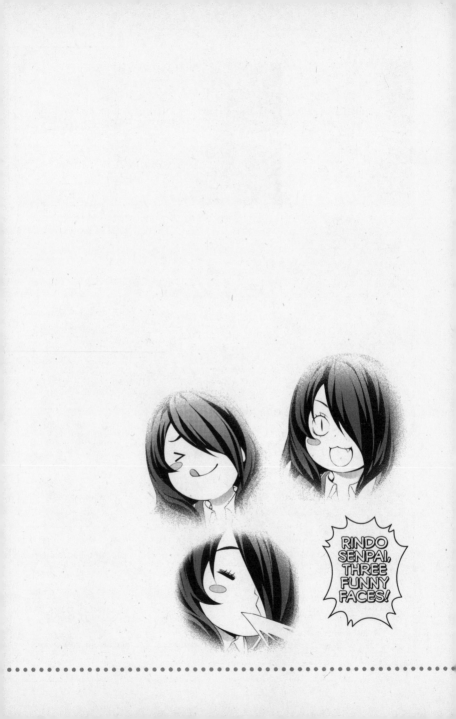

194 THE PRICE

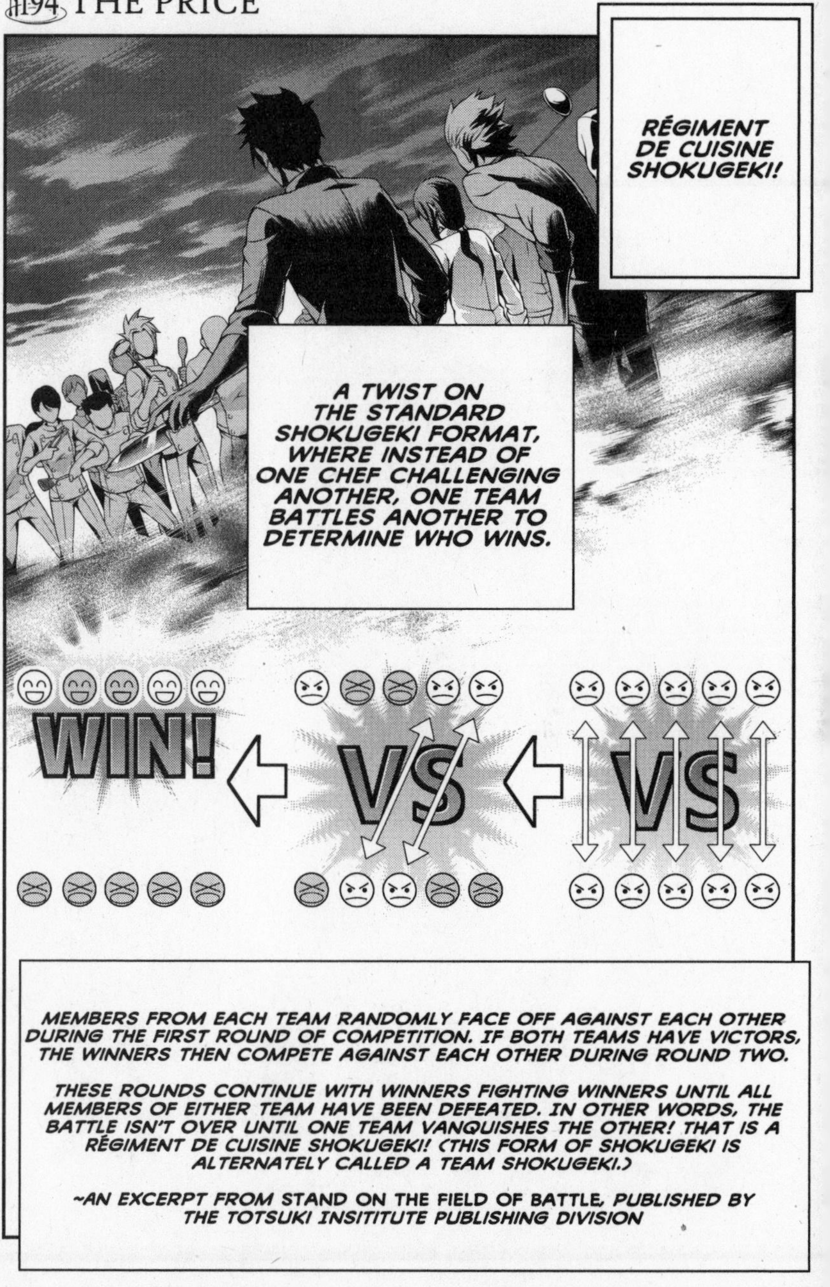
RÉGIMENT DE CUISINE SHOKUGEKI!
A TWIST ON THE STANDARD SHOKUGEKI FORMAT, WHERE INSTEAD OF ONE CHEF CHALLENGING ANOTHER, ONE TEAM BATTLES ANOTHER TO DETERMINE WHO WINS.
VS
VS
WIN!
MEMBERS FROM EACH TEAM RANDOMLY FACE OFF AGAINST EACH OTHER DURING THE FIRST ROUND OF COMPETITION. IF BOTH TEAMS HAVE VICTORS, THE WINNERS THEN COMPETE AGAINST EACH OTHER DURING ROUND TWO.
THESE ROUNDS CONTINUE WITH WINNERS FIGHTING WINNERS UNTIL ALL MEMBERS OF EITHER TEAM HAVE BEEN DEFEATED. IN OTHER WORDS, THE BATTLE ISN'T OVER UNTIL ONE TEAM VANQUISHES THE OTHER! THAT IS A RÉGIMENT DE CUISINE SHOKUGEKI! (THIS FORM OF SHOKUGEKI IS ALTERNATELY CALLED A TEAM SHOKUGEKI.)
~AN EXCERPT FROM STAND ON THE FIELD OF BATTLE, PUBLISHED BY THE TOTSUKI INSITITUTE PUBLISHING DIVISION

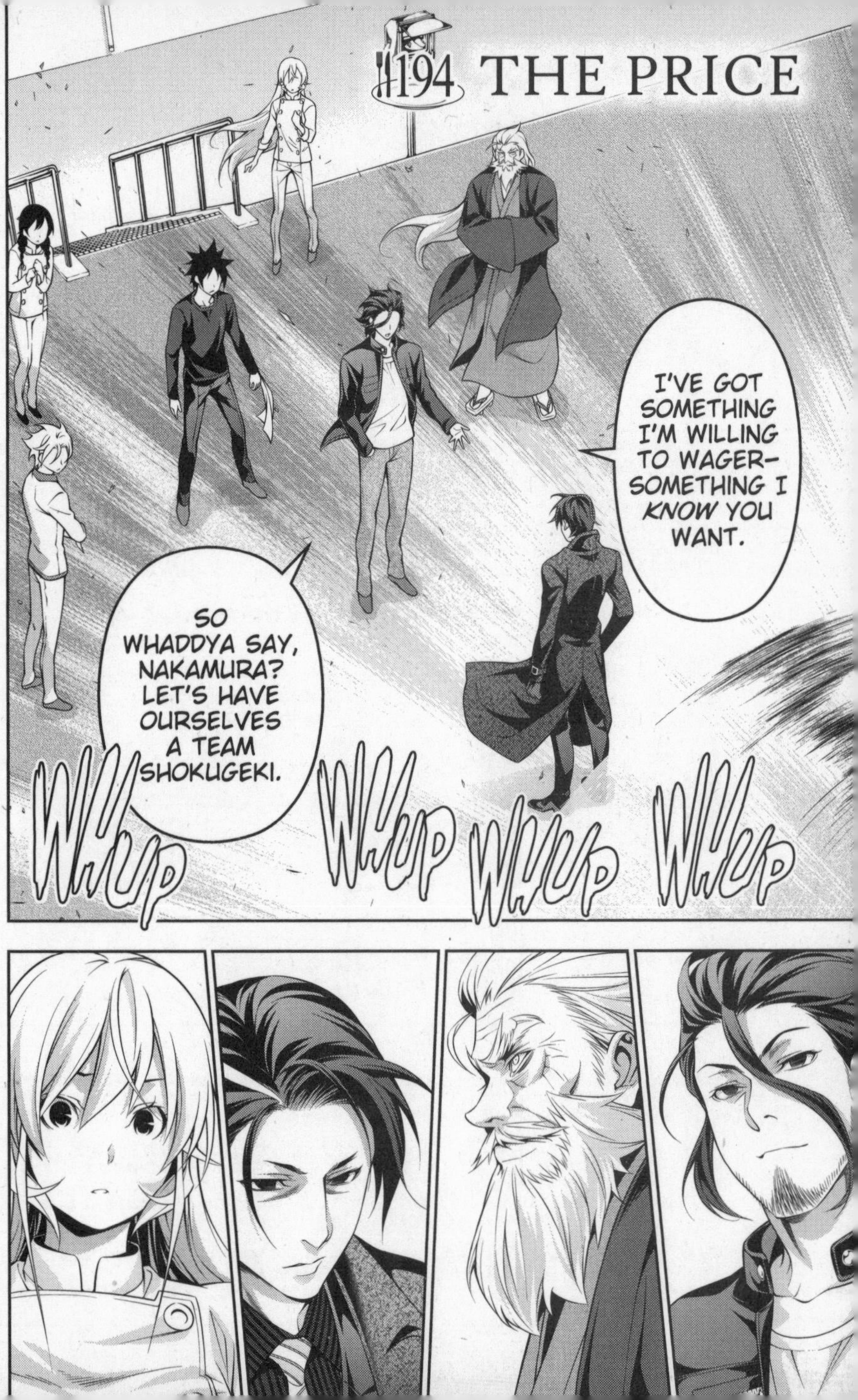
194 THE PRICE
I'VE GOT SOMETHING I'M WILLING TO WAGER—SOMETHING I *KNOW* YOU WANT.
SO WHADDYA SAY, NAKAMURA? LET'S HAVE OURSELVES A TEAM SHOKUGEKI.
WHUP
WHUP
WHUP
WHUP

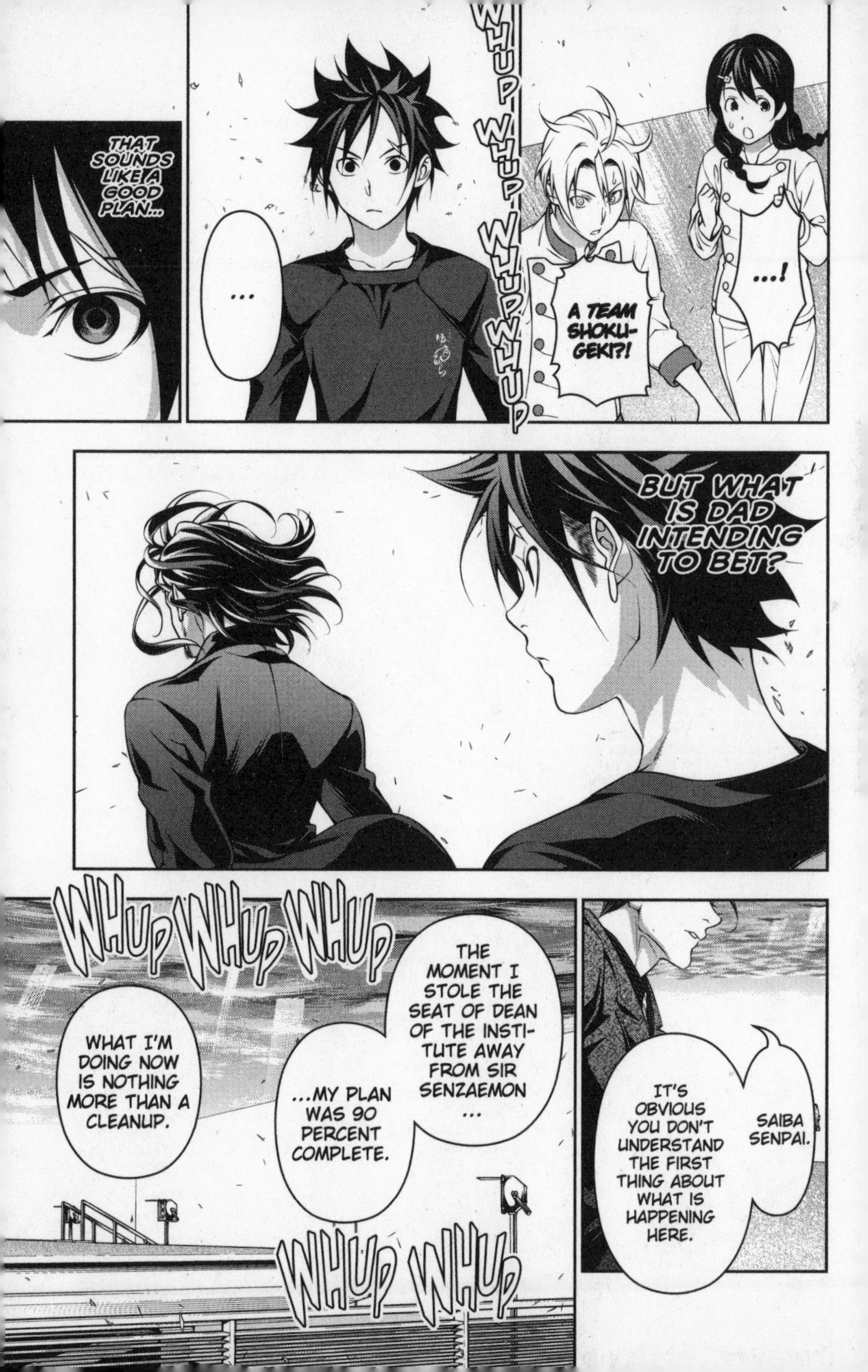
...!
A TEAM SHOKUGEKI?!
WHUP WHUP WHUP WHUP WHUP
...
THAT SOUNDS LIKE A GOOD PLAN...
BUT WHAT IS DAD INTENDING TO BET?
SAIBA SENPAI.
IT'S OBVIOUS YOU DON'T UNDERSTAND THE FIRST THING ABOUT WHAT IS HAPPENING HERE.
THE MOMENT I STOLE THE SEAT OF DEAN OF THE INSTITUTE AWAY FROM SIR SENZAEMON...
...MY PLAN WAS 90 PERCENT COMPLETE.
WHAT I'M DOING NOW IS NOTHING MORE THAN A CLEANUP.
WHUP WHUP WHUP
WHUP WHUP

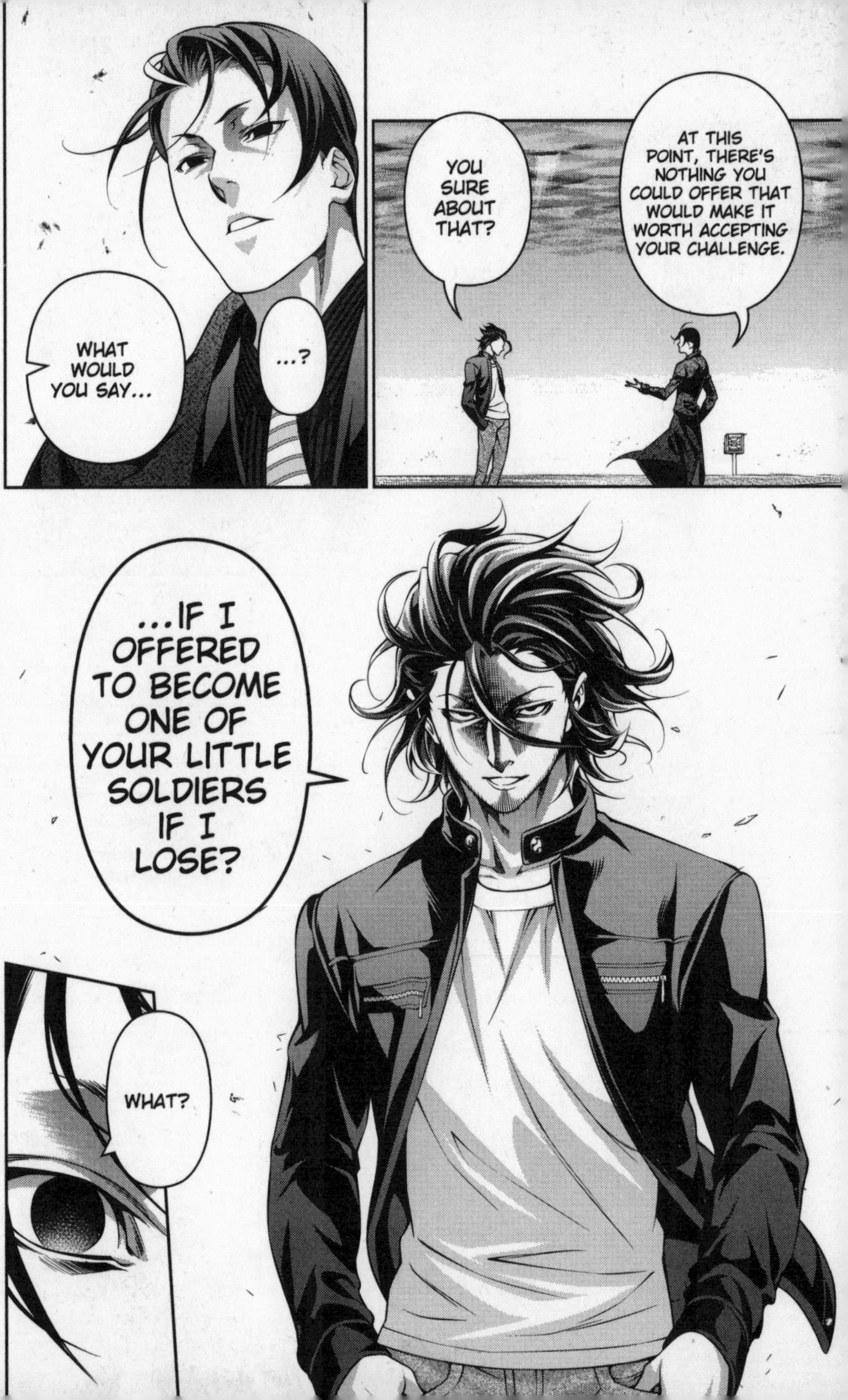
AT THIS POINT, THERE'S NOTHING YOU COULD OFFER THAT WOULD MAKE IT WORTH ACCEPTING YOUR CHALLENGE.
YOU SURE ABOUT THAT?
...?
WHAT WOULD YOU SAY...
...IF I OFFERED TO BECOME ONE OF YOUR LITTLE SOLDIERS IF I LOSE?
WHAT?

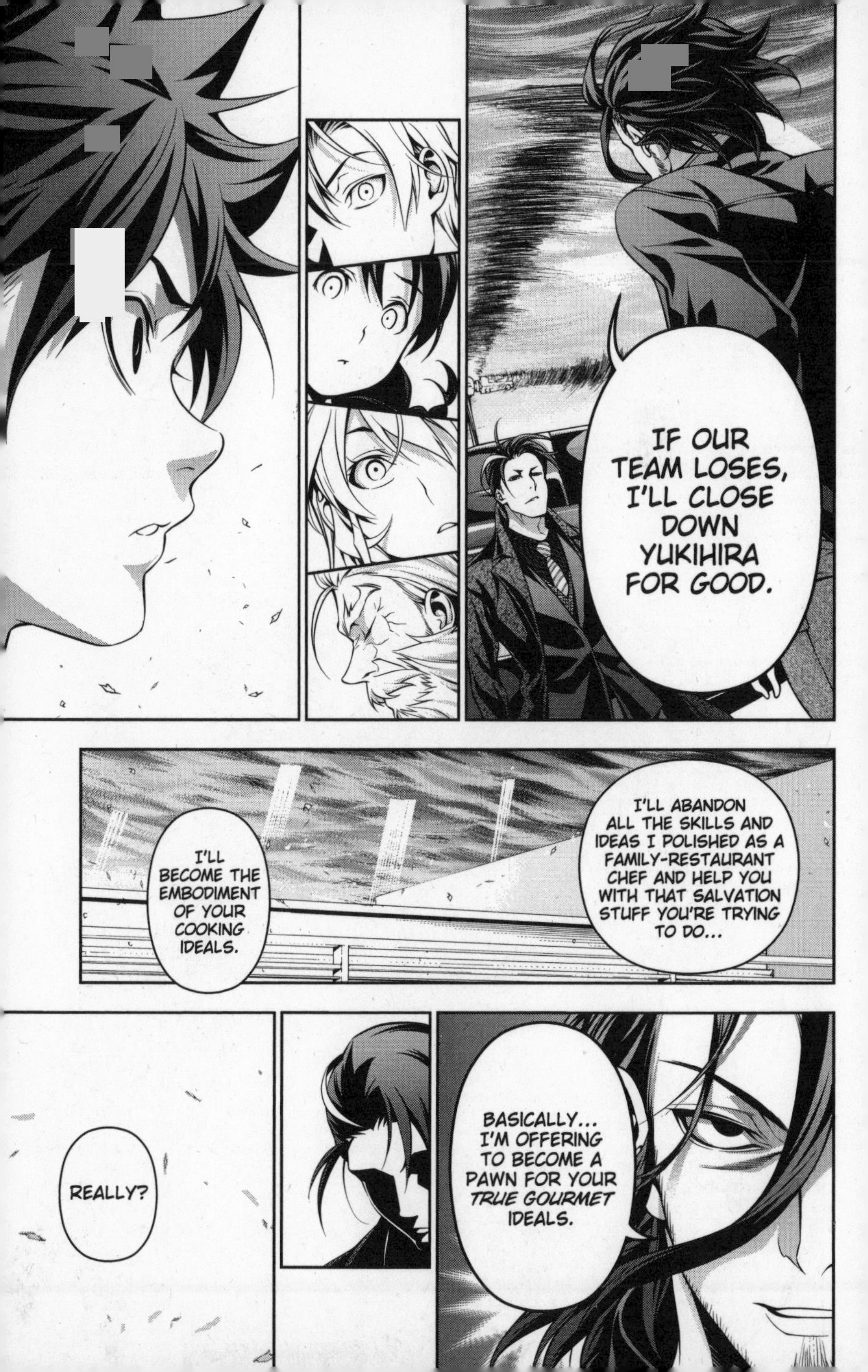
IF OUR TEAM LOSES, I'LL CLOSE DOWN YUKIHIRA FOR GOOD.
I'LL ABANDON ALL THE SKILLS AND IDEAS I POLISHED AS A FAMILY-RESTAURANT CHEF AND HELP YOU WITH THAT SALVATION STUFF YOU'RE TRYING TO DO...
I'LL BECOME THE EMBODIMENT OF YOUR COOKING IDEALS.
BASICALLY... I'M OFFERING TO BECOME A PAWN FOR YOUR *TRUE GOURMET* IDEALS.
REALLY?

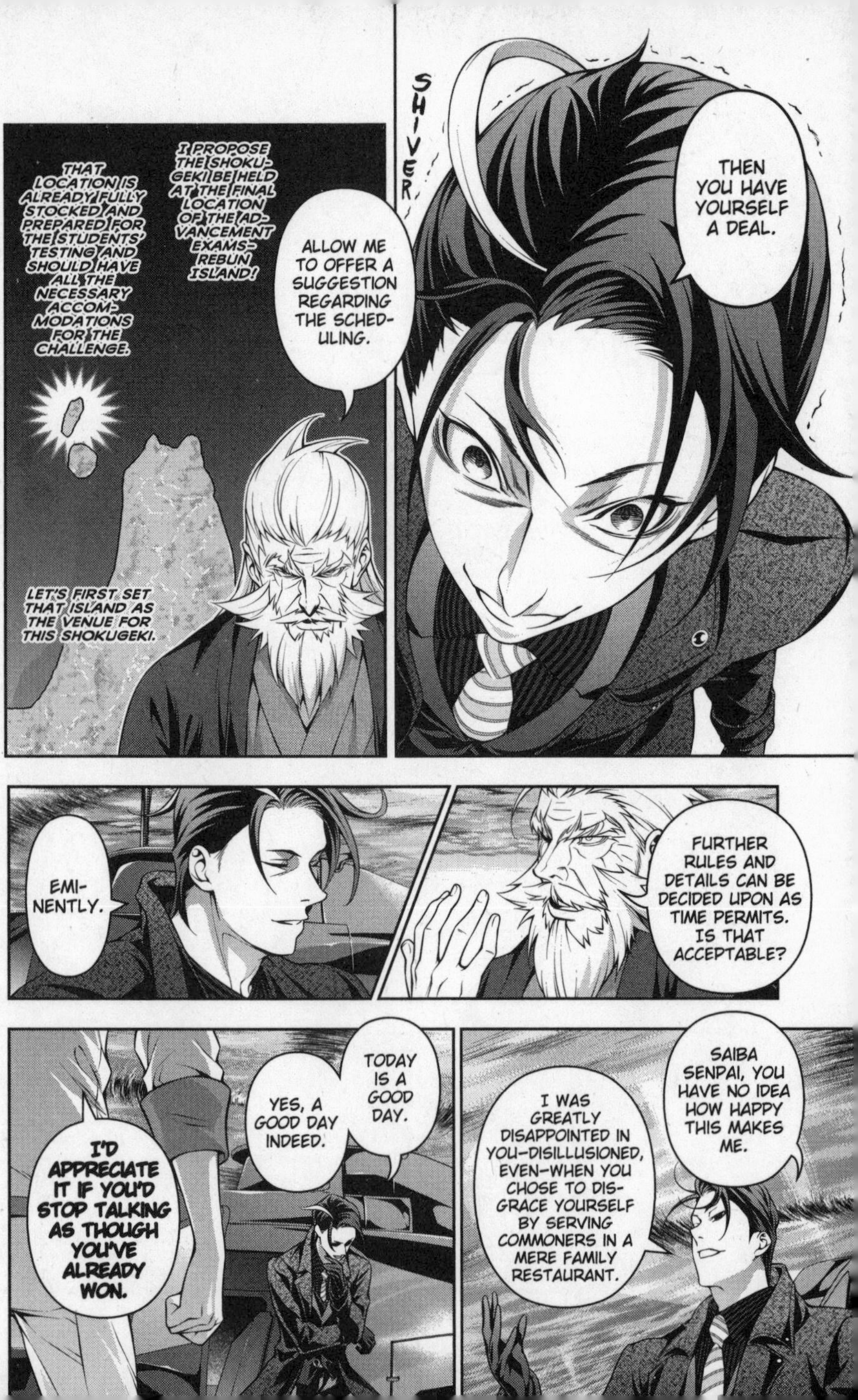
SHIVER
THEN YOU HAVE YOURSELF A DEAL.
ALLOW ME TO OFFER A SUGGESTION REGARDING THE SCHEDULING.
I PROPOSE THE SHOKUGEKI BE HELD AT THE FINAL LOCATION OF THE ADVANCEMENT EXAMS— REBUN ISLAND!
THAT LOCATION IS ALREADY FULLY STOCKED AND PREPARED FOR THE STUDENTS' TESTING AND SHOULD HAVE ALL THE NECESSARY ACCOMMODATIONS FOR THE CHALLENGE.
LET'S FIRST SET THAT ISLAND AS THE VENUE FOR THIS SHOKUGEKI.
FURTHER RULES AND DETAILS CAN BE DECIDED UPON AS TIME PERMITS. IS THAT ACCEPTABLE?
EMINENTLY.
SAIBA SENPAI, YOU HAVE NO IDEA HOW HAPPY THIS MAKES ME.
I WAS GREATLY DISAPPOINTED IN YOU—DISILLUSIONED, EVEN—WHEN YOU CHOSE TO DISGRACE YOURSELF BY SERVING COMMONERS IN A MERE FAMILY RESTAURANT.
TODAY IS A GOOD DAY.
YES, A GOOD DAY INDEED.
I'D APPRECIATE IT IF YOU'D STOP TALKING AS THOUGH YOU'VE ALREADY WON.

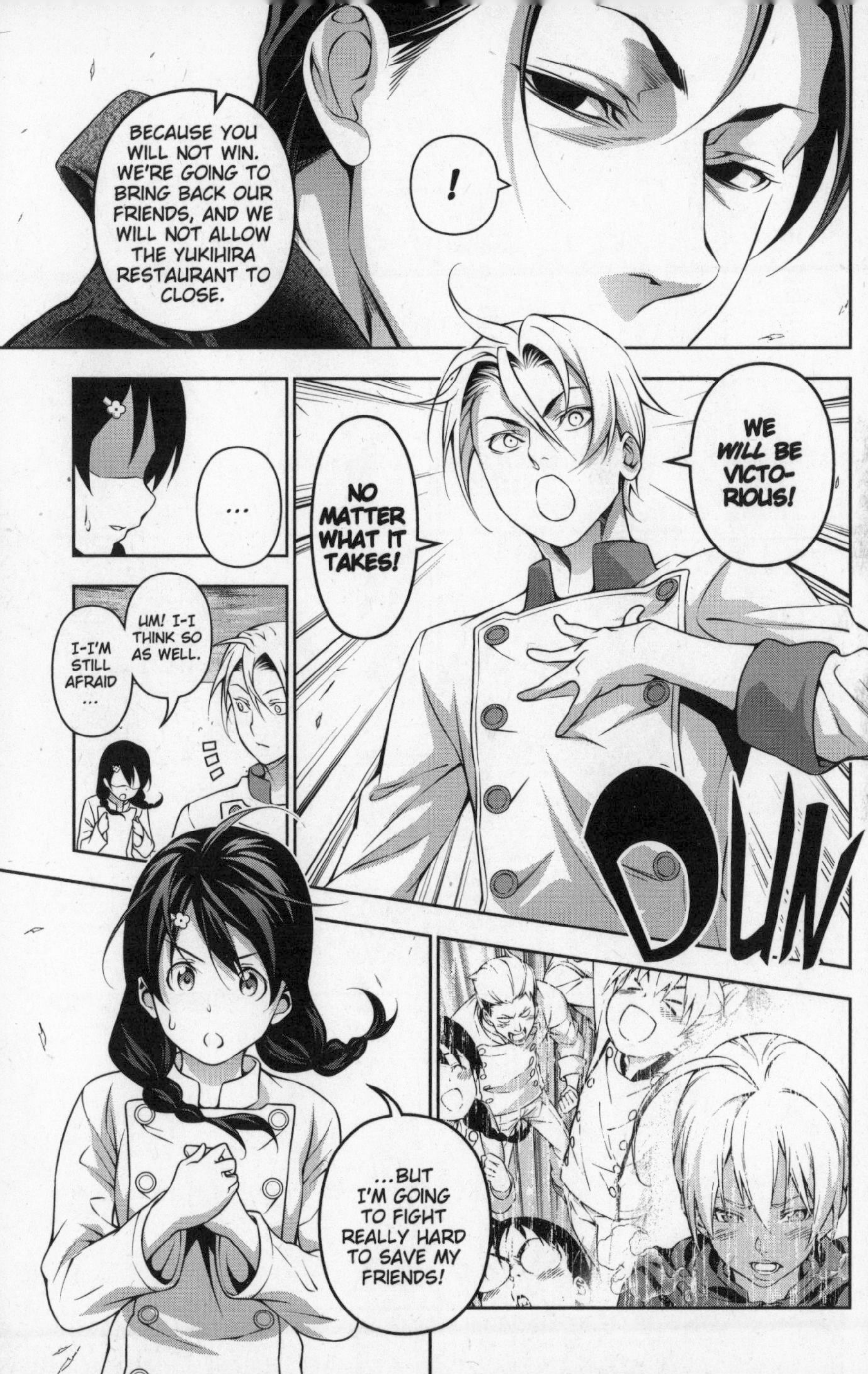
BECAUSE YOU WILL NOT WIN. WE'RE GOING TO BRING BACK OUR FRIENDS, AND WE WILL NOT ALLOW THE YUKIHIRA RESTAURANT TO CLOSE.
!
WE WILL BE VICTORIOUS!
NO MATTER WHAT IT TAKES!
DUN
...
UM! I-I THINK SO AS WELL.
I-I'M STILL AFRAID ...
...BUT I'M GOING TO FIGHT REALLY HARD TO SAVE MY FRIENDS!

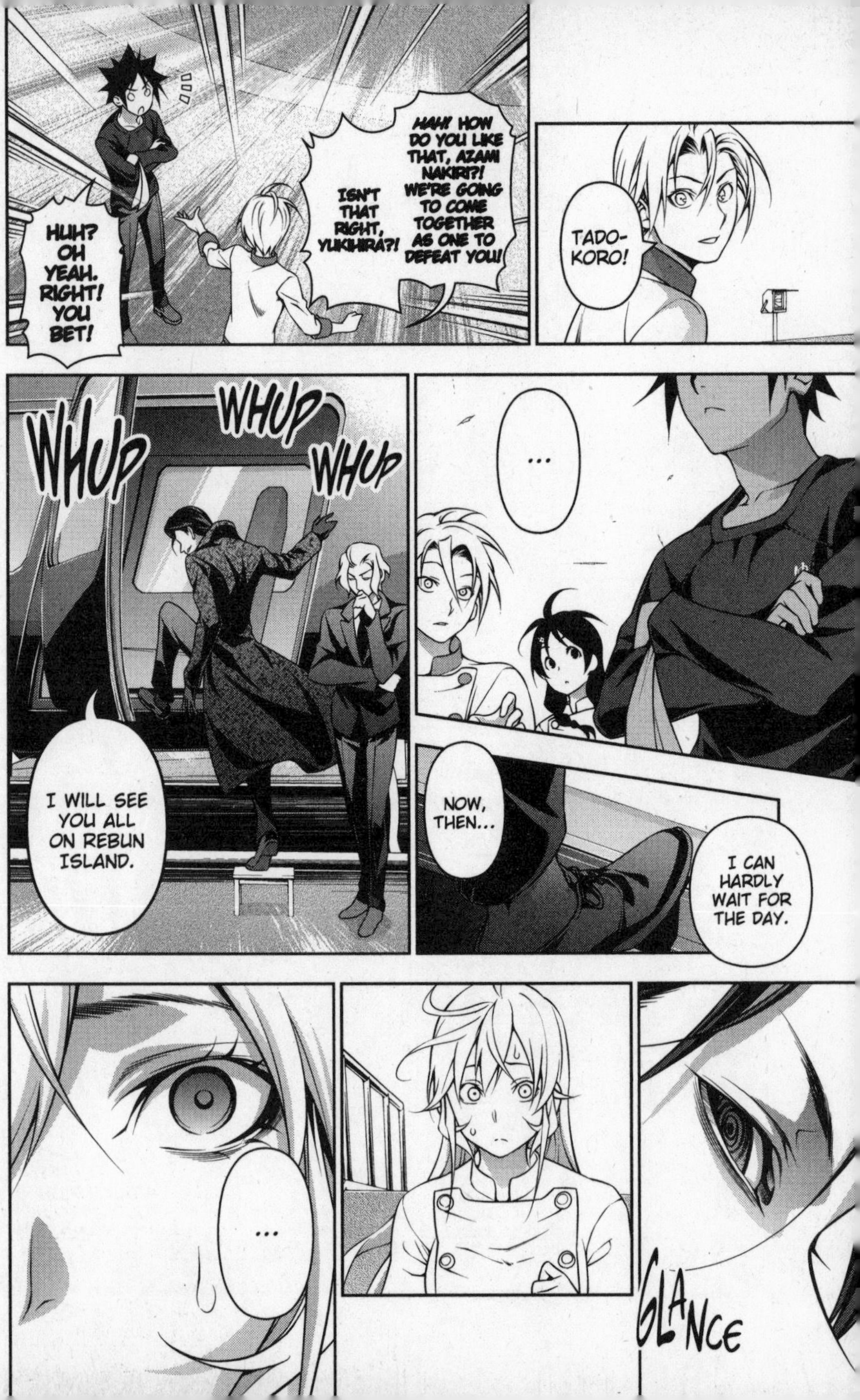
TADO-KORO!
HAH! HOW DO YOU LIKE THAT, AZAMI NAKIRI?! WE'RE GOING TO COME TOGETHER AS ONE TO DEFEAT YOU!
ISN'T THAT RIGHT, YUKIHIRA?!
HUH? OH YEAH. RIGHT! YOU BET!
...
NOW, THEN...
I CAN HARDLY WAIT FOR THE DAY.
WHUP
WHUP
WHUP
I WILL SEE YOU ALL ON REBUN ISLAND.
GLANCE
...

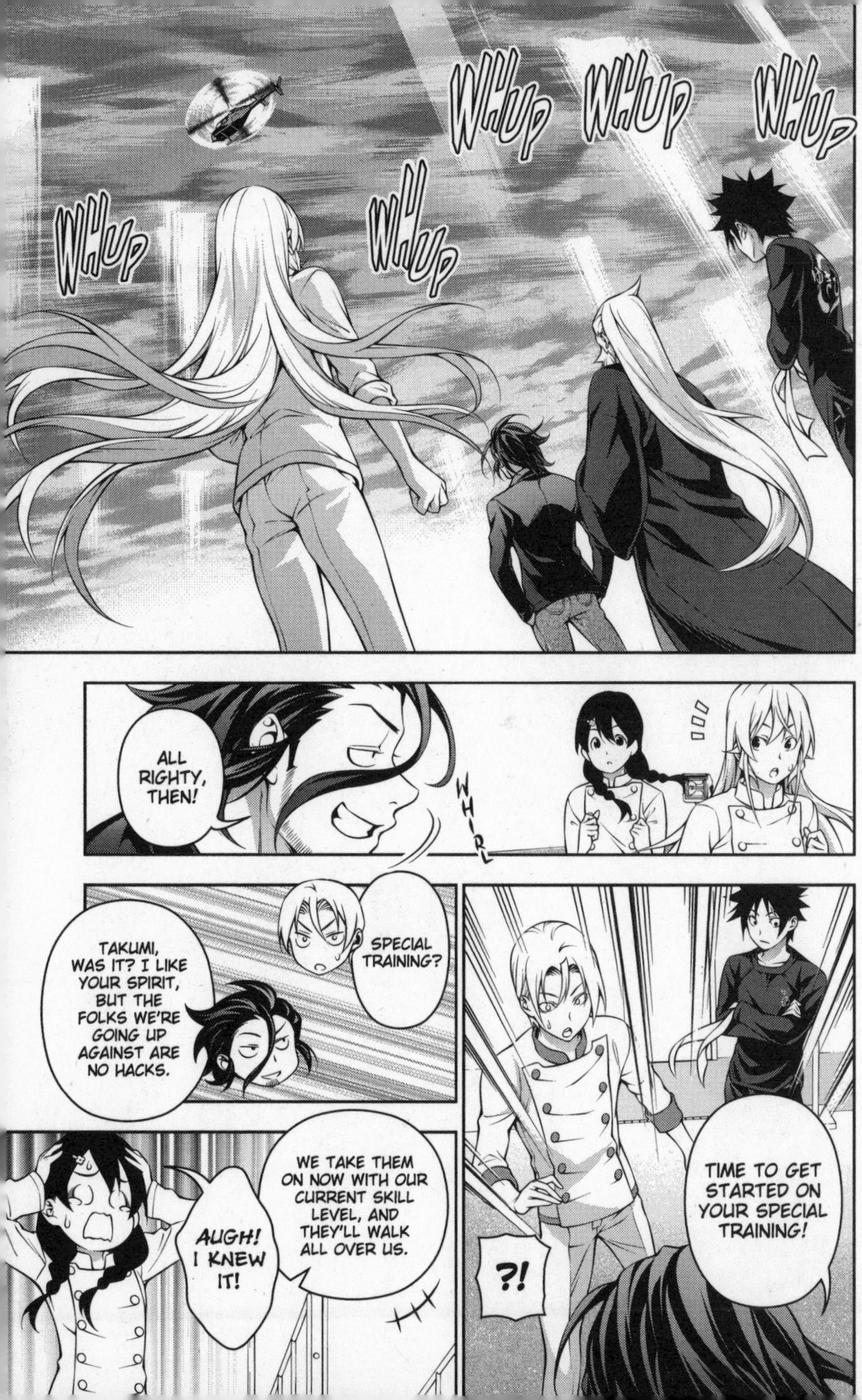
WHUP
WHUP
WHUP
WHUP
WHUP
ALL RIGHTY, THEN!
WHIRL
TIME TO GET STARTED ON YOUR SPECIAL TRAINING!
?!
SPECIAL TRAINING?
TAKUMI, WAS IT? I LIKE YOUR SPIRIT, BUT THE FOLKS WE'RE GOING UP AGAINST ARE NO HACKS.
WE TAKE THEM ON NOW WITH OUR CURRENT SKILL LEVEL, AND THEY'LL WALK ALL OVER US.
AUGH! I KNEW IT!

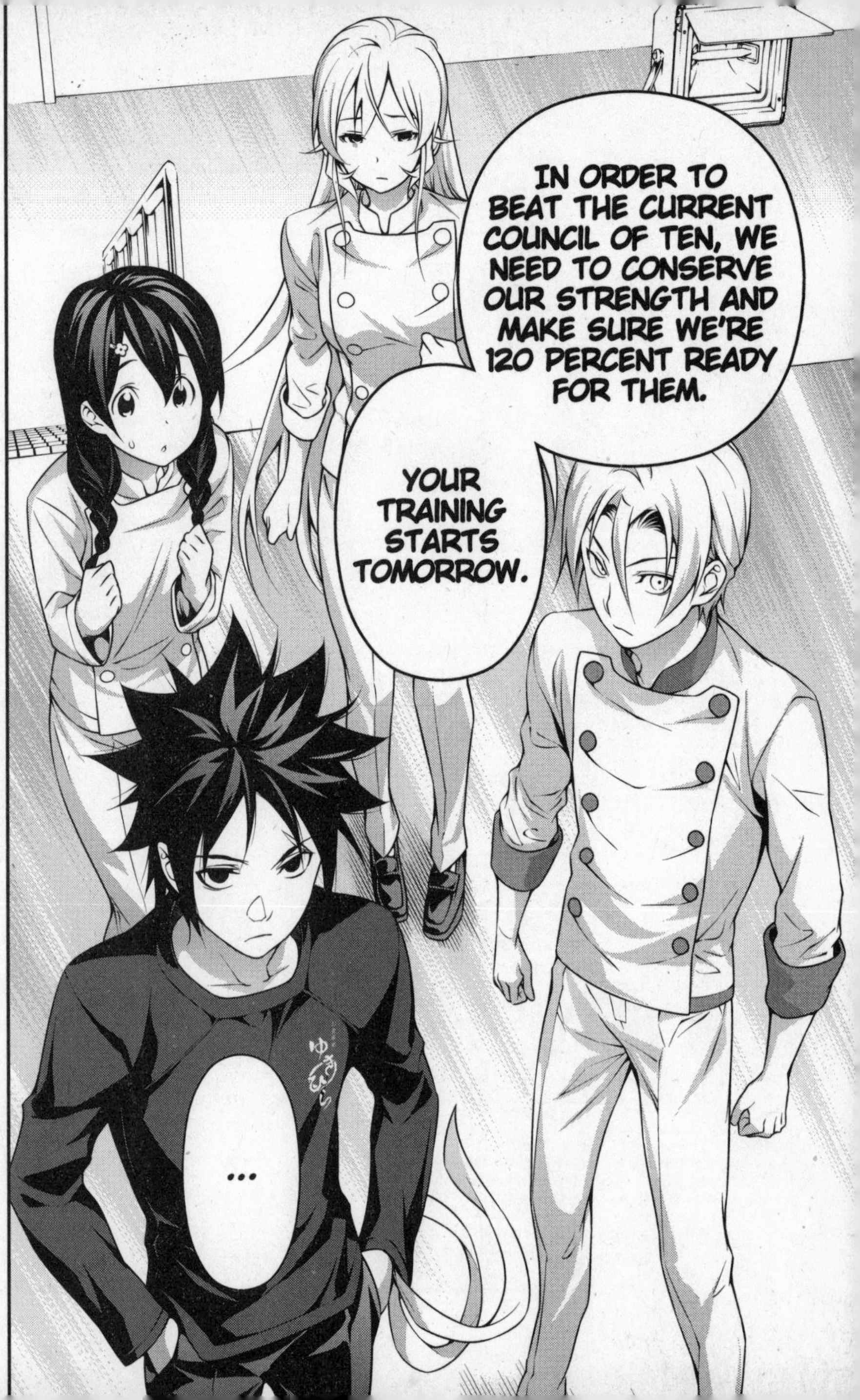
IN ORDER TO BEAT THE CURRENT COUNCIL OF TEN, WE NEED TO CONSERVE OUR STRENGTH AND MAKE SURE WE'RE 120 PERCENT READY FOR THEM.
YOUR TRAINING STARTS TOMORROW.
...

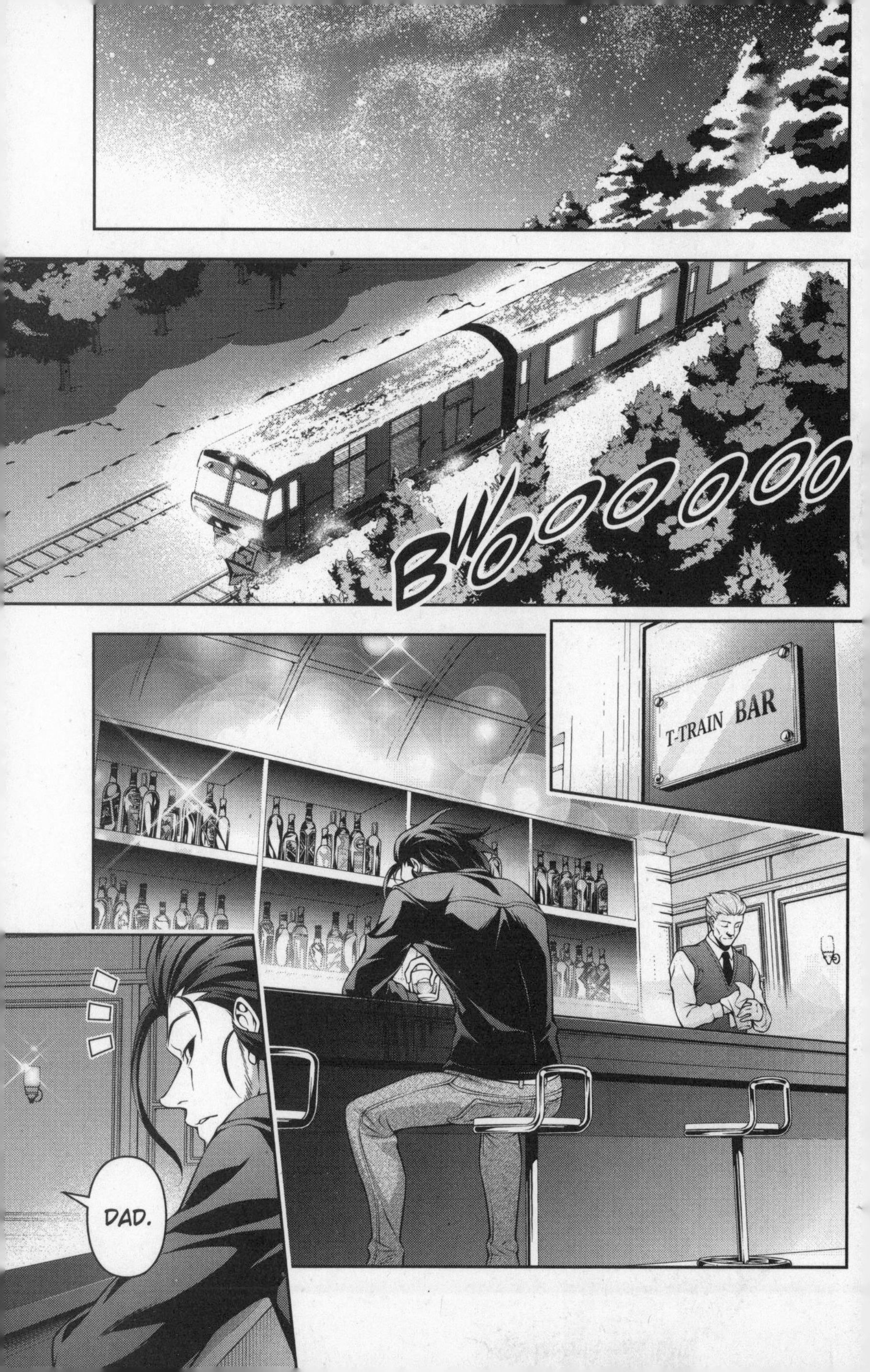
BWOOOOOO
T-TRAIN BAR
DAD.

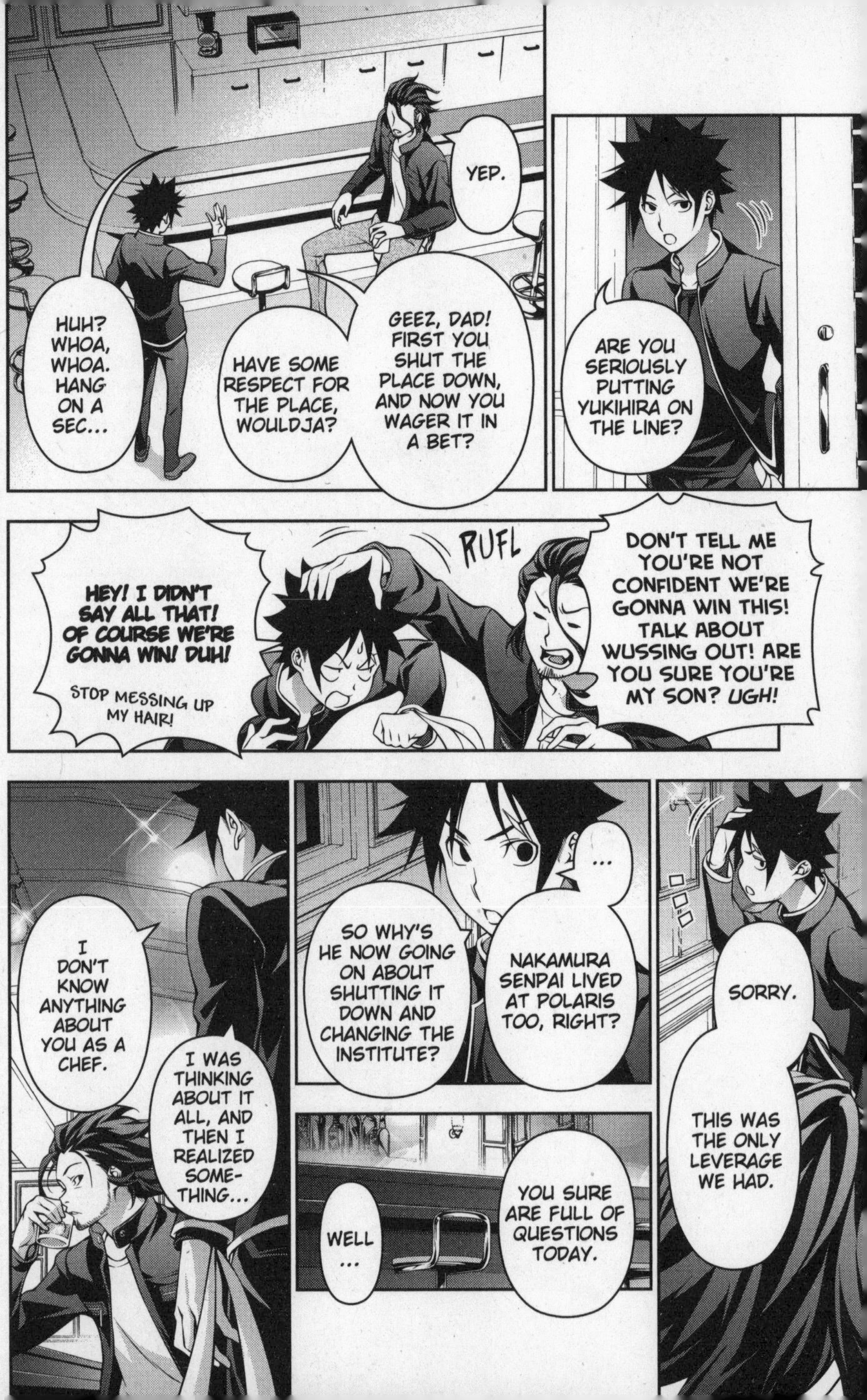
ARE YOU SERIOUSLY PUTTING YUKIHIRA ON THE LINE?
YEP.
GEEZ, DAD! FIRST YOU SHUT THE PLACE DOWN, AND NOW YOU WAGER IT IN A BET?
HAVE SOME RESPECT FOR THE PLACE, WOULDJA?
HUH? WHOA, WHOA. HANG ON A SEC...
DON'T TELL ME YOU'RE NOT CONFIDENT WE'RE GONNA WIN THIS! TALK ABOUT WUSSING OUT! ARE YOU SURE YOU'RE MY SON? UGH!
RUFL
HEY! I DIDN'T SAY ALL THAT! OF COURSE WE'RE GONNA WIN! DUH!
STOP MESSING UP MY HAIR!
SORRY.
THIS WAS THE ONLY LEVERAGE WE HAD.
...
NAKAMURA SENPAI LIVED AT POLARIS TOO, RIGHT?
SO WHY'S HE NOW GOING ON ABOUT SHUTTING IT DOWN AND CHANGING THE INSTITUTE?
YOU SURE ARE FULL OF QUESTIONS TODAY.
WELL ...
I WAS THINKING ABOUT IT ALL, AND THEN I REALIZED SOME-THING...
I DON'T KNOW ANYTHING ABOUT YOU AS A CHEF.

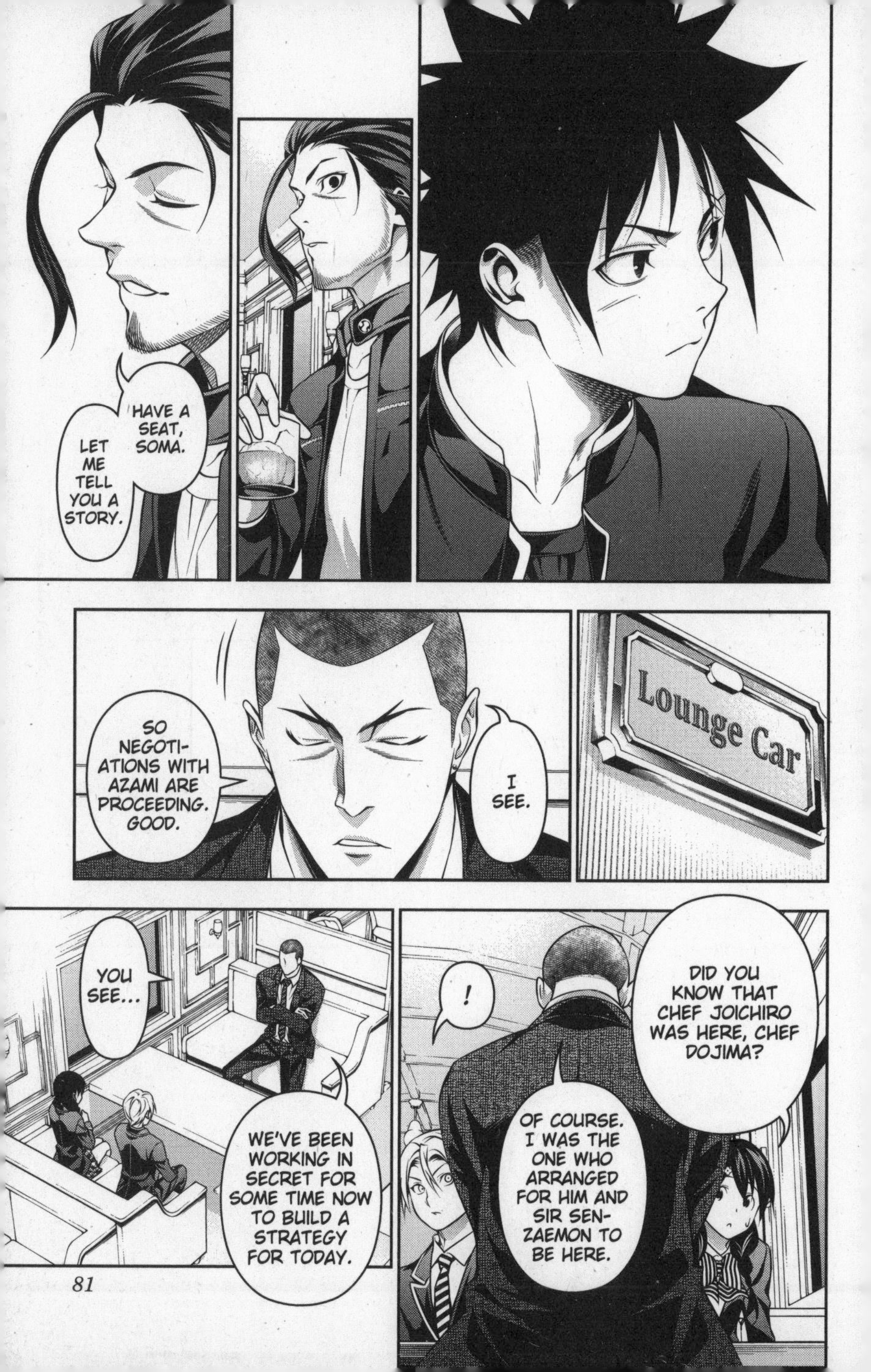
HAVE A SEAT, SOMA.
LET ME TELL YOU A STORY.
Lounge Car
I SEE.
SO NEGOTIATIONS WITH AZAMI ARE PROCEEDING. GOOD.
DID YOU KNOW THAT CHEF JOICHIRO WAS HERE, CHEF DOJIMA?
!
OF COURSE. I WAS THE ONE WHO ARRANGED FOR HIM AND SIR SENZAEMON TO BE HERE.
YOU SEE...
WE'VE BEEN WORKING IN SECRET FOR SOME TIME NOW TO BUILD A STRATEGY FOR TODAY.

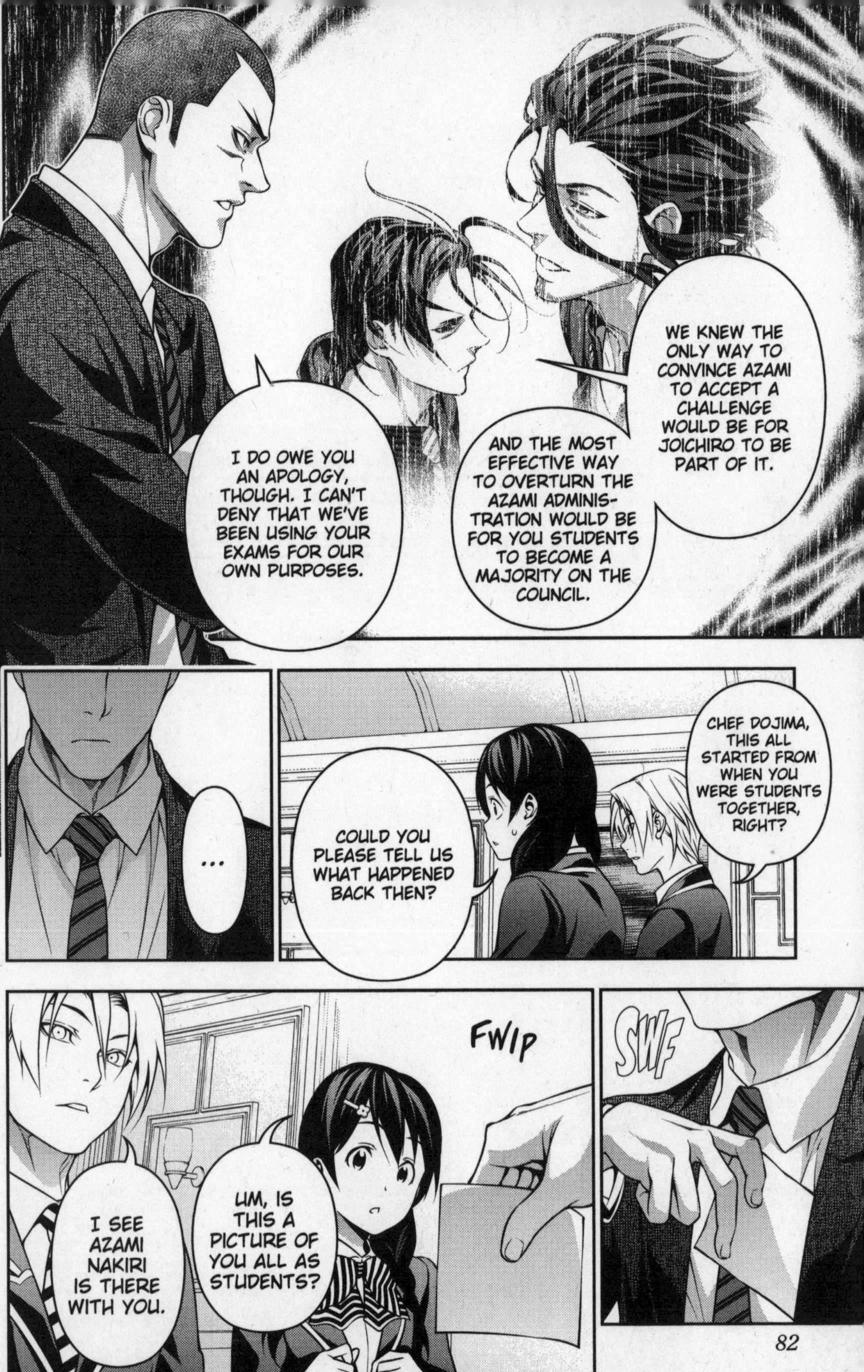
WE KNEW THE ONLY WAY TO CONVINCE AZAMI TO ACCEPT A CHALLENGE WOULD BE FOR JOICHIRO TO BE PART OF IT.
AND THE MOST EFFECTIVE WAY TO OVERTURN THE AZAMI ADMINIS-TRATION WOULD BE FOR YOU STUDENTS TO BECOME A MAJORITY ON THE COUNCIL.
I DO OWE YOU AN APOLOGY, THOUGH. I CAN'T DENY THAT WE'VE BEEN USING YOUR EXAMS FOR OUR OWN PURPOSES.
CHEF DOJIMA, THIS ALL STARTED FROM WHEN YOU WERE STUDENTS TOGETHER, RIGHT?
COULD YOU PLEASE TELL US WHAT HAPPENED BACK THEN?
...
SWF
FWIP
UM, IS THIS A PICTURE OF YOU ALL AS STUDENTS?
I SEE AZAMI NAKIRI IS THERE WITH YOU.

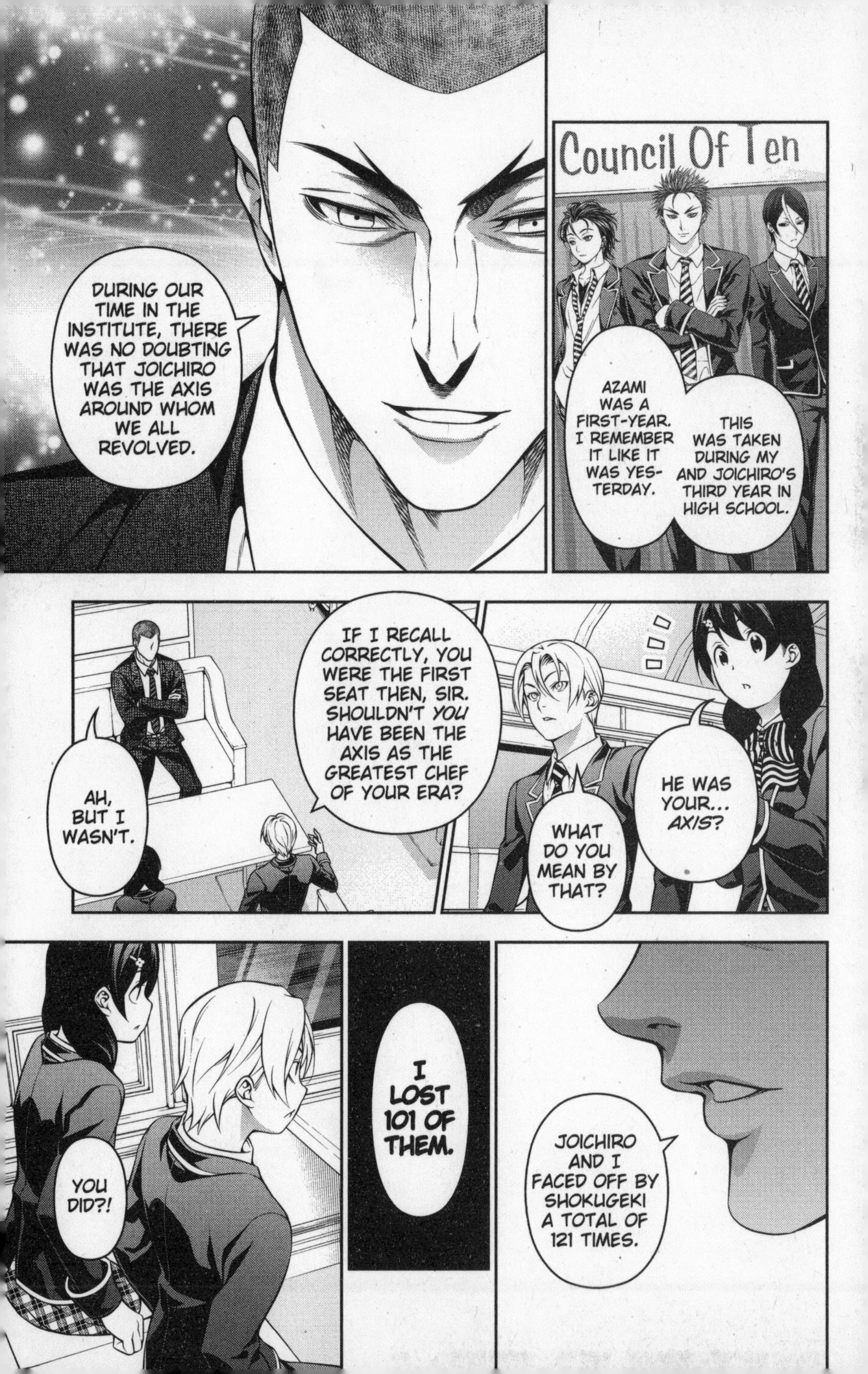
Council Of Ten
THIS WAS TAKEN DURING MY AND JOICHIRO'S THIRD YEAR IN HIGH SCHOOL.
AZAMI WAS A FIRST-YEAR. I REMEMBER IT LIKE IT WAS YES-TERDAY.
DURING OUR TIME IN THE INSTITUTE, THERE WAS NO DOUBTING THAT JOICHIRO WAS THE AXIS AROUND WHOM WE ALL REVOLVED.
HE WAS YOUR... *AXIS*?
WHAT DO YOU MEAN BY THAT?
IF I RECALL CORRECTLY, YOU WERE THE FIRST SEAT THEN, SIR. SHOULDN'T *YOU* HAVE BEEN THE AXIS AS THE GREATEST CHEF OF YOUR ERA?
AH, BUT I WASN'T.
JOICHIRO AND I FACED OFF BY SHOKUGEKI A TOTAL OF 121 TIMES.
I LOST 101 OF THEM.
YOU DID?!

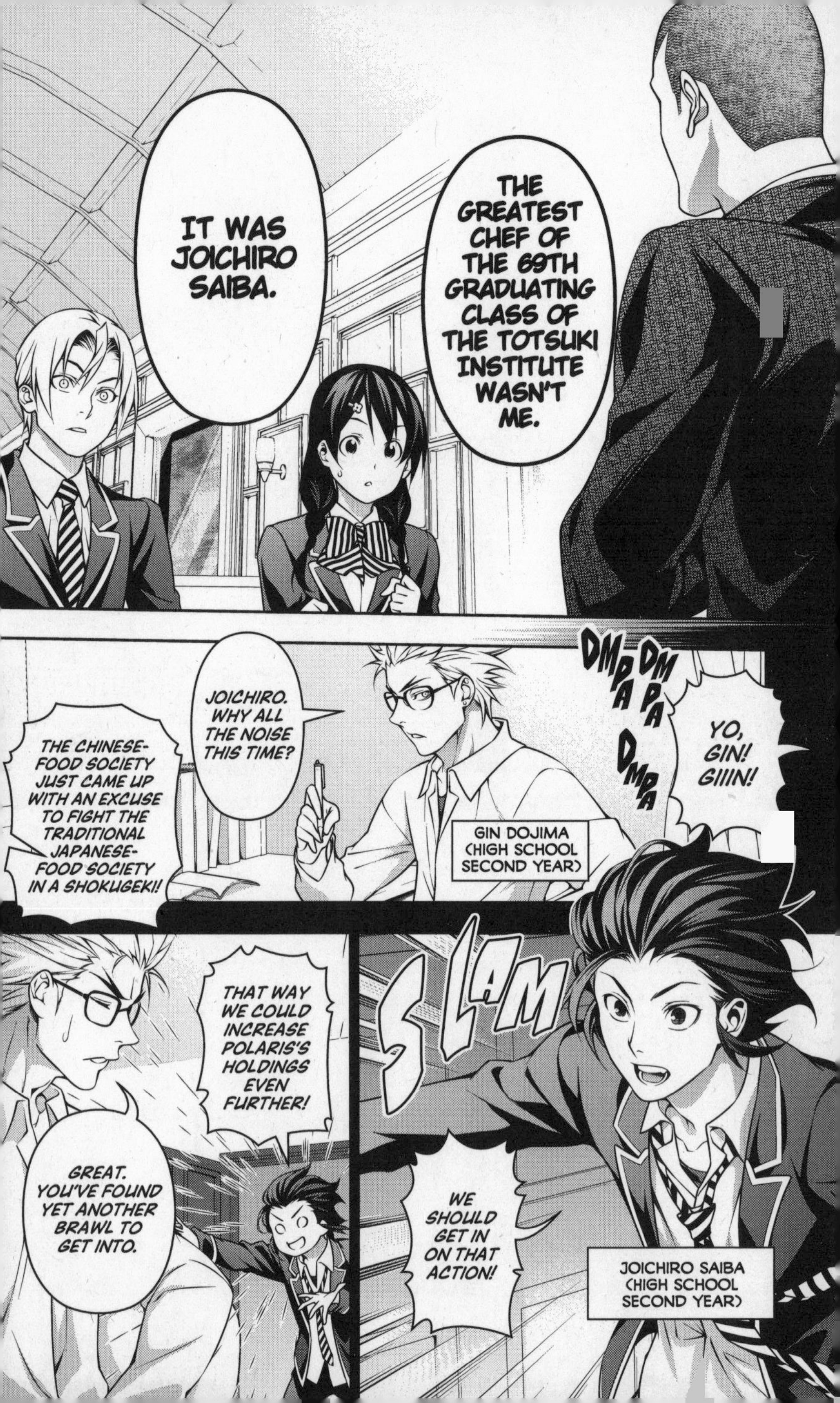
THE GREATEST CHEF OF THE 69TH GRADUATING CLASS OF THE TOTSUKI INSTITUTE WASN'T ME.
IT WAS JOICHIRO SAIBA.
DMPA DMPA DMPA
YO, GIN! GIIIN!
JOICHIRO. WHY ALL THE NOISE THIS TIME?
GIN DOJIMA (HIGH SCHOOL SECOND YEAR)
THE CHINESE-FOOD SOCIETY JUST CAME UP WITH AN EXCUSE TO FIGHT THE TRADITIONAL JAPANESE-FOOD SOCIETY IN A SHOKUGEKI!
SLAM
WE SHOULD GET IN ON THAT ACTION!
JOICHIRO SAIBA (HIGH SCHOOL SECOND YEAR)
THAT WAY WE COULD INCREASE POLARIS'S HOLDINGS EVEN FURTHER!
GREAT. YOU'VE FOUND YET ANOTHER BRAWL TO GET INTO.

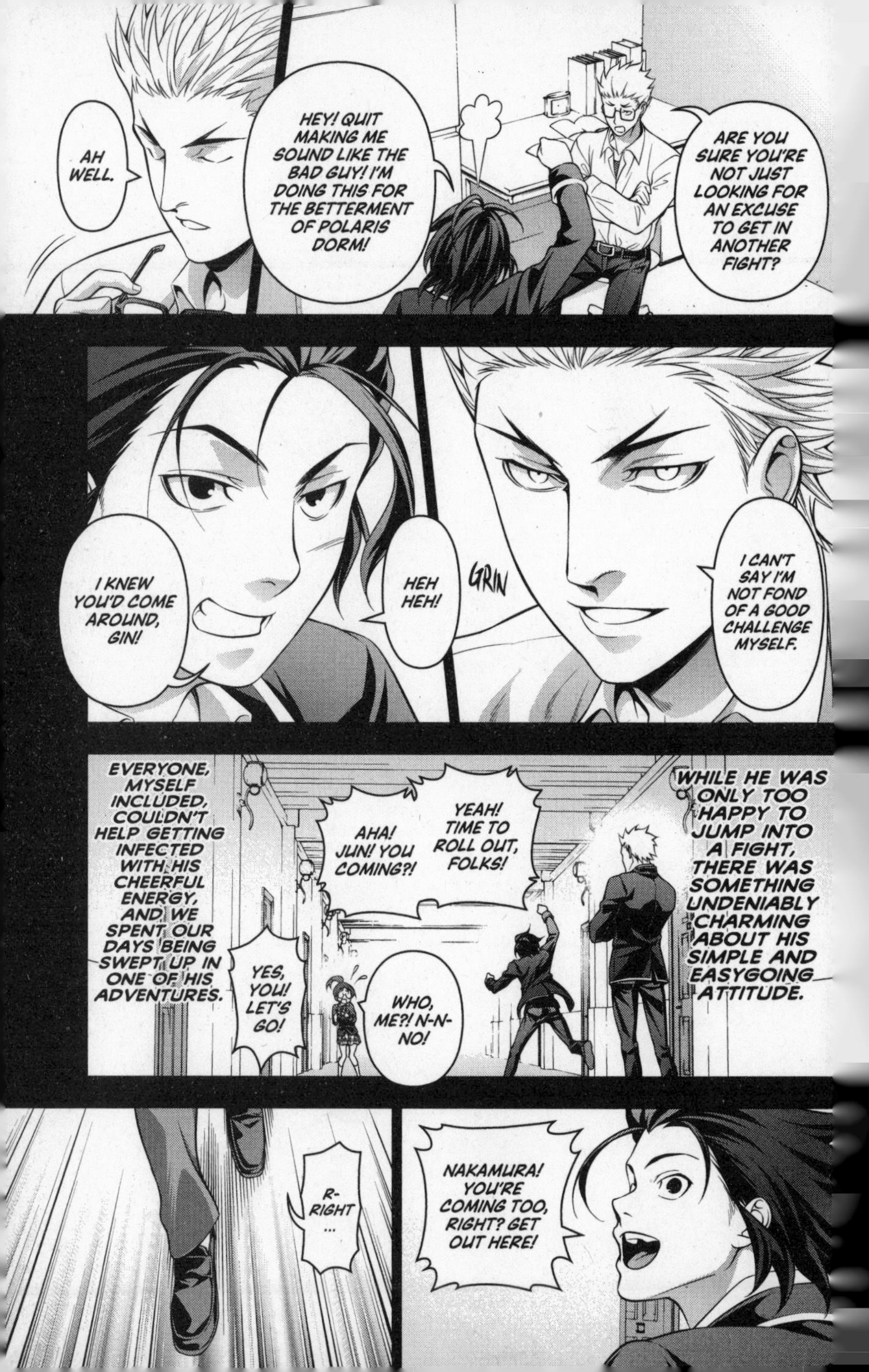
ARE YOU SURE YOU'RE NOT JUST LOOKING FOR AN EXCUSE TO GET IN ANOTHER FIGHT?
HEY! QUIT MAKING ME SOUND LIKE THE BAD GUY! I'M DOING THIS FOR THE BETTERMENT OF POLARIS DORM!
AH WELL.
I CAN'T SAY I'M NOT FOND OF A GOOD CHALLENGE MYSELF.
GRIN
HEH HEH!
I KNEW YOU'D COME AROUND, GIN!
WHILE HE WAS ONLY TOO HAPPY TO JUMP INTO A FIGHT, THERE WAS SOMETHING UNDENIABLY CHARMING ABOUT HIS SIMPLE AND EASYGOING ATTITUDE.
YEAH! TIME TO ROLL OUT, FOLKS!
AHA! JUN! YOU COMING?!
WHO, ME?! N-N-NO!
YES, YOU! LET'S GO!
EVERYONE, MYSELF INCLUDED, COULDN'T HELP GETTING INFECTED WITH HIS CHEERFUL ENERGY, AND WE SPENT OUR DAYS BEING SWEPT UP IN ONE OF HIS ADVENTURES.
NAKAMURA! YOU'RE COMING TOO, RIGHT? GET OUT HERE!
R-RIGHT...

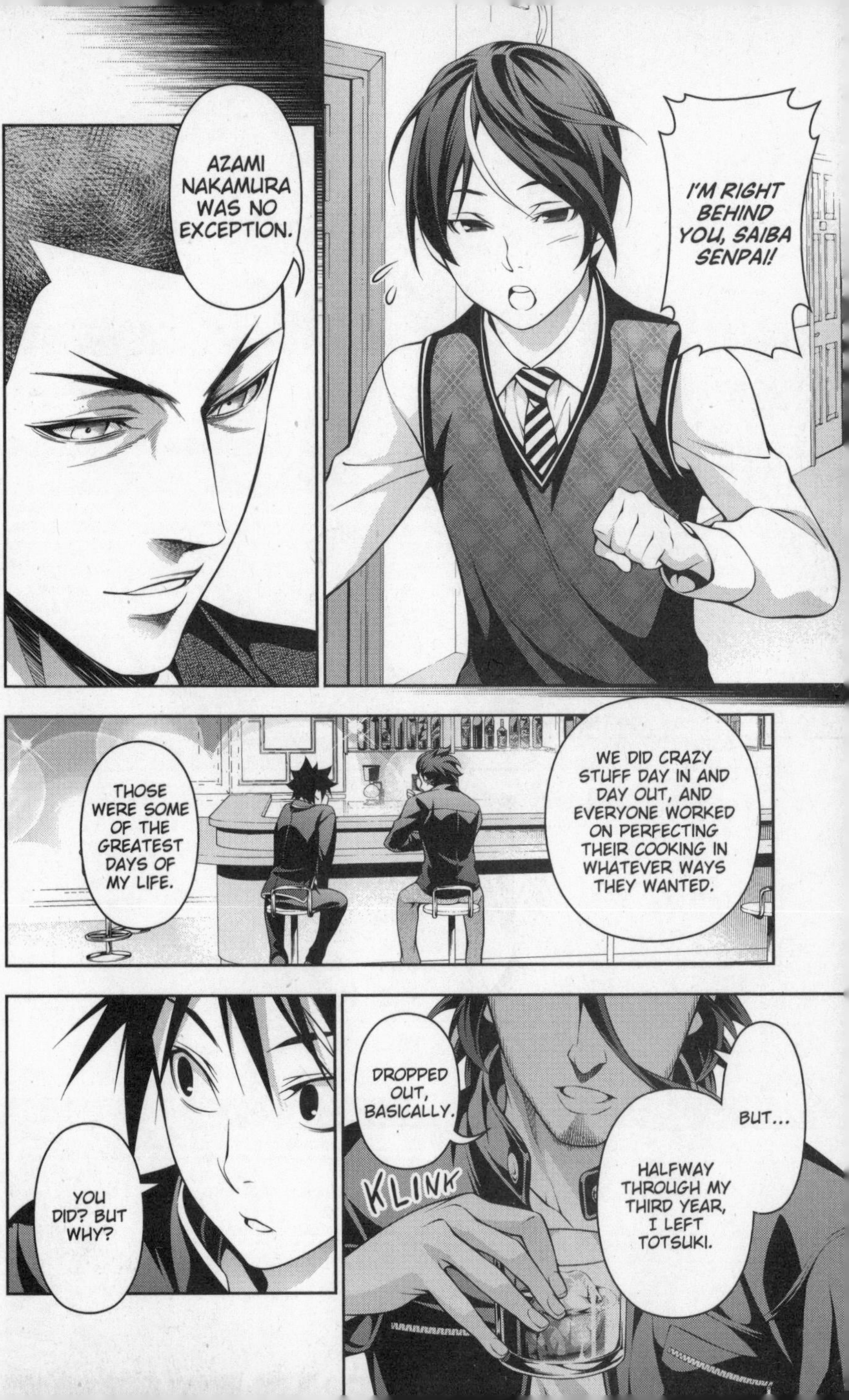
I'M RIGHT BEHIND YOU, SAIBA SENPAI!
AZAMI NAKAMURA WAS NO EXCEPTION.
WE DID CRAZY STUFF DAY IN AND DAY OUT, AND EVERYONE WORKED ON PERFECTING THEIR COOKING IN WHATEVER WAYS THEY WANTED.
THOSE WERE SOME OF THE GREATEST DAYS OF MY LIFE.
BUT...
HALFWAY THROUGH MY THIRD YEAR, I LEFT TOTSUKI.
DROPPED OUT, BASICALLY.
KLINK
YOU DID? BUT WHY?

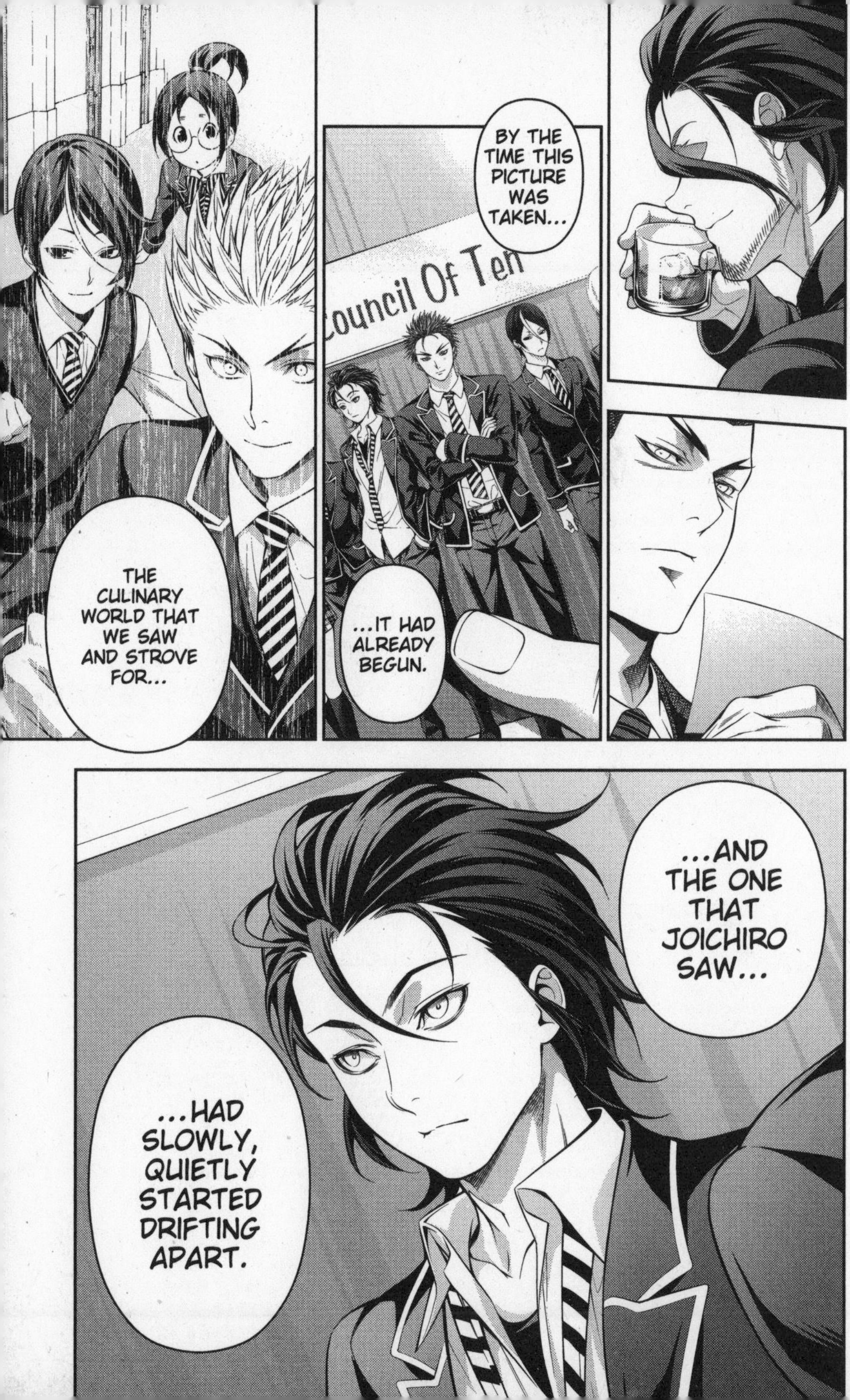
BY THE TIME THIS PICTURE WAS TAKEN...
Council Of Ten
...IT HAD ALREADY BEGUN.
THE CULINARY WORLD THAT WE SAW AND STROVE FOR...
...AND THE ONE THAT JOICHIRO SAW...
...HAD SLOWLY, QUIETLY STARTED DRIFTING APART.

SHOKUGEKI COLUMN

~ORIGIN OF THE NAME RÉGIMENT DE CUISINE~

From the late 19th to the early 20th century, French chef Auguste Escoffier revolutionized cooking management across the world. Before then, running a kitchen was a very disorganized and inefficient affair, with no standardized systems or methods. He developed a system and hierarchy for managing large kitchens, delineating specific positions like *entremetier*, *saucier*, *rôtisseur*, etc., and codifying their duties. This system, called the Brigade de de Cuisine (effectively meaning "the Kitchen Brigade") forms the basis for how kitchens are managed even in the modern day.

An official from the Totsuki Institute, deciding the term *team shokugeki* was too dull, chose to rename them with a name inspired by that system, trading *brigade* for another French military-unit name, *régiment*. And thus the name *Régiment de Cuisine* was born.

Excerpt from *The History of Totsuki*, Totsuki Institute Publishing

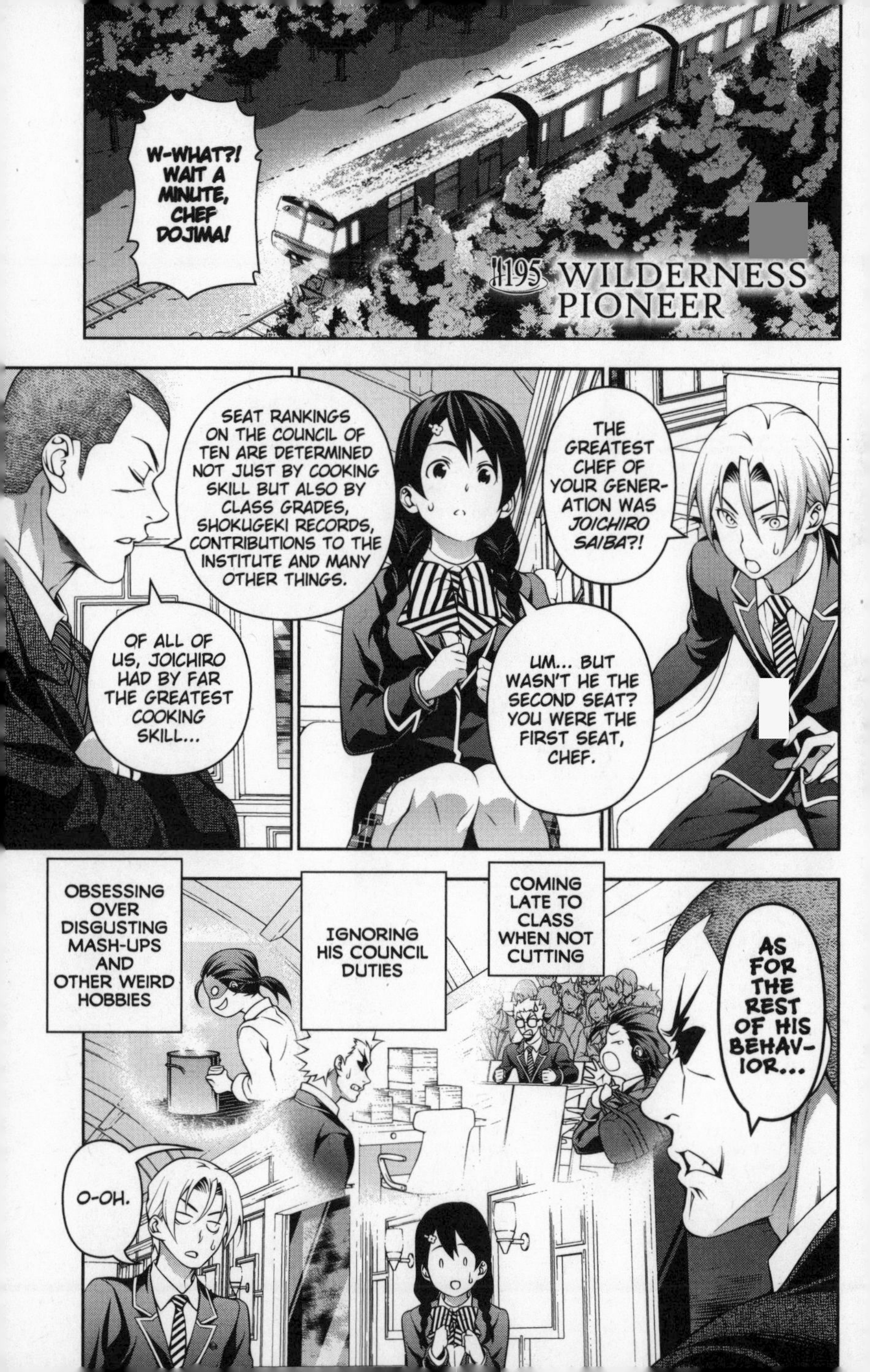
#195 WILDERNESS PIONEER
W-WHAT?! WAIT A MINUTE, CHEF DOJIMA!
THE GREATEST CHEF OF YOUR GENERATION WAS JOICHIRO SAIBA?!
UM... BUT WASN'T HE THE SECOND SEAT? YOU WERE THE FIRST SEAT, CHEF.
SEAT RANKINGS ON THE COUNCIL OF TEN ARE DETERMINED NOT JUST BY COOKING SKILL BUT ALSO BY CLASS GRADES, SHOKUGEKI RECORDS, CONTRIBUTIONS TO THE INSTITUTE AND MANY OTHER THINGS.
OF ALL OF US, JOICHIRO HAD BY FAR THE GREATEST COOKING SKILL...
AS FOR THE REST OF HIS BEHAVIOR...
COMING LATE TO CLASS WHEN NOT CUTTING
IGNORING HIS COUNCIL DUTIES
OBSESSING OVER DISGUSTING MASH-UPS AND OTHER WEIRD HOBBIES
O-OH.

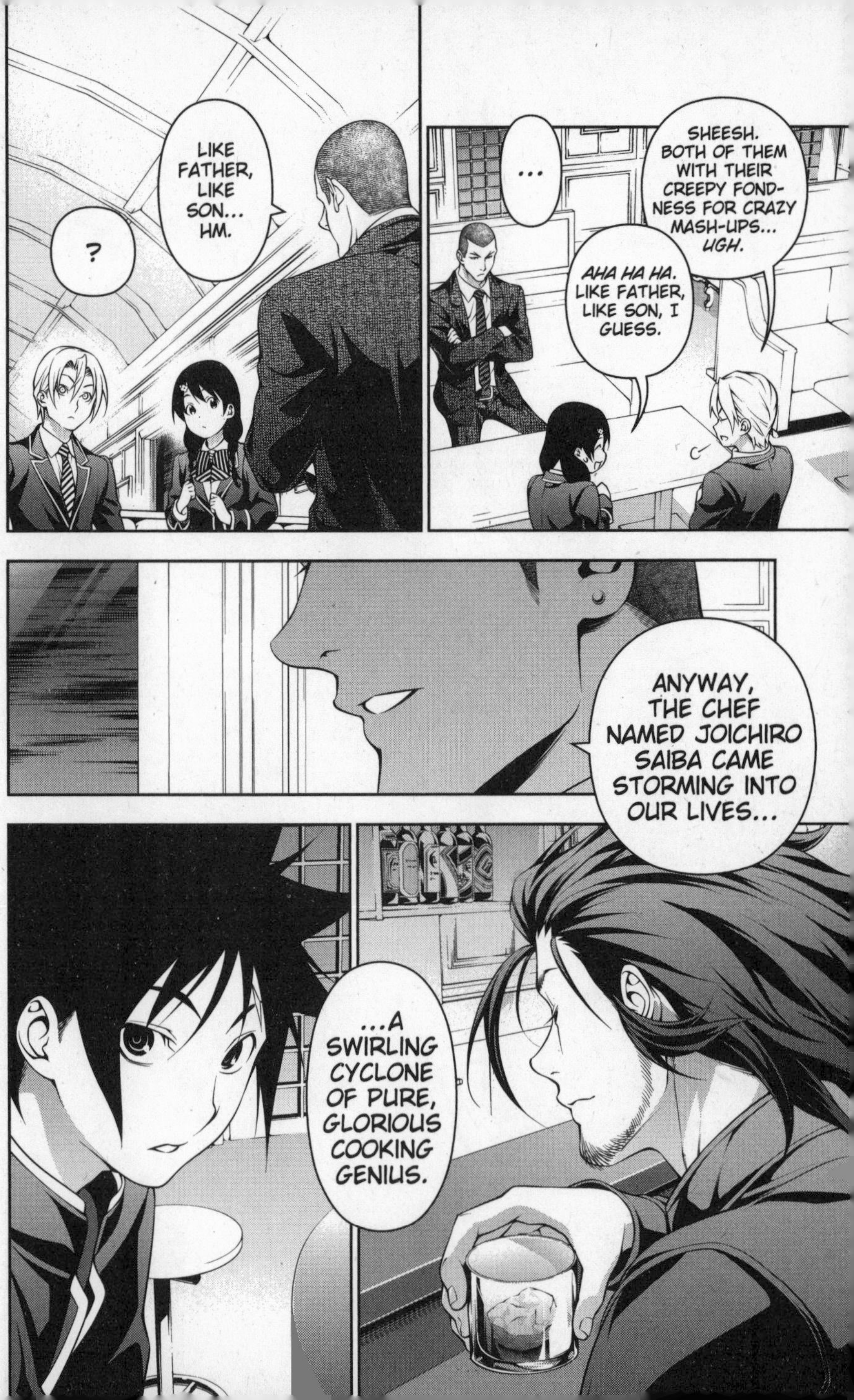
SHEESH. BOTH OF THEM WITH THEIR CREEPY FONDNESS FOR CRAZY MASH-UPS... UGH.
...
AHA HA HA. LIKE FATHER, LIKE SON, I GUESS.
LIKE FATHER, LIKE SON... HM.
?
ANYWAY, THE CHEF NAMED JOICHIRO SAIBA CAME STORMING INTO OUR LIVES...
...A SWIRLING CYCLONE OF PURE, GLORIOUS COOKING GENIUS.

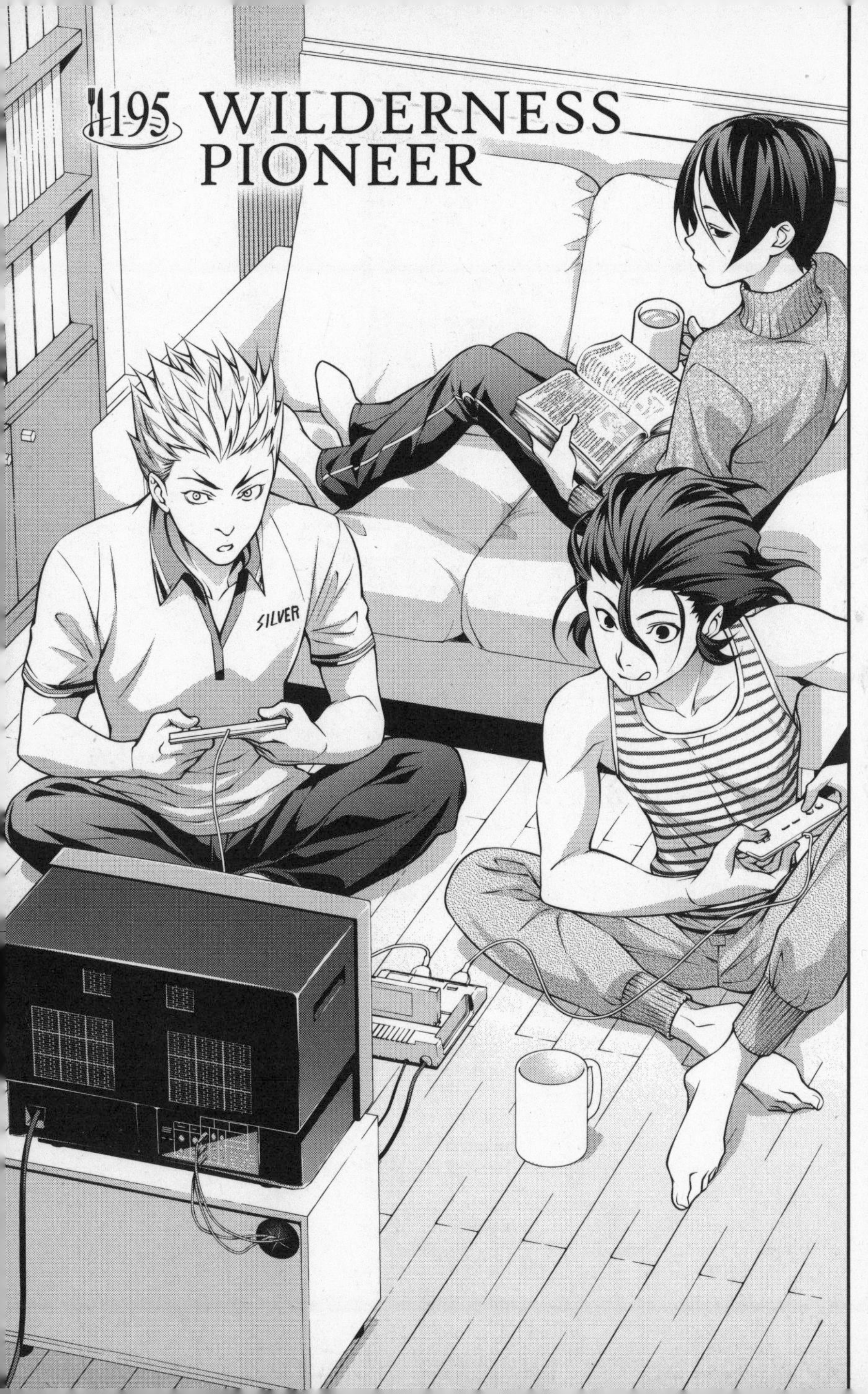
195 WILDERNESS PIONEER
SILVER

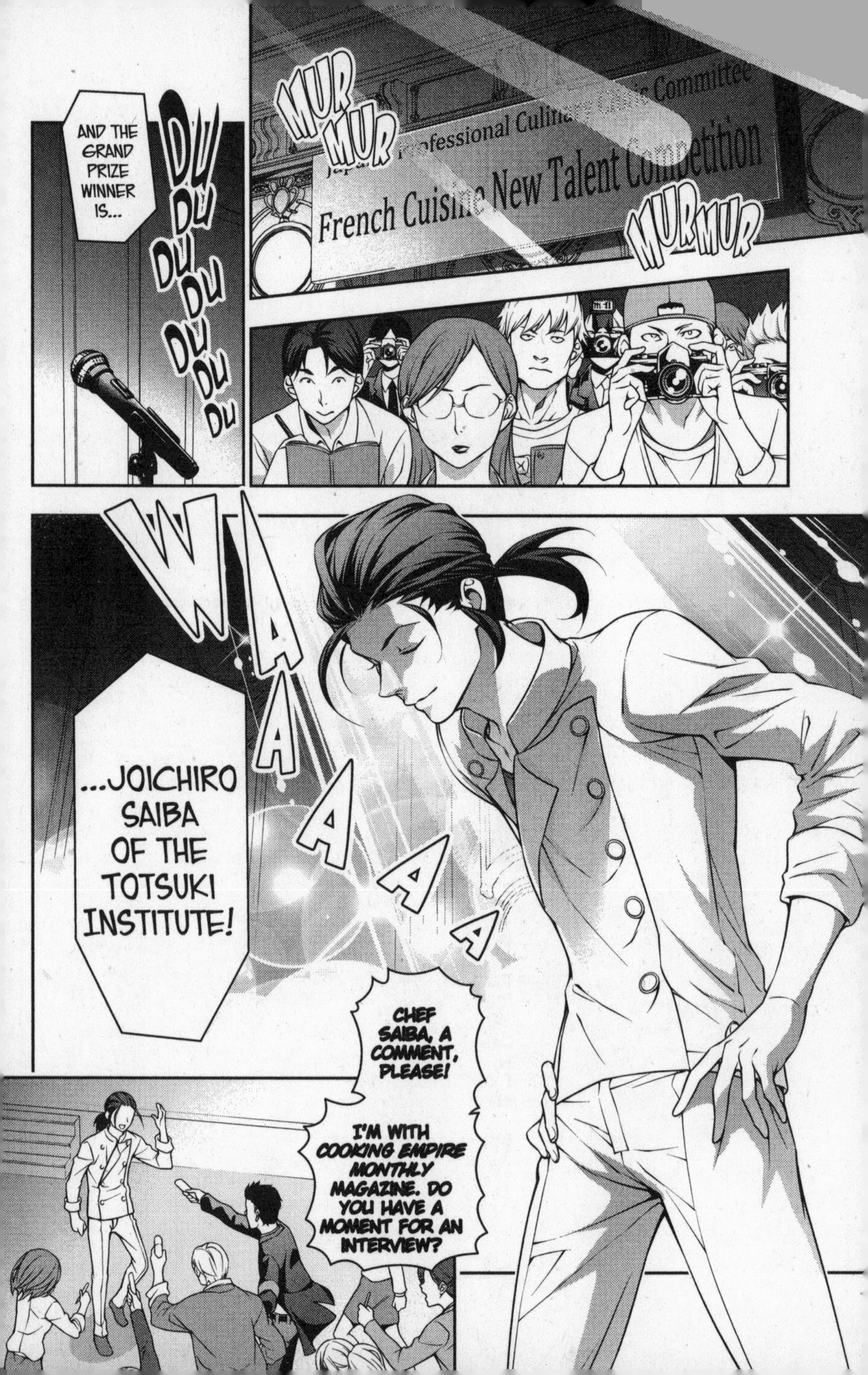
Committee
French Cuisine New Talent Competition
MUR MUR
MURMUR
AND THE GRAND PRIZE WINNER IS...
DU DU DU DU DU DU DU DU
WAAAAAA
...JOICHIRO SAIBA OF THE TOTSUKI INSTITUTE!
CHEF SAIBA, A COMMENT, PLEASE!
I'M WITH COOKING EMPIRE MONTHLY MAGAZINE. DO YOU HAVE A MOMENT FOR AN INTERVIEW?

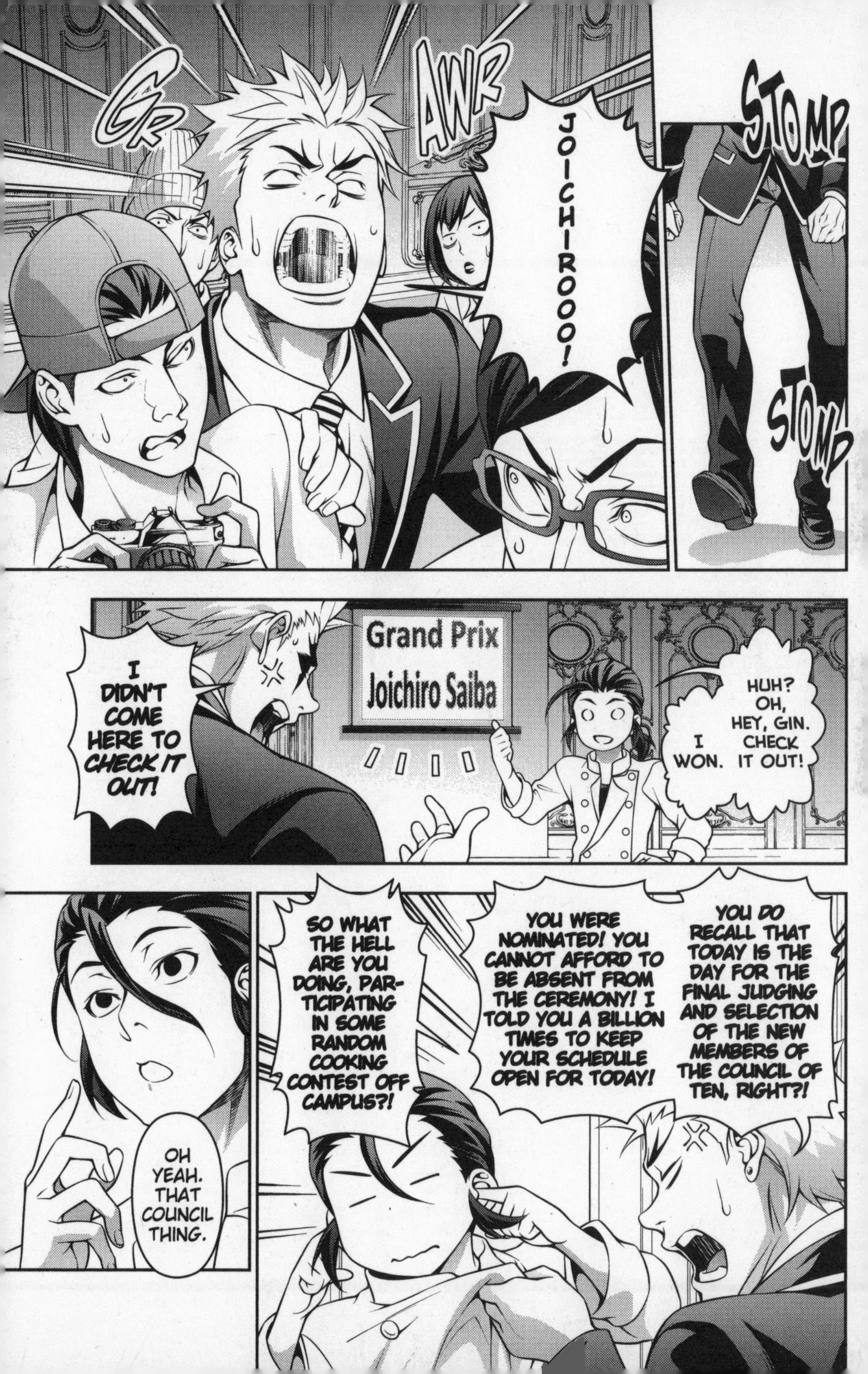
STOMP
STOMP
JOICHIROOOO!
AWR
GR
HUH? OH, HEY, GIN. I WON. CHECK IT OUT!
Grand Prix
Joichiro Saiba
I DIDN'T COME HERE TO CHECK IT OUT!
YOU DO RECALL THAT TODAY IS THE DAY FOR THE FINAL JUDGING AND SELECTION OF THE NEW MEMBERS OF THE COUNCIL OF TEN, RIGHT?!
YOU WERE NOMINATED! YOU CANNOT AFFORD TO BE ABSENT FROM THE CEREMONY! I TOLD YOU A BILLION TIMES TO KEEP YOUR SCHEDULE OPEN FOR TODAY!
SO WHAT THE HELL ARE YOU DOING, PARTICIPATING IN SOME RANDOM COOKING CONTEST OFF CAMPUS?!
OH YEAH. THAT COUNCIL THING.

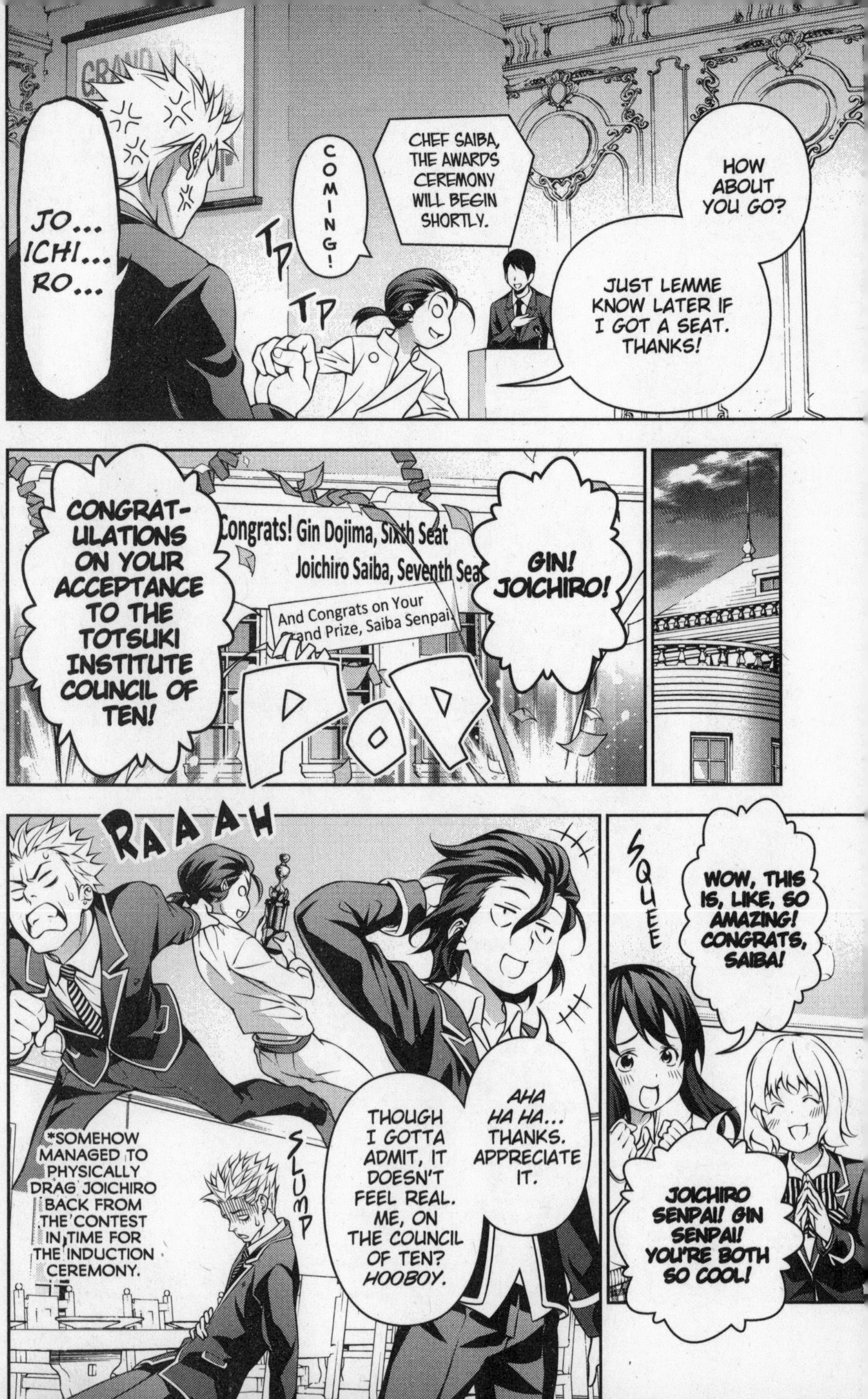
HOW ABOUT YOU GO?
JUST LEMME KNOW LATER IF I GOT A SEAT. THANKS!
CHEF SAIBA, THE AWARDS CEREMONY WILL BEGIN SHORTLY.
COMING!
TP TP
JO... ICHI... RO...
GIN! JOICHIRO!
Congrats! Gin Dojima, Sixth Seat
Joichiro Saiba, Seventh Sea
And Congrats on Your
rand Prize, Saiba Senpai!
POP
CONGRATULATIONS ON YOUR ACCEPTANCE TO THE TOTSUKI INSTITUTE COUNCIL OF TEN!
SQUEE
WOW, THIS IS, LIKE, SO AMAZING! CONGRATS, SAIBA!
JOICHIRO SENPAI! GIN SENPAI! YOU'RE BOTH SO COOL!
RAAAH
AHA HA HA... THANKS. APPRECIATE IT.
THOUGH I GOTTA ADMIT, IT DOESN'T FEEL REAL. ME, ON THE COUNCIL OF TEN? HOOBOY.
SLUMP
*SOMEHOW MANAGED TO PHYSICALLY DRAG JOICHIRO BACK FROM THE CONTEST IN TIME FOR THE INDUCTION CEREMONY.

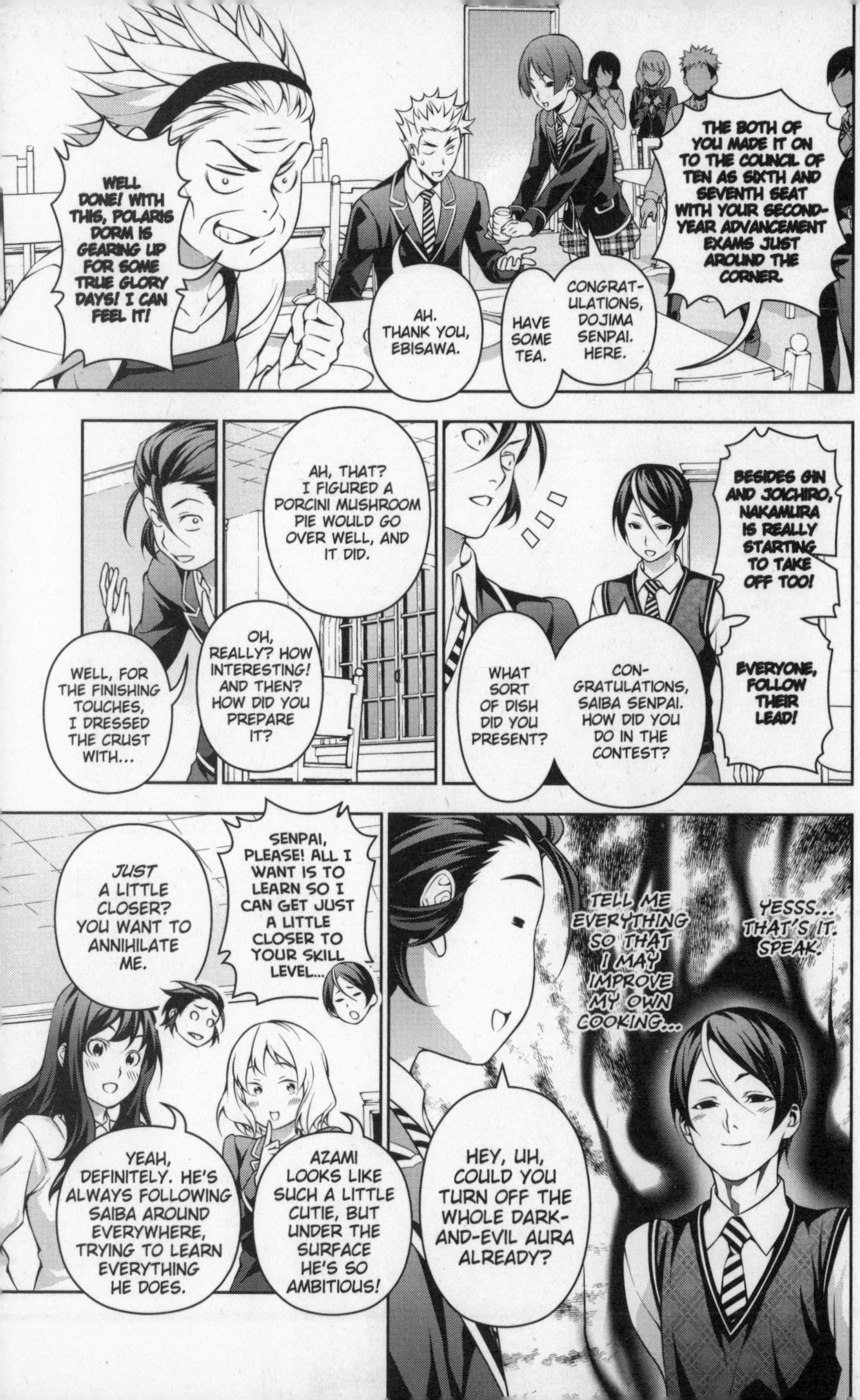
THE BOTH OF YOU MADE IT ON TO THE COUNCIL OF TEN AS SIXTH AND SEVENTH SEAT WITH YOUR SECOND-YEAR ADVANCEMENT EXAMS JUST AROUND THE CORNER.
CONGRAT-ULATIONS, DOJIMA SENPAI. HERE.
HAVE SOME TEA.
AH. THANK YOU, EBISAWA.
WELL DONE! WITH THIS, POLARIS DORM IS GEARING UP FOR SOME TRUE GLORY DAYS! I CAN FEEL IT!
BESIDES GIN AND JOICHIRO, NAKAMURA IS REALLY STARTING TO TAKE OFF TOO!
EVERYONE, FOLLOW THEIR LEAD!
CON-GRATULATIONS, SAIBA SENPAI. HOW DID YOU DO IN THE CONTEST?
WHAT SORT OF DISH DID YOU PRESENT?
AH, THAT? I FIGURED A PORCINI MUSHROOM PIE WOULD GO OVER WELL, AND IT DID.
OH, REALLY? HOW INTERESTING! AND THEN? HOW DID YOU PREPARE IT?
WELL, FOR THE FINISHING TOUCHES, I DRESSED THE CRUST WITH...
YESSS... THAT'S IT. SPEAK.
TELL ME EVERYTHING SO THAT I MAY IMPROVE MY OWN COOKING...
HEY, UH, COULD YOU TURN OFF THE WHOLE DARK-AND-EVIL AURA ALREADY?
SENPAI, PLEASE! ALL I WANT IS TO LEARN SO I CAN GET JUST A LITTLE CLOSER TO YOUR SKILL LEVEL...
JUST A LITTLE CLOSER? YOU WANT TO ANNIHILATE ME.
AZAMI LOOKS LIKE SUCH A LITTLE CUTIE, BUT UNDER THE SURFACE HE'S SO AMBITIOUS!
YEAH, DEFINITELY. HE'S ALWAYS FOLLOWING SAIBA AROUND EVERYWHERE, TRYING TO LEARN EVERYTHING HE DOES.

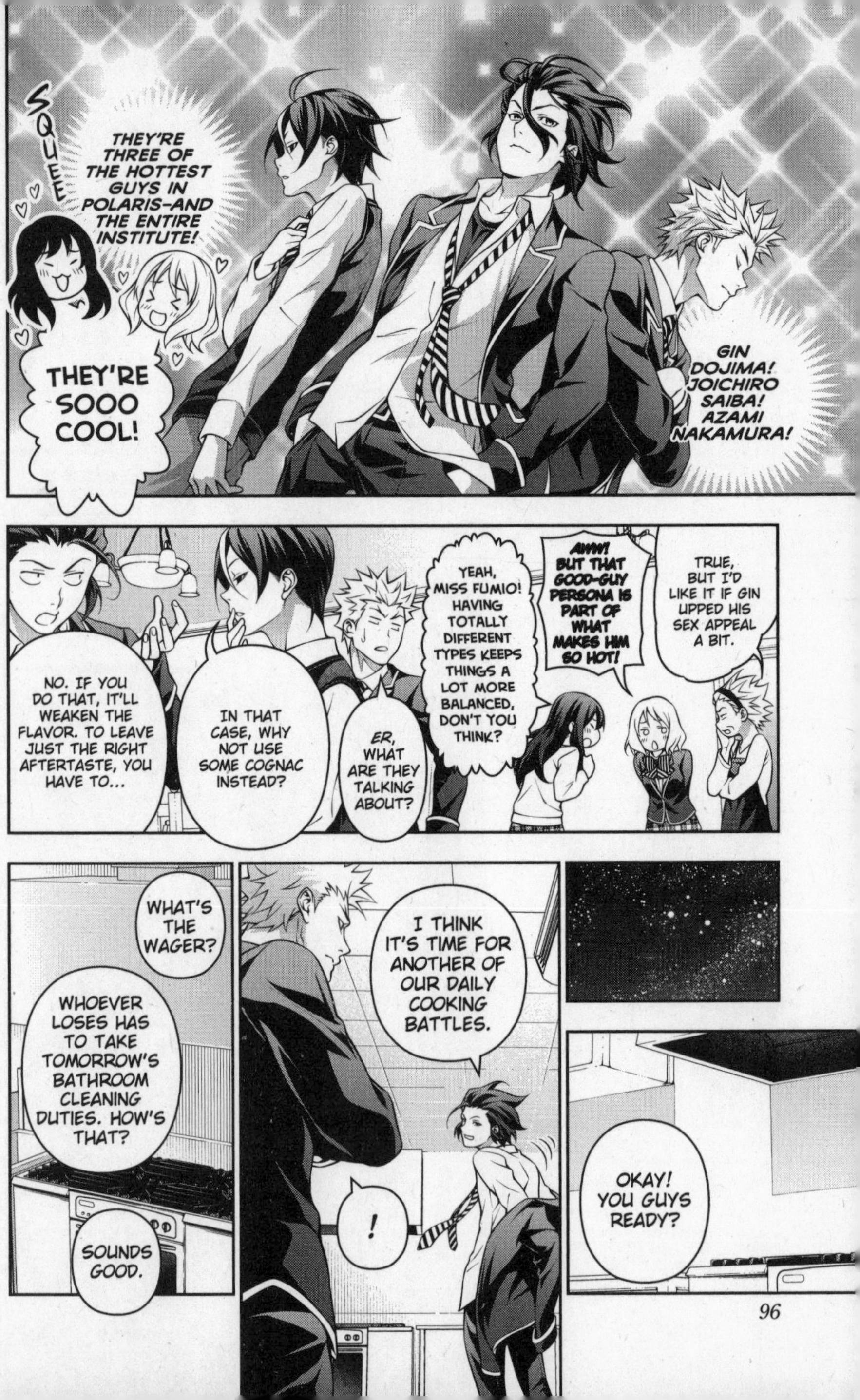

GIN DOJIMA! JOICHIRO SAIBA! AZAMI NAKAMURA!
SQUEE
THEY'RE THREE OF THE HOTTEST GUYS IN POLARIS—AND THE ENTIRE INSTITUTE!
THEY'RE SOOO COOL!
TRUE, BUT I'D LIKE IT IF GIN UPPED HIS SEX APPEAL A BIT.
AWW! BUT THAT GOOD-GUY PERSONA IS PART OF WHAT MAKES HIM SO HOT!
YEAH, MISS FUMIO! HAVING TOTALLY DIFFERENT TYPES KEEPS THINGS A LOT MORE BALANCED, DON'T YOU THINK?
ER, WHAT ARE THEY TALKING ABOUT?
IN THAT CASE, WHY NOT USE SOME COGNAC INSTEAD?
NO. IF YOU DO THAT, IT'LL WEAKEN THE FLAVOR. TO LEAVE JUST THE RIGHT AFTERTASTE, YOU HAVE TO...
OKAY! YOU GUYS READY?
I THINK IT'S TIME FOR ANOTHER OF OUR DAILY COOKING BATTLES.
!
WHAT'S THE WAGER?
WHOEVER LOSES HAS TO TAKE TOMORROW'S BATHROOM CLEANING DUTIES. HOW'S THAT?
SOUNDS GOOD.

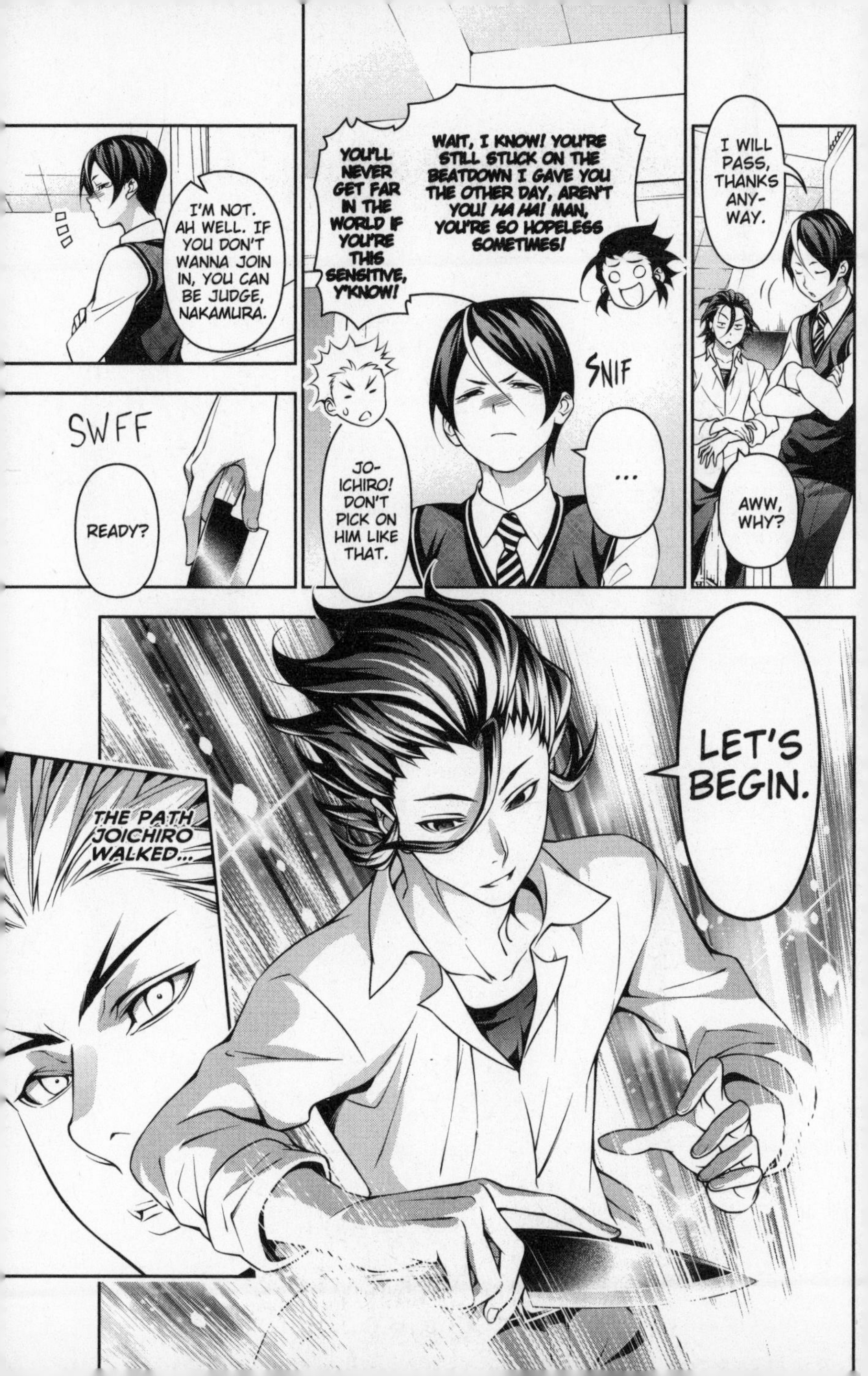
I WILL PASS, THANKS ANY-WAY.
AWW, WHY?
WAIT, I KNOW! YOU'RE STILL STUCK ON THE BEATDOWN I GAVE YOU THE OTHER DAY, AREN'T YOU! HA HA! MAN, YOU'RE SO HOPELESS SOMETIMES!
YOU'LL NEVER GET FAR IN THE WORLD IF YOU'RE THIS SENSITIVE, Y'KNOW!
SNIF
...
JO-ICHIRO! DON'T PICK ON HIM LIKE THAT.
I'M NOT. AH WELL. IF YOU DON'T WANNA JOIN IN, YOU CAN BE JUDGE, NAKAMURA.
SWFF
READY?
LET'S BEGIN.
THE PATH JOICHIRO WALKED...

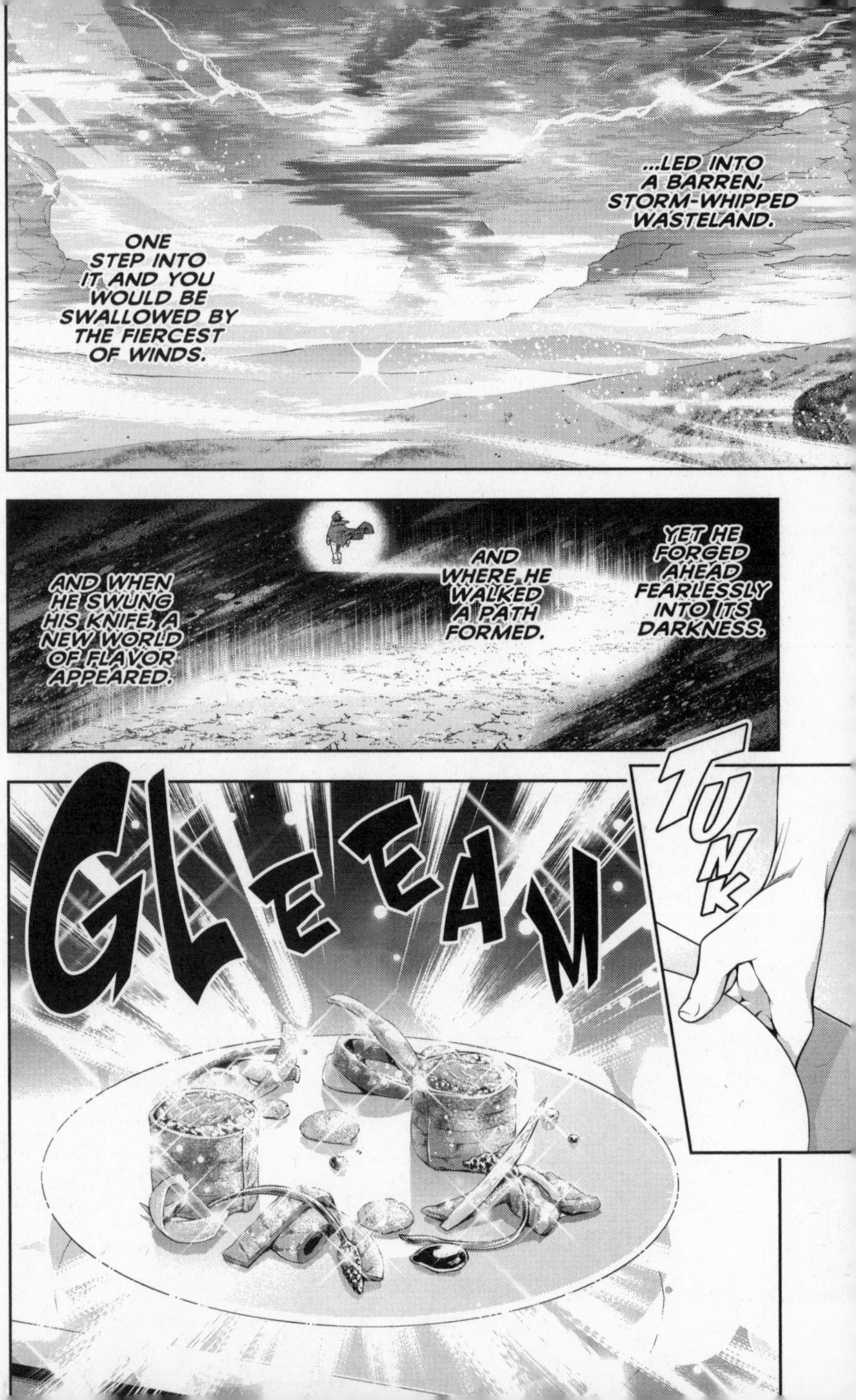
...LED INTO A BARREN, STORM-WHIPPED WASTELAND.
ONE STEP INTO IT AND YOU WOULD BE SWALLOWED BY THE FIERCEST OF WINDS.
YET HE FORGED AHEAD FEARLESSLY INTO ITS DARKNESS.
AND WHERE HE WALKED A PATH FORMED.
AND WHEN HE SWUNG HIS KNIFE, A NEW WORLD OF FLAVOR APPEARED.
TUNK
GLEEAM

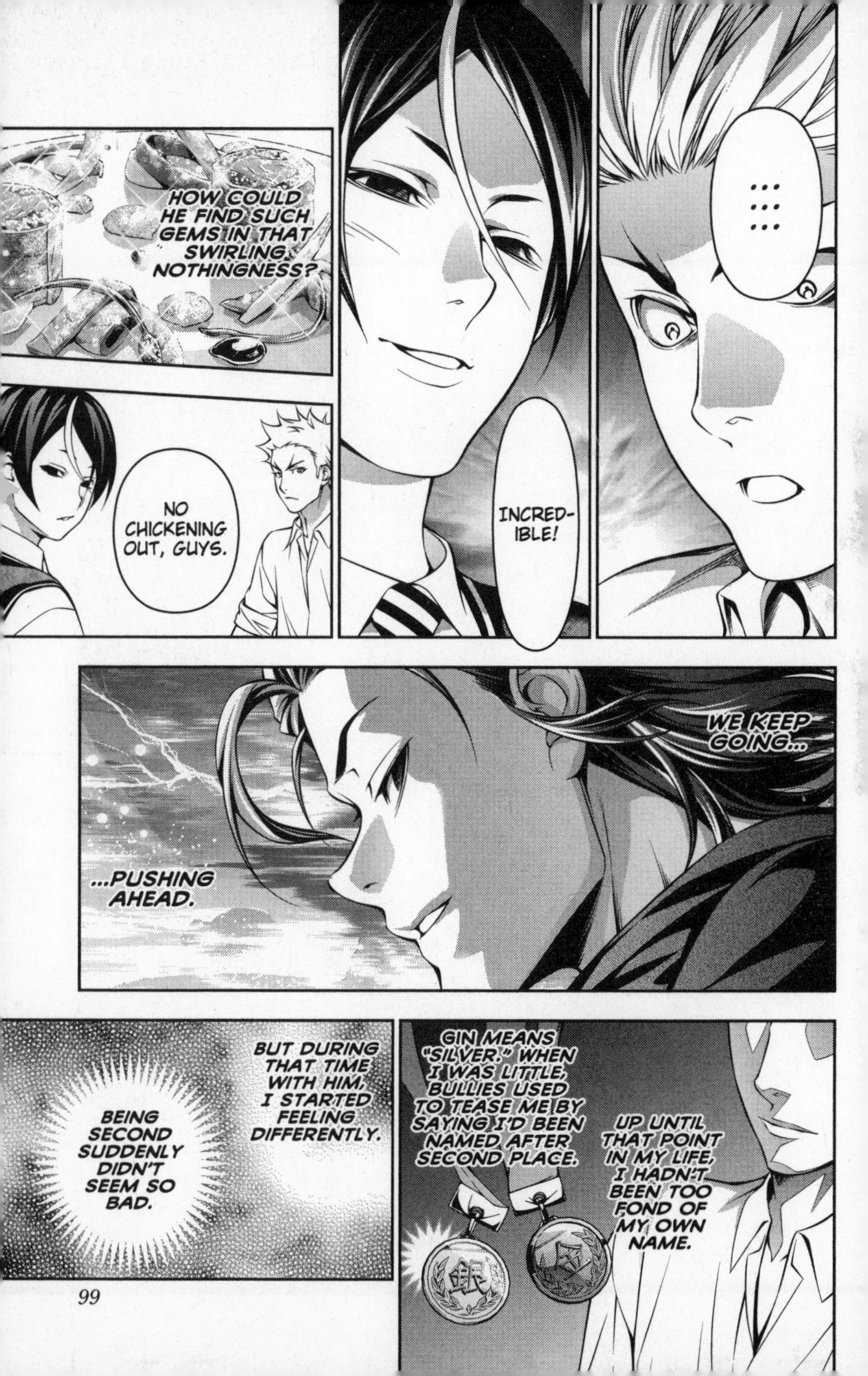
......
INCRED-IBLE!
HOW COULD HE FIND SUCH GEMS IN THAT SWIRLING NOTHINGNESS?
NO CHICKENING OUT, GUYS.
WE KEEP GOING...
...PUSHING AHEAD.
GIN MEANS "SILVER." WHEN I WAS LITTLE, BULLIES USED TO TEASE ME BY SAYING I'D BEEN NAMED AFTER SECOND PLACE.
UP UNTIL THAT POINT IN MY LIFE, I HADN'T BEEN TOO FOND OF MY OWN NAME.
BUT DURING THAT TIME WITH HIM, I STARTED FEELING DIFFERENTLY.
BEING SECOND SUDDENLY DIDN'T SEEM SO BAD.

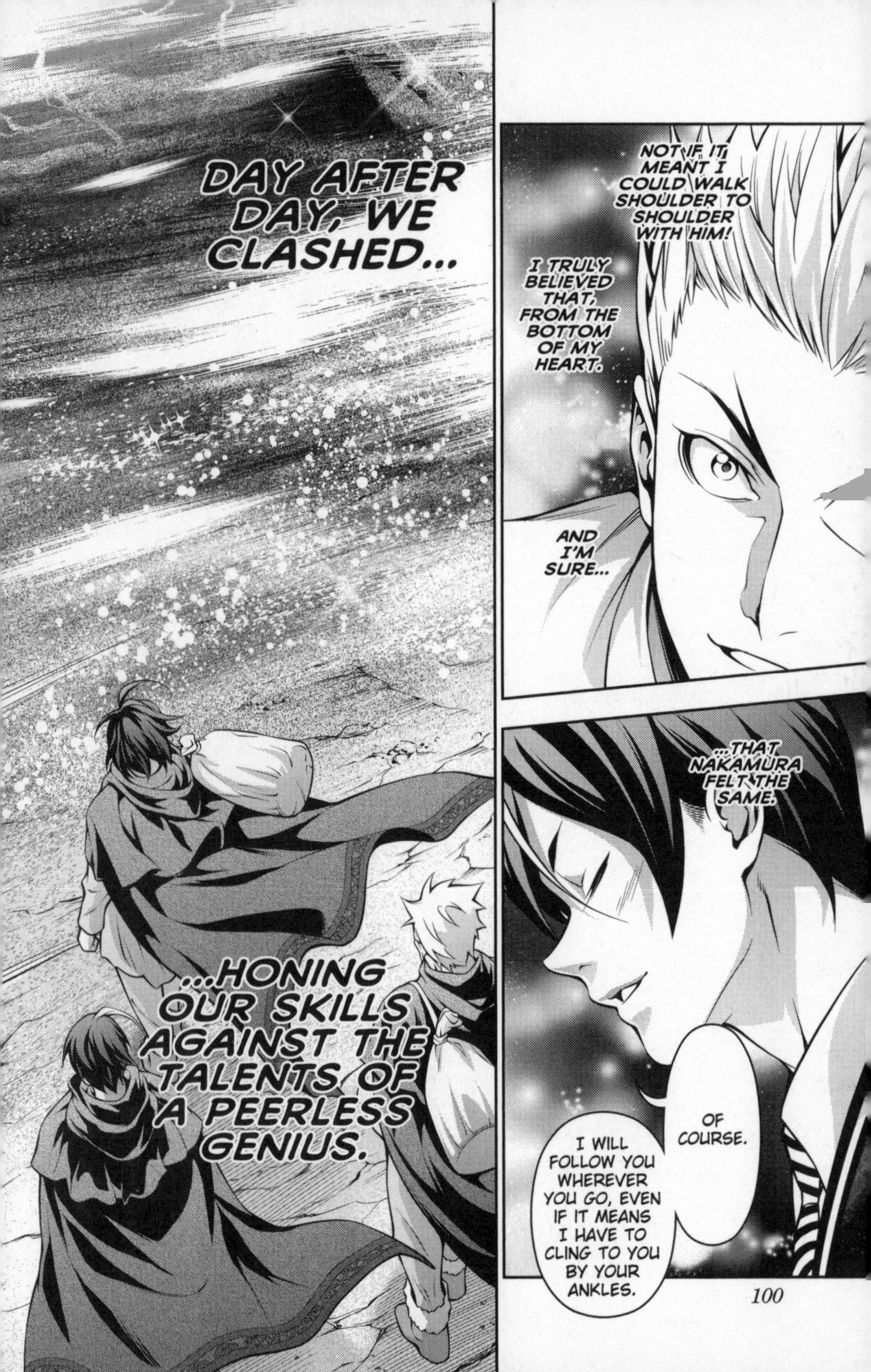
NOT IF IT MEANT I COULD WALK SHOULDER TO SHOULDER WITH HIM!
I TRULY BELIEVED THAT, FROM THE BOTTOM OF MY HEART.
AND I'M SURE...
...THAT NAKAMURA FELT THE SAME.
OF COURSE.
I WILL FOLLOW YOU WHEREVER YOU GO, EVEN IF IT MEANS I HAVE TO CLING TO YOU BY YOUR ANKLES.
DAY AFTER DAY, WE CLASHED...
...HONING OUR SKILLS AGAINST THE TALENTS OF A PEERLESS GENIUS.

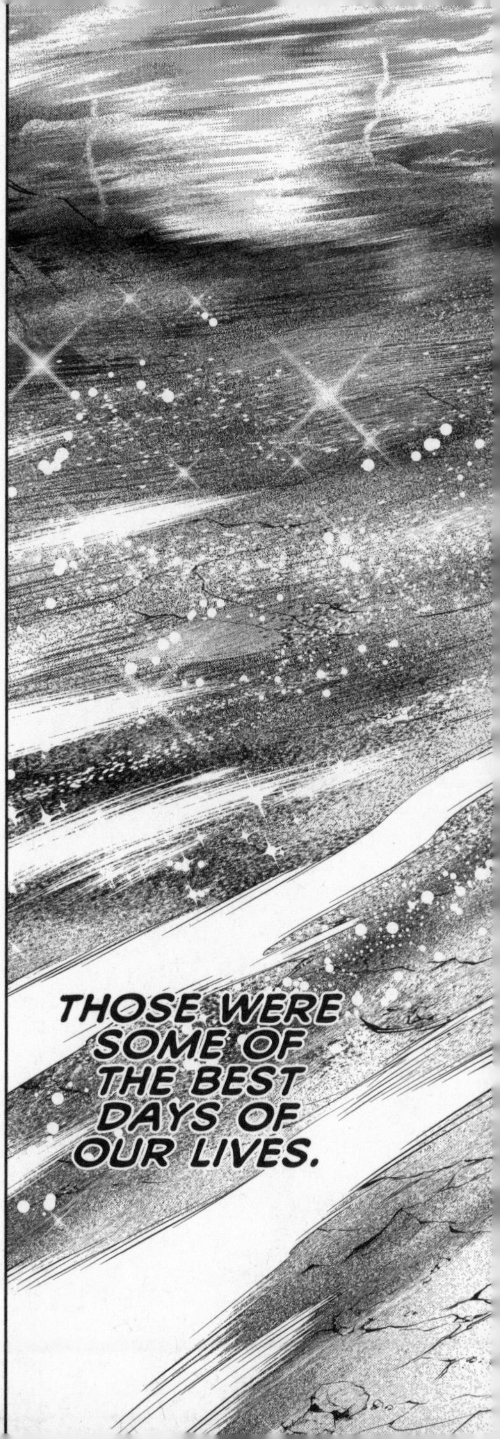
THOSE WERE SOME OF THE BEST DAYS OF OUR LIVES.

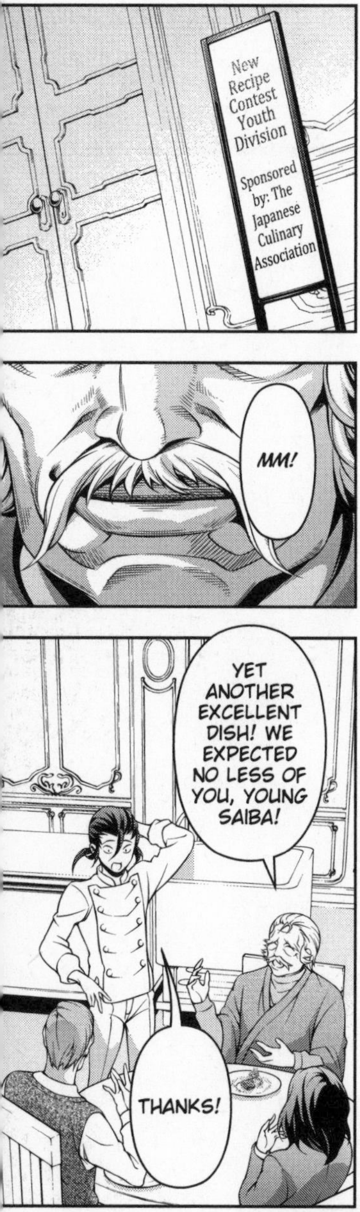
New Recipe Contest Youth Division
Sponsored by: The Japanese Culinary Association
MM!
YET ANOTHER EXCELLENT DISH! WE EXPECTED NO LESS OF YOU, YOUNG SAIBA!
THANKS!

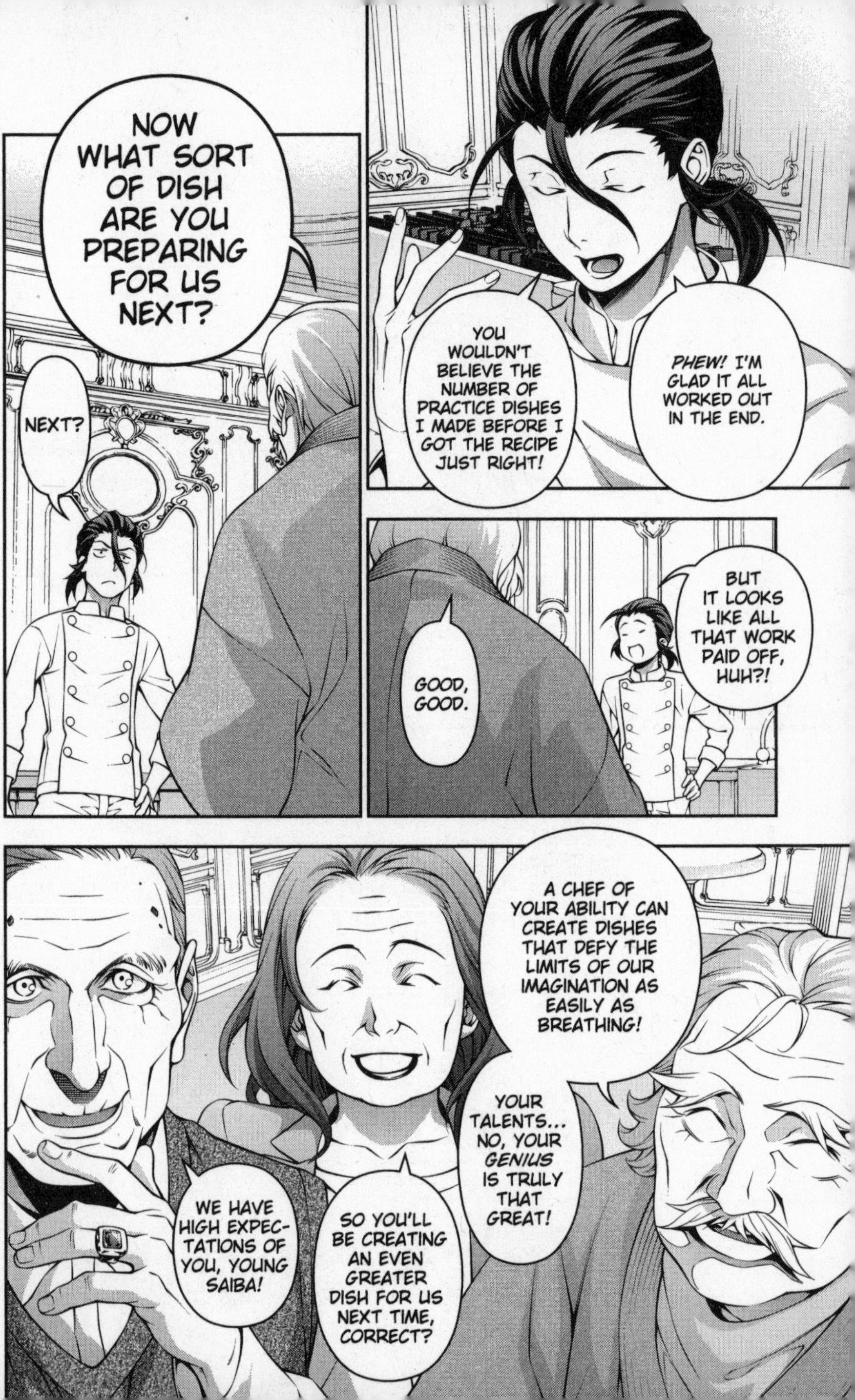
PHEW! I'M GLAD IT ALL WORKED OUT IN THE END.
YOU WOULDN'T BELIEVE THE NUMBER OF PRACTICE DISHES I MADE BEFORE I GOT THE RECIPE JUST RIGHT!
BUT IT LOOKS LIKE ALL THAT WORK PAID OFF, HUH?!
GOOD, GOOD.
NOW WHAT SORT OF DISH ARE YOU PREPARING FOR US NEXT?
NEXT?
A CHEF OF YOUR ABILITY CAN CREATE DISHES THAT DEFY THE LIMITS OF OUR IMAGINATION AS EASILY AS BREATHING!
YOUR TALENTS... NO, YOUR *GENIUS* IS TRULY THAT GREAT!
SO YOU'LL BE CREATING AN EVEN GREATER DISH FOR US NEXT TIME, CORRECT?
WE HAVE HIGH EXPECTATIONS OF YOU, YOUNG SAIBA!

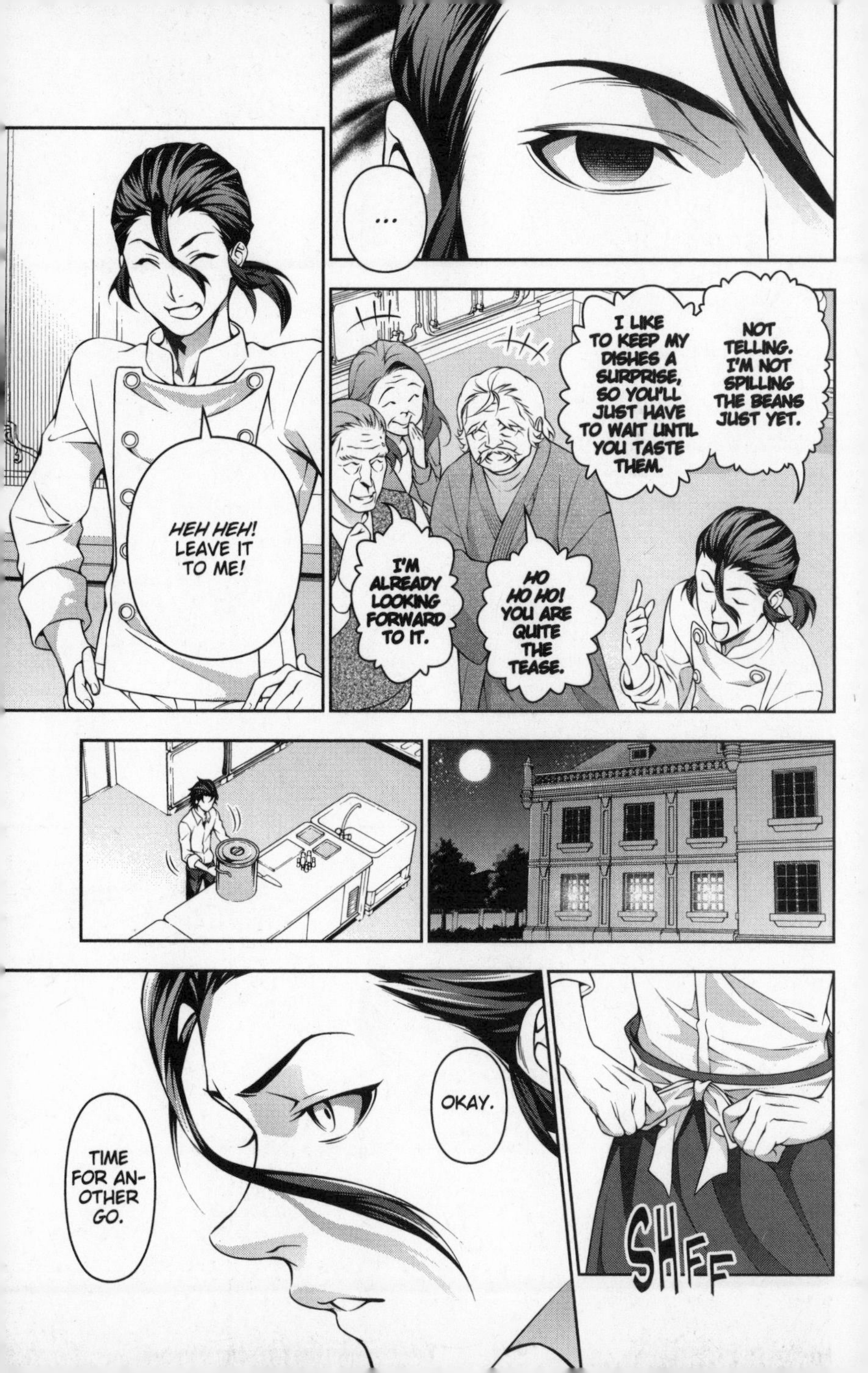
...
NOT TELLING. I'M NOT SPILLING THE BEANS JUST YET.
I LIKE TO KEEP MY DISHES A SURPRISE, SO YOU'LL JUST HAVE TO WAIT UNTIL YOU TASTE THEM.
HO HO HO! YOU ARE QUITE THE TEASE.
I'M ALREADY LOOKING FORWARD TO IT.
HEH HEH! LEAVE IT TO ME!
SHFF
OKAY.
TIME FOR AN-OTHER GO.

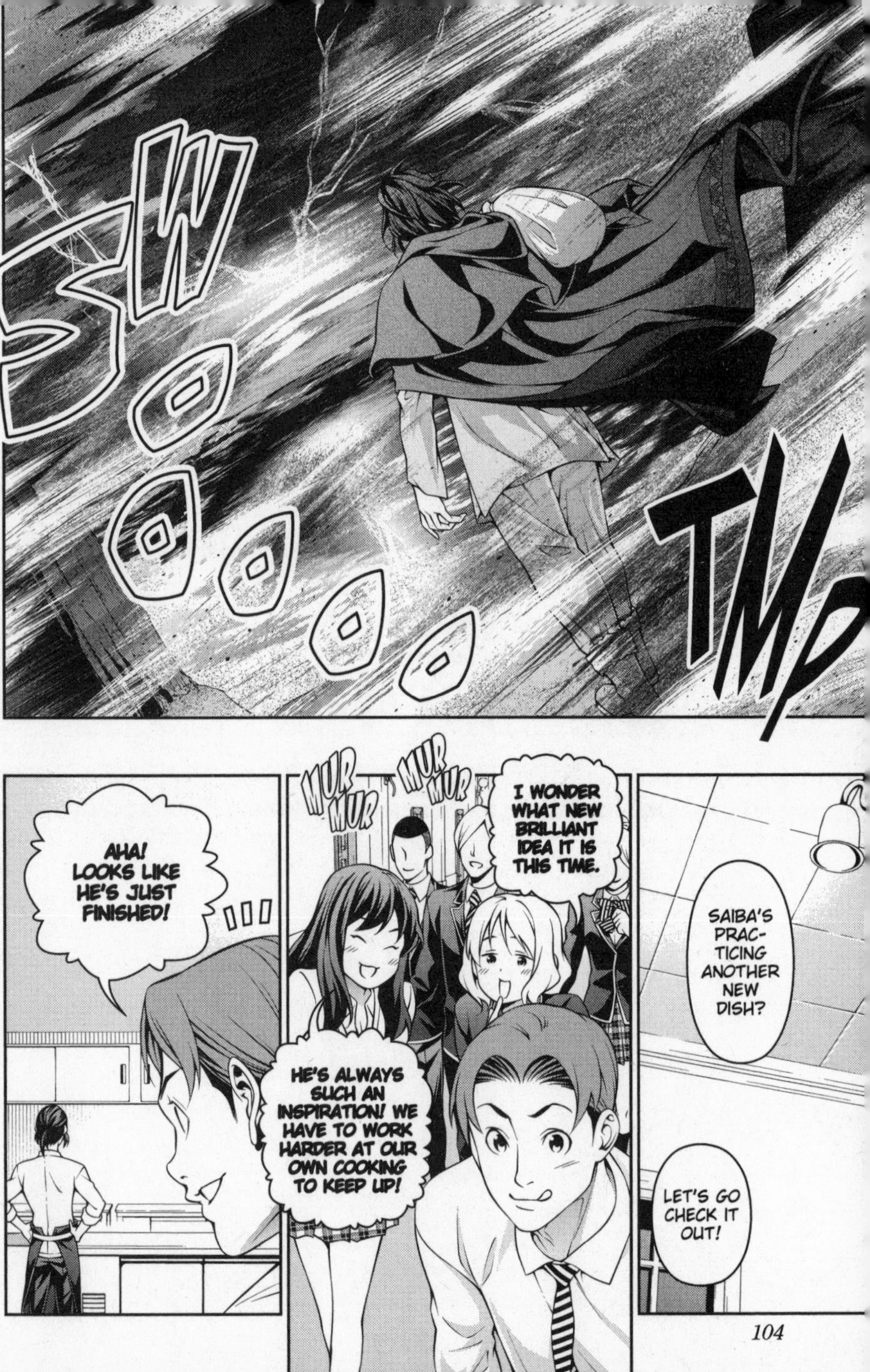
SWOOOOOO
TMP
SAIBA'S PRAC-TICING ANOTHER NEW DISH?
LET'S GO CHECK IT OUT!
MUR MUR
MUR MUR
I WONDER WHAT NEW BRILLIANT IDEA IT IS THIS TIME.
HE'S ALWAYS SUCH AN INSPIRATION! WE HAVE TO WORK HARDER AT OUR OWN COOKING TO KEEP UP!
AHA! LOOKS LIKE HE'S JUST FINISHED!
!!!

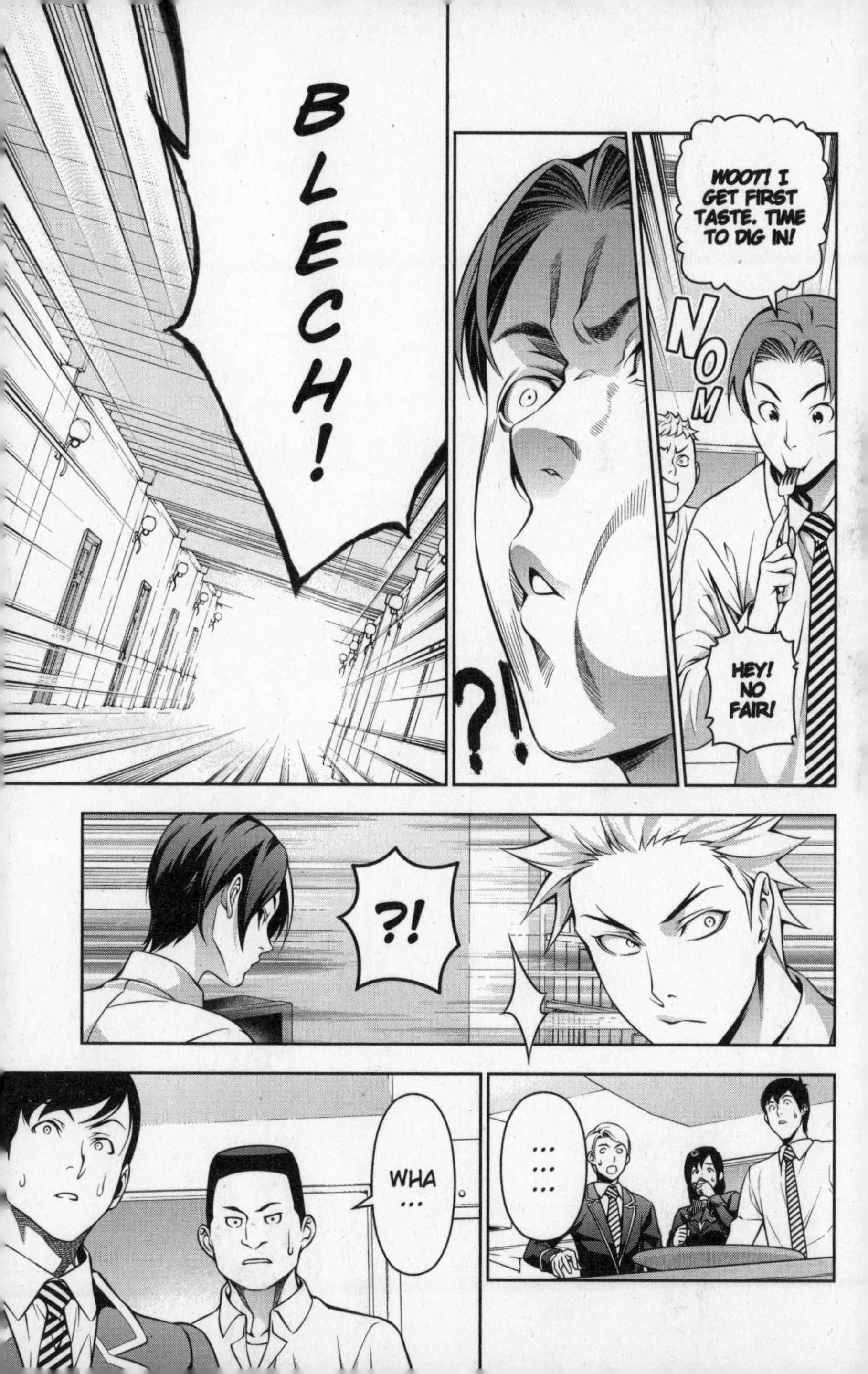
WOOT! I GET FIRST TASTE. TIME TO DIG IN!
NOM
HEY! NO FAIR!
?!
BLECH!
?!
....
WHA...

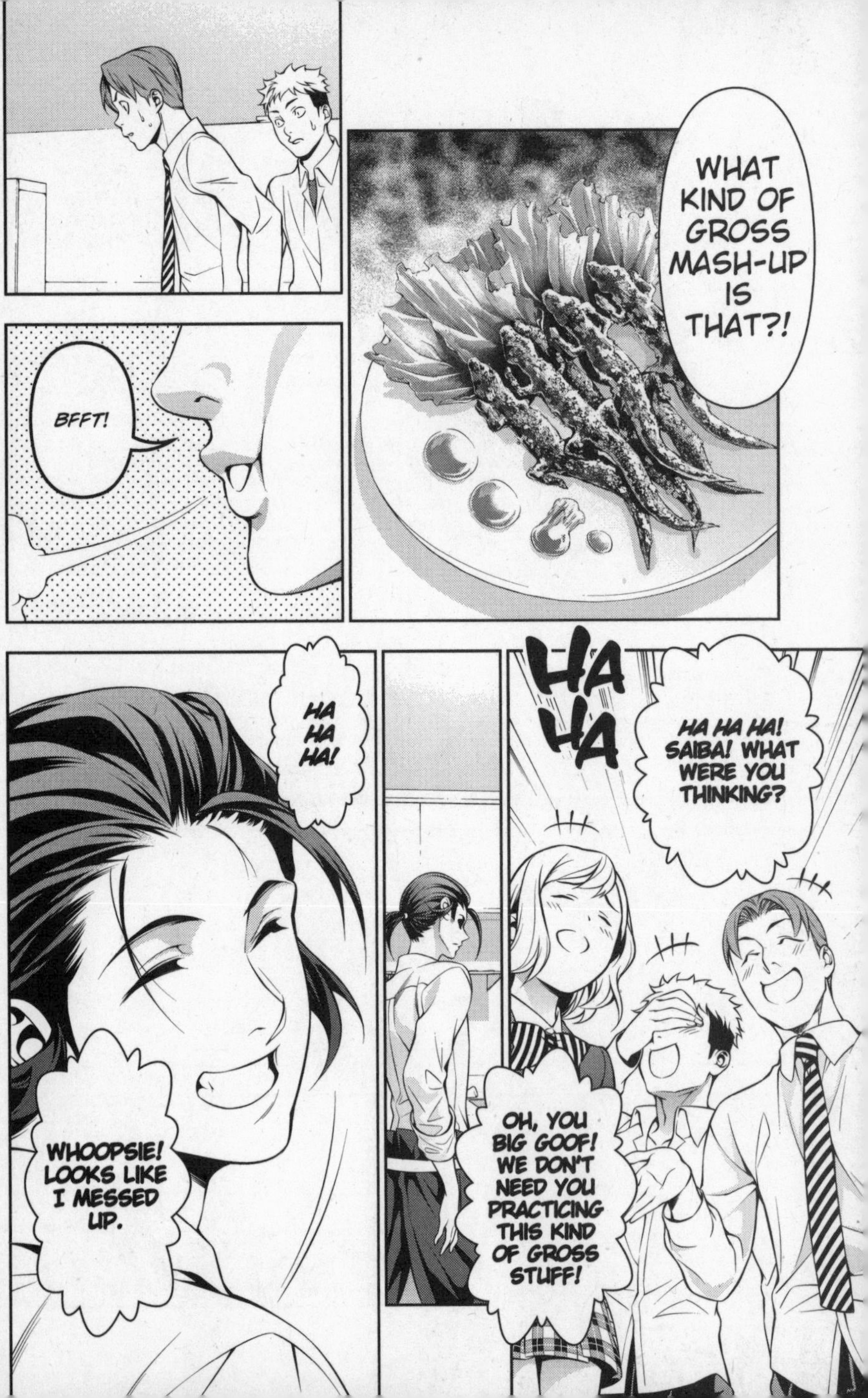
WHAT KIND OF GROSS MASH-UP IS THAT?!
BFFT!
HA HA
HA HA HA! SAIBA! WHAT WERE YOU THINKING?
OH, YOU BIG GOOF! WE DON'T NEED YOU PRACTICING THIS KIND OF GROSS STUFF!
HA HA HA!
WHOOPSIE! LOOKS LIKE I MESSED UP.

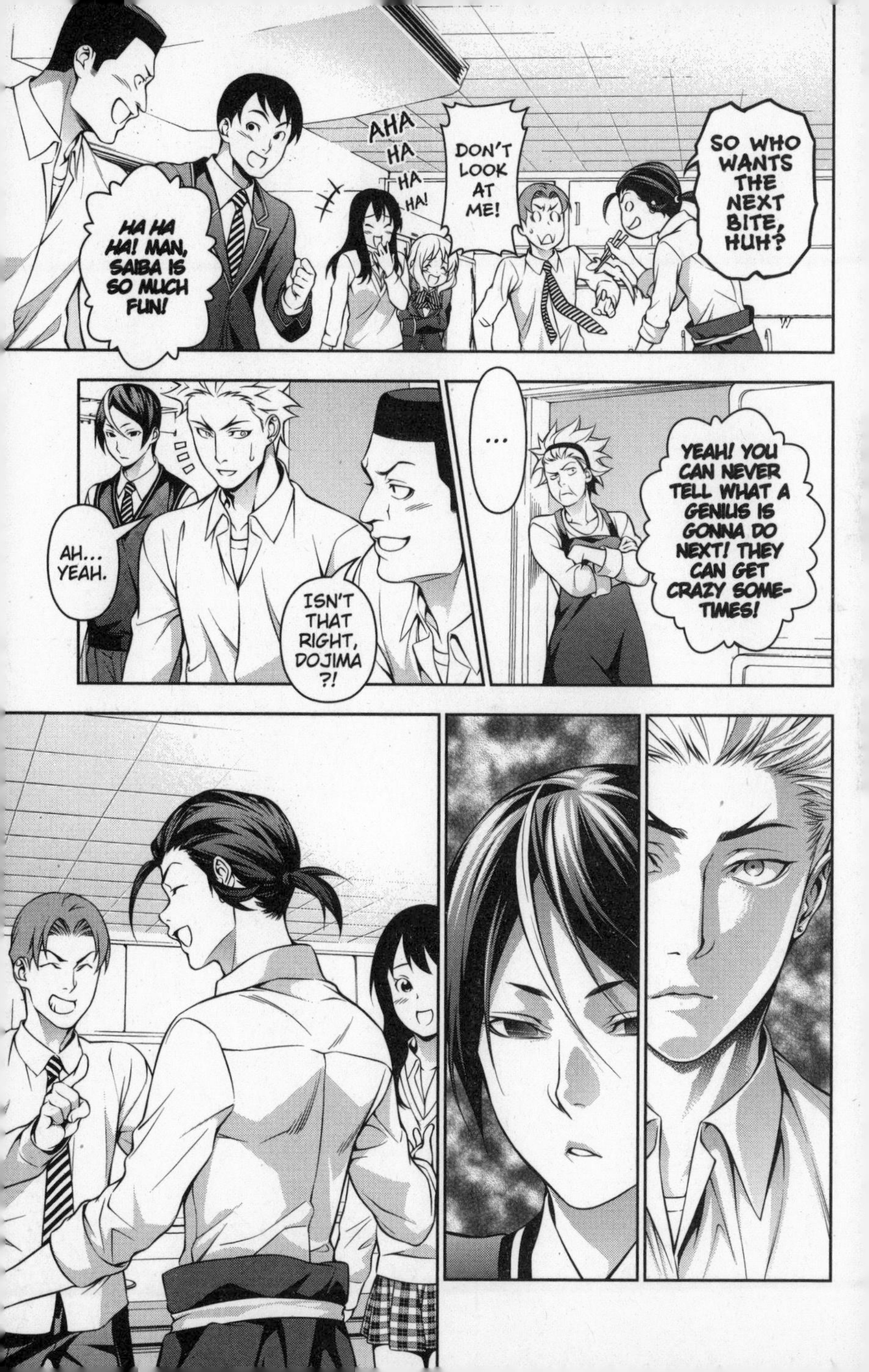
SO WHO WANTS THE NEXT BITE, HUH?
DON'T LOOK AT ME!
AHA HA HA HA!
HA HA HA! MAN, SAIBA IS SO MUCH FUN!
YEAH! YOU CAN NEVER TELL WHAT A GENIUS IS GONNA DO NEXT! THEY CAN GET CRAZY SOME-TIMES!
...
ISN'T THAT RIGHT, DOJIMA?!
AH... YEAH.

YOUNG
JOICHIRO
PIONEER
OUTFIT

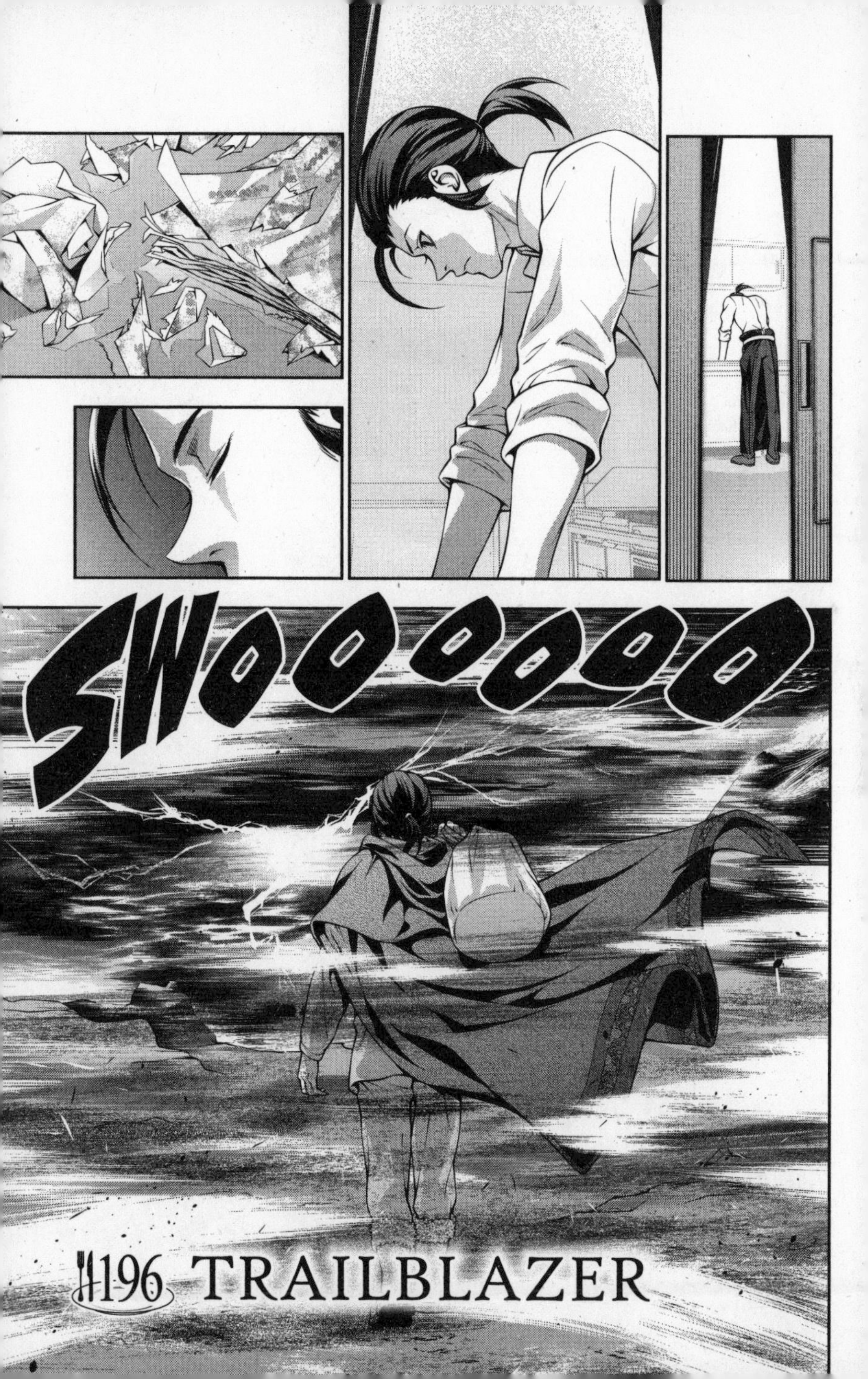
SWOOOOOO
196 TRAILBLAZER

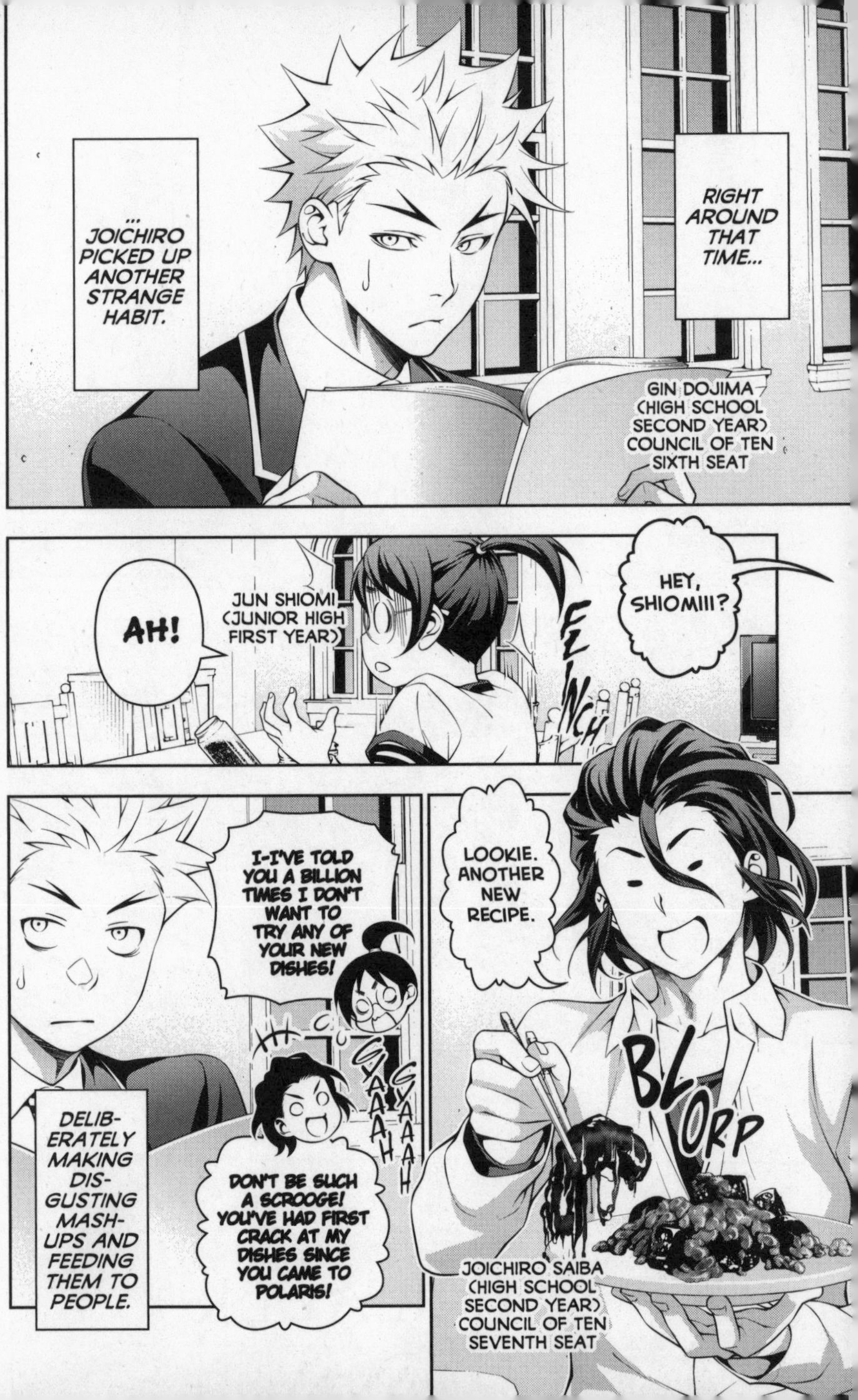
RIGHT AROUND THAT TIME...
...JOICHIRO PICKED UP ANOTHER STRANGE HABIT.
GIN DOJIMA (HIGH SCHOOL SECOND YEAR) COUNCIL OF TEN SIXTH SEAT
HEY, SHIOMIII?
FLINCH
JUN SHIOMI (JUNIOR HIGH FIRST YEAR)
AH!
LOOKIE. ANOTHER NEW RECIPE.
BLORP
JOICHIRO SAIBA (HIGH SCHOOL SECOND YEAR) COUNCIL OF TEN SEVENTH SEAT
I-I'VE TOLD YOU A BILLION TIMES I DON'T WANT TO TRY ANY OF YOUR NEW DISHES!
GYAAAH GYAAAH
DON'T BE SUCH A SCROOGE! YOU'VE HAD FIRST CRACK AT MY DISHES SINCE YOU CAME TO POLARIS!
DELIB-ERATELY MAKING DIS-GUSTING MASH-UPS AND FEEDING THEM TO PEOPLE.

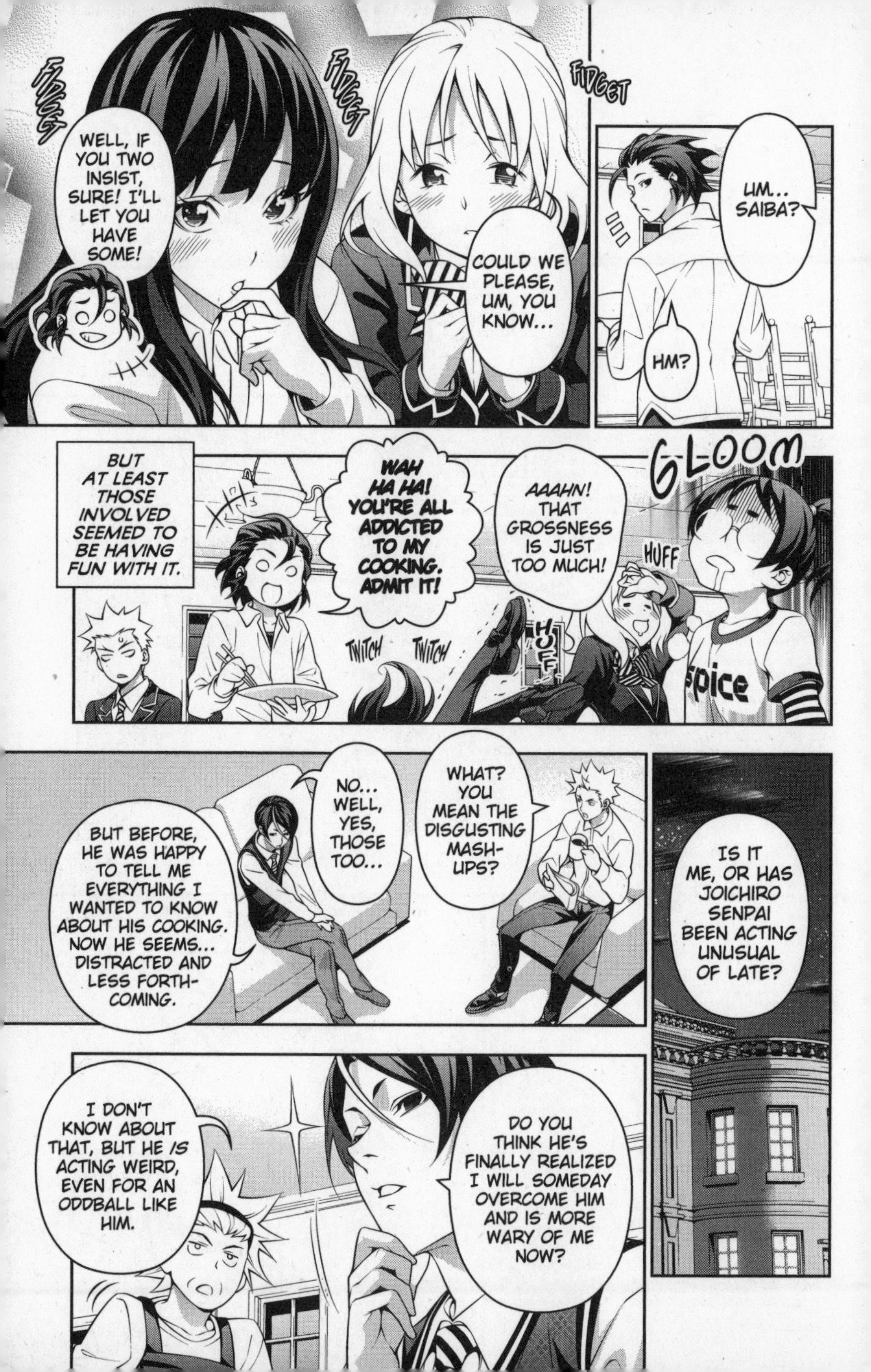
UM... SAIBA?
HM?
FIDGET
COULD WE PLEASE, UM, YOU KNOW...
FIDGET
FIDGET
WELL, IF YOU TWO INSIST, SURE! I'LL LET YOU HAVE SOME!
GLOOM
AAAHN! THAT GROSSNESS IS JUST TOO MUCH!
HUFF
HUFF
WAH HA HA! YOU'RE ALL ADDICTED TO MY COOKING. ADMIT IT!
TWITCH
TWITCH
BUT AT LEAST THOSE INVOLVED SEEMED TO BE HAVING FUN WITH IT.
IS IT ME, OR HAS JOICHIRO SENPAI BEEN ACTING UNUSUAL OF LATE?
WHAT? YOU MEAN THE DISGUSTING MASH-UPS?
NO... WELL, YES, THOSE TOO...
BUT BEFORE, HE WAS HAPPY TO TELL ME EVERYTHING I WANTED TO KNOW ABOUT HIS COOKING. NOW HE SEEMS... DISTRACTED AND LESS FORTH-COMING.
DO YOU THINK HE'S FINALLY REALIZED I WILL SOMEDAY OVERCOME HIM AND IS MORE WARY OF ME NOW?
I DON'T KNOW ABOUT THAT, BUT HE *IS* ACTING WEIRD, EVEN FOR AN ODDBALL LIKE HIM.
spice

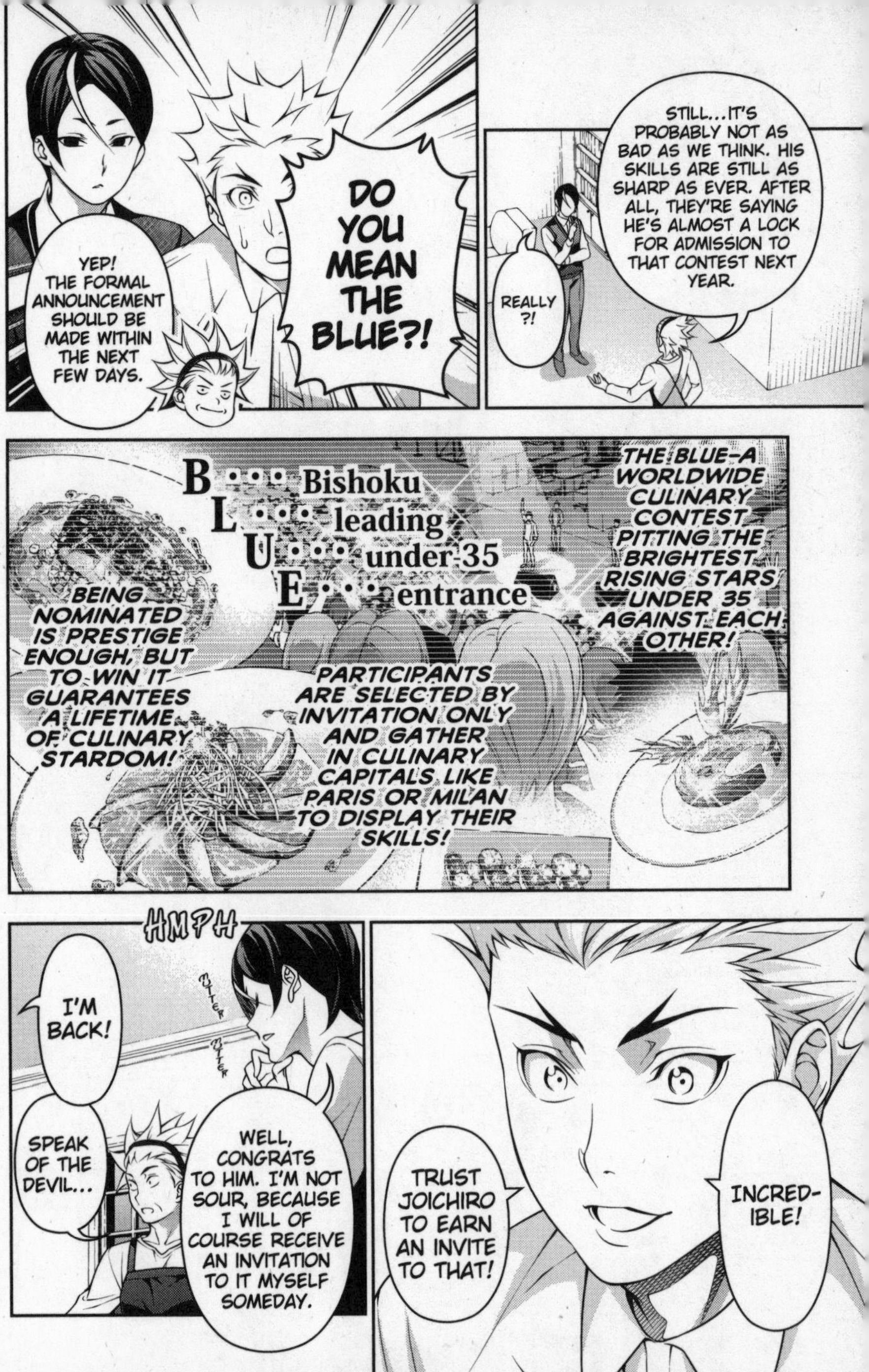

STILL...IT'S PROBABLY NOT AS BAD AS WE THINK. HIS SKILLS ARE STILL AS SHARP AS EVER. AFTER ALL, THEY'RE SAYING HE'S ALMOST A LOCK FOR ADMISSION TO THAT CONTEST NEXT YEAR.
REALLY ?!
DO YOU MEAN THE BLUE?!
YEP! THE FORMAL ANNOUNCEMENT SHOULD BE MADE WITHIN THE NEXT FEW DAYS.
THE BLUE—A WORLDWIDE CULINARY CONTEST PITTING THE BRIGHTEST RISING STARS UNDER 35 AGAINST EACH OTHER!
B ••• Bishoku
L ••• leading
U ••• under-35
E ••• entrance
PARTICIPANTS ARE SELECTED BY INVITATION ONLY AND GATHER IN CULINARY CAPITALS LIKE PARIS OR MILAN TO DISPLAY THEIR SKILLS!
BEING NOMINATED IS PRESTIGE ENOUGH, BUT TO WIN IT GUARANTEES A LIFETIME OF CULINARY STARDOM!
INCRED-IBLE!
TRUST JOICHIRO TO EARN AN INVITE TO THAT!
HMPH
WELL, CONGRATS TO HIM. I'M NOT SOUR, BECAUSE I WILL OF COURSE RECEIVE AN INVITATION TO IT MYSELF SOMEDAY.
MUTTER
MUTTER
I'M BACK!
SPEAK OF THE DEVIL...

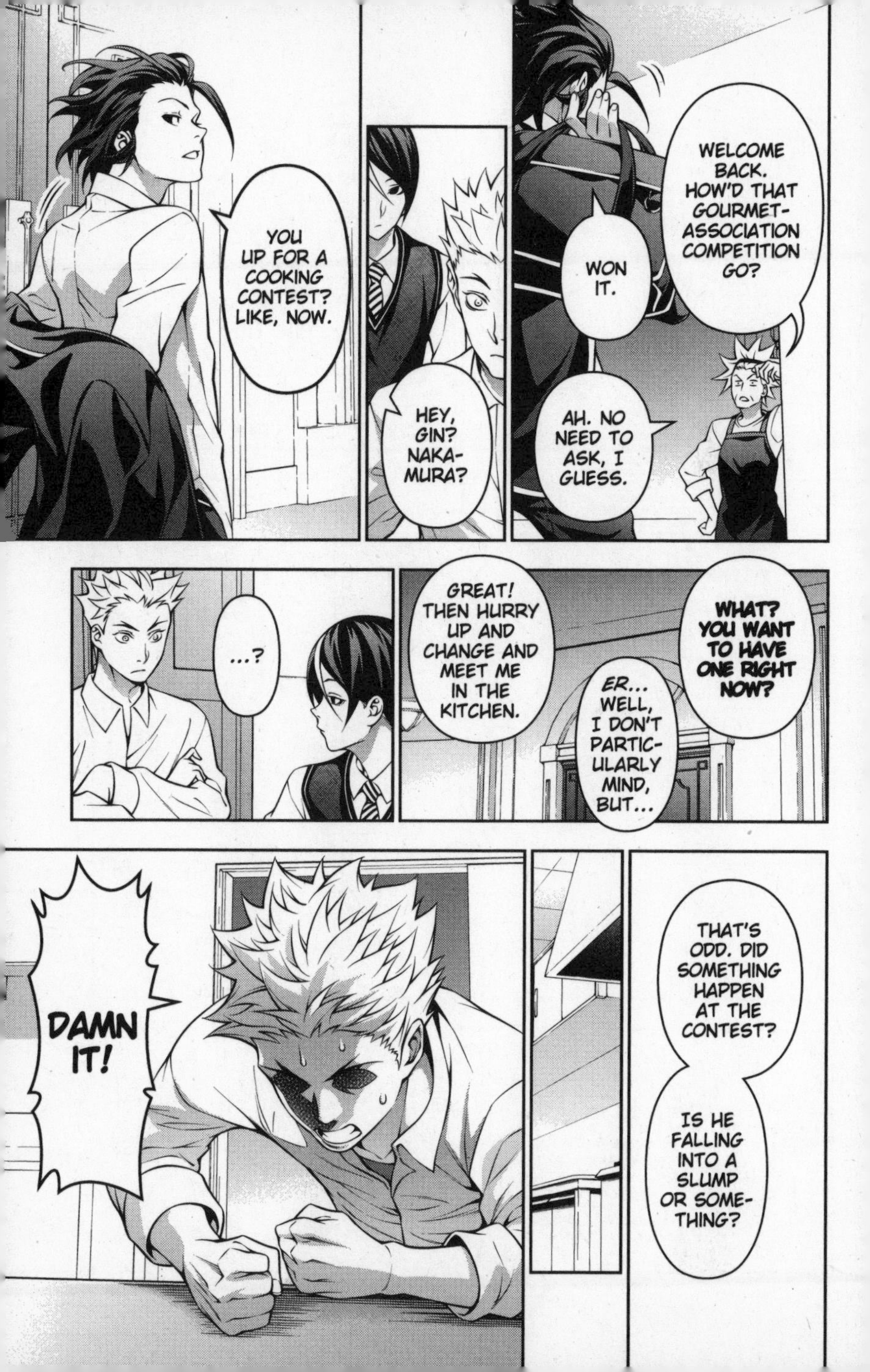
WELCOME BACK. HOW'D THAT GOURMET-ASSOCIATION COMPETITION GO?
WON IT.
AH. NO NEED TO ASK, I GUESS.
HEY, GIN? NAKAMURA?
YOU UP FOR A COOKING CONTEST? LIKE, NOW.
WHAT? YOU WANT TO HAVE ONE RIGHT NOW?
ER... WELL, I DON'T PARTICULARLY MIND, BUT...
GREAT! THEN HURRY UP AND CHANGE AND MEET ME IN THE KITCHEN.
...?
THAT'S ODD. DID SOMETHING HAPPEN AT THE CONTEST?
IS HE FALLING INTO A SLUMP OR SOMETHING?
DAMN IT!

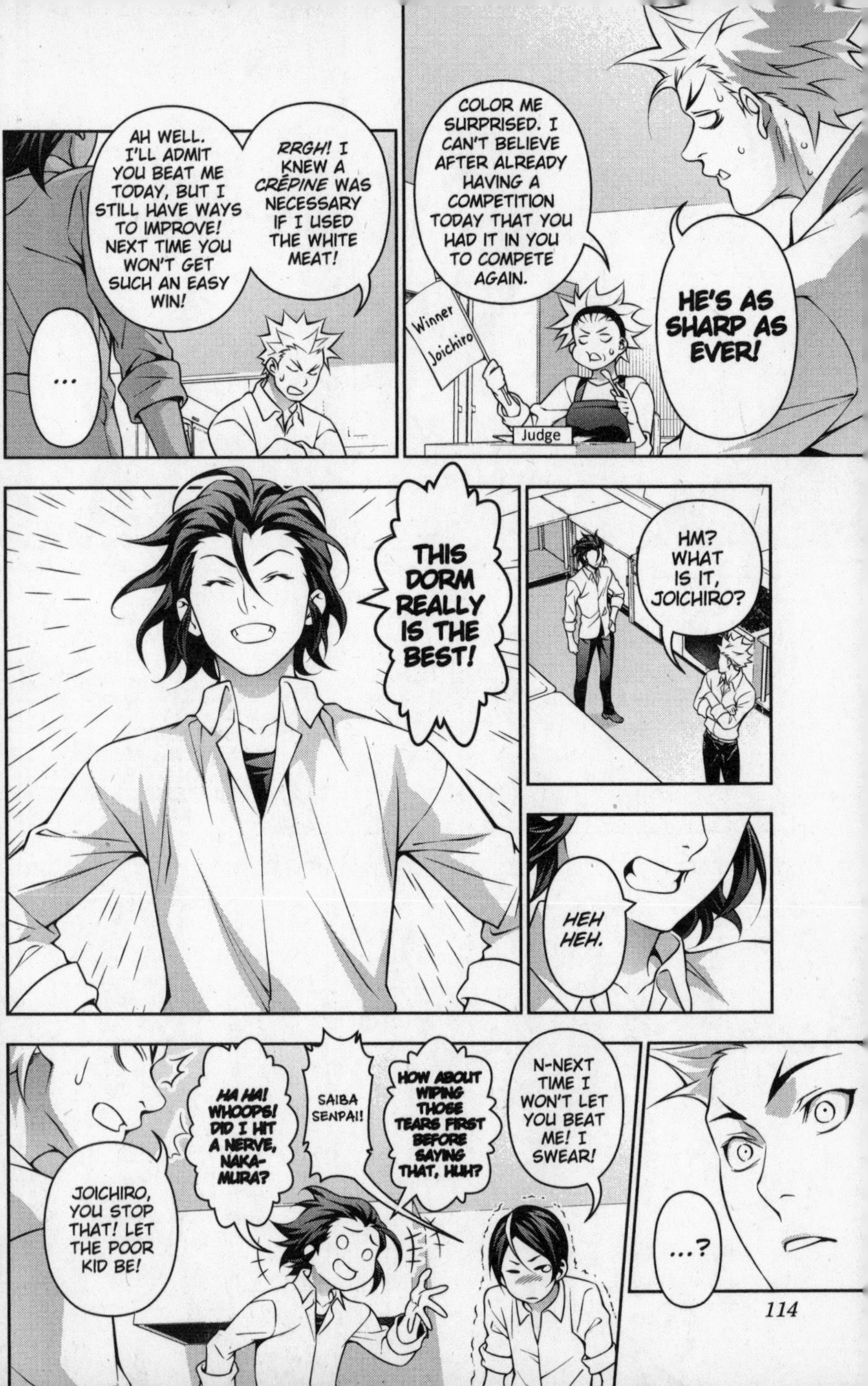
COLOR ME SURPRISED. I CAN'T BELIEVE AFTER ALREADY HAVING A COMPETITION TODAY THAT YOU HAD IT IN YOU TO COMPETE AGAIN.
HE'S AS SHARP AS EVER!
Winner Joichiro
Judge
RRGH! I KNEW A CRÊPINE WAS NECESSARY IF I USED THE WHITE MEAT!
AH WELL. I'LL ADMIT YOU BEAT ME TODAY, BUT I STILL HAVE WAYS TO IMPROVE! NEXT TIME YOU WON'T GET SUCH AN EASY WIN!
...
HM? WHAT IS IT, JOICHIRO?
HEH HEH.
THIS DORM REALLY IS THE BEST!
...?
N-NEXT TIME I WON'T LET YOU BEAT ME! I SWEAR!
HOW ABOUT WIPING THOSE TEARS FIRST BEFORE SAYING THAT, HUH?
SAIBA SENPAI!
HA HA! WHOOPS! DID I HIT A NERVE, NAKAMURA?
JOICHIRO, YOU STOP THAT! LET THE POOR KID BE!

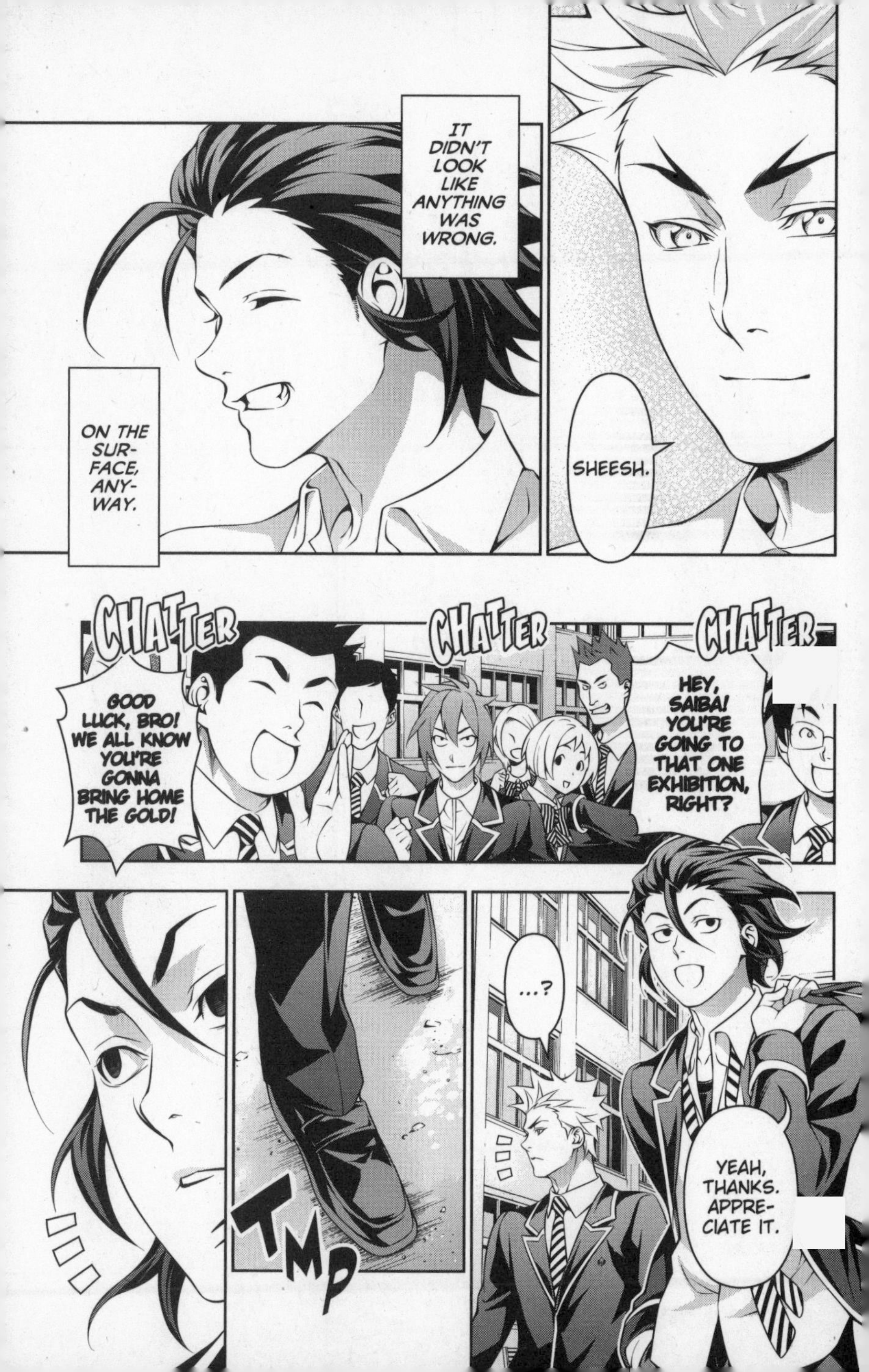
SHEESH.
IT DIDN'T LOOK LIKE ANYTHING WAS WRONG.
ON THE SURFACE, ANYWAY.
CHATTER
CHATTER
CHATTER
HEY, SAIBA! YOU'RE GOING TO THAT ONE EXHIBITION, RIGHT?
GOOD LUCK, BRO! WE ALL KNOW YOU'RE GONNA BRING HOME THE GOLD!
YEAH, THANKS. APPRECIATE IT.
...?
TMP

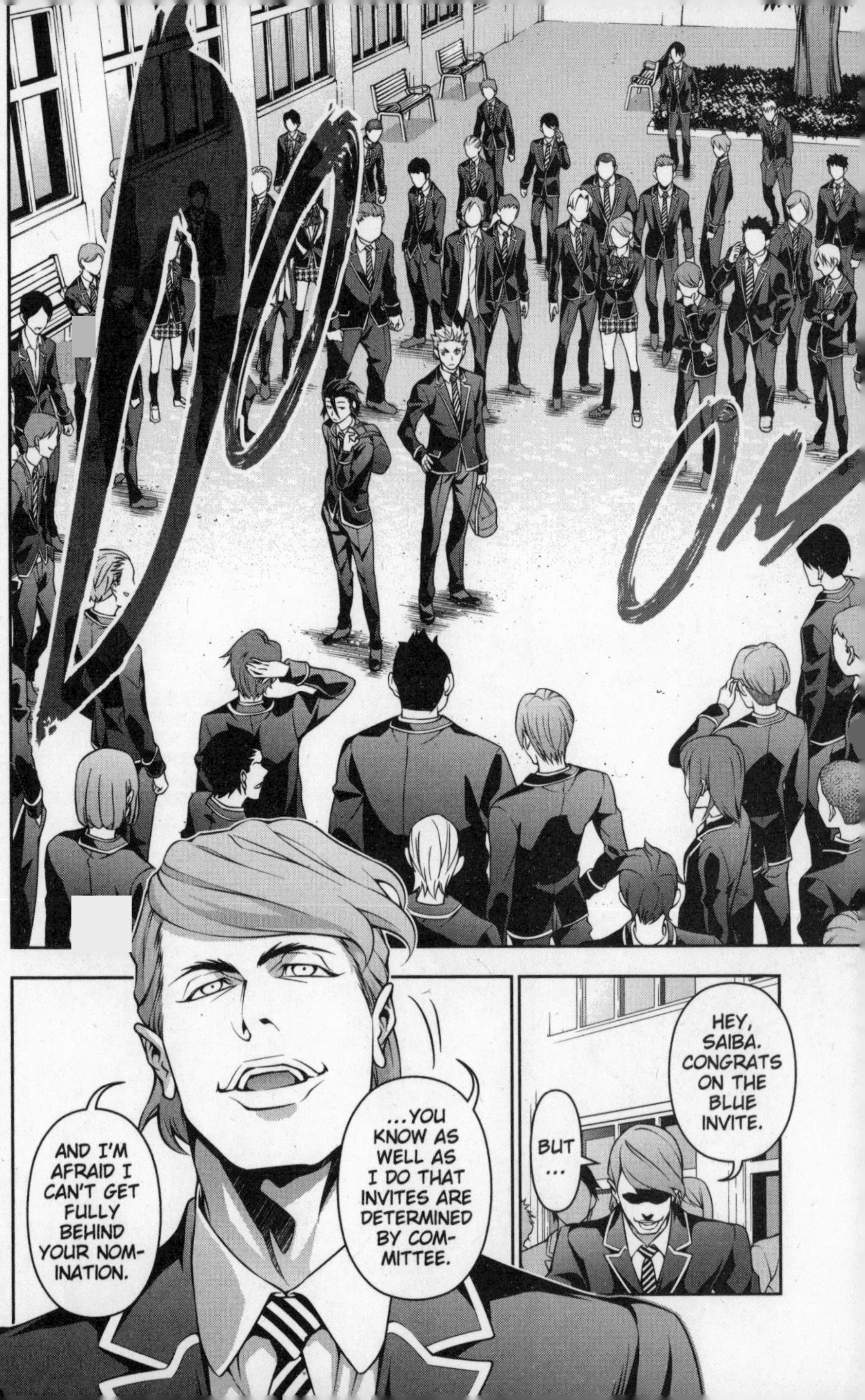
HEY, SAIBA. CONGRATS ON THE BLUE INVITE.
BUT...
...YOU KNOW AS WELL AS I DO THAT INVITES ARE DETERMINED BY COM-MITTEE.
AND I'M AFRAID I CAN'T GET FULLY BEHIND YOUR NOM-INATION.

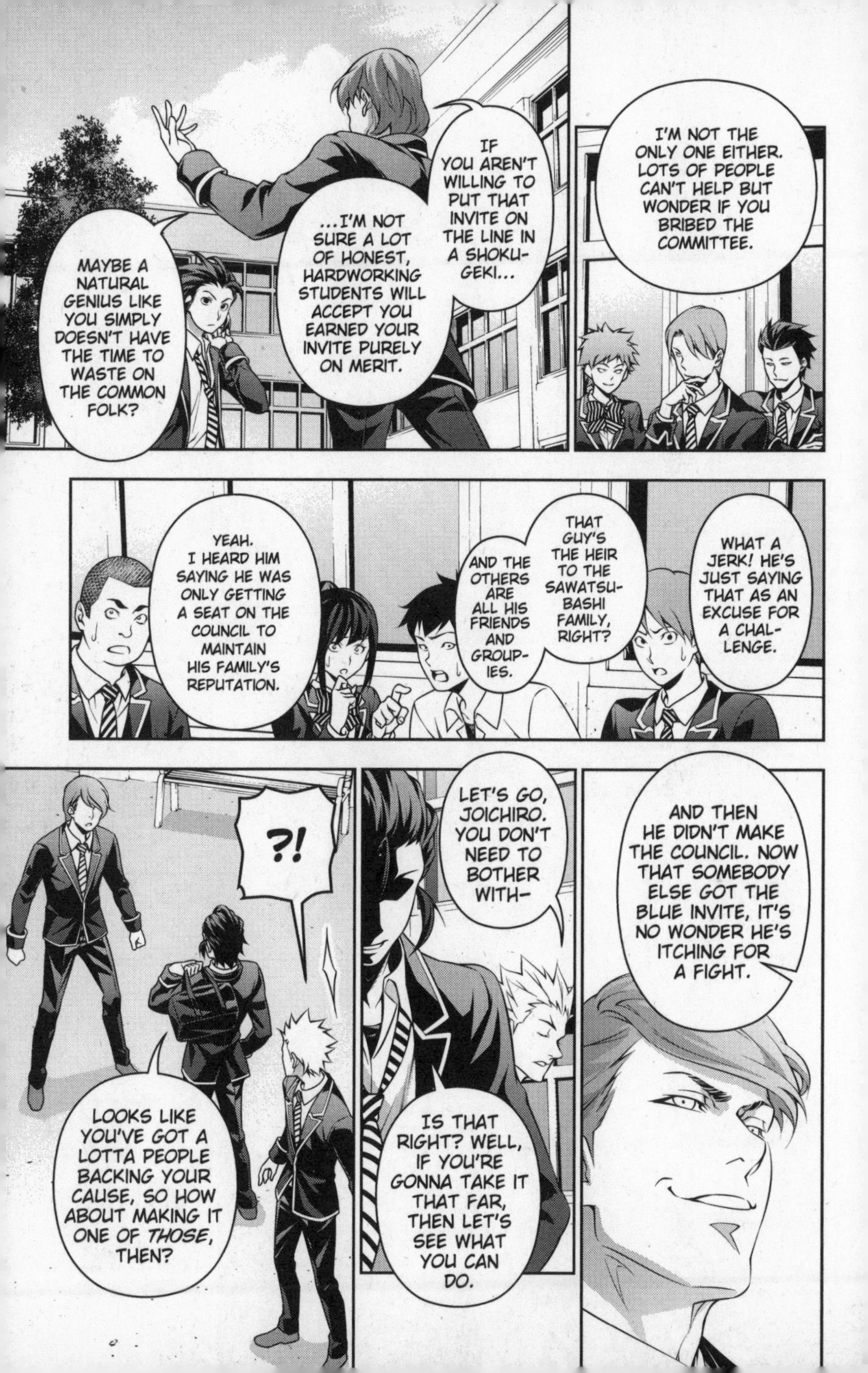
I'M NOT THE ONLY ONE EITHER. LOTS OF PEOPLE CAN'T HELP BUT WONDER IF YOU BRIBED THE COMMITTEE.
IF YOU AREN'T WILLING TO PUT THAT INVITE ON THE LINE IN A SHOKU-GEKI...
...I'M NOT SURE A LOT OF HONEST, HARDWORKING STUDENTS WILL ACCEPT YOU EARNED YOUR INVITE PURELY ON MERIT.
MAYBE A NATURAL GENIUS LIKE YOU SIMPLY DOESN'T HAVE THE TIME TO WASTE ON THE COMMON FOLK?
WHAT A JERK! HE'S JUST SAYING THAT AS AN EXCUSE FOR A CHAL-LENGE.
THAT GUY'S THE HEIR TO THE SAWATSU-BASHI FAMILY, RIGHT?
AND THE OTHERS ARE ALL HIS FRIENDS AND GROUP-IES.
YEAH. I HEARD HIM SAYING HE WAS ONLY GETTING A SEAT ON THE COUNCIL TO MAINTAIN HIS FAMILY'S REPUTATION.
AND THEN HE DIDN'T MAKE THE COUNCIL. NOW THAT SOMEBODY ELSE GOT THE BLUE INVITE, IT'S NO WONDER HE'S ITCHING FOR A FIGHT.
LET'S GO, JOICHIRO. YOU DON'T NEED TO BOTHER WITH-
IS THAT RIGHT? WELL, IF YOU'RE GONNA TAKE IT THAT FAR, THEN LET'S SEE WHAT YOU CAN DO.
?!
LOOKS LIKE YOU'VE GOT A LOTTA PEOPLE BACKING YOUR CAUSE, SO HOW ABOUT MAKING IT ONE OF *THOSE*, THEN?

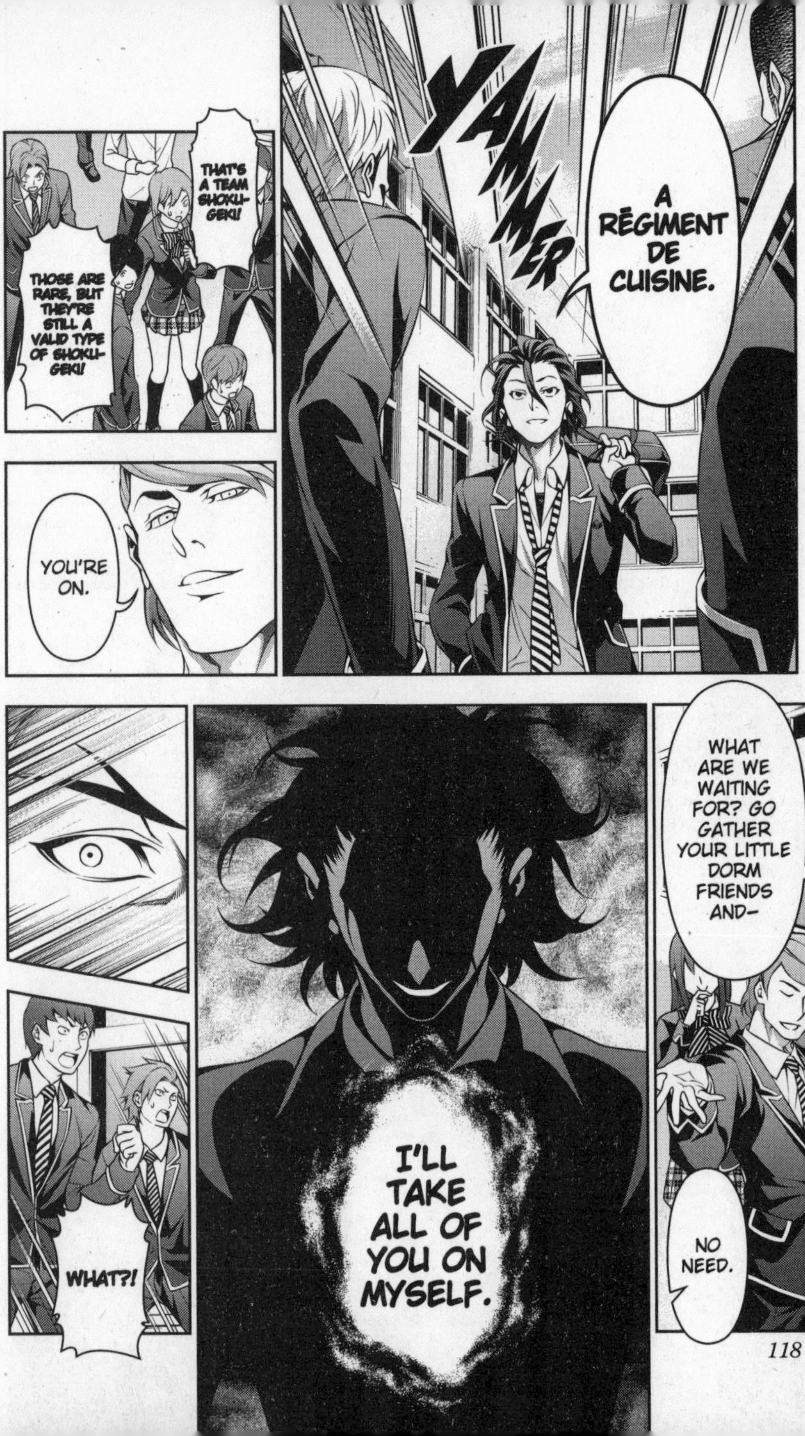
YAMMER
A RÉGIMENT DE CUISINE.
THAT'S A TEAM SHOKUGEKI!
THOSE ARE RARE, BUT THEY'RE STILL A VALID TYPE OF SHOKUGEKI!
YOU'RE ON.
WHAT ARE WE WAITING FOR? GO GATHER YOUR LITTLE DORM FRIENDS AND—
NO NEED.
I'LL TAKE ALL OF YOU ON MYSELF.
WHAT?!

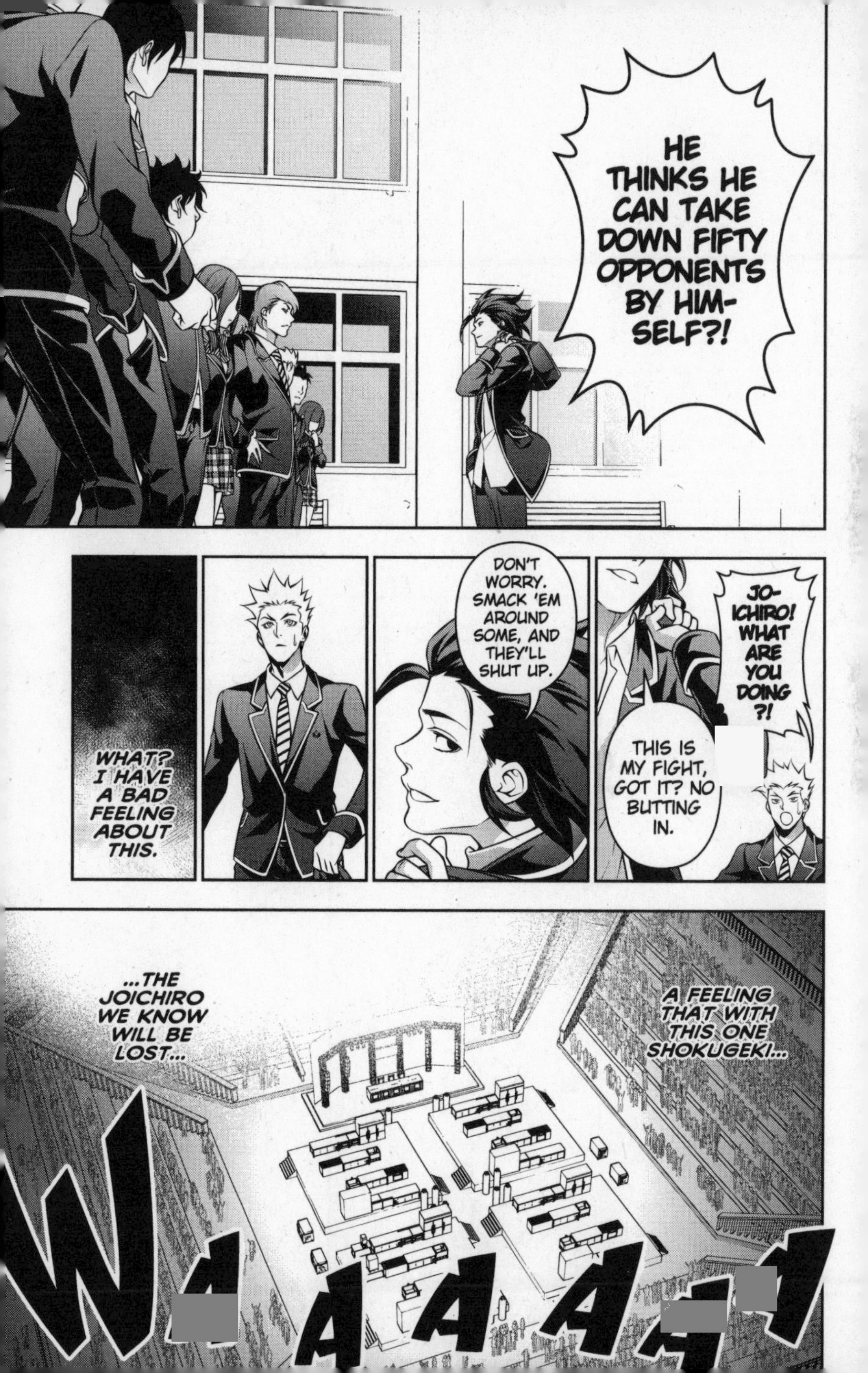
HE THINKS HE CAN TAKE DOWN FIFTY OPPONENTS BY HIM-SELF?!
JO-ICHIRO! WHAT ARE YOU DOING?!
THIS IS MY FIGHT, GOT IT? NO BUTTING IN.
DON'T WORRY. SMACK 'EM AROUND SOME, AND THEY'LL SHUT UP.
WHAT? I HAVE A BAD FEELING ABOUT THIS.
A FEELING THAT WITH THIS ONE SHOKUGEKI...
...THE JOICHIRO WE KNOW WILL BE LOST...
WAAAAA!!

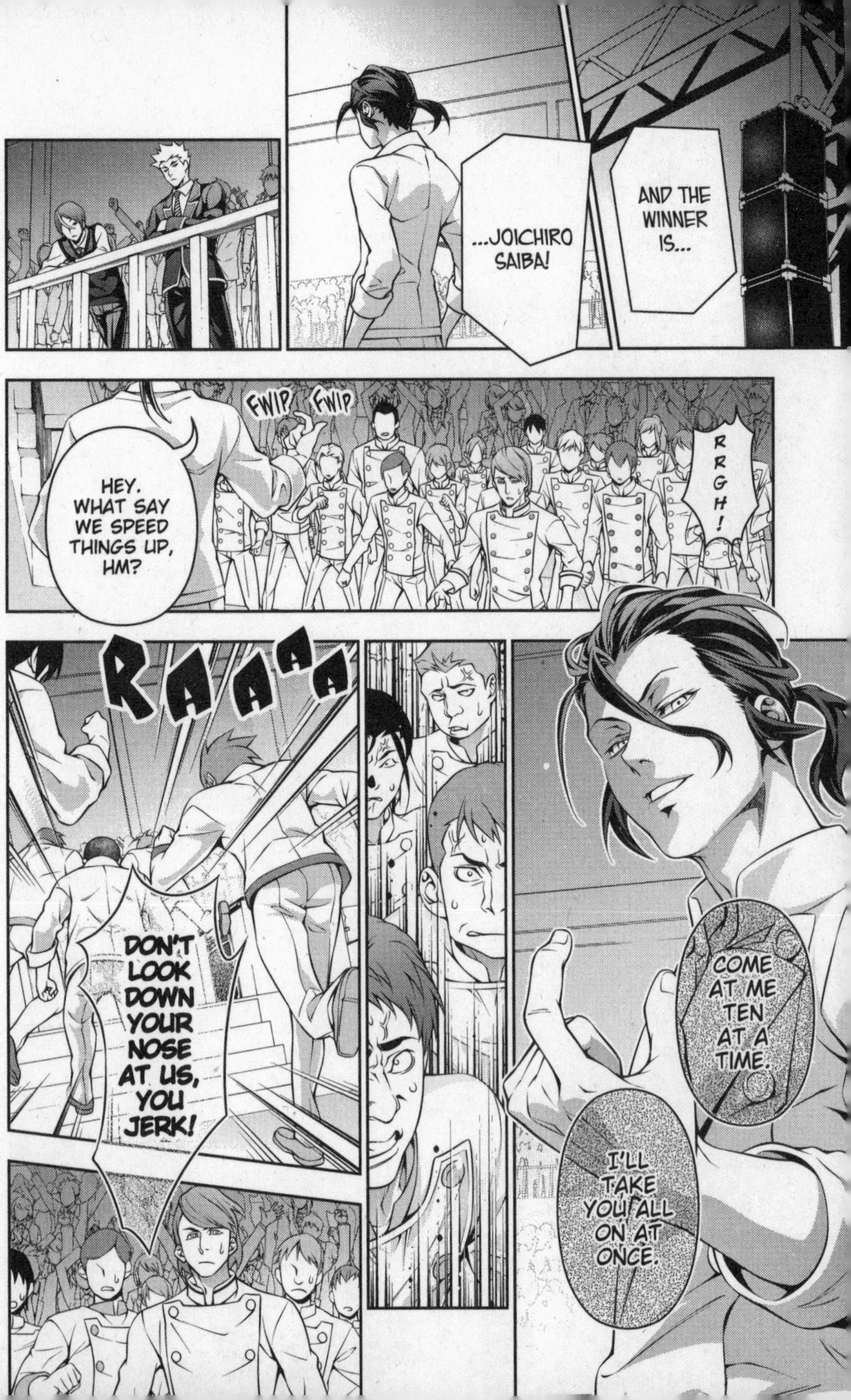
AND THE WINNER IS...
...JOICHIRO SAIBA!
RRGH!
FWIP FWIP
HEY. WHAT SAY WE SPEED THINGS UP, HM?
COME AT ME TEN AT A TIME.
I'LL TAKE YOU ALL ON AT ONCE.
RAAAA
DON'T LOOK DOWN YOUR NOSE AT US, YOU JERK!

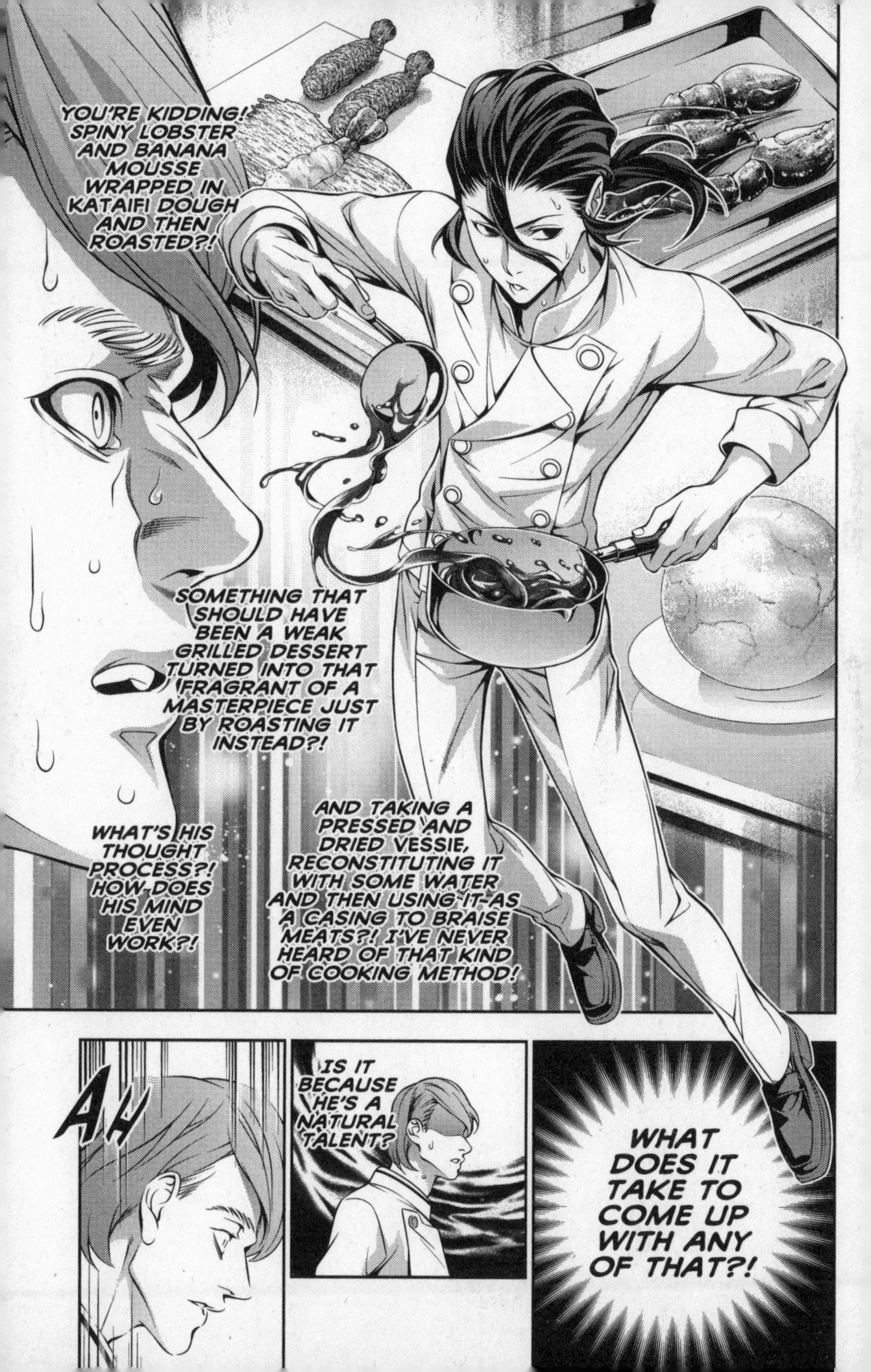
YOU'RE KIDDING! SPINY LOBSTER AND BANANA MOUSSE WRAPPED IN KATAIFI DOUGH AND THEN ROASTED?!
SOMETHING THAT SHOULD HAVE BEEN A WEAK GRILLED DESSERT TURNED INTO THAT FRAGRANT OF A MASTERPIECE JUST BY ROASTING IT INSTEAD?!
AND TAKING A PRESSED AND DRIED VESSIE, RECONSTITUTING IT WITH SOME WATER AND THEN USING IT AS A CASING TO BRAISE MEATS?! I'VE NEVER HEARD OF THAT KIND OF COOKING METHOD!
WHAT'S HIS THOUGHT PROCESS?! HOW DOES HIS MIND EVEN WORK?!
WHAT DOES IT TAKE TO COME UP WITH ANY OF THAT?!
IS IT BECAUSE HE'S A NATURAL TALENT?
AH

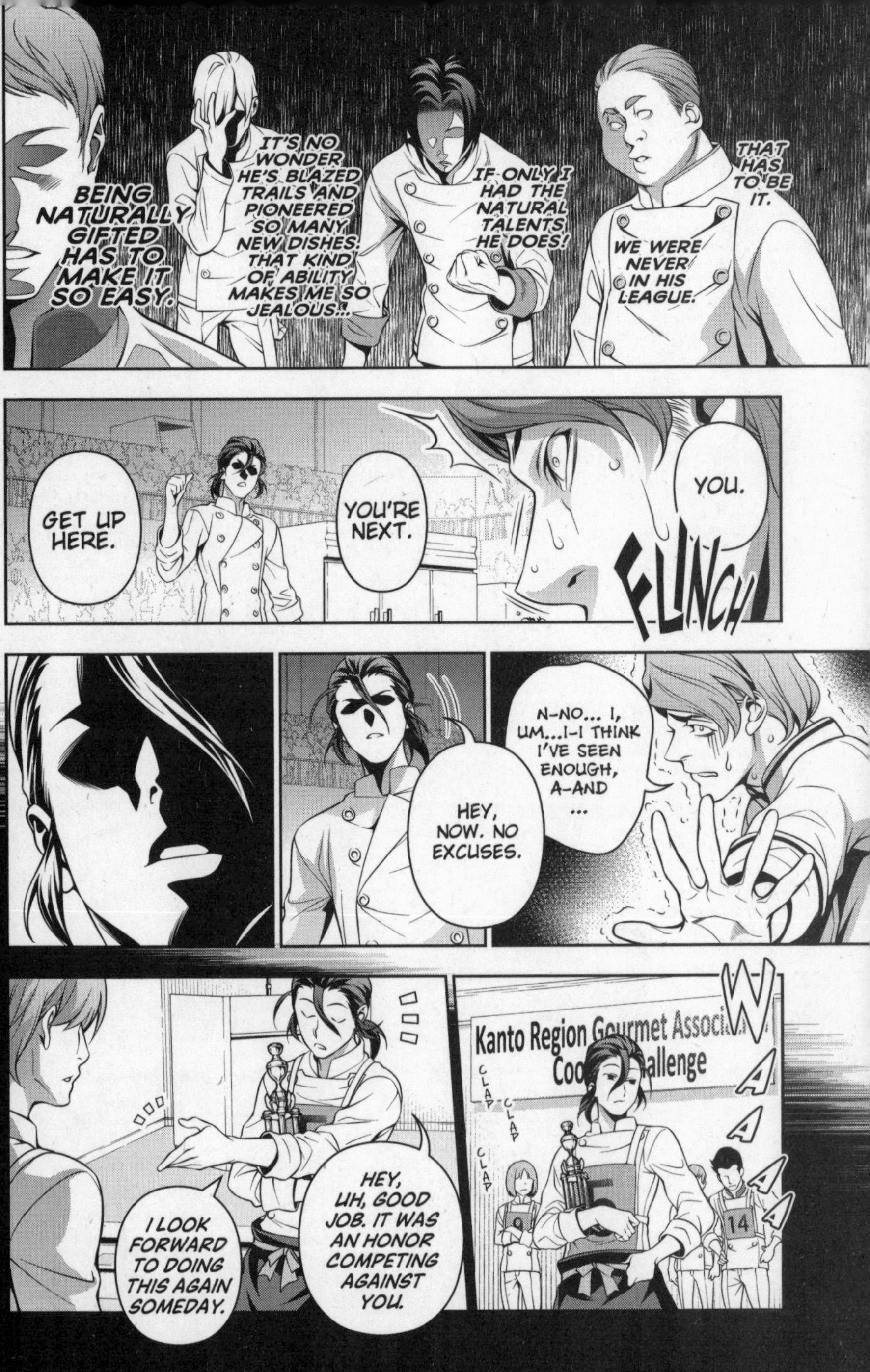
THAT HAS TO BE IT.
WE WERE NEVER IN HIS LEAGUE.
IF ONLY I HAD THE NATURAL TALENTS HE DOES!
IT'S NO WONDER HE'S BLAZED TRAILS AND PIONEERED SO MANY NEW DISHES. THAT KIND OF ABILITY MAKES ME SO JEALOUS...
BEING NATURALLY GIFTED HAS TO MAKE IT SO EASY.
YOU.
FLINCH
YOU'RE NEXT.
GET UP HERE.
N-NO... I, UM...I-I THINK I'VE SEEN ENOUGH, A-AND ...
HEY, NOW. NO EXCUSES.
WAAAAA
Kanto Region Gourmet
CLAP
CLAP
CLAP
CLAP
14
HEY, UH, GOOD JOB. IT WAS AN HONOR COMPETING AGAINST YOU.
I LOOK FORWARD TO DOING THIS AGAIN SOMEDAY.

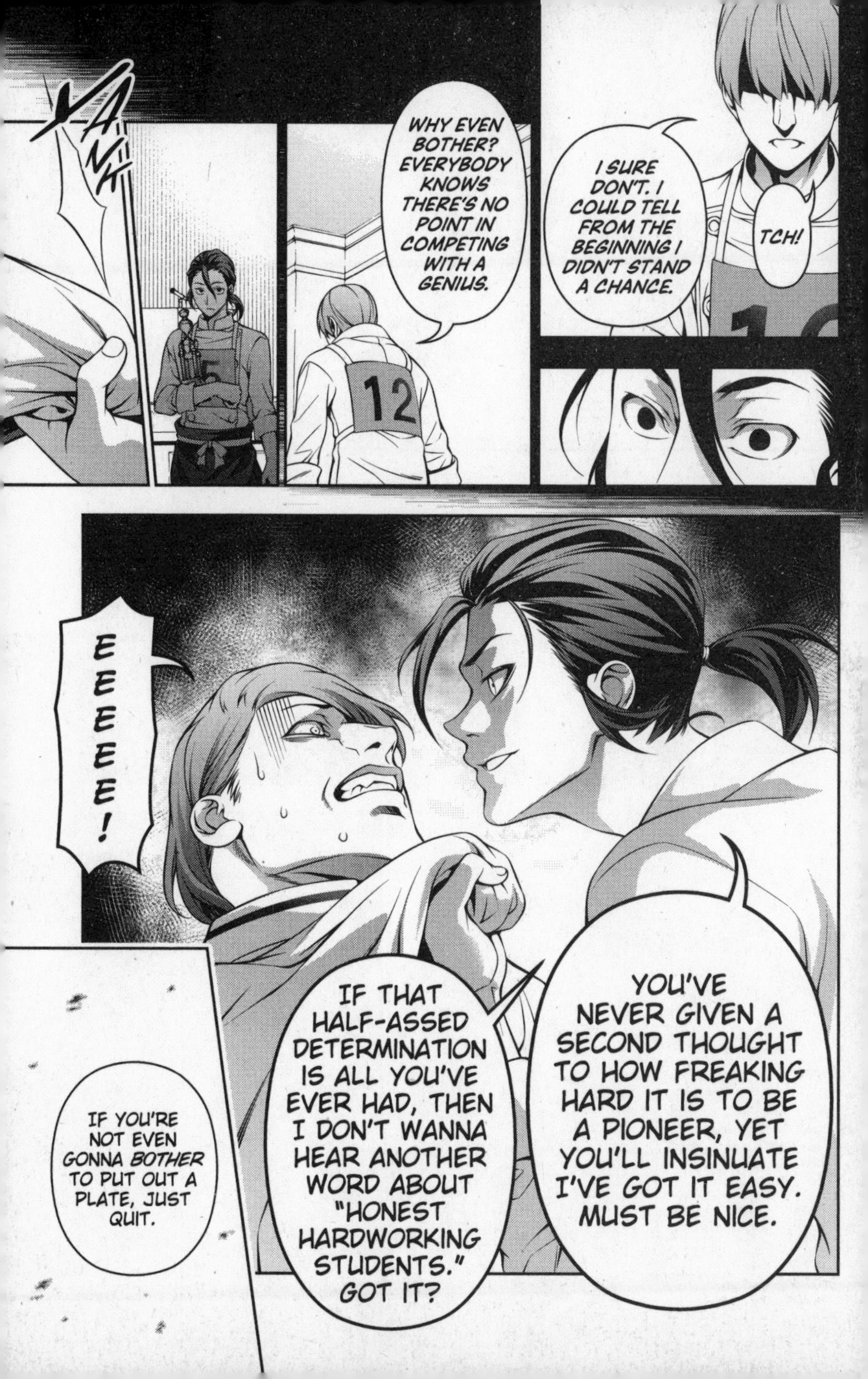
I SURE DON'T. I COULD TELL FROM THE BEGINNING I DIDN'T STAND A CHANCE.
TCH!
WHY EVEN BOTHER? EVERYBODY KNOWS THERE'S NO POINT IN COMPETING WITH A GENIUS.
YANK
EEEEEE!
YOU'VE NEVER GIVEN A SECOND THOUGHT TO HOW FREAKING HARD IT IS TO BE A PIONEER, YET YOU'LL INSINUATE I'VE GOT IT EASY. MUST BE NICE.
IF THAT HALF-ASSED DETERMINATION IS ALL YOU'VE EVER HAD, THEN I DON'T WANNA HEAR ANOTHER WORD ABOUT "HONEST HARDWORKING STUDENTS." GOT IT?
IF YOU'RE NOT EVEN GONNA *BOTHER* TO PUT OUT A PLATE, JUST QUIT.

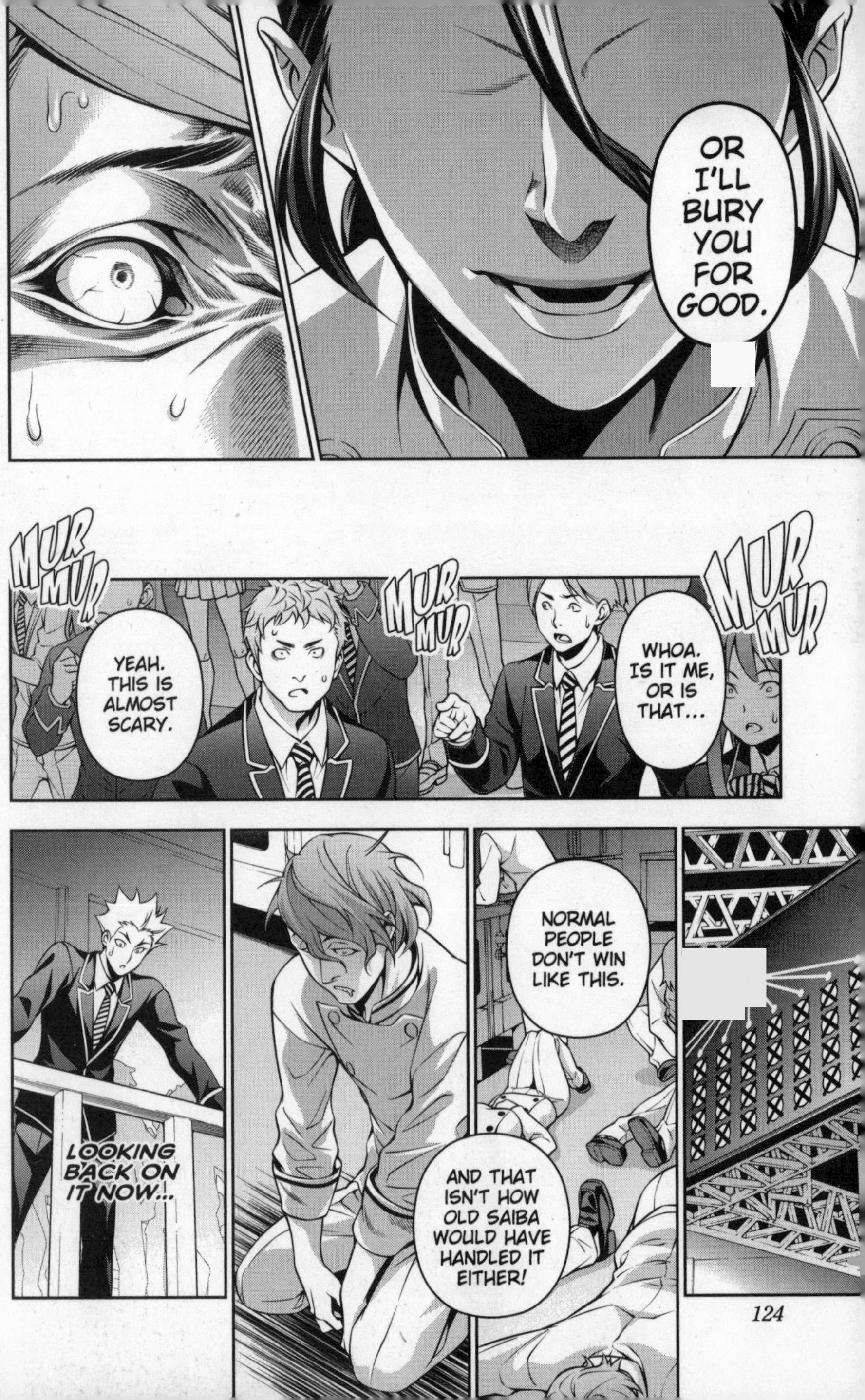

OR I'LL BURY YOU FOR GOOD.
MUR MUR
WHOA. IS IT ME, OR IS THAT...
MUR MUR
YEAH. THIS IS ALMOST SCARY.
MUR MUR
NORMAL PEOPLE DON'T WIN LIKE THIS.
AND THAT ISN'T HOW OLD SAIBA WOULD HAVE HANDLED IT EITHER!
LOOKING BACK ON IT NOW...

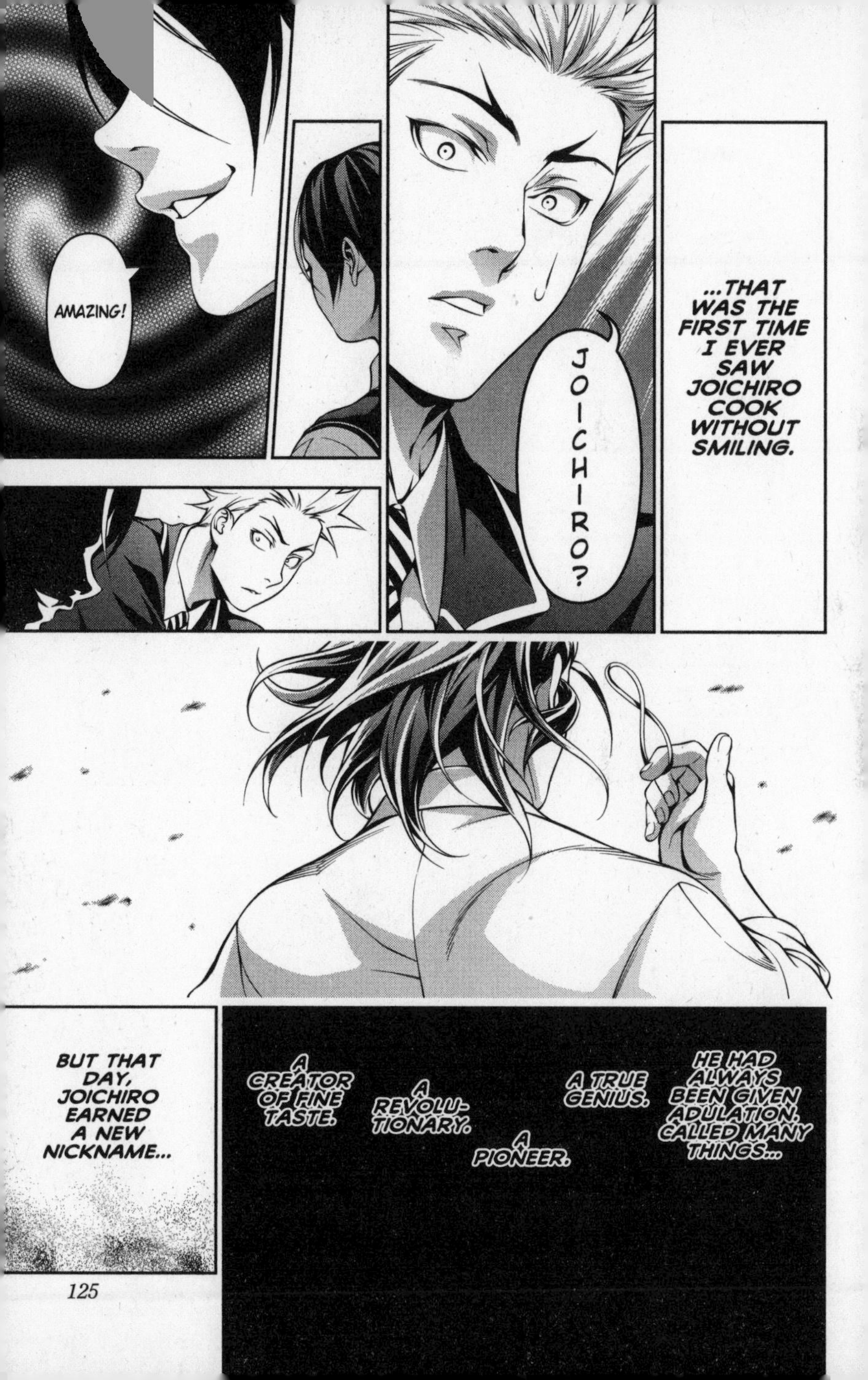
...THAT WAS THE FIRST TIME I EVER SAW JOICHIRO COOK WITHOUT SMILING.
JOICHIRO?
AMAZING!
HE HAD ALWAYS BEEN GIVEN ADULATION, CALLED MANY THINGS...
A TRUE GENIUS.
A PIONEER.
A REVOLUTIONARY.
A CREATOR OF FINE TASTE.
BUT THAT DAY, JOICHIRO EARNED A NEW NICKNAME...

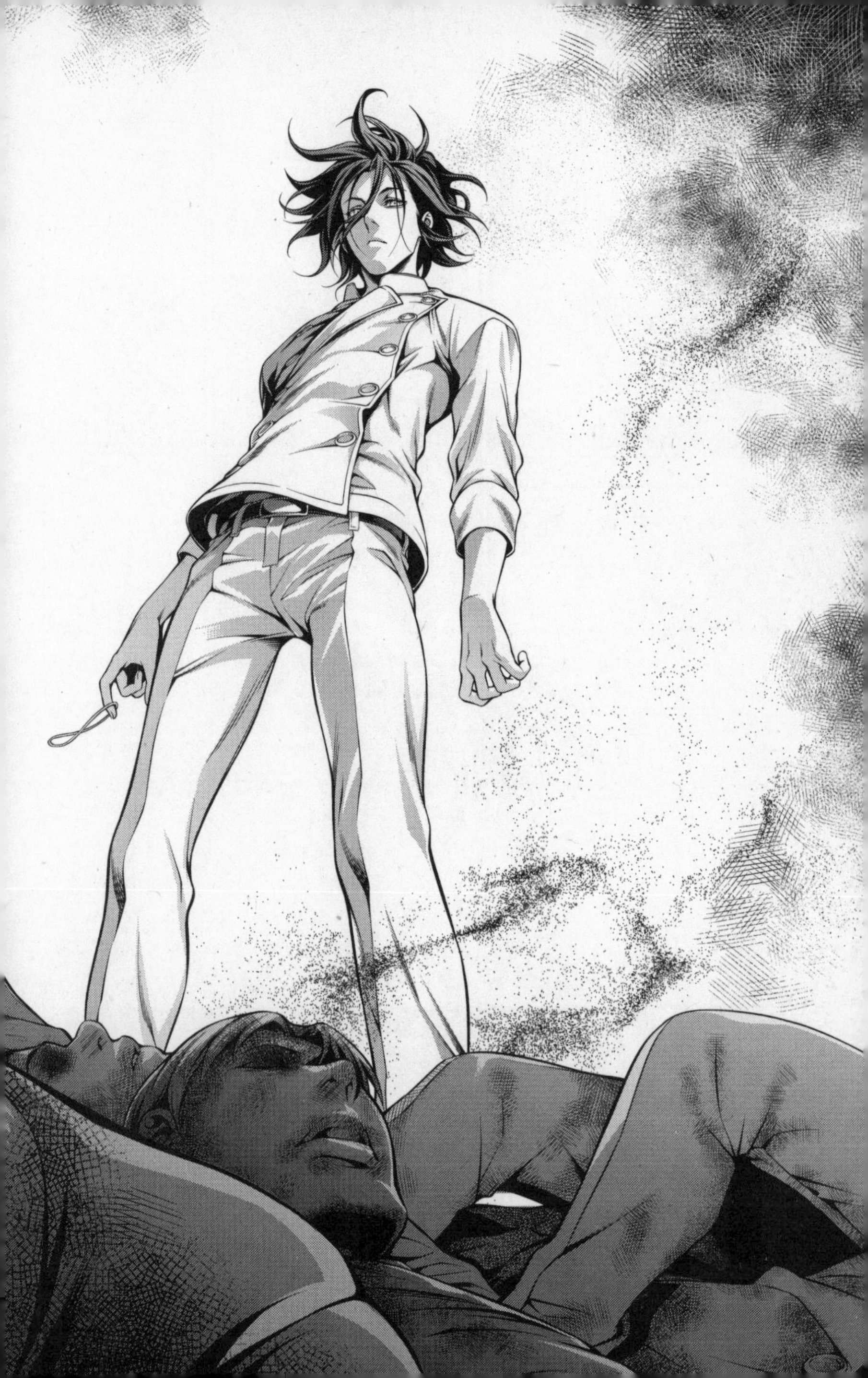

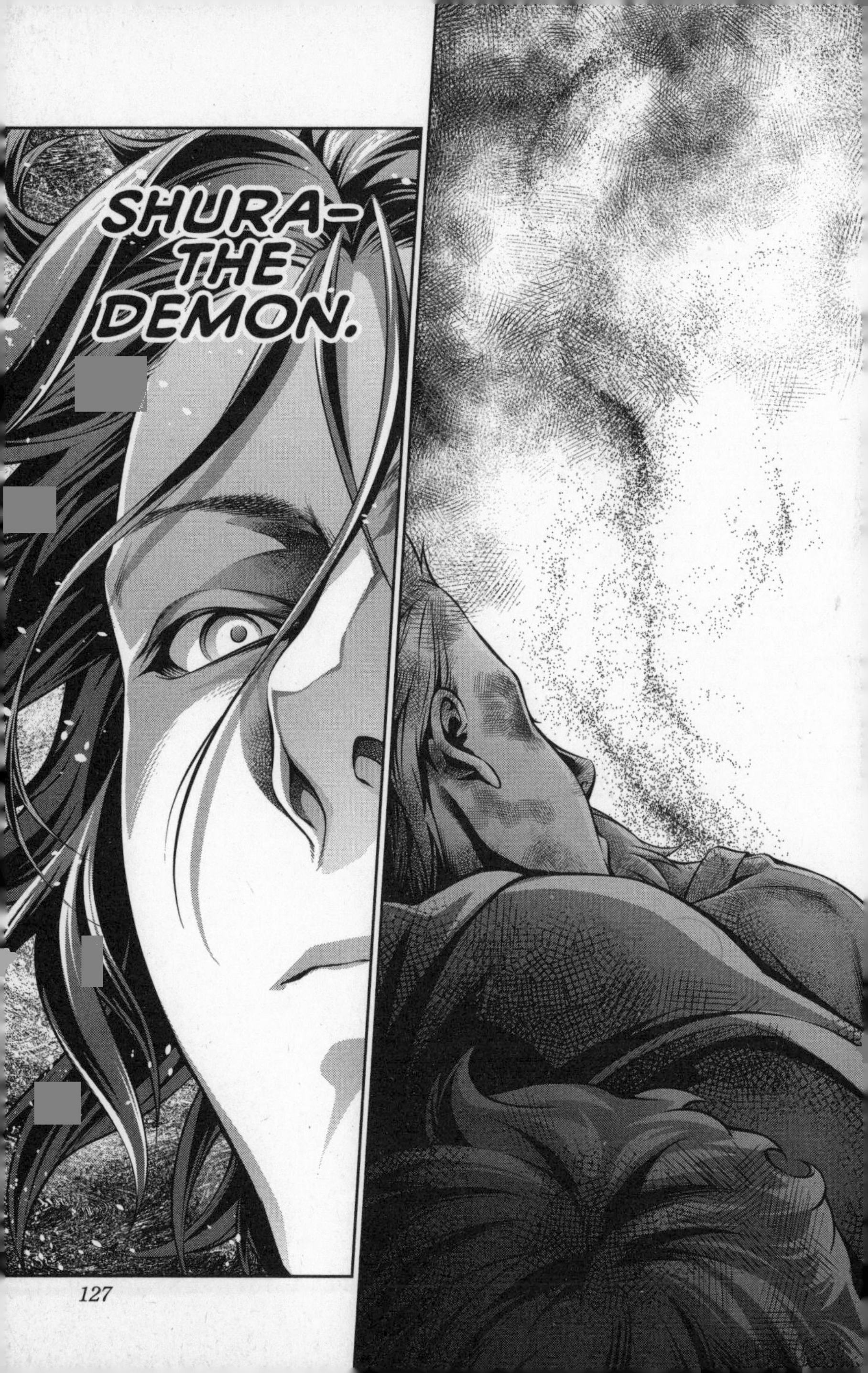
SHURA—
THE
DEMON.

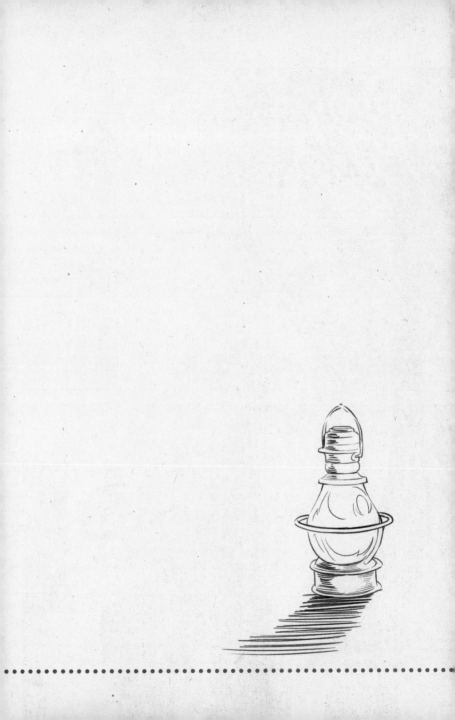

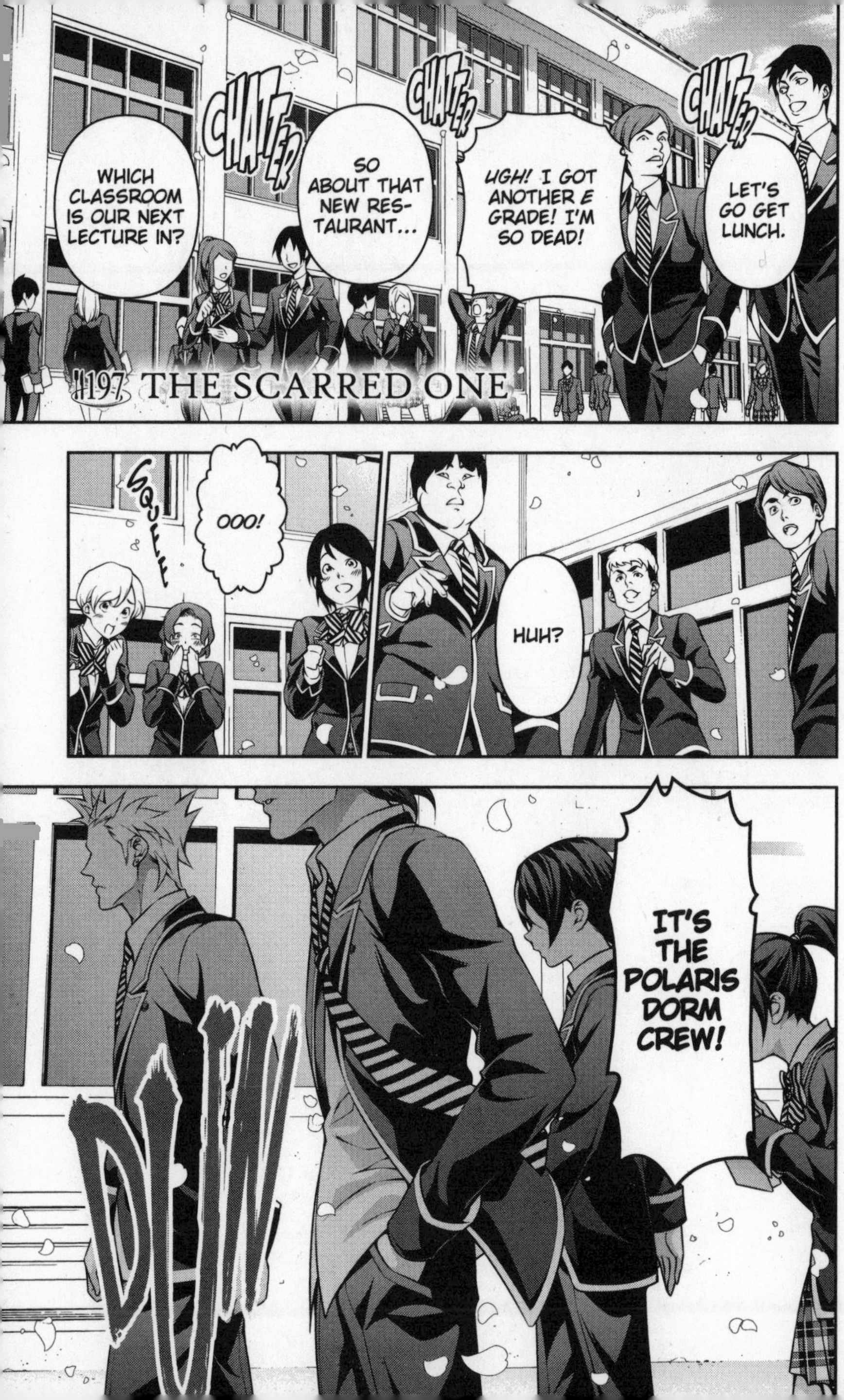
LET'S GO GET LUNCH.
CHATTER
UGH! I GOT ANOTHER E GRADE! I'M SO DEAD!
CHATTER
SO ABOUT THAT NEW RES-TAURANT...
CHATTER
WHICH CLASSROOM IS OUR NEXT LECTURE IN?
#197 THE SCARRED ONE
HUH?
OOO!
SQUEEE
IT'S THE POLARIS DORM CREW!

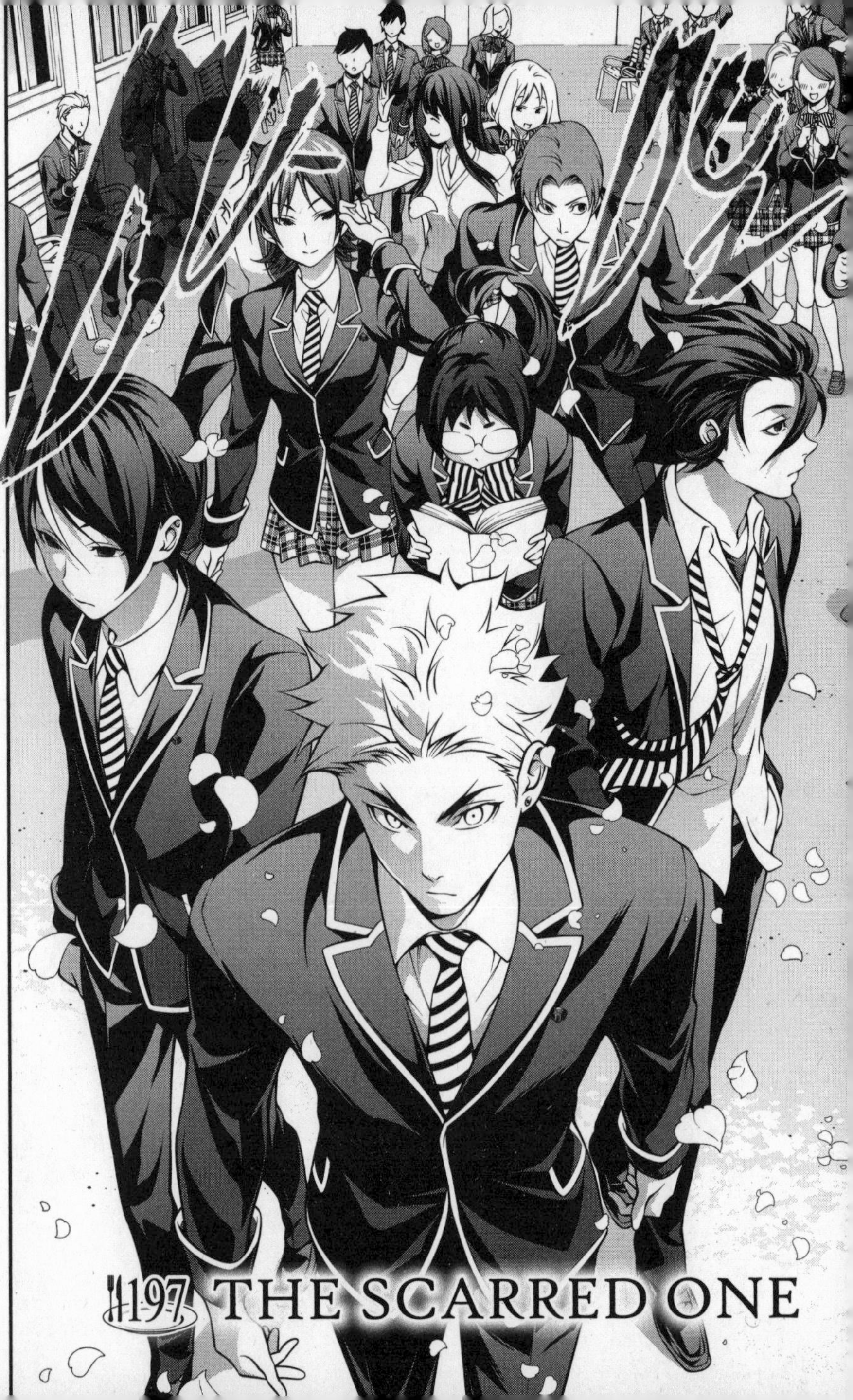
197 THE SCARRED ONE

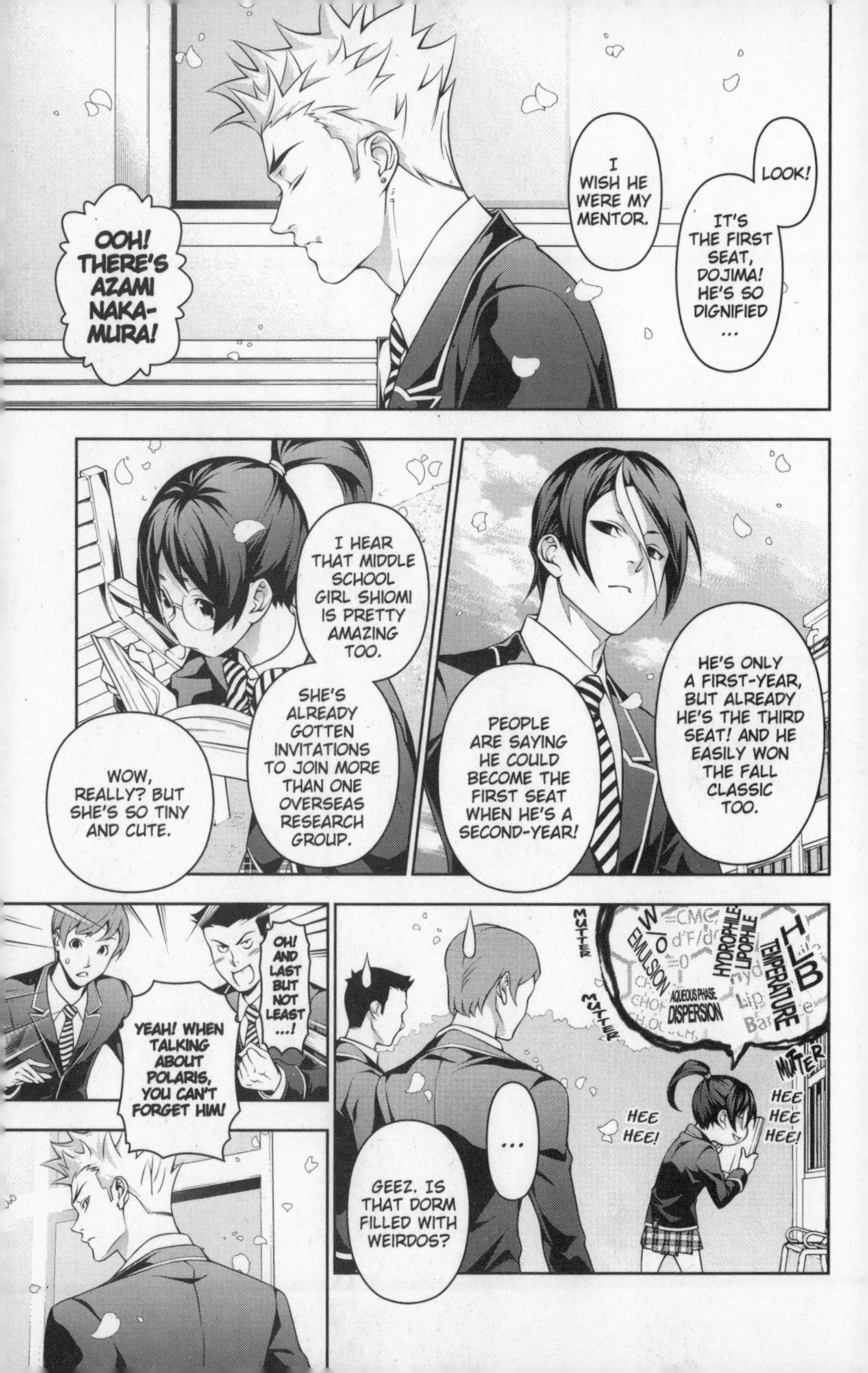
LOOK!
IT'S THE FIRST SEAT, DOJIMA! HE'S SO DIGNIFIED...
I WISH HE WERE MY MENTOR.
OOH! THERE'S AZAMI NAKAMURA!
HE'S ONLY A FIRST-YEAR, BUT ALREADY HE'S THE THIRD SEAT! AND HE EASILY WON THE FALL CLASSIC TOO.
PEOPLE ARE SAYING HE COULD BECOME THE FIRST SEAT WHEN HE'S A SECOND-YEAR!
I HEAR THAT MIDDLE SCHOOL GIRL SHIOMI IS PRETTY AMAZING TOO.
SHE'S ALREADY GOTTEN INVITATIONS TO JOIN MORE THAN ONE OVERSEAS RESEARCH GROUP.
WOW, REALLY? BUT SHE'S SO TINY AND CUTE.
MUTTER
HLB
TEMPERATURE
HYDROPHILE
LIPOPHILE
W/O
EMULSION
AQUEOUS PHASE
DISPERSION
MUTTER
MUTTER
HEE HEE HEE!
HEE HEE!
...
GEEZ. IS THAT DORM FILLED WITH WEIRDOS?
OH! AND LAST BUT NOT LEAST...!
YEAH! WHEN TALKING ABOUT POLARIS, YOU CAN'T FORGET HIM!

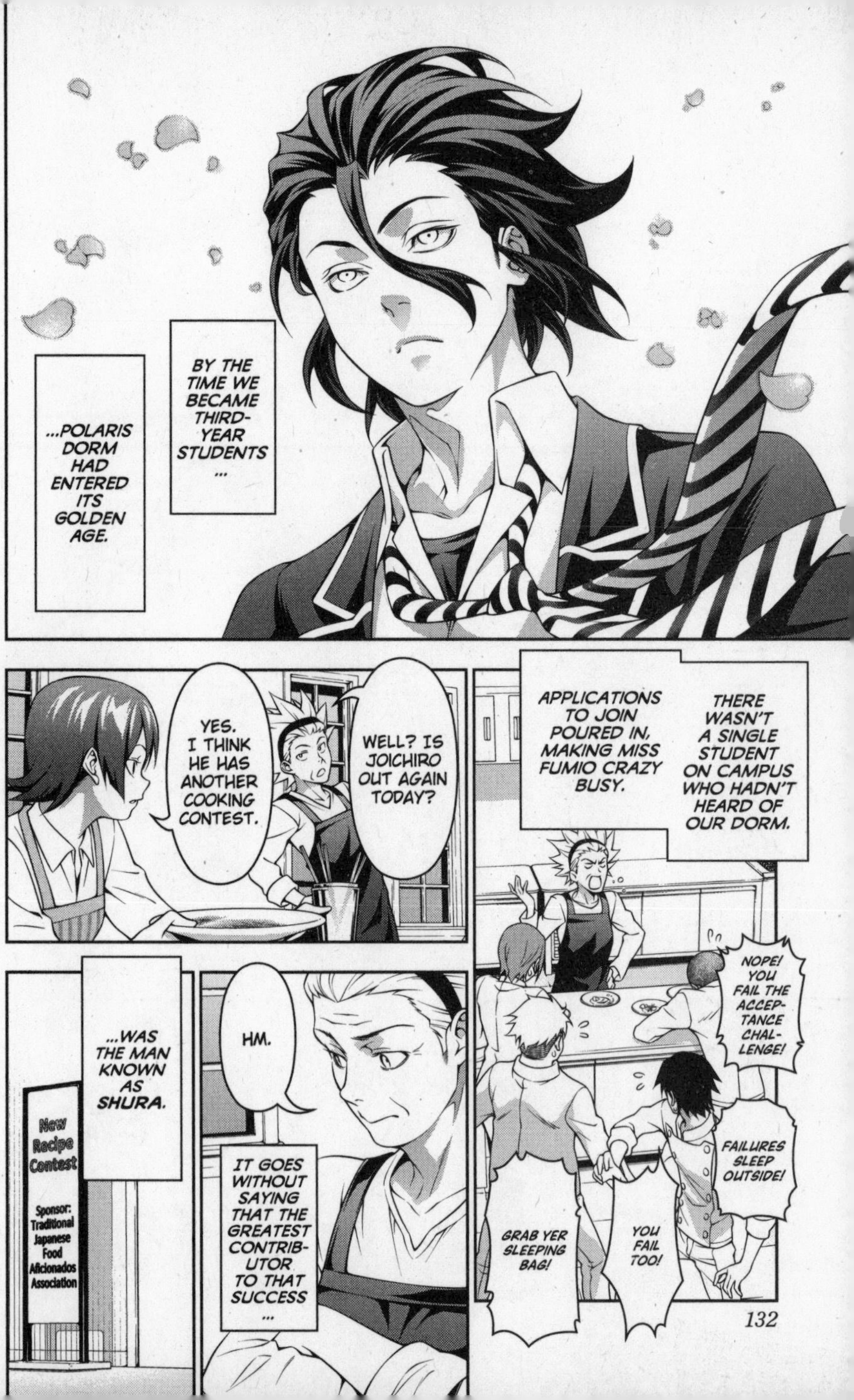
BY THE TIME WE BECAME THIRD-YEAR STUDENTS...
...POLARIS DORM HAD ENTERED ITS GOLDEN AGE.
THERE WASN'T A SINGLE STUDENT ON CAMPUS WHO HADN'T HEARD OF OUR DORM.
APPLICATIONS TO JOIN POURED IN, MAKING MISS FUMIO CRAZY BUSY.
NOPE! YOU FAIL THE ACCEPTANCE CHALLENGE!
FAILURES SLEEP OUTSIDE!
YOU FAIL TOO!
GRAB YER SLEEPING BAG!
WELL? IS JOICHIRO OUT AGAIN TODAY?
YES. I THINK HE HAS ANOTHER COOKING CONTEST.
HM.
IT GOES WITHOUT SAYING THAT THE GREATEST CONTRIBUTOR TO THAT SUCCESS...
...WAS THE MAN KNOWN AS SHURA.
New Recipe Contest
Sponsor: Traditional Japanese Food Aficionados Association

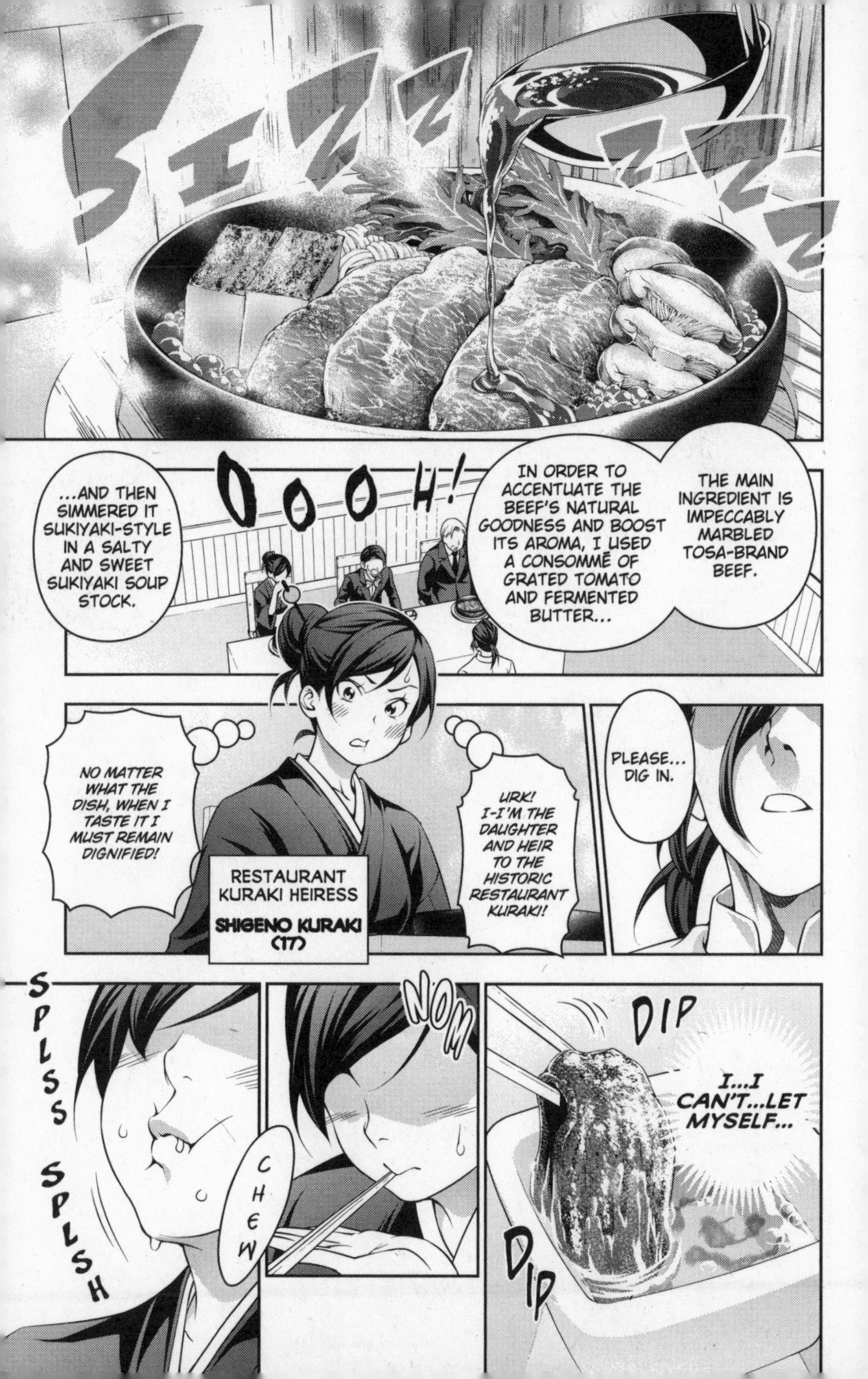
SIZZZZZZ
THE MAIN INGREDIENT IS IMPECCABLY MARBLED TOSA-BRAND BEEF.
IN ORDER TO ACCENTUATE THE BEEF'S NATURAL GOODNESS AND BOOST ITS AROMA, I USED A CONSOMMÉ OF GRATED TOMATO AND FERMENTED BUTTER...
OOOH!
...AND THEN SIMMERED IT SUKIYAKI-STYLE IN A SALTY AND SWEET SUKIYAKI SOUP STOCK.
PLEASE... DIG IN.
URK! I-I'M THE DAUGHTER AND HEIR TO THE HISTORIC RESTAURANT KURAKI!
RESTAURANT KURAKI HEIRESS
SHIGENO KURAKI (17)
NO MATTER WHAT THE DISH, WHEN I TASTE IT I MUST REMAIN DIGNIFIED!
DIP
I...I CAN'T...LET MYSELF...
DIP
NOM
CHEW
SPLSS
SPLSH

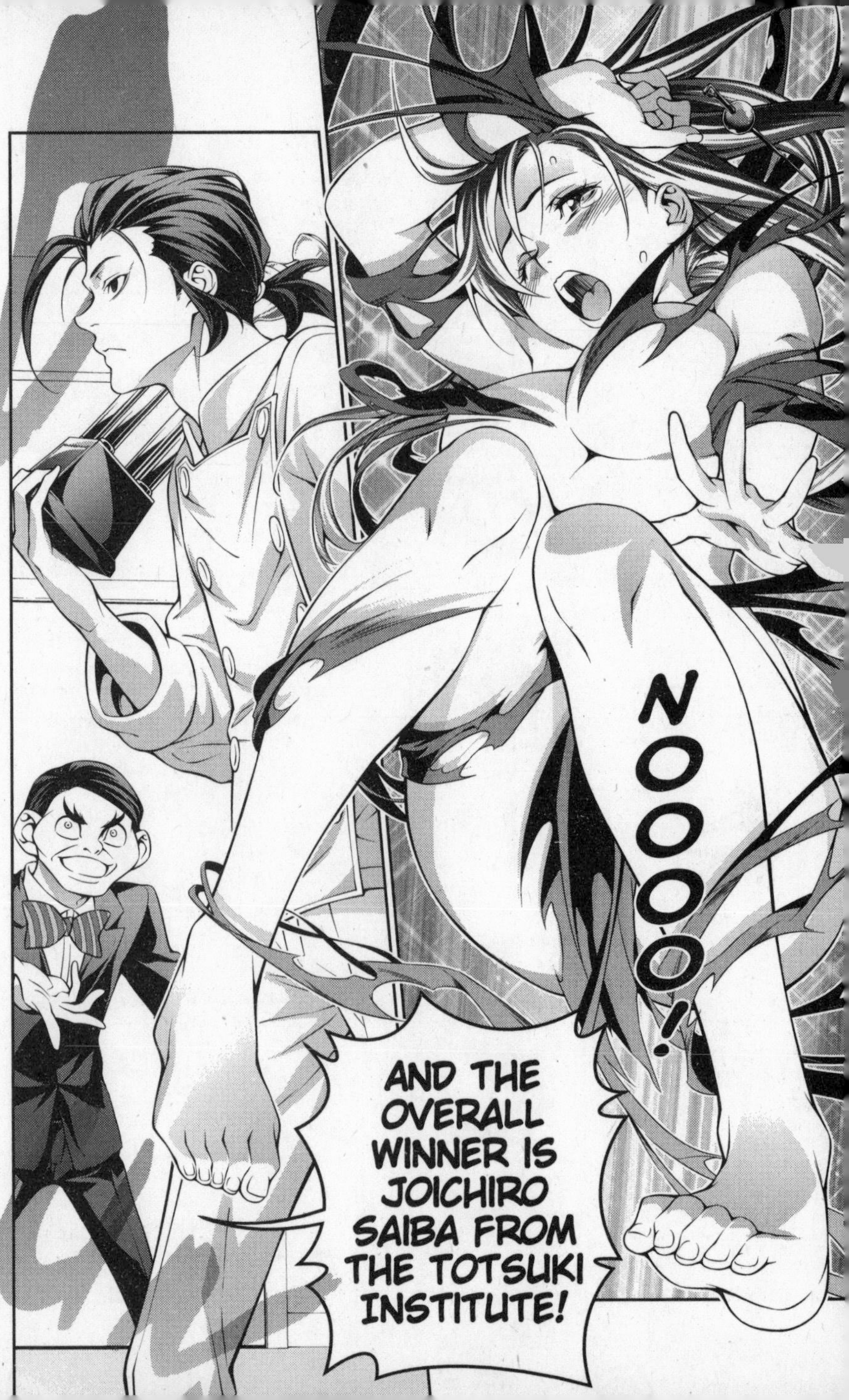
NOOOOO!
AND THE OVERALL WINNER IS JOICHIRO SAIBA FROM THE TOTSUKI INSTITUTE!

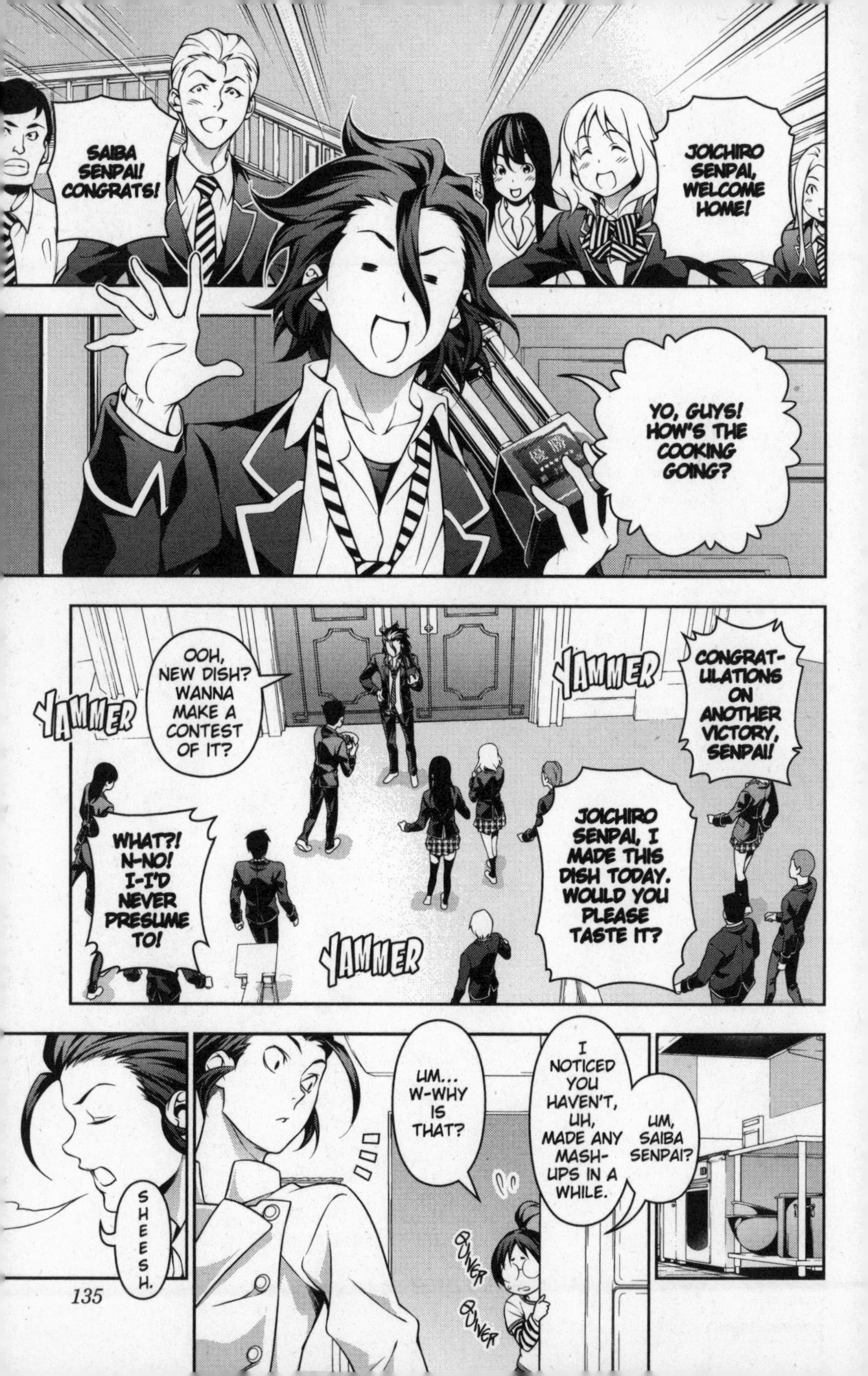
JOICHIRO SENPAI, WELCOME HOME!
SAIBA SENPAI! CONGRATS!
YO, GUYS! HOW'S THE COOKING GOING?
YAMMER
CONGRATULATIONS ON ANOTHER VICTORY, SENPAI!
JOICHIRO SENPAI, I MADE THIS DISH TODAY. WOULD YOU PLEASE TASTE IT?
OOH, NEW DISH? WANNA MAKE A CONTEST OF IT?
YAMMER
WHAT?! N-NO! I-I'D NEVER PRESUME TO!
YAMMER
UM, SAIBA SENPAI?
I NOTICED YOU HAVEN'T, UH, MADE ANY MASH-UPS IN A WHILE.
QUIVER
QUIVER
UM... W-WHY IS THAT?
SHEESH.

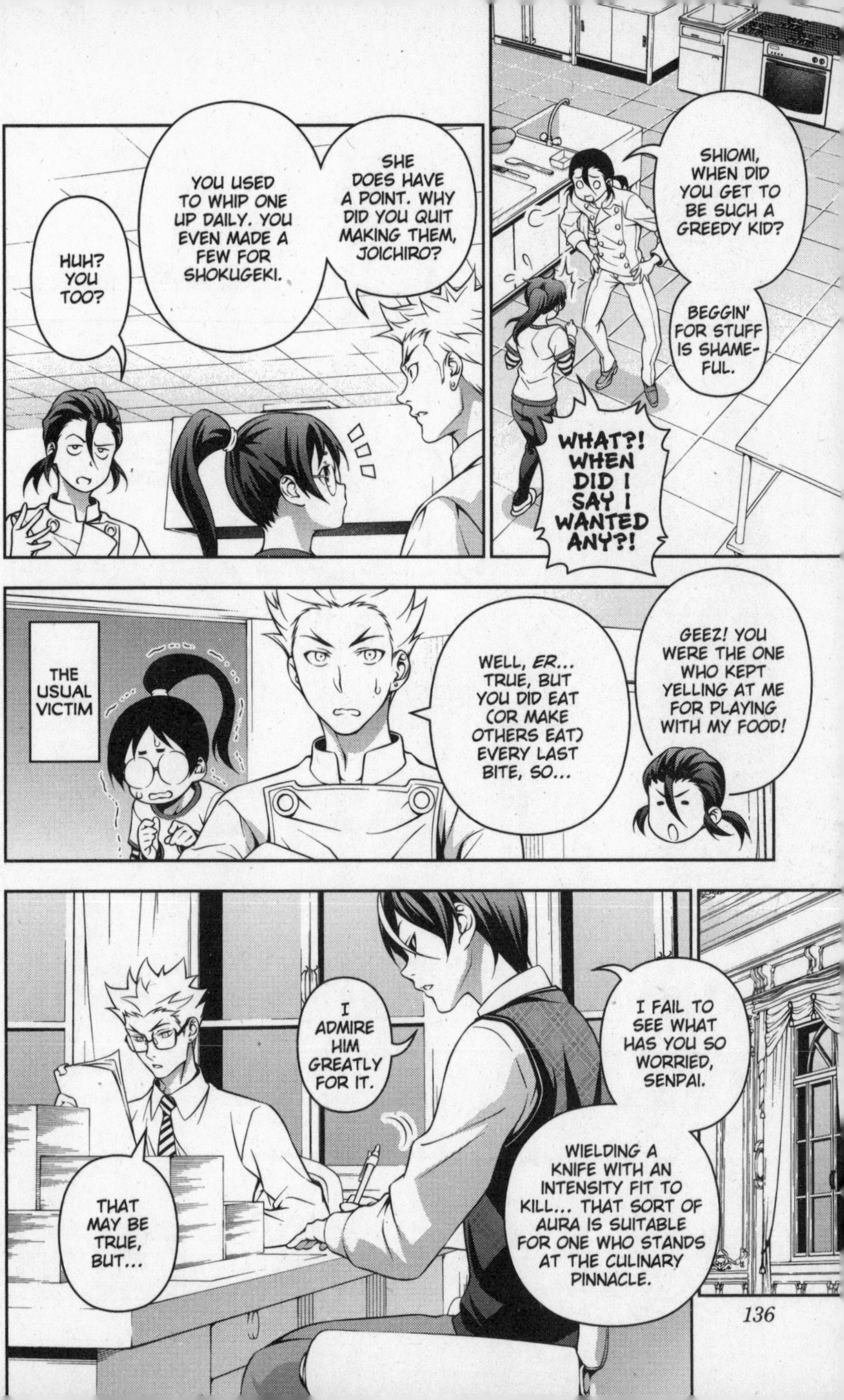
SHIOMI, WHEN DID YOU GET TO BE SUCH A GREEDY KID?
BEGGIN' FOR STUFF IS SHAMEFUL.
WHAT?! WHEN DID I SAY I WANTED ANY?!
SHE DOES HAVE A POINT. WHY DID YOU QUIT MAKING THEM, JOICHIRO?
YOU USED TO WHIP ONE UP DAILY. YOU EVEN MADE A FEW FOR SHOKUGEKI.
HUH? YOU TOO?
GEEZ! YOU WERE THE ONE WHO KEPT YELLING AT ME FOR PLAYING WITH MY FOOD!
WELL, *ER*... TRUE, BUT YOU DID EAT (OR MAKE OTHERS EAT) EVERY LAST BITE, SO...
THE USUAL VICTIM
I FAIL TO SEE WHAT HAS YOU SO WORRIED, SENPAI.
I ADMIRE HIM GREATLY FOR IT.
WIELDING A KNIFE WITH AN INTENSITY FIT TO KILL... THAT SORT OF AURA IS SUITABLE FOR ONE WHO STANDS AT THE CULINARY PINNACLE.
THAT MAY BE TRUE, BUT...

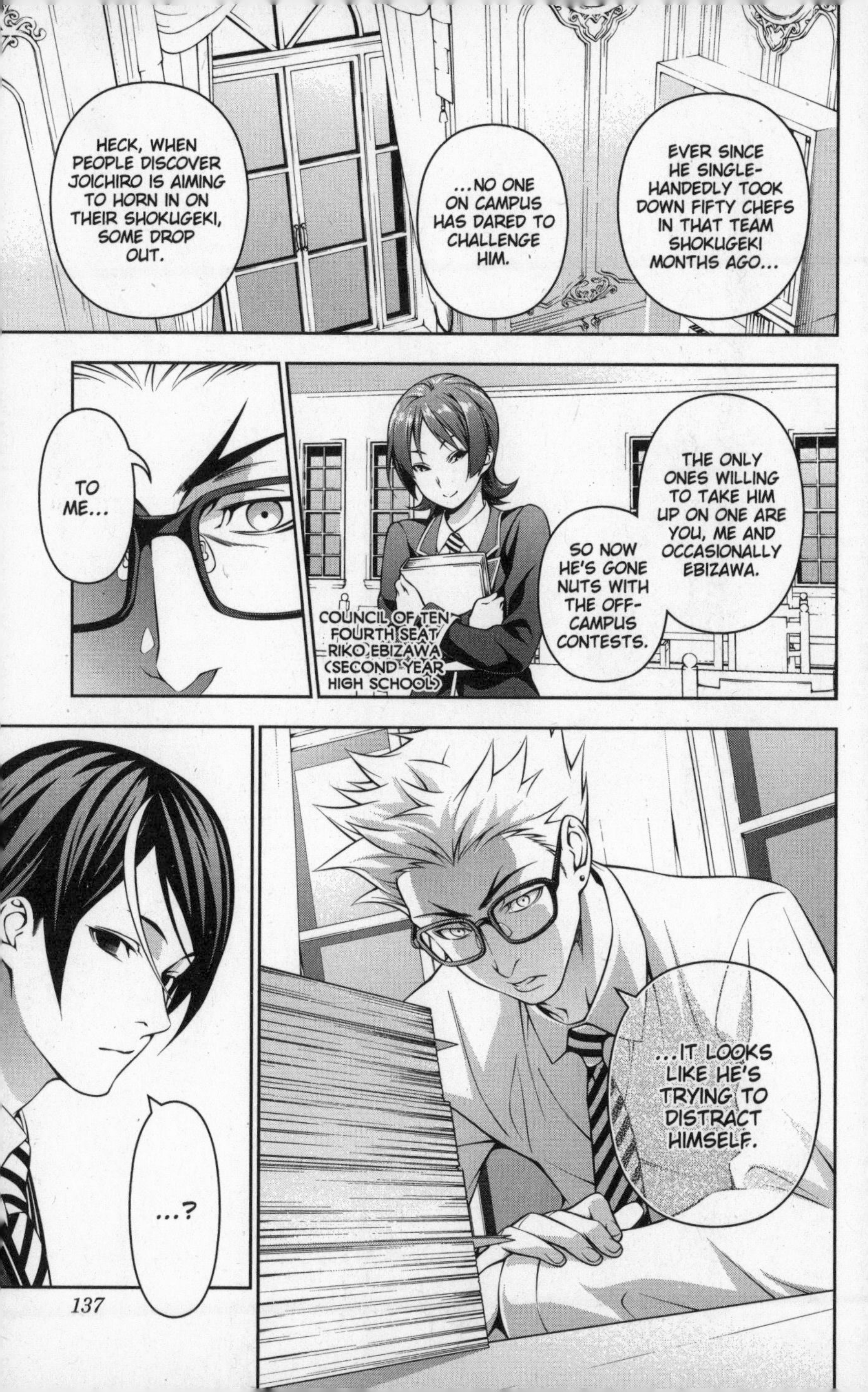
EVER SINCE HE SINGLE-HANDEDLY TOOK DOWN FIFTY CHEFS IN THAT TEAM SHOKUGEKI MONTHS AGO...
...NO ONE ON CAMPUS HAS DARED TO CHALLENGE HIM.
HECK, WHEN PEOPLE DISCOVER JOICHIRO IS AIMING TO HORN IN ON THEIR SHOKUGEKI, SOME DROP OUT.
THE ONLY ONES WILLING TO TAKE HIM UP ON ONE ARE YOU, ME AND OCCASIONALLY EBIZAWA.
SO NOW HE'S GONE NUTS WITH THE OFF-CAMPUS CONTESTS.
COUNCIL OF TEN FOURTH SEAT RIKO EBIZAWA (SECOND YEAR HIGH SCHOOL)
TO ME...
...IT LOOKS LIKE HE'S TRYING TO DISTRACT HIMSELF.
...?

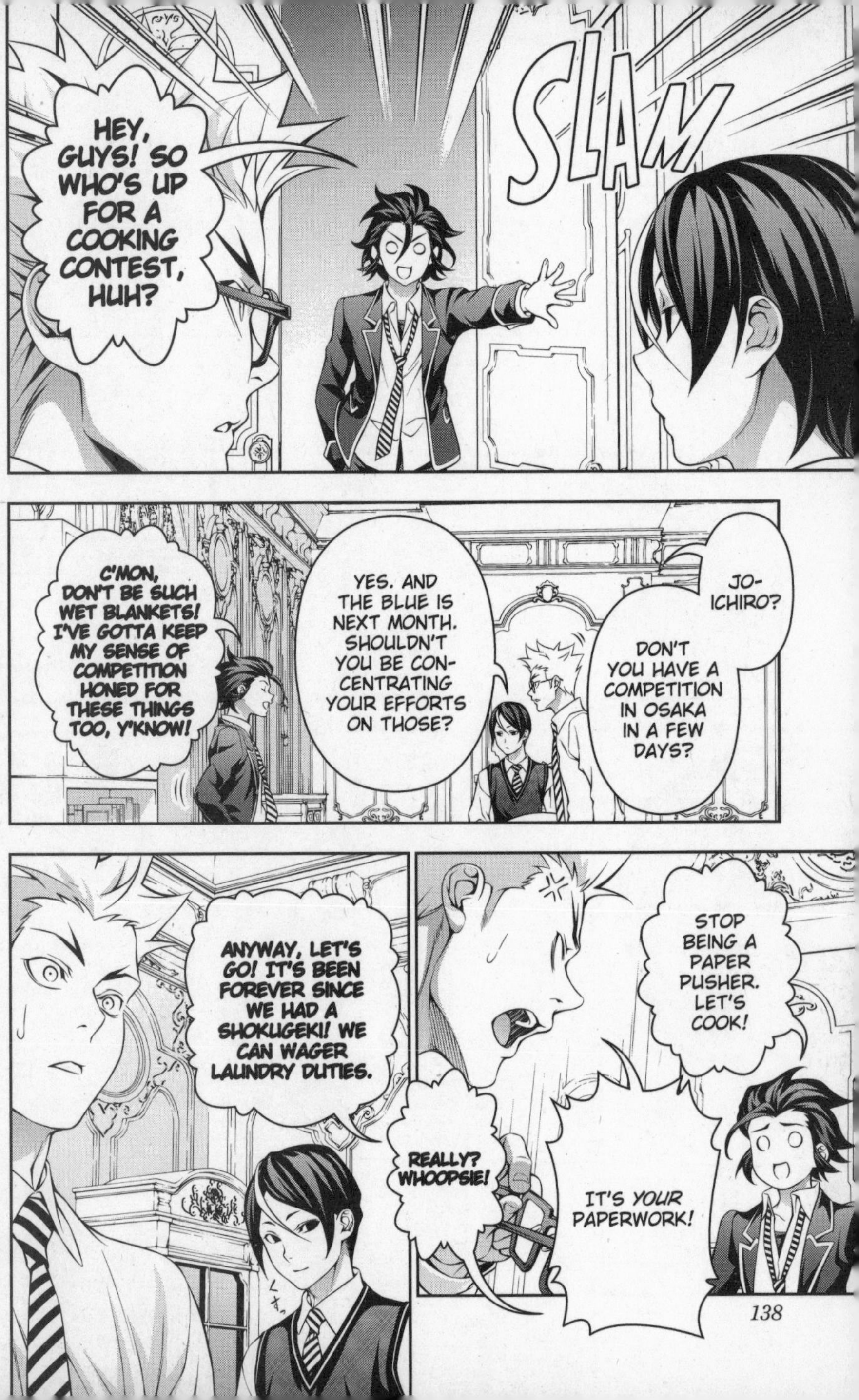
SLAM
HEY, GUYS! SO WHO'S UP FOR A COOKING CONTEST, HUH?
JO-ICHIRO?
DON'T YOU HAVE A COMPETITION IN OSAKA IN A FEW DAYS?
YES. AND THE BLUE IS NEXT MONTH. SHOULDN'T YOU BE CON-CENTRATING YOUR EFFORTS ON THOSE?
C'MON, DON'T BE SUCH WET BLANKETS! I'VE GOTTA KEEP MY SENSE OF COMPETITION HONED FOR THESE THINGS TOO, Y'KNOW!
STOP BEING A PAPER PUSHER. LET'S COOK!
IT'S *YOUR* PAPERWORK!
REALLY? WHOOPSIE!
ANYWAY, LET'S GO! IT'S BEEN FOREVER SINCE WE HAD A SHOKUGEKI! WE CAN WAGER LAUNDRY DUTIES.

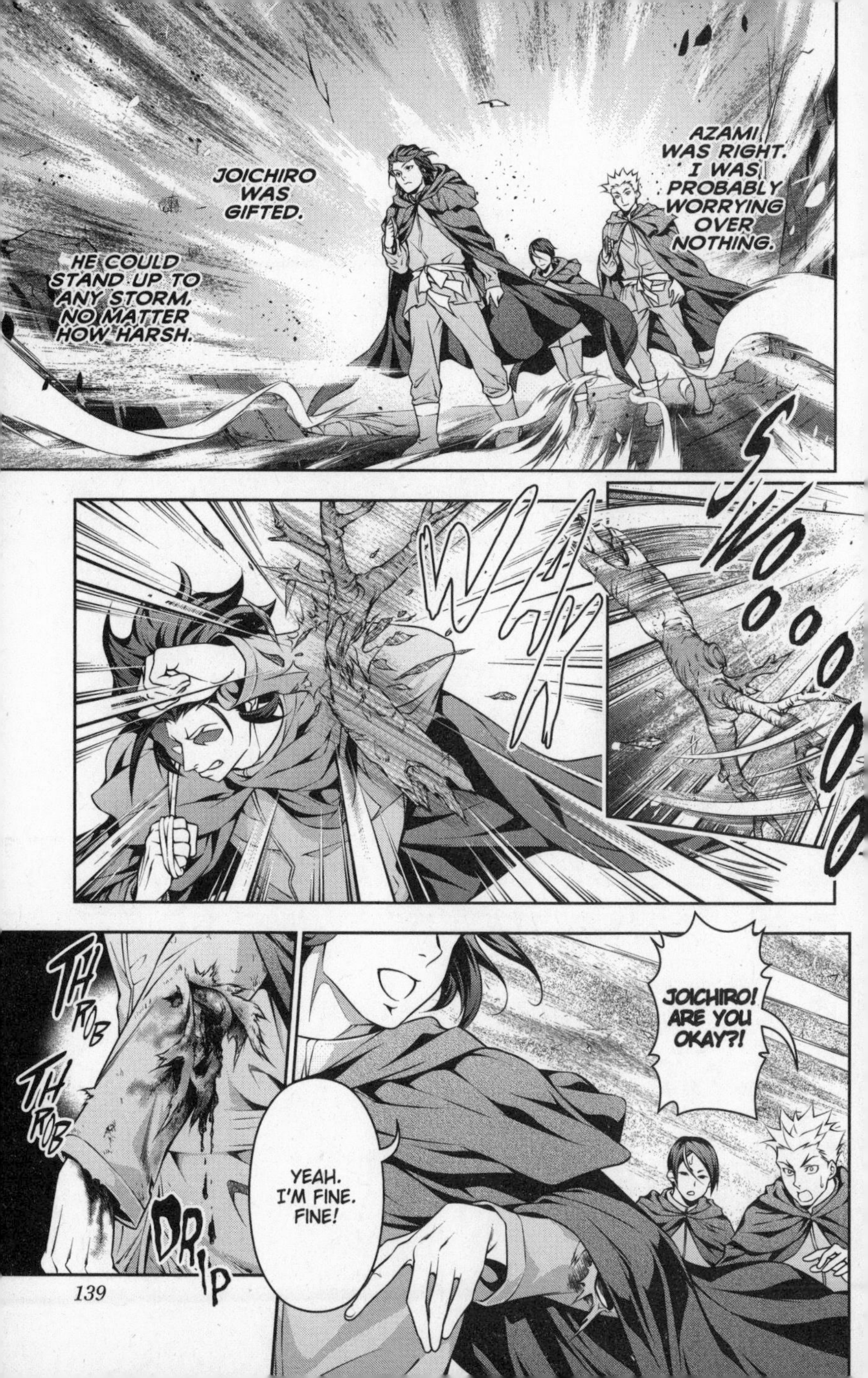
AZAMI WAS RIGHT. I WAS PROBABLY WORRYING OVER NOTHING.
JOICHIRO WAS GIFTED.
HE COULD STAND UP TO ANY STORM, NO MATTER HOW HARSH.
SWOOOOOOOO
WHAM
JOICHIRO! ARE YOU OKAY?!
YEAH. I'M FINE. FINE!
THROB
THROB
DRIP

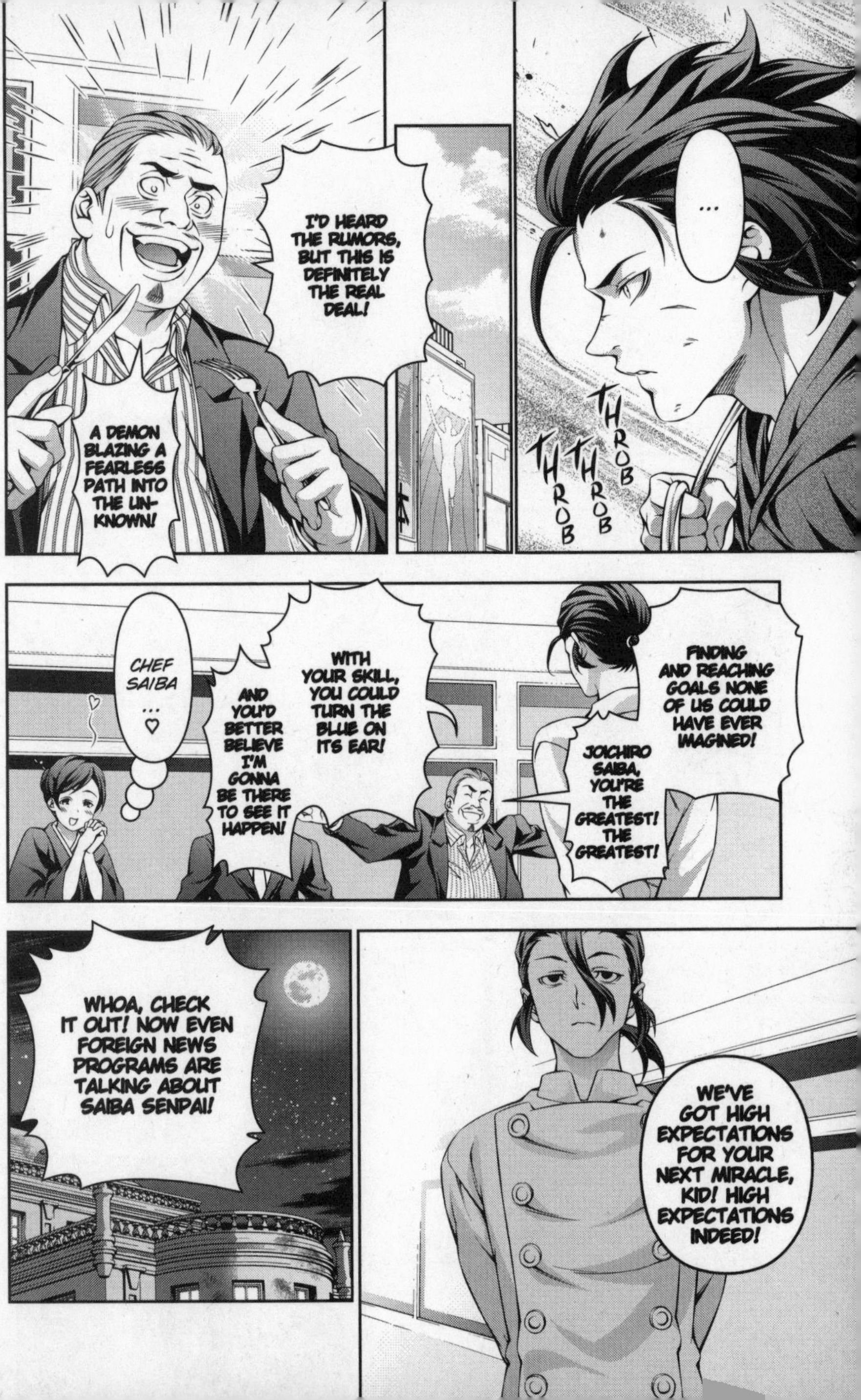
...
THROB THROB THROB
I'D HEARD THE RUMORS, BUT THIS IS DEFINITELY THE REAL DEAL!
A DEMON BLAZING A FEARLESS PATH INTO THE UN-KNOWN!
FINDING AND REACHING GOALS NONE OF US COULD HAVE EVER IMAGINED!
JOICHIRO SAIBA, YOU'RE THE GREATEST! THE GREATEST!
WITH YOUR SKILL, YOU COULD TURN THE BLUE ON ITS EAR!
AND YOU'D BETTER BELIEVE I'M GONNA BE THERE TO SEE IT HAPPEN!
CHEF SAIBA ... ♡
WE'VE GOT HIGH EXPECTATIONS FOR YOUR NEXT MIRACLE, KID! HIGH EXPECTATIONS INDEED!
WHOA, CHECK IT OUT! NOW EVEN FOREIGN NEWS PROGRAMS ARE TALKING ABOUT SAIBA SENPAI!

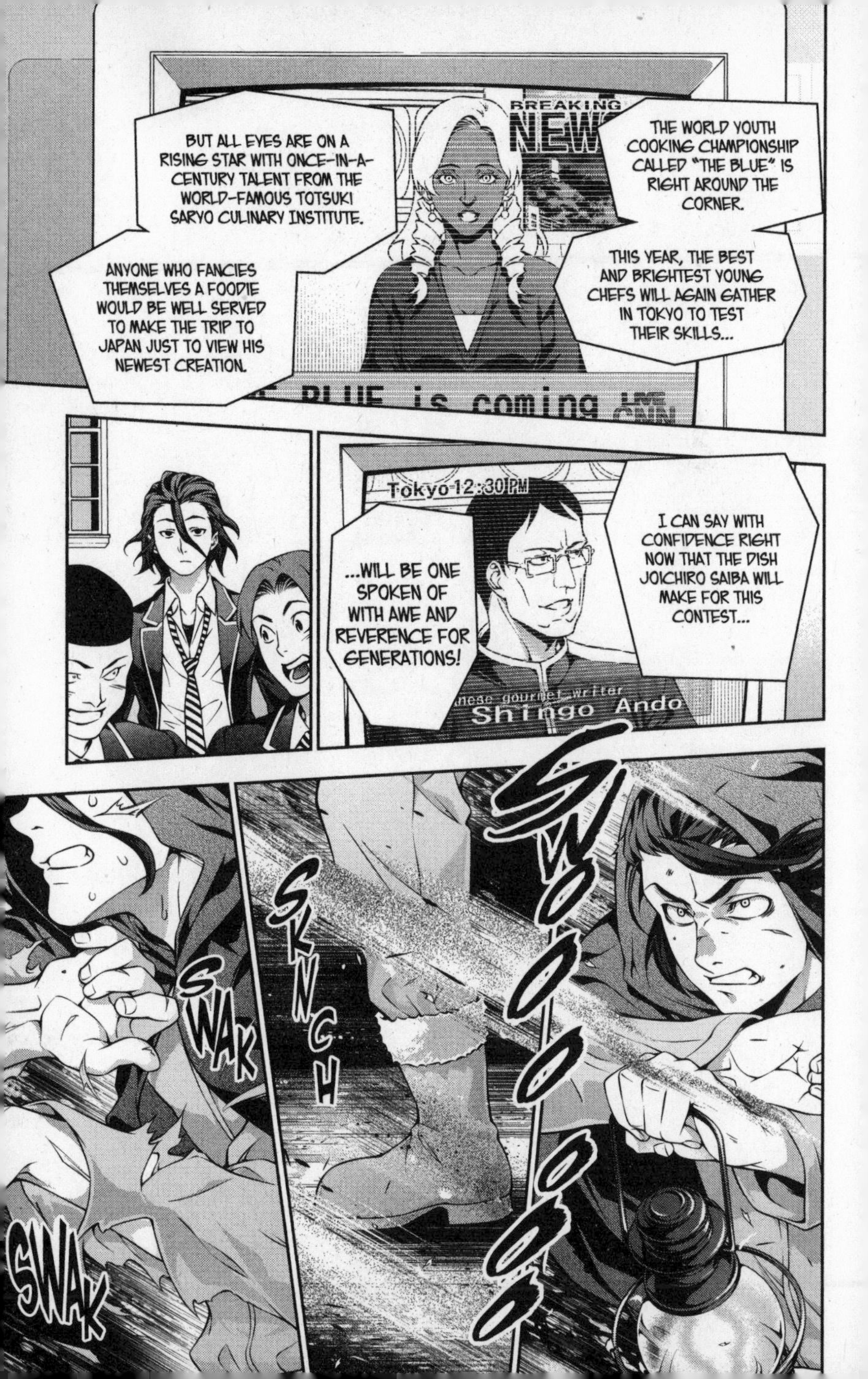
BREAKING
THE WORLD YOUTH COOKING CHAMPIONSHIP CALLED "THE BLUE" IS RIGHT AROUND THE CORNER.
THIS YEAR, THE BEST AND BRIGHTEST YOUNG CHEFS WILL AGAIN GATHER IN TOKYO TO TEST THEIR SKILLS...
BUT ALL EYES ARE ON A RISING STAR WITH ONCE-IN-A-CENTURY TALENT FROM THE WORLD-FAMOUS TOTSUKI SARYO CULINARY INSTITUTE.
ANYONE WHO FANCIES THEMSELVES A FOODIE WOULD BE WELL SERVED TO MAKE THE TRIP TO JAPAN JUST TO VIEW HIS NEWEST CREATION.
is coming
Tokyo 12:30PM
I CAN SAY WITH CONFIDENCE RIGHT NOW THAT THE DISH JOICHIRO SAIBA WILL MAKE FOR THIS CONTEST...
...WILL BE ONE SPOKEN OF WITH AWE AND REVERENCE FOR GENERATIONS!
gourmet writer
Shingo Ando
SWOOOOOOOO
SKNCH
SWAK
SWAK

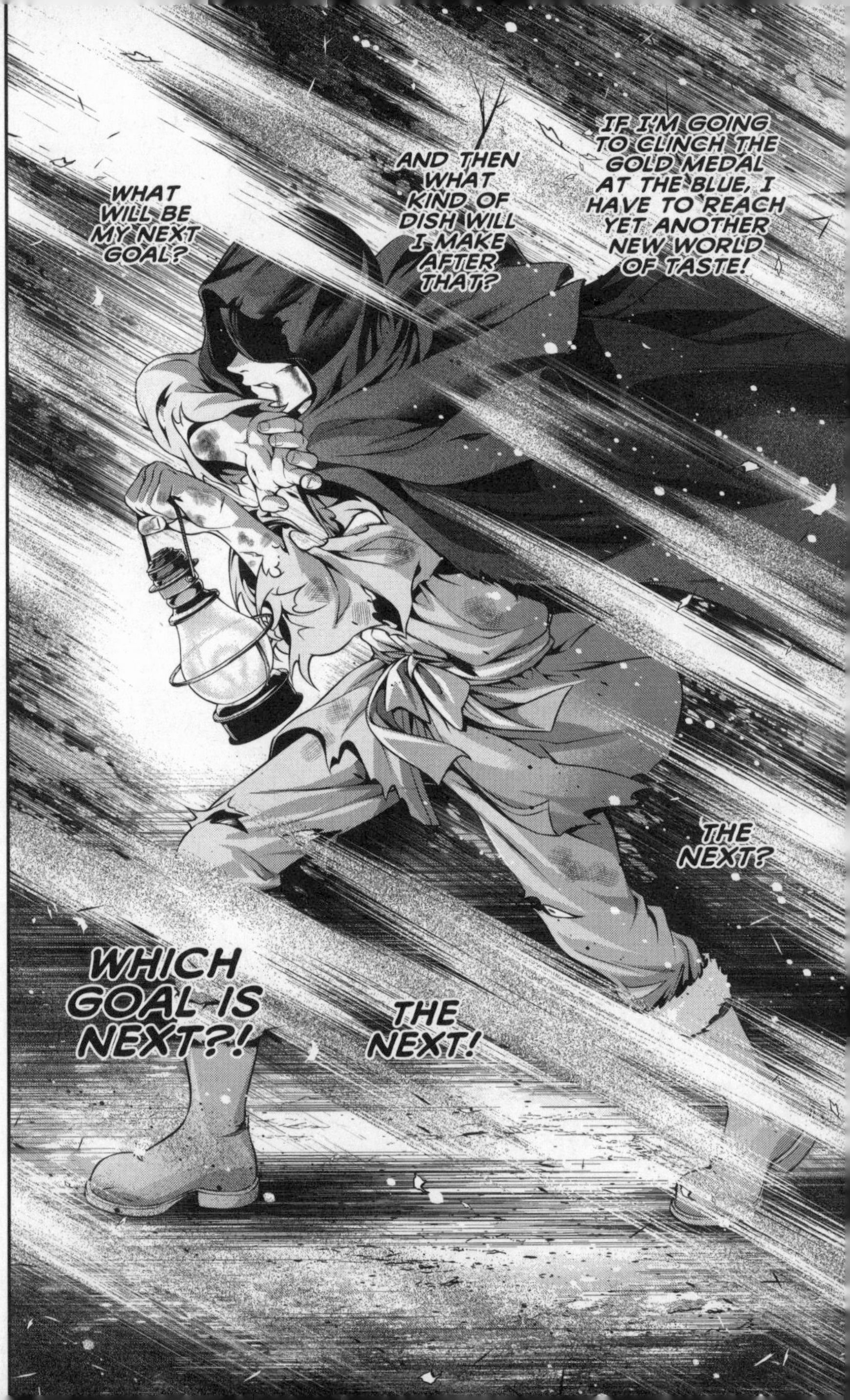
IF I'M GOING TO CLINCH THE GOLD MEDAL AT THE BLUE, I HAVE TO REACH YET ANOTHER NEW WORLD OF TASTE!
AND THEN WHAT KIND OF DISH WILL I MAKE AFTER THAT?
WHAT WILL BE MY NEXT GOAL?
THE NEXT?
THE NEXT!
WHICH GOAL IS NEXT?!

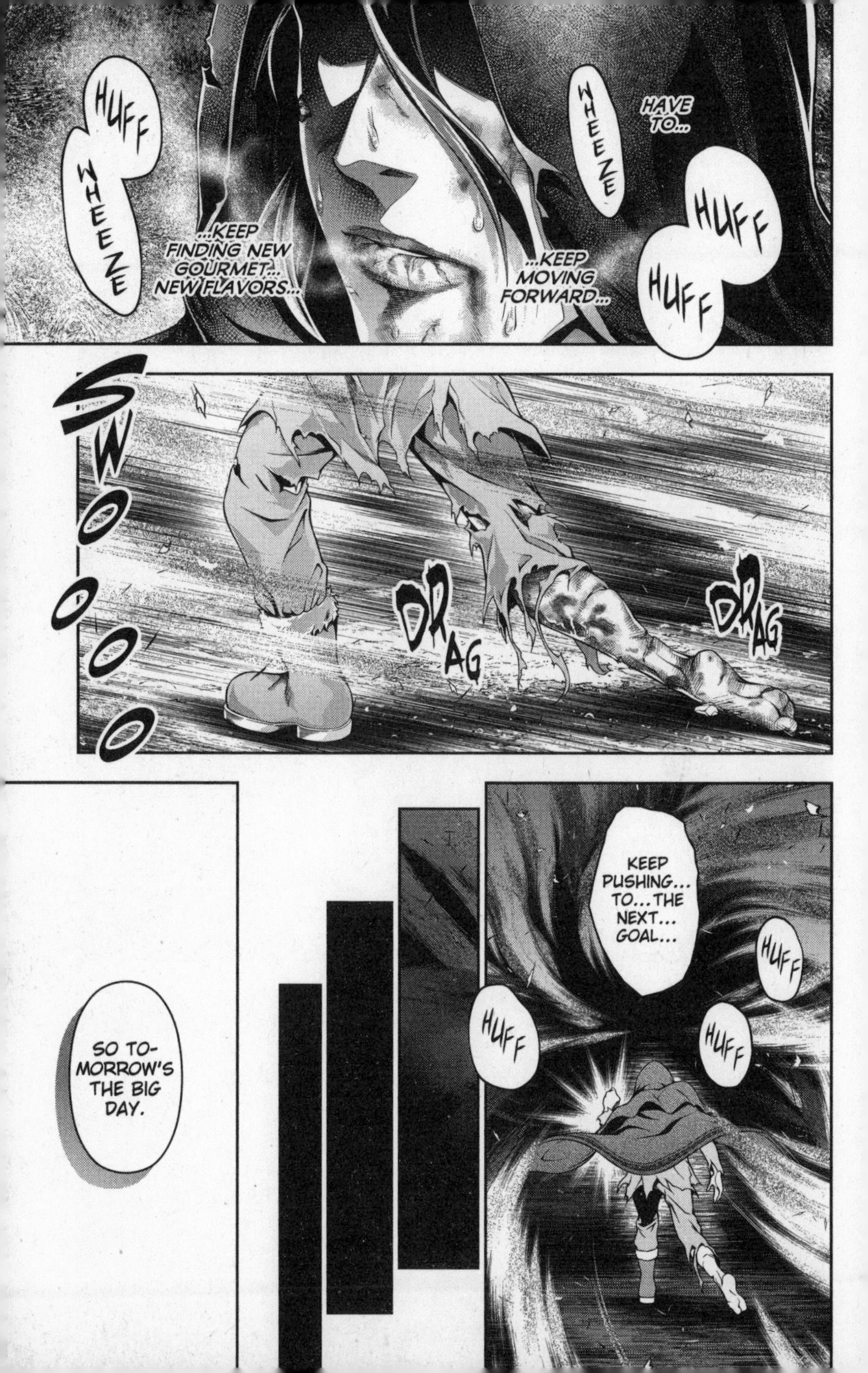
HAVE TO...
HUFF HUFF
WHEEZE
...KEEP MOVING FORWARD...
...KEEP FINDING NEW GOURMET... NEW FLAVORS...
HUFF WHEEZE
DRAG
DRAG
SWOOOOOOO
KEEP PUSHING... TO... THE NEXT... GOAL...
HUFF
HUFF
HUFF
SO TO-MORROW'S THE BIG DAY.

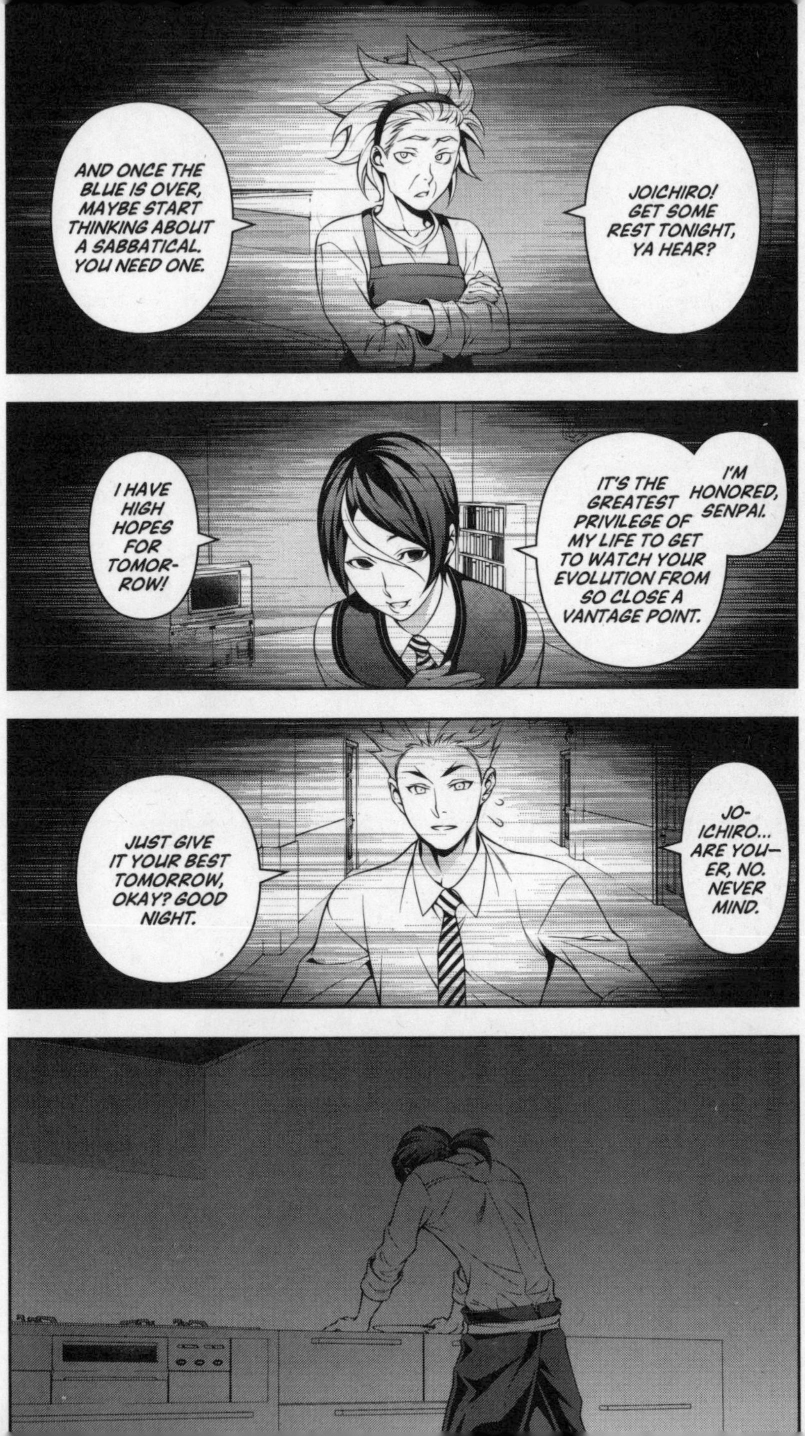
JOICHIRO! GET SOME REST TONIGHT, YA HEAR?
AND ONCE THE BLUE IS OVER, MAYBE START THINKING ABOUT A SABBATICAL. YOU NEED ONE.
I'M HONORED, SENPAI.
IT'S THE GREATEST PRIVILEGE OF MY LIFE TO GET TO WATCH YOUR EVOLUTION FROM SO CLOSE A VANTAGE POINT.
I HAVE HIGH HOPES FOR TOMORROW!
JO-ICHIRO... ARE YOU—ER, NO. NEVER MIND.
JUST GIVE IT YOUR BEST TOMORROW, OKAY? GOOD NIGHT.

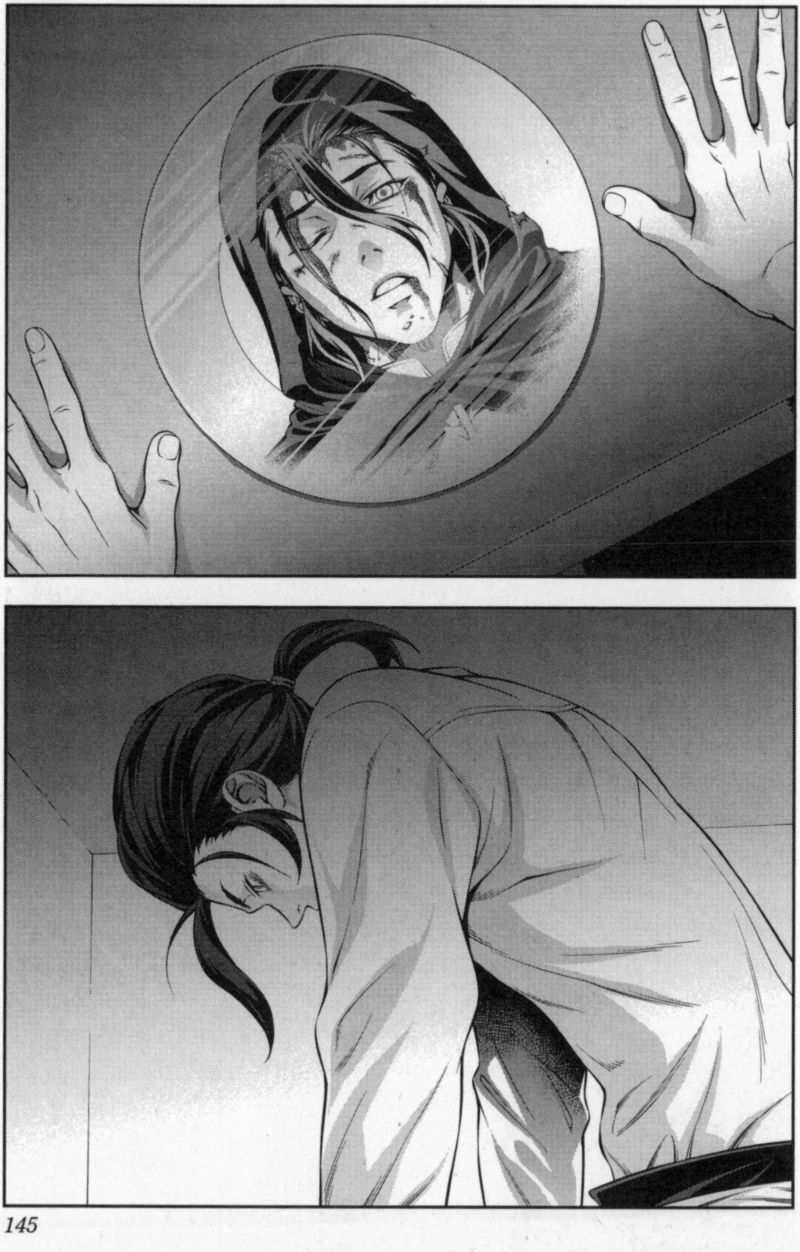

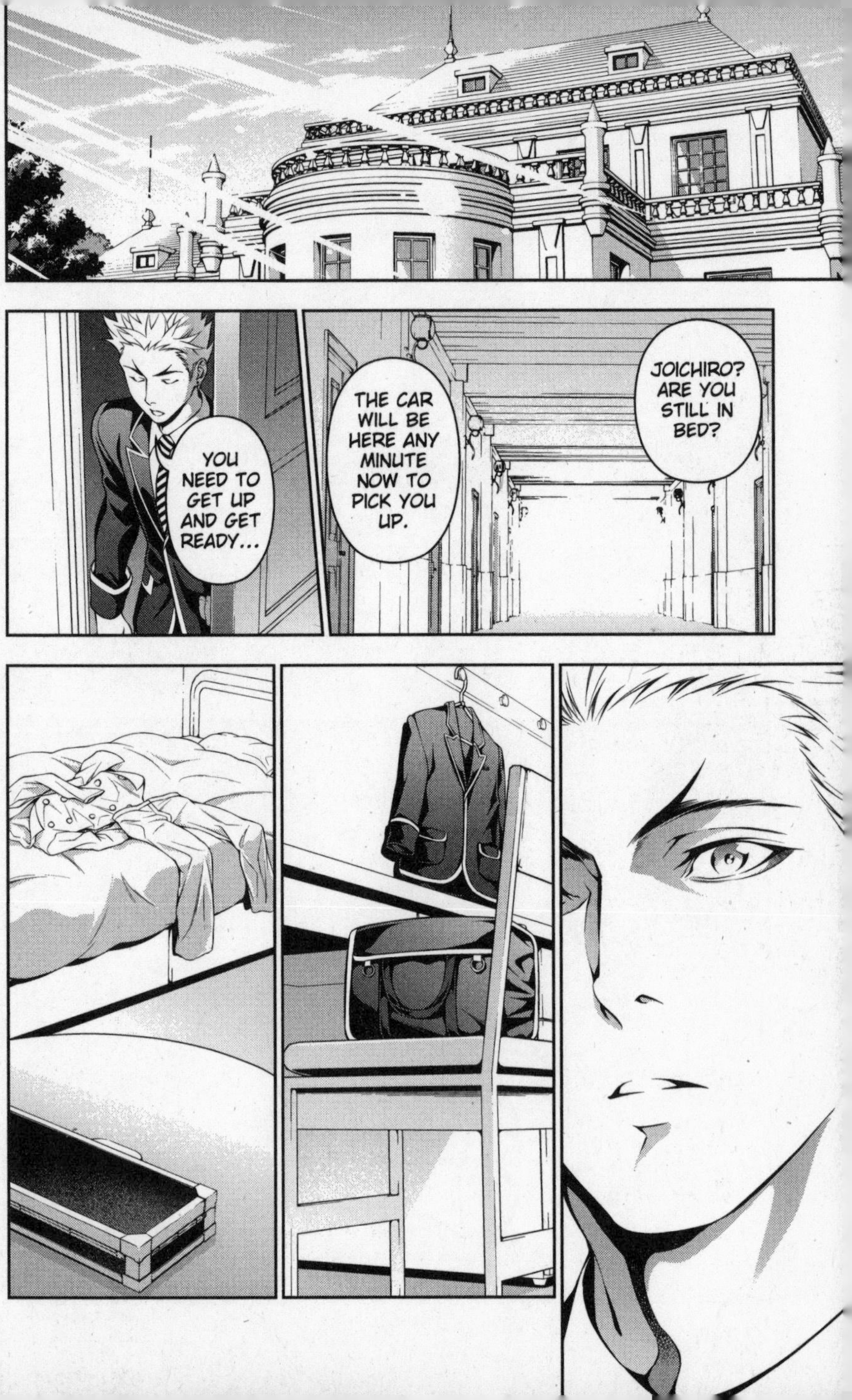
JOICHIRO? ARE YOU STILL IN BED?
THE CAR WILL BE HERE ANY MINUTE NOW TO PICK YOU UP.
YOU NEED TO GET UP AND GET READY...

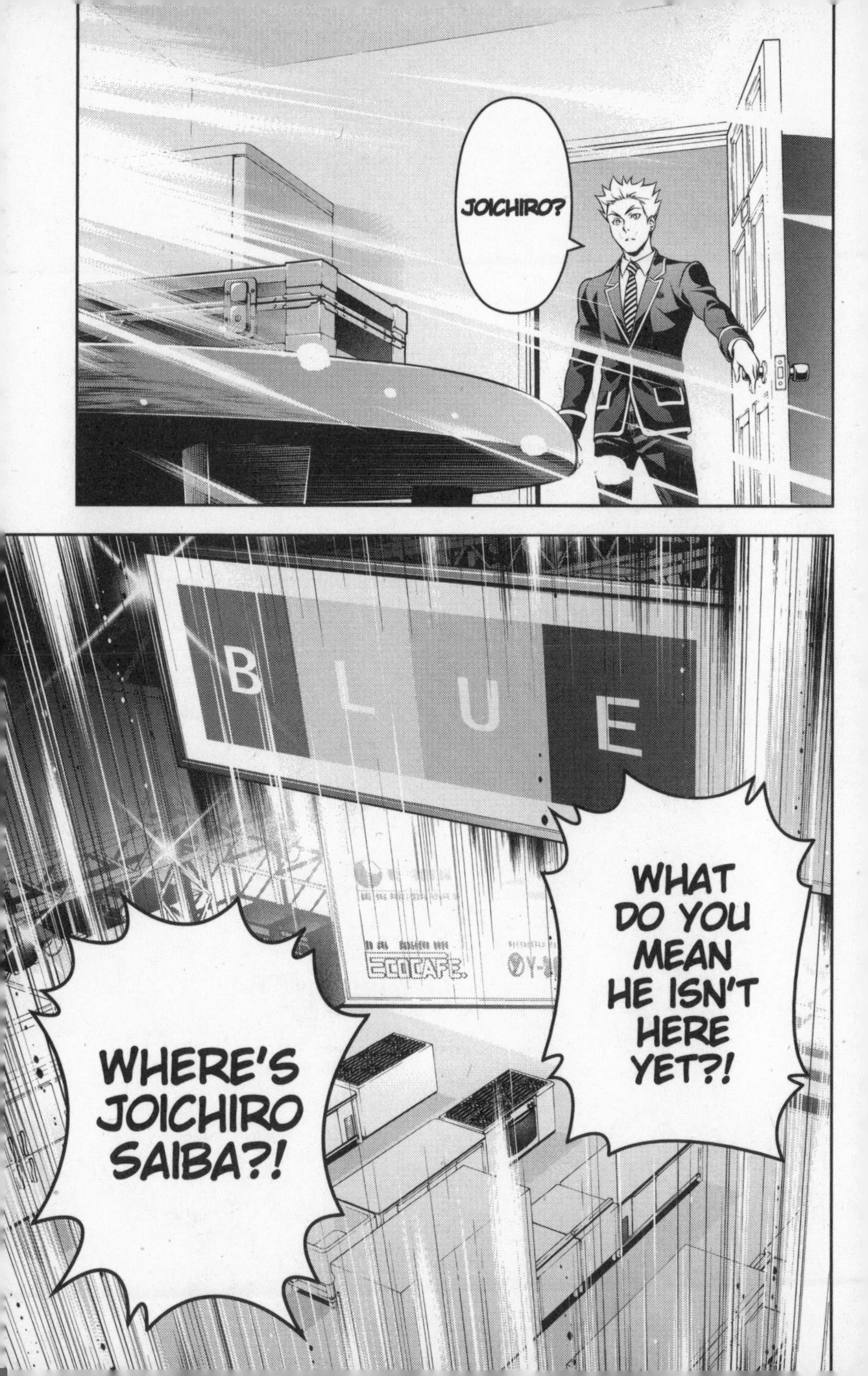
JOICHIRO?
BLUE
ECOCAFE.
WHAT DO YOU MEAN HE ISN'T HERE YET?!
WHERE'S JOICHIRO SAIBA?!

BEFORE
AFTER
SHIGENO
KURAKI
OSAJI
KITA
SHINGO
ANDO
KAKINOSHIN
OHIZUMI

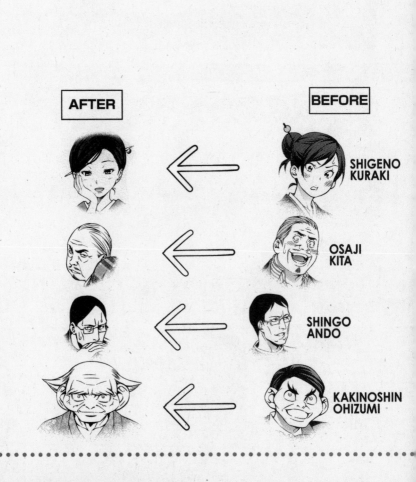

198 EXHAUSTION

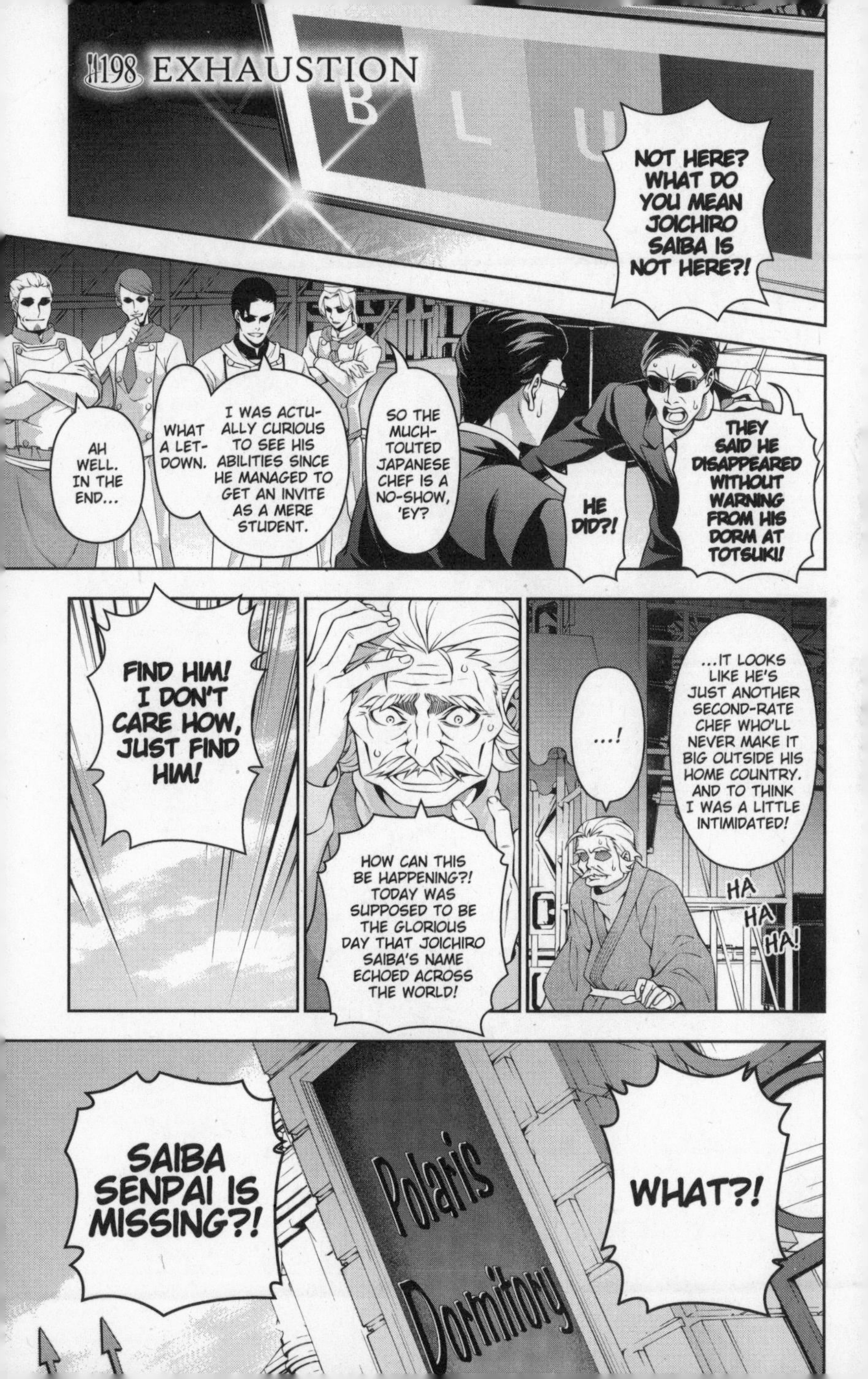
B L U
NOT HERE? WHAT DO YOU MEAN JOICHIRO SAIBA IS NOT HERE?!
THEY SAID HE DISAPPEARED WITHOUT WARNING FROM HIS DORM AT TOTSUKI!
HE DID?!
SO THE MUCH-TOUTED JAPANESE CHEF IS A NO-SHOW, 'EY?
I WAS ACTU-ALLY CURIOUS TO SEE HIS ABILITIES SINCE HE MANAGED TO GET AN INVITE AS A MERE STUDENT.
WHAT A LET-DOWN.
AH WELL. IN THE END...
...IT LOOKS LIKE HE'S JUST ANOTHER SECOND-RATE CHEF WHO'LL NEVER MAKE IT BIG OUTSIDE HIS HOME COUNTRY. AND TO THINK I WAS A LITTLE INTIMIDATED!
...!
HA HA HA!
HOW CAN THIS BE HAPPENING?! TODAY WAS SUPPOSED TO BE THE GLORIOUS DAY THAT JOICHIRO SAIBA'S NAME ECHOED ACROSS THE WORLD!
FIND HIM! I DON'T CARE HOW, JUST FIND HIM!
WHAT?!
Polaris Dormitory
SAIBA SENPAI IS MISSING?!

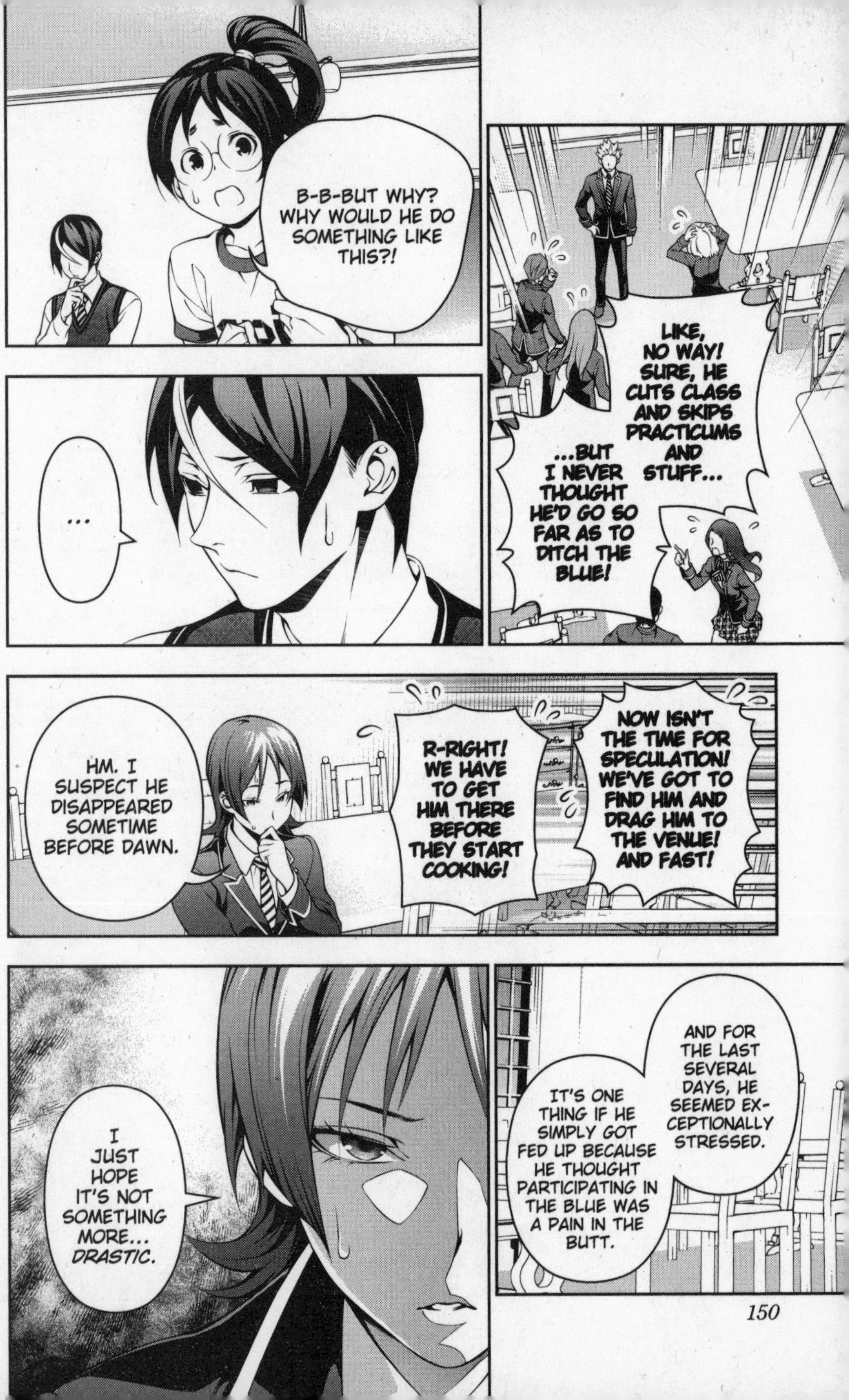
LIKE, NO WAY! SURE, HE CUTS CLASS AND SKIPS PRACTICUMS AND STUFF...
...BUT I NEVER THOUGHT HE'D GO SO FAR AS TO DITCH THE BLUE!
B-B-BUT WHY? WHY WOULD HE DO SOMETHING LIKE THIS?!
...
NOW ISN'T THE TIME FOR SPECULATION! WE'VE GOT TO FIND HIM AND DRAG HIM TO THE VENUE! AND FAST!
R-RIGHT! WE HAVE TO GET HIM THERE BEFORE THEY START COOKING!
HM. I SUSPECT HE DISAPPEARED SOMETIME BEFORE DAWN.
AND FOR THE LAST SEVERAL DAYS, HE SEEMED EX-CEPTIONALLY STRESSED.
IT'S ONE THING IF HE SIMPLY GOT FED UP BECAUSE HE THOUGHT PARTICIPATING IN THE BLUE WAS A PAIN IN THE BUTT.
I JUST HOPE IT'S NOT SOMETHING MORE... *DRASTIC*.

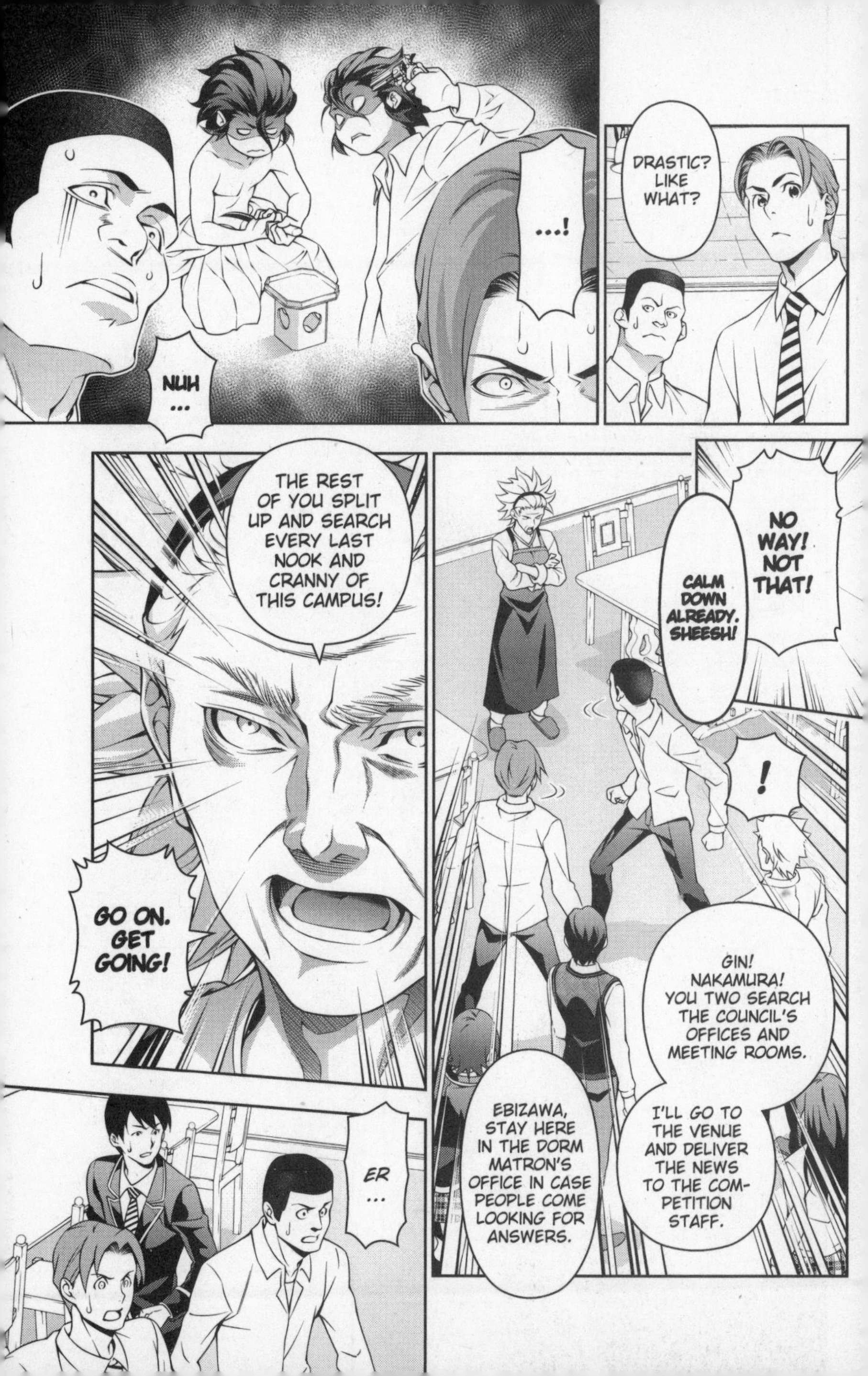
DRASTIC? LIKE WHAT?
...!
NUH ...
NO WAY! NOT THAT!
CALM DOWN ALREADY. SHEESH!
!
GIN! NAKAMURA! YOU TWO SEARCH THE COUNCIL'S OFFICES AND MEETING ROOMS.
I'LL GO TO THE VENUE AND DELIVER THE NEWS TO THE COM-PETITION STAFF.
EBIZAWA, STAY HERE IN THE DORM MATRON'S OFFICE IN CASE PEOPLE COME LOOKING FOR ANSWERS.
THE REST OF YOU SPLIT UP AND SEARCH EVERY LAST NOOK AND CRANNY OF THIS CAMPUS!
GO ON. GET GOING!
ER ...

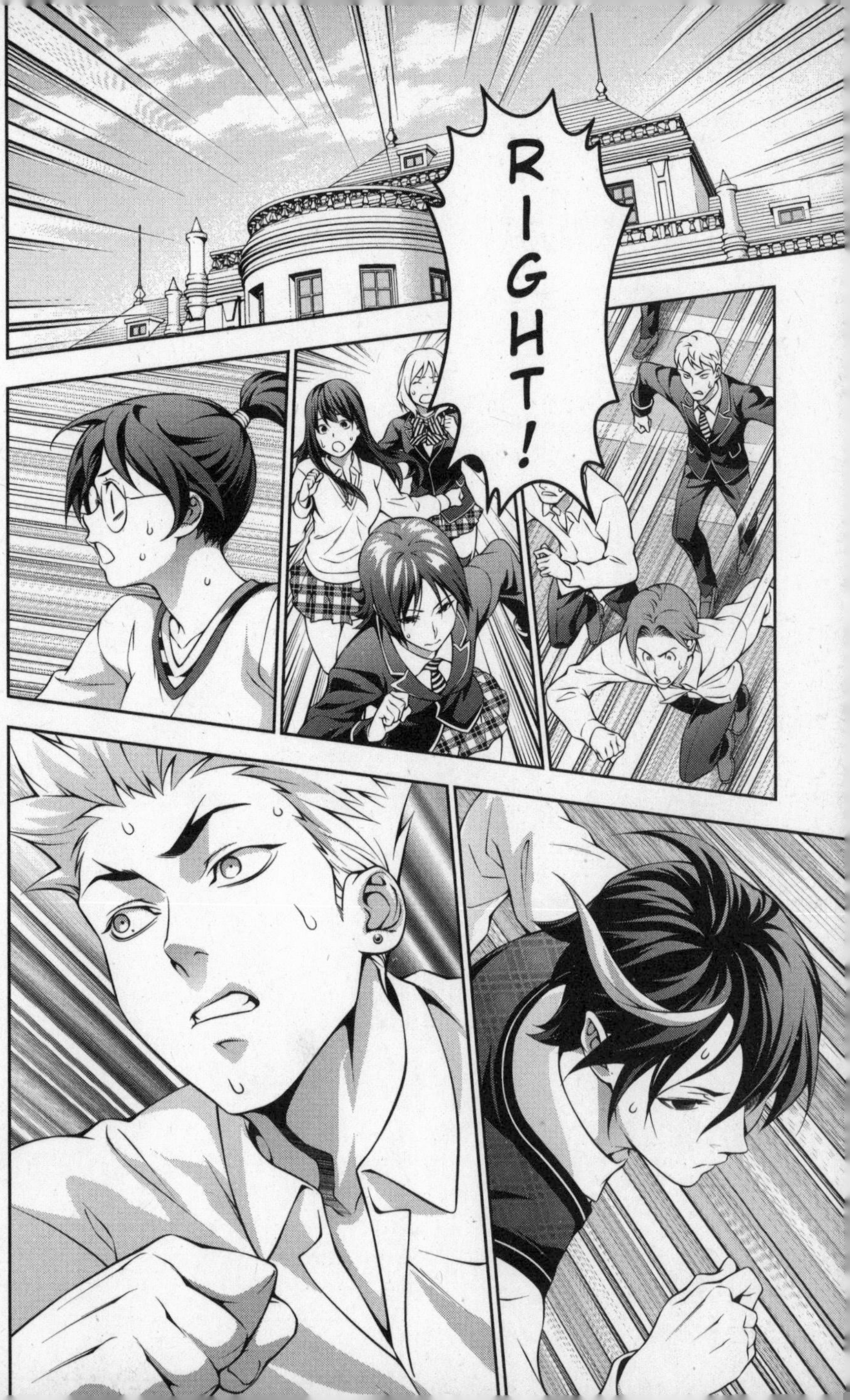
RIGHT!

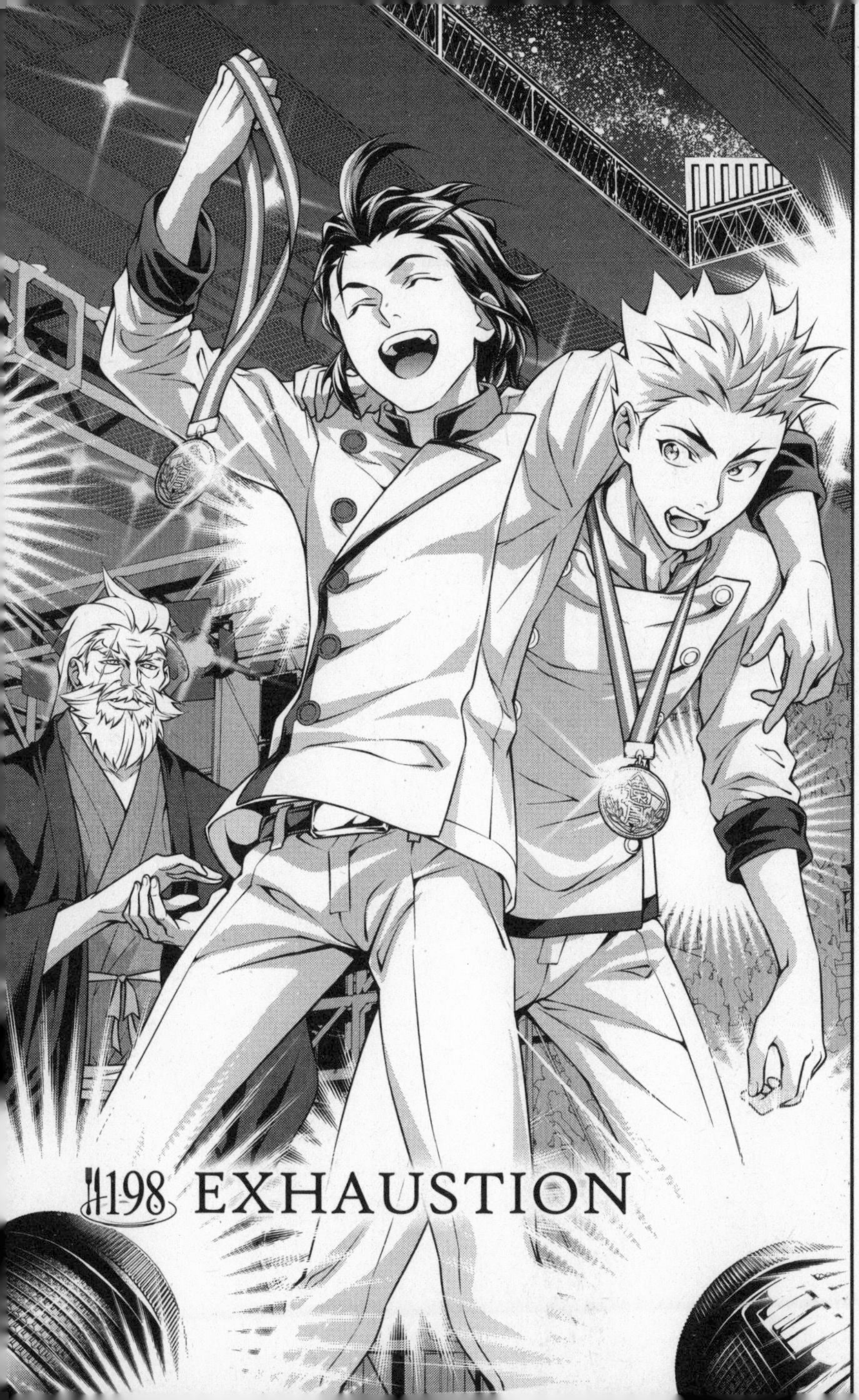
198 EXHAUSTION

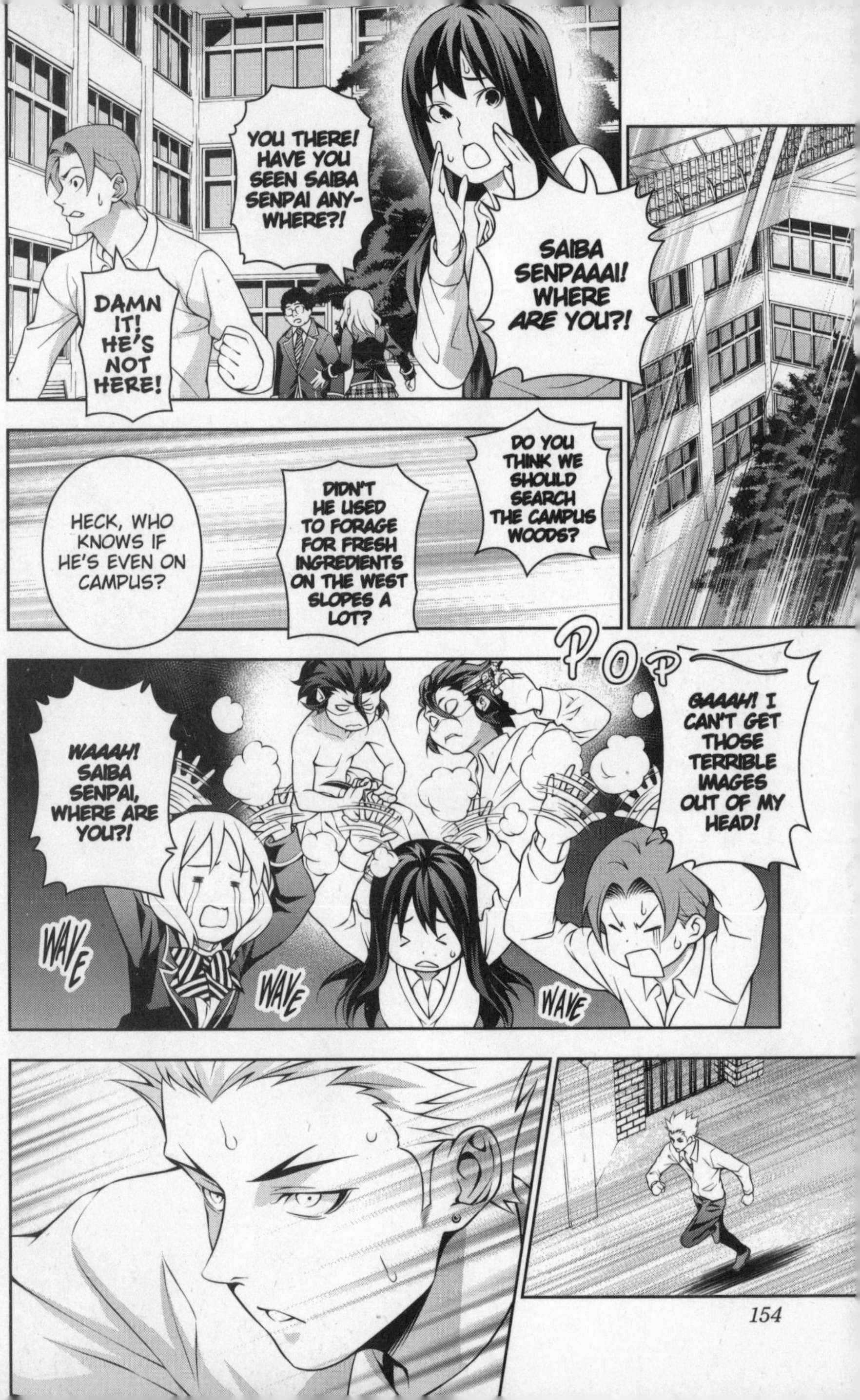
SAIBA SENPAAAI! WHERE ARE YOU?!
YOU THERE! HAVE YOU SEEN SAIBA SENPAI ANY-WHERE?!
DAMN IT! HE'S NOT HERE!
DO YOU THINK WE SHOULD SEARCH THE CAMPUS WOODS?
DIDN'T HE USED TO FORAGE FOR FRESH INGREDIENTS ON THE WEST SLOPES A LOT?
HECK, WHO KNOWS IF HE'S EVEN ON CAMPUS?
POP
GAAAH! I CAN'T GET THOSE TERRIBLE IMAGES OUT OF MY HEAD!
WAAAH! SAIBA SENPAI, WHERE ARE YOU?!
WAVE
WAVE
WAVE

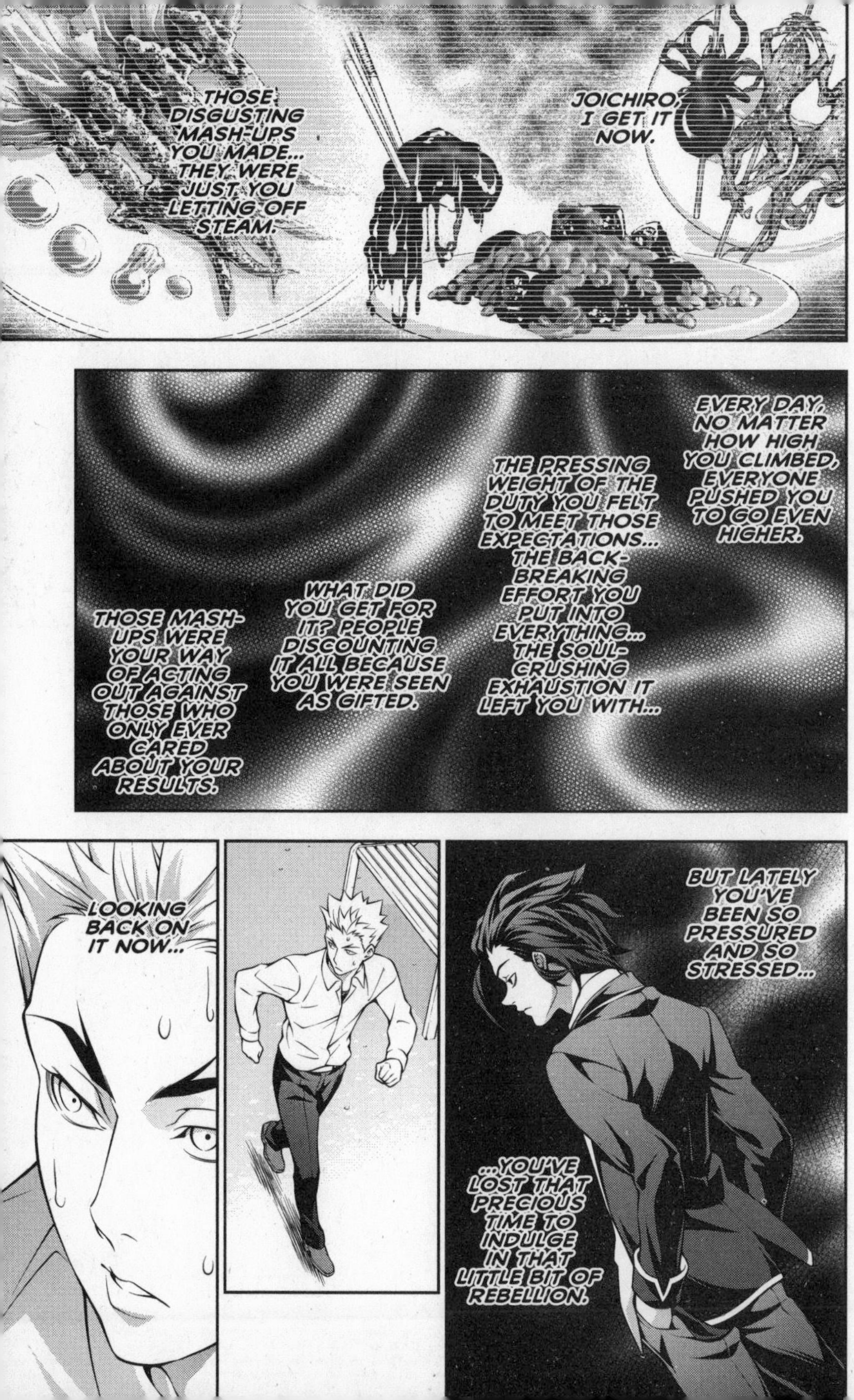
JOICHIRO, I GET IT NOW.
THOSE DISGUSTING MASH-UPS YOU MADE... THEY WERE JUST YOU LETTING OFF STEAM.
EVERY DAY, NO MATTER HOW HIGH YOU CLIMBED, EVERYONE PUSHED YOU TO GO EVEN HIGHER.
THE PRESSING WEIGHT OF THE DUTY YOU FELT TO MEET THOSE EXPECTATIONS... THE BACK-BREAKING EFFORT YOU PUT INTO EVERYTHING... THE SOUL-CRUSHING EXHAUSTION IT LEFT YOU WITH...
WHAT DID YOU GET FOR IT? PEOPLE DISCOUNTING IT ALL BECAUSE YOU WERE SEEN AS GIFTED.
THOSE MASH-UPS WERE YOUR WAY OF ACTING OUT AGAINST THOSE WHO ONLY EVER CARED ABOUT YOUR RESULTS.
BUT LATELY YOU'VE BEEN SO PRESSURED AND SO STRESSED...
...YOU'VE LOST THAT PRECIOUS TIME TO INDULGE IN THAT LITTLE BIT OF REBELLION.
LOOKING BACK ON IT NOW...

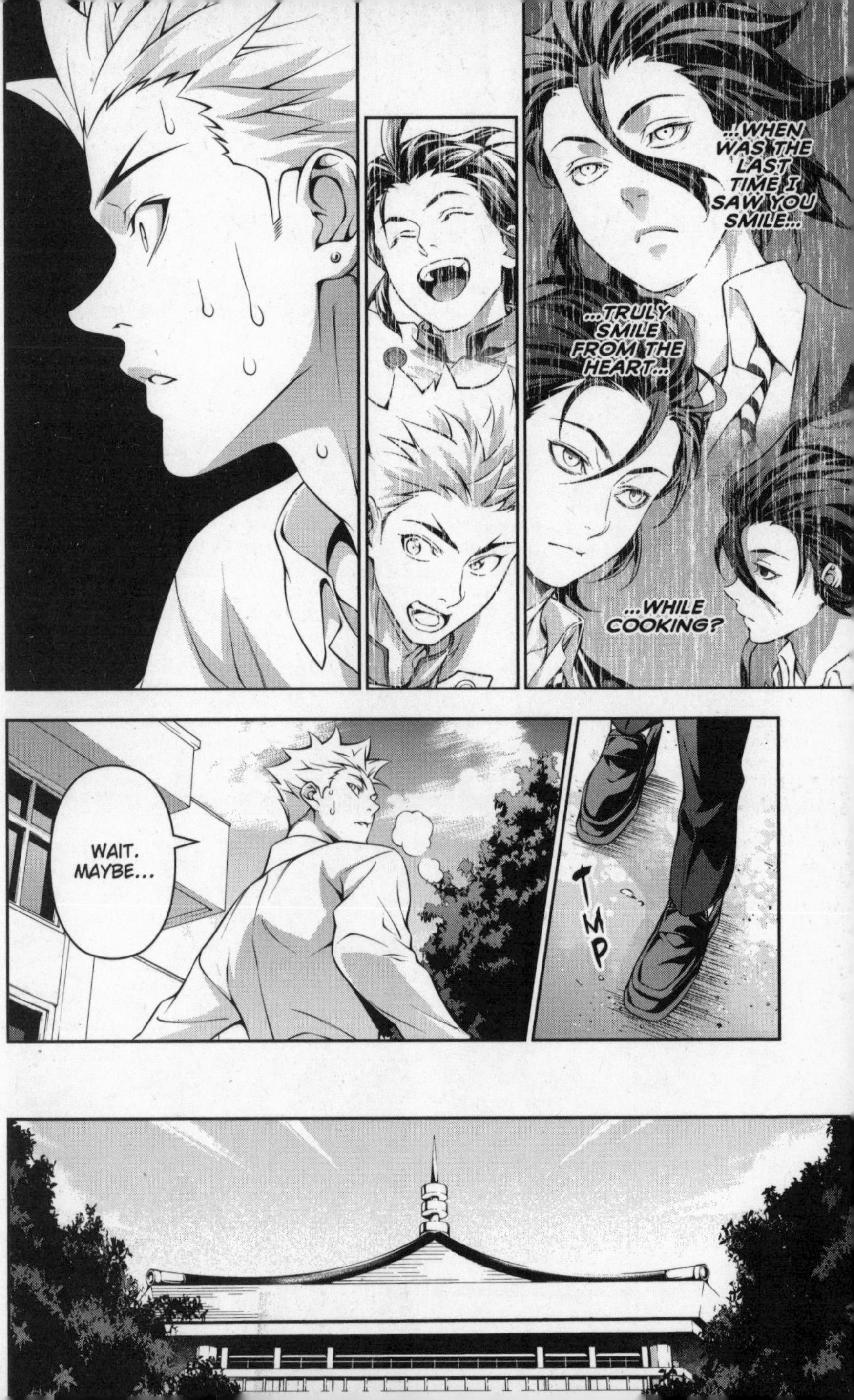
...WHEN WAS THE LAST TIME I SAW YOU SMILE...
...TRULY SMILE FROM THE HEART...
...WHILE COOKING?
TMP
WAIT. MAYBE...

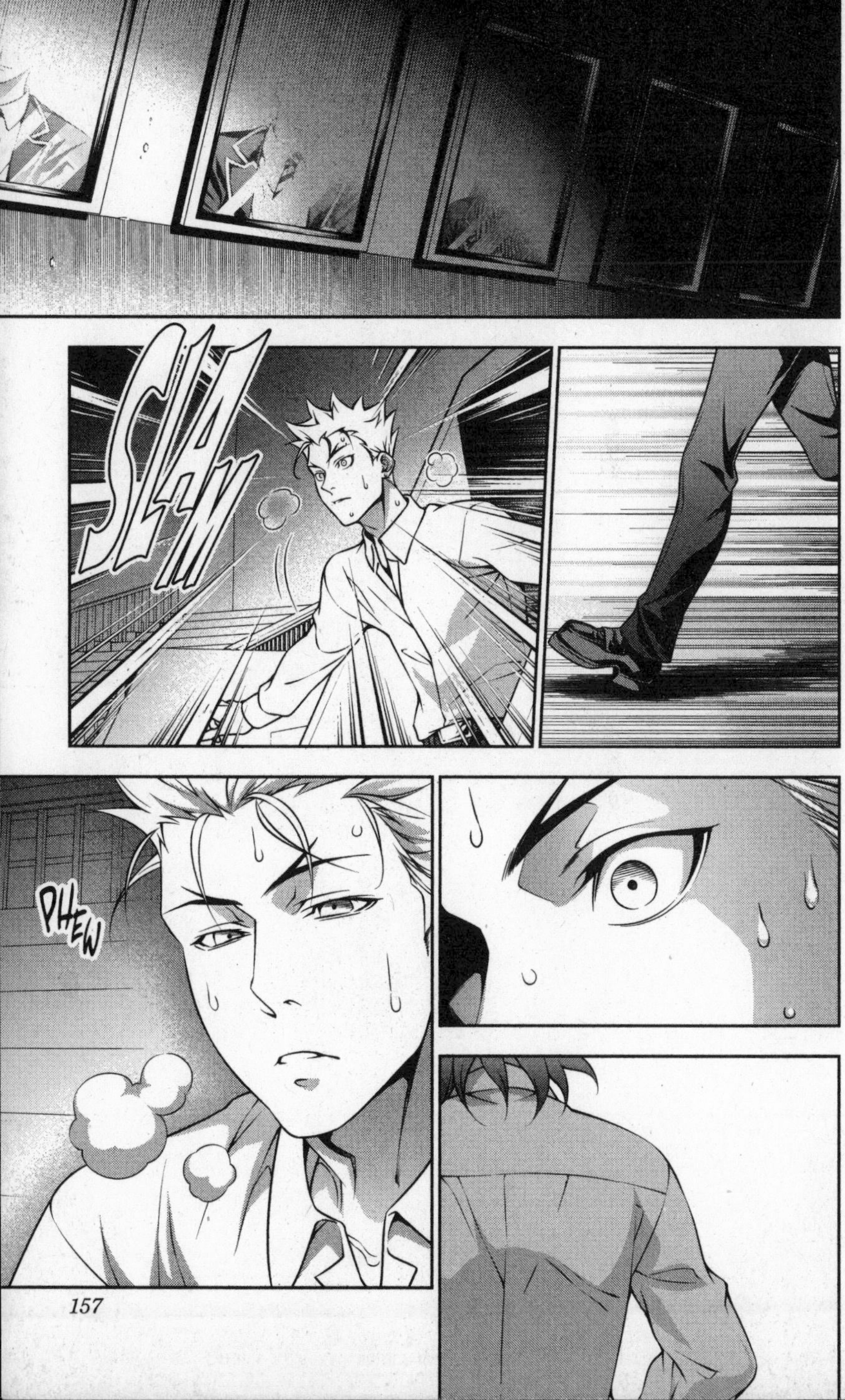
SLAM
PHEW

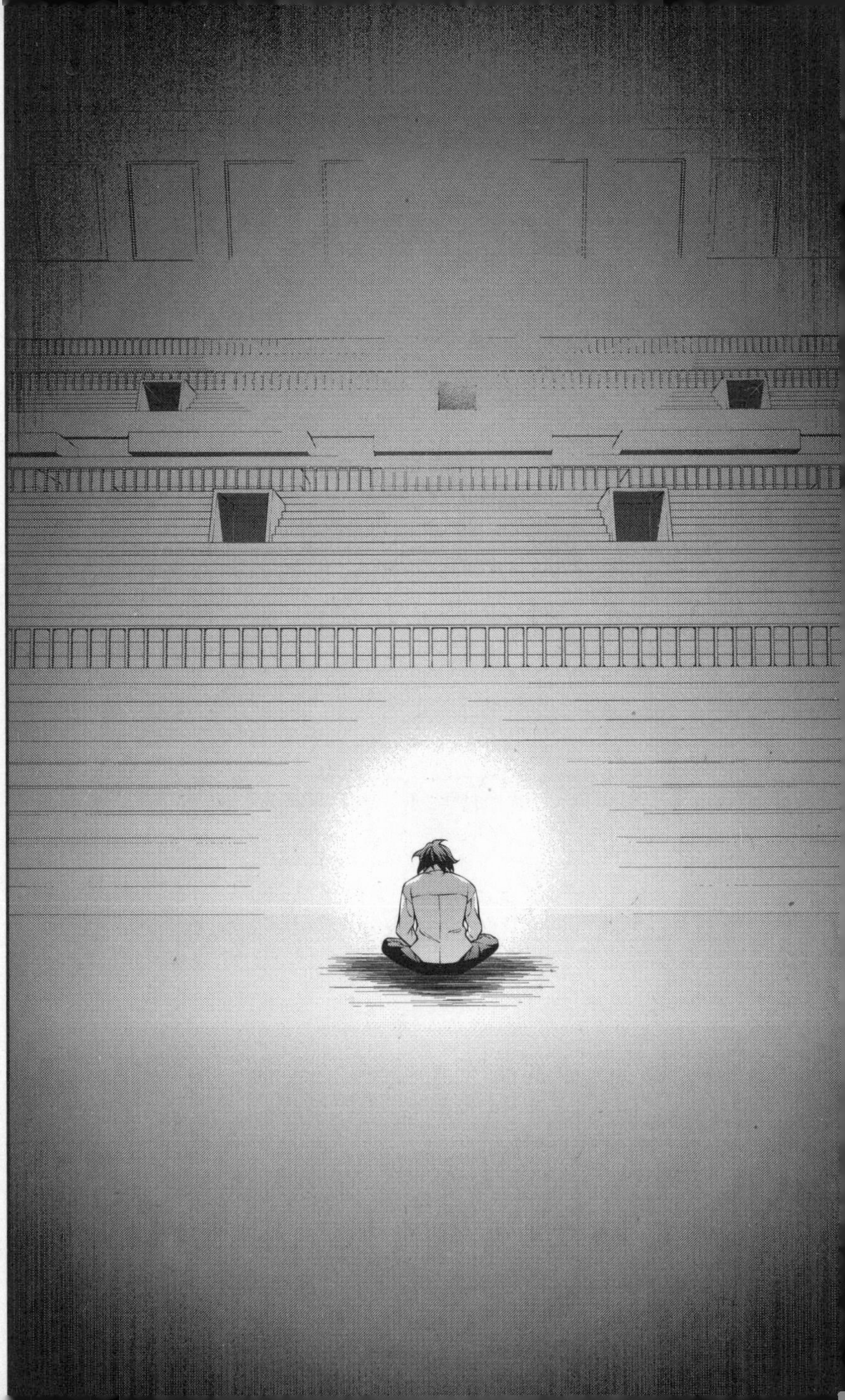

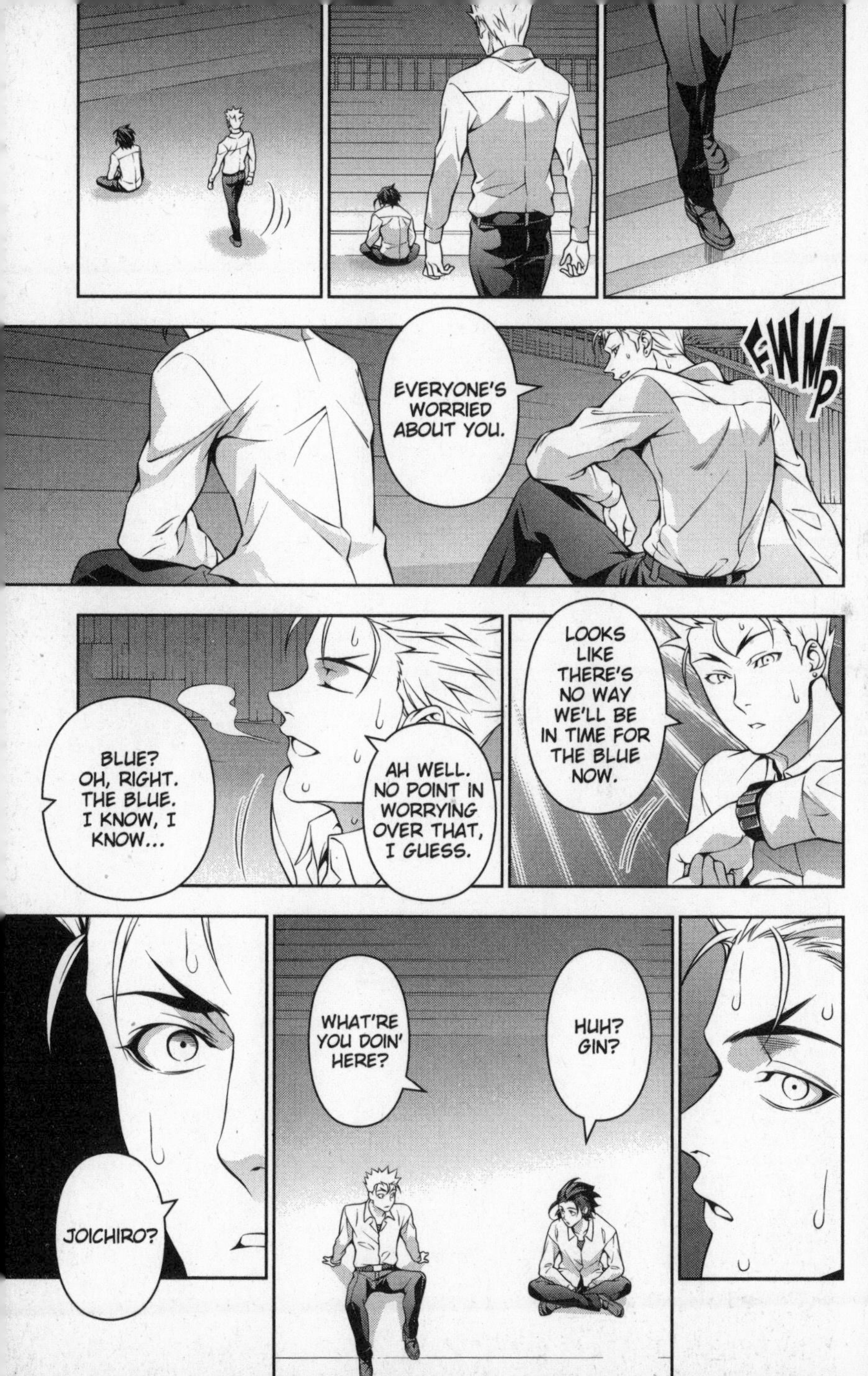
FWMP
EVERYONE'S WORRIED ABOUT YOU.
LOOKS LIKE THERE'S NO WAY WE'LL BE IN TIME FOR THE BLUE NOW.
BLUE? OH, RIGHT. THE BLUE. I KNOW, I KNOW...
AH WELL. NO POINT IN WORRYING OVER THAT, I GUESS.
HUH? GIN?
WHAT'RE YOU DOIN' HERE?
JOICHIRO?

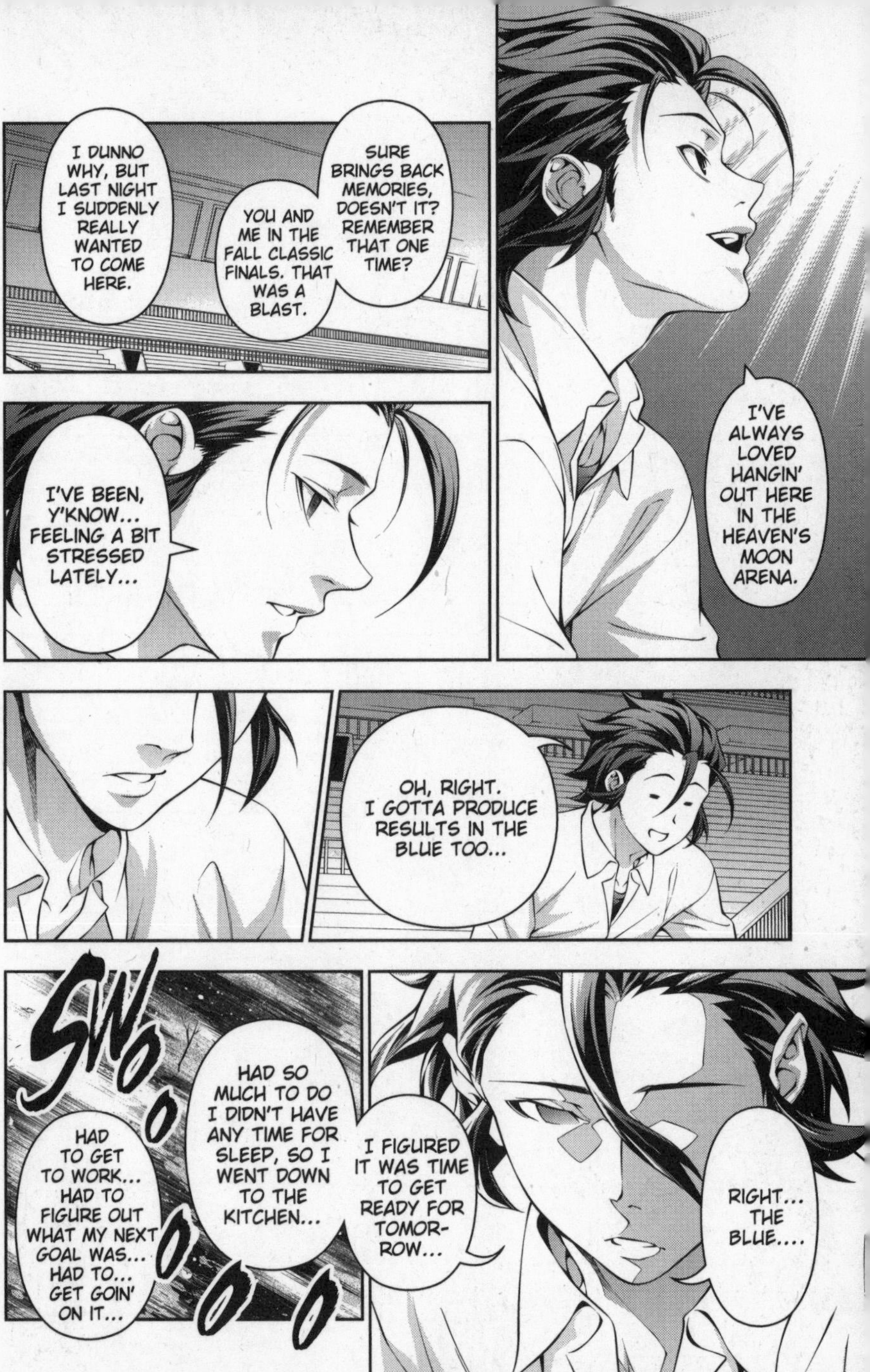
I'VE ALWAYS LOVED HANGIN' OUT HERE IN THE HEAVEN'S MOON ARENA.
SURE BRINGS BACK MEMORIES, DOESN'T IT? REMEMBER THAT ONE TIME?
YOU AND ME IN THE FALL CLASSIC FINALS. THAT WAS A BLAST.
I DUNNO WHY, BUT LAST NIGHT I SUDDENLY REALLY WANTED TO COME HERE.
I'VE BEEN, Y'KNOW... FEELING A BIT STRESSED LATELY...
OH, RIGHT. I GOTTA PRODUCE RESULTS IN THE BLUE TOO...
RIGHT... THE BLUE....
I FIGURED IT WAS TIME TO GET READY FOR TOMOR-ROW...
HAD SO MUCH TO DO I DIDN'T HAVE ANY TIME FOR SLEEP, SO I WENT DOWN TO THE KITCHEN...
HAD TO GET TO WORK... HAD TO FIGURE OUT WHAT MY NEXT GOAL WAS... HAD TO... GET GOIN' ON IT...
SWOOOOOO

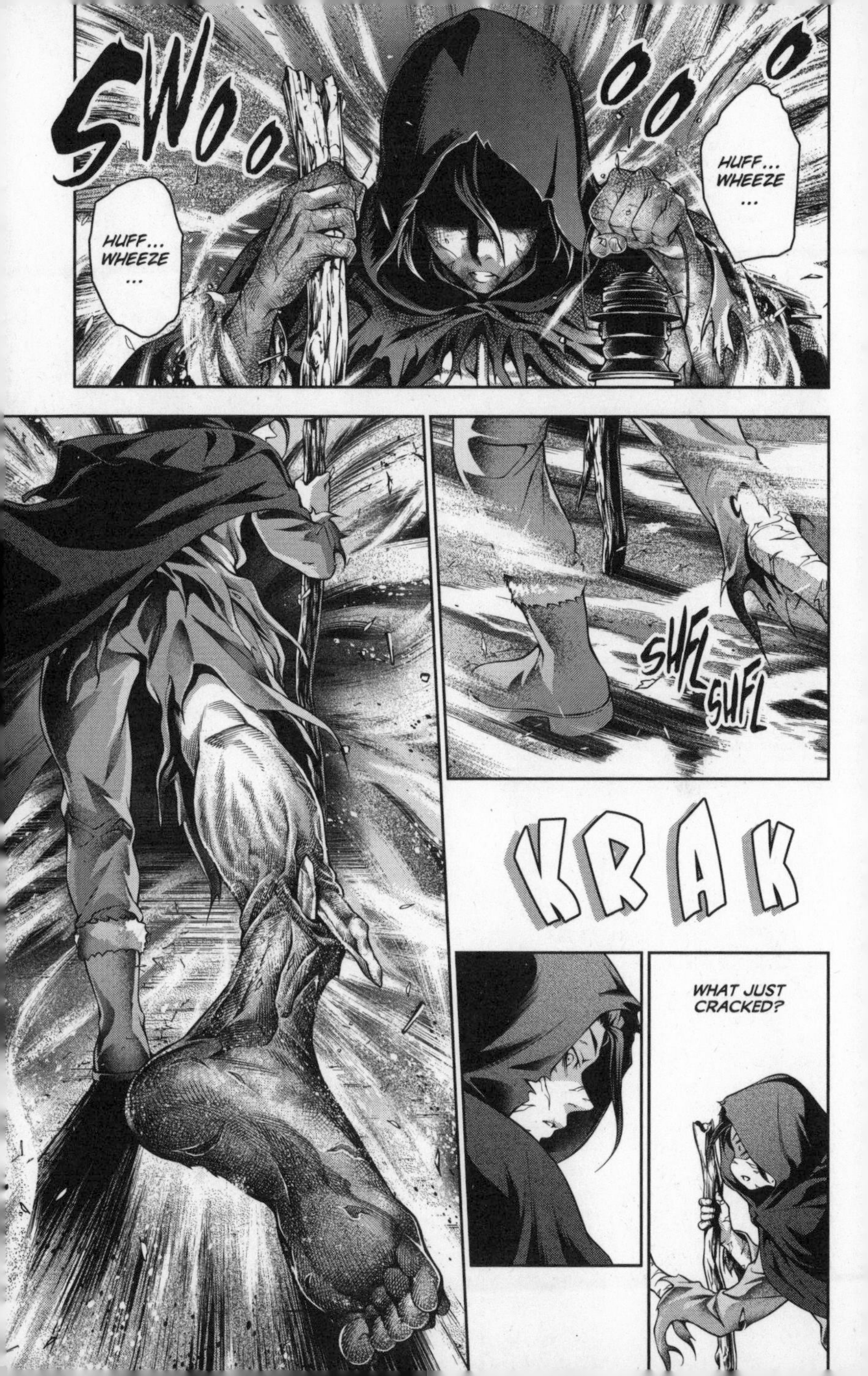
SWOOOOOO
HUFF... WHEEZE ...
HUFF... WHEEZE ...
SHFL SHFL
KRAK
WHAT JUST CRACKED?

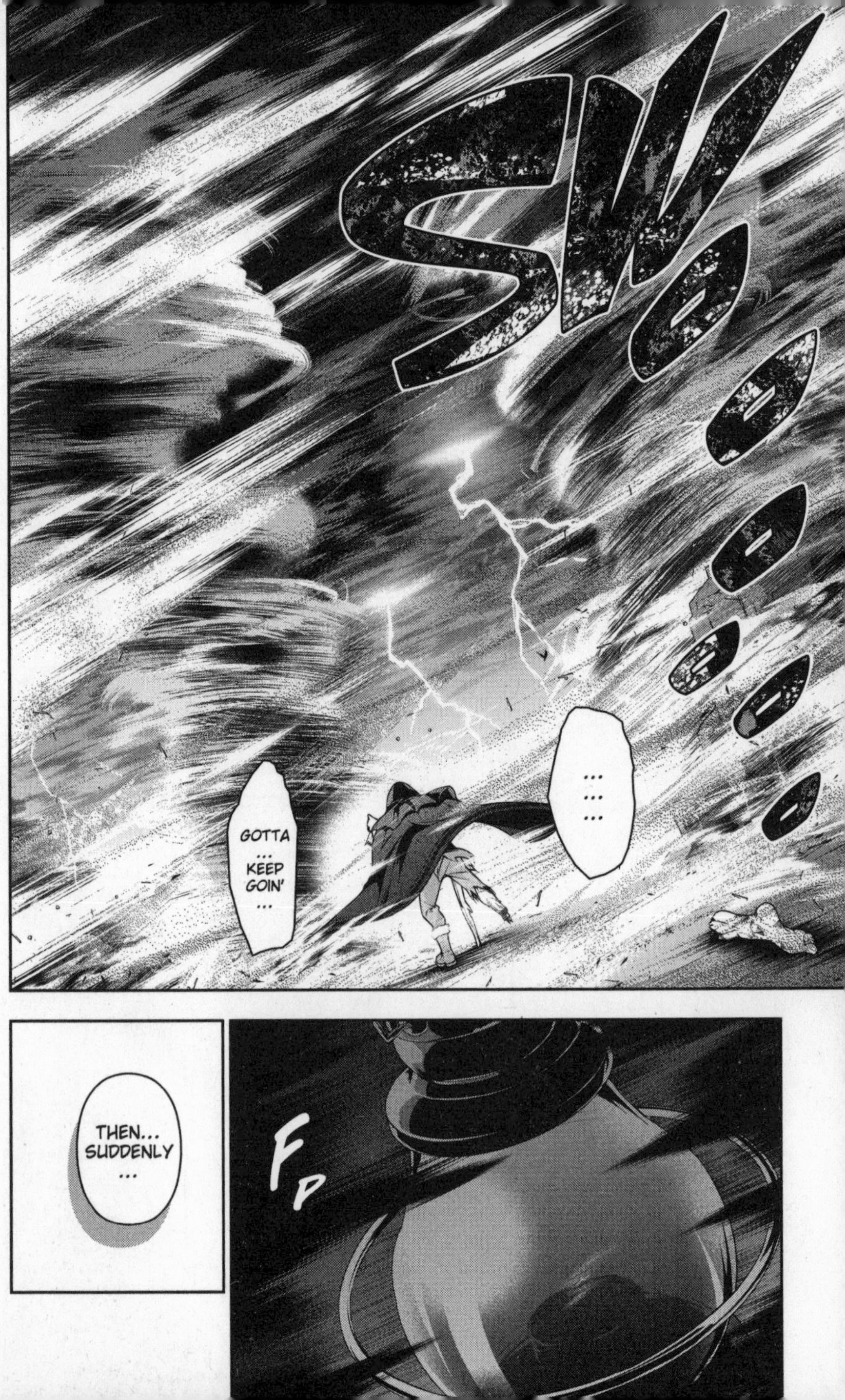
SHOOOOOO
...
...
...
GOTTA ... KEEP GOIN' ...
Fp
THEN... SUDDENLY ...

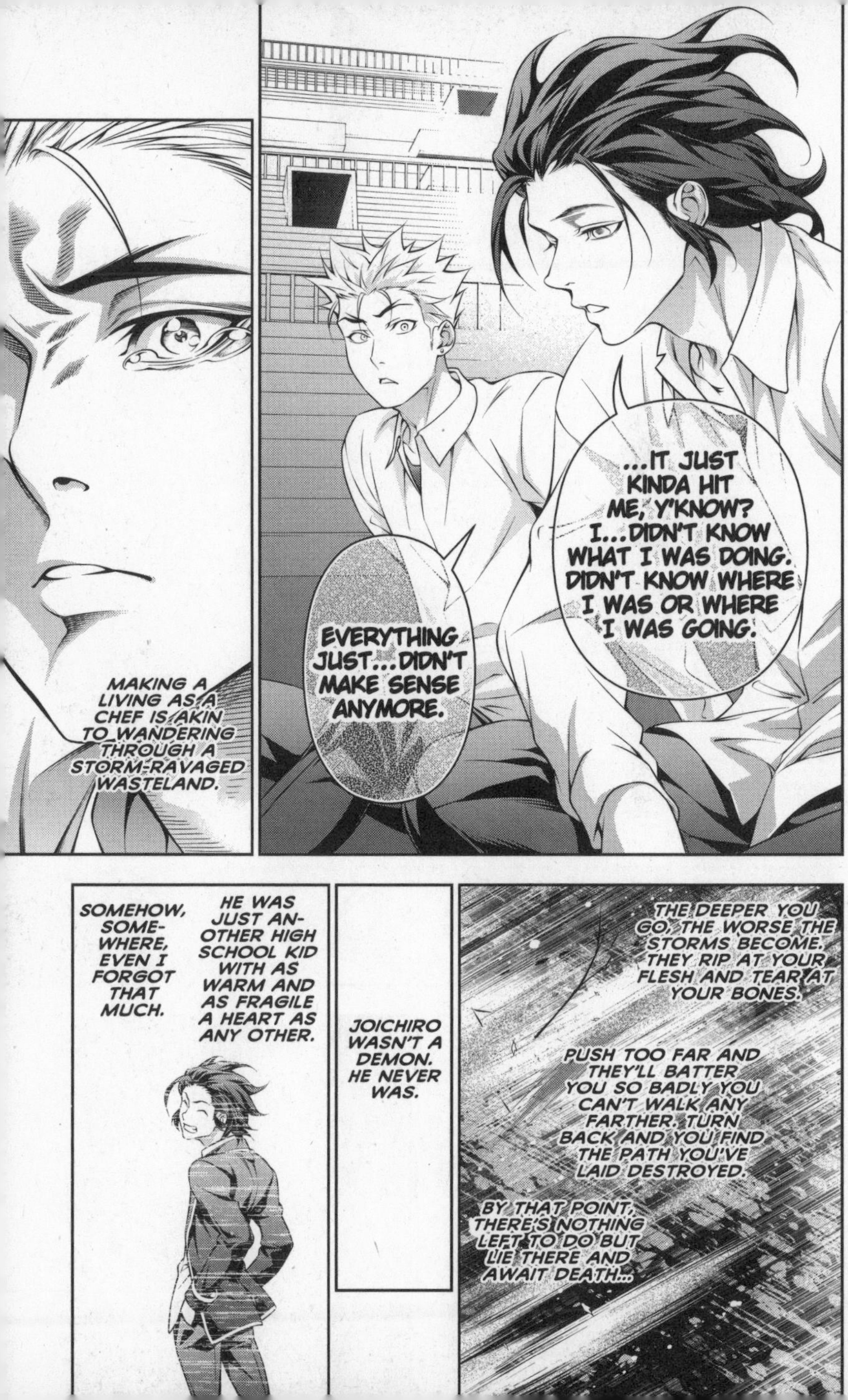
...IT JUST KINDA HIT ME, Y'KNOW? I...DIDN'T KNOW WHAT I WAS DOING. DIDN'T KNOW WHERE I WAS OR WHERE I WAS GOING.
EVERYTHING JUST...DIDN'T MAKE SENSE ANYMORE.
MAKING A LIVING AS A CHEF IS AKIN TO WANDERING THROUGH A STORM-RAVAGED WASTELAND.
THE DEEPER YOU GO, THE WORSE THE STORMS BECOME. THEY RIP AT YOUR FLESH AND TEAR AT YOUR BONES.
PUSH TOO FAR AND THEY'LL BATTER YOU SO BADLY YOU CAN'T WALK ANY FARTHER. TURN BACK AND YOU FIND THE PATH YOU'VE LAID DESTROYED.
BY THAT POINT, THERE'S NOTHING LEFT TO DO BUT LIE THERE AND AWAIT DEATH...
JOICHIRO WASN'T A DEMON. HE NEVER WAS.
HE WAS JUST AN-OTHER HIGH SCHOOL KID WITH AS WARM AND AS FRAGILE A HEART AS ANY OTHER.
SOMEHOW, SOME-WHERE, EVEN I FORGOT THAT MUCH.

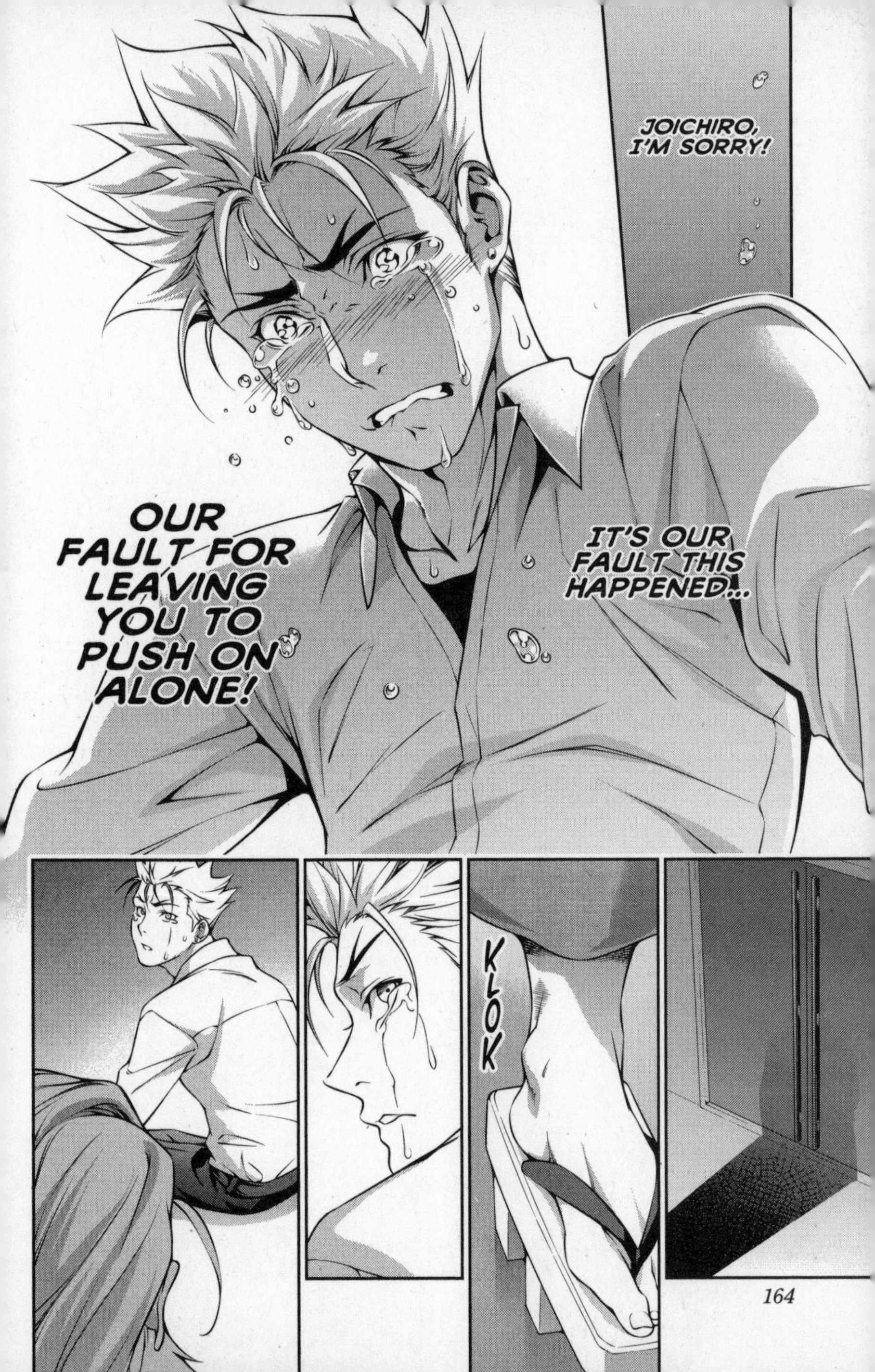
JOICHIRO, I'M SORRY!
IT'S OUR FAULT THIS HAPPENED...
OUR FAULT FOR LEAVING YOU TO PUSH ON ALONE!
KLOK

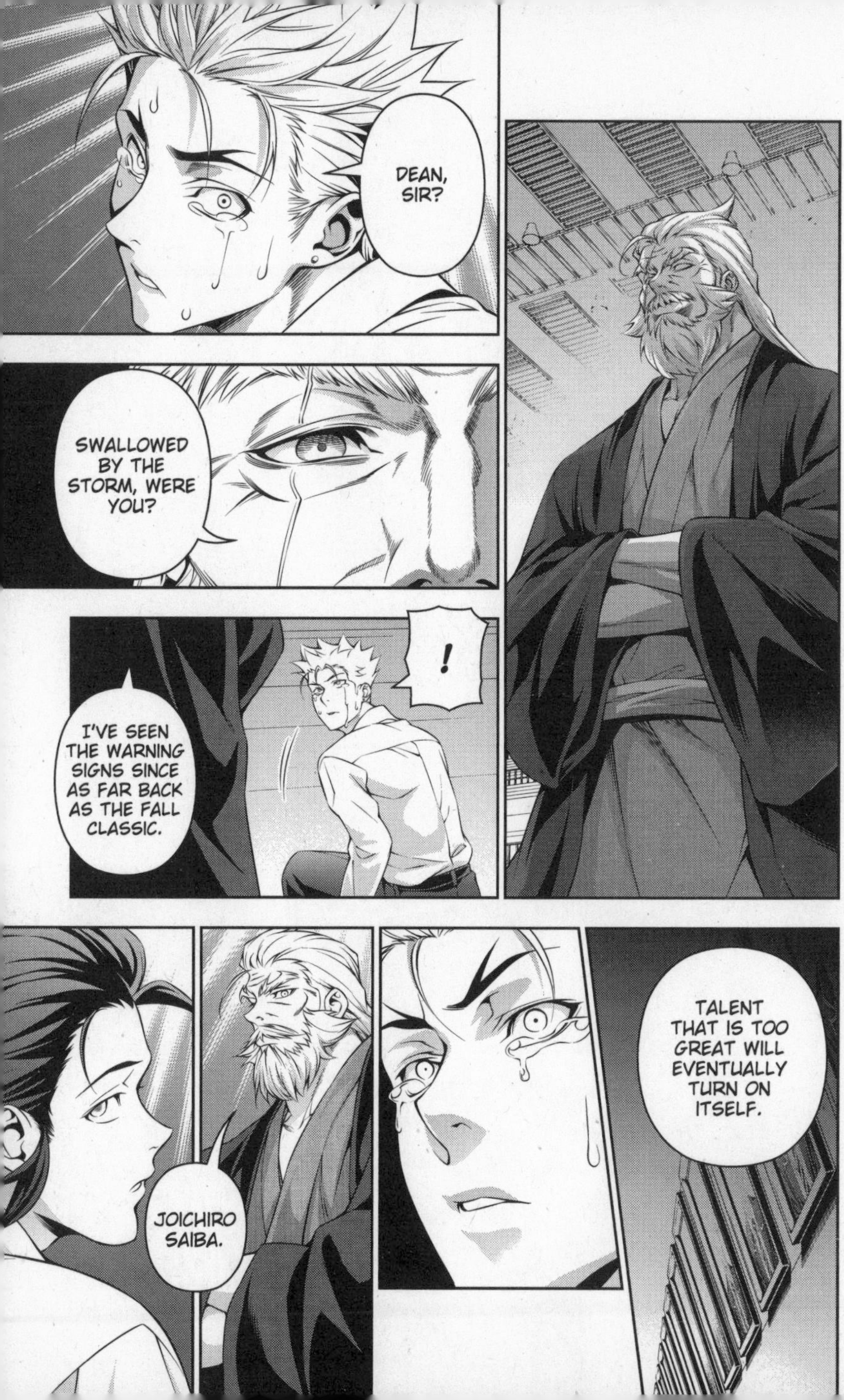
DEAN, SIR?
SWALLOWED BY THE STORM, WERE YOU?
!
I'VE SEEN THE WARNING SIGNS SINCE AS FAR BACK AS THE FALL CLASSIC.
TALENT THAT IS TOO GREAT WILL EVENTUALLY TURN ON ITSELF.
JOICHIRO SAIBA.

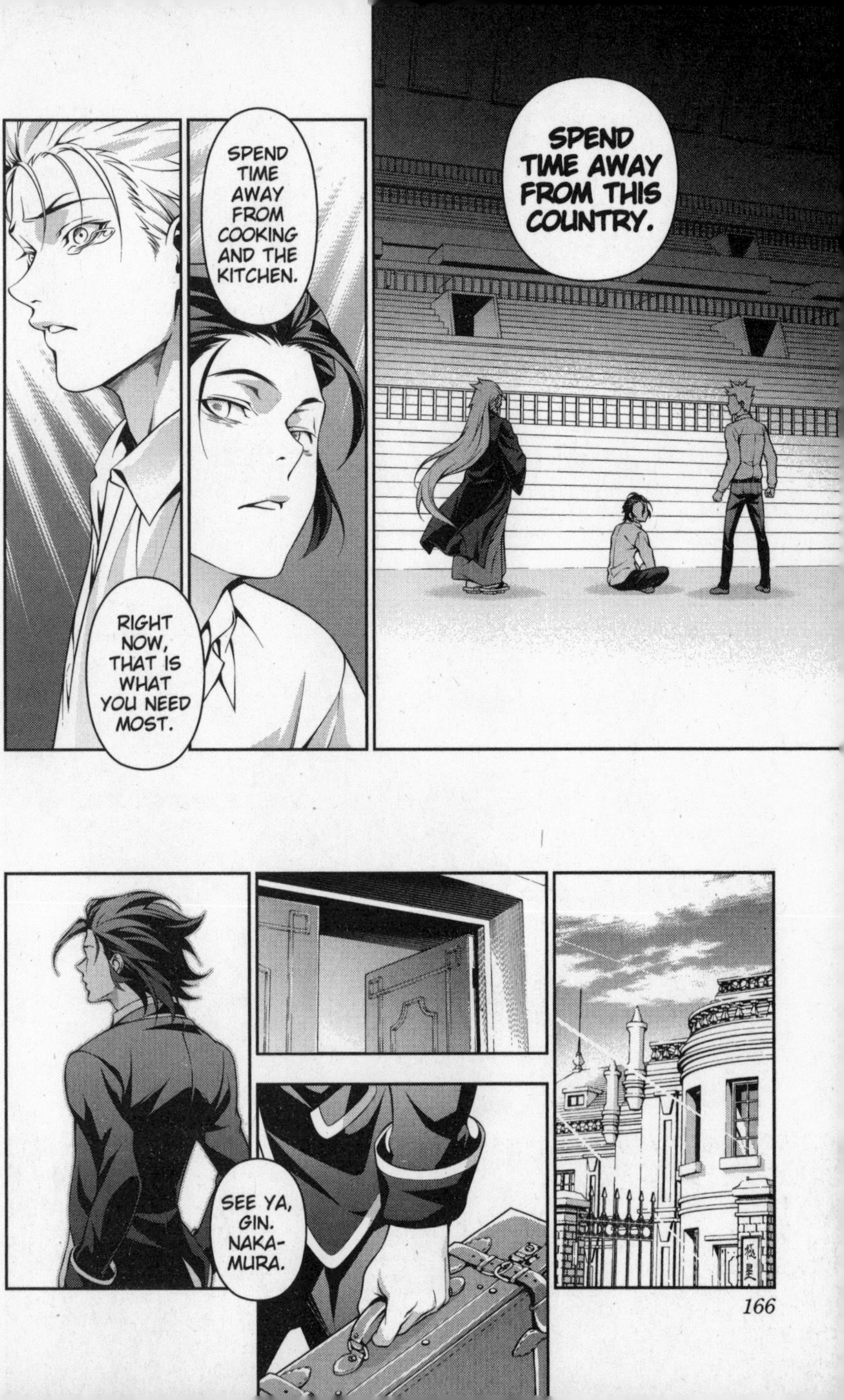
SPEND TIME AWAY FROM THIS COUNTRY.
SPEND TIME AWAY FROM COOKING AND THE KITCHEN.
RIGHT NOW, THAT IS WHAT YOU NEED MOST.
SEE YA, GIN. NAKA-MURA.

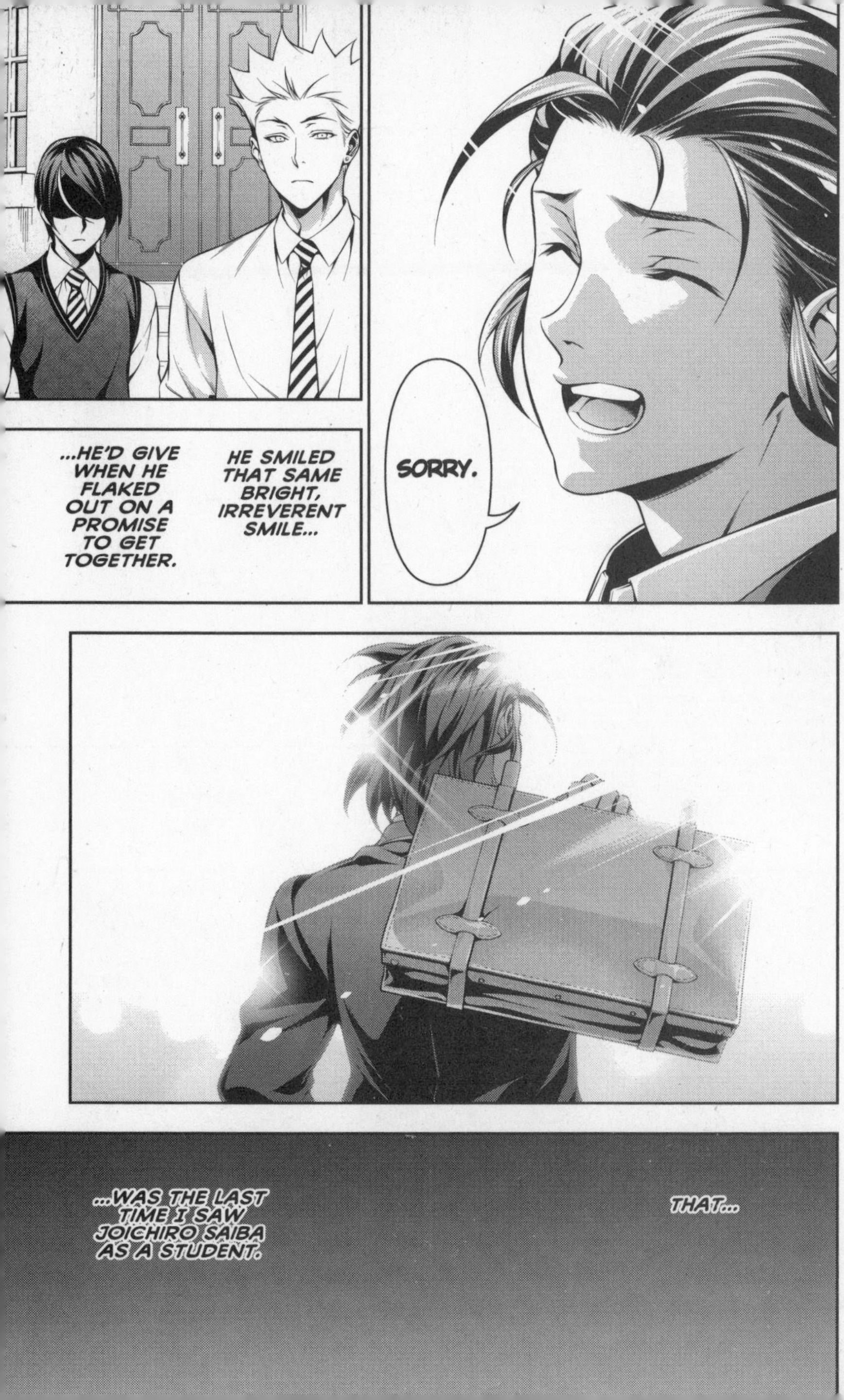
SORRY.
HE SMILED THAT SAME BRIGHT, IRREVERENT SMILE...
...HE'D GIVE WHEN HE FLAKED OUT ON A PROMISE TO GET TOGETHER.
THAT...
...WAS THE LAST TIME I SAW JOICHIRO SAIBA AS A STUDENT.

HEH HEH HEH ... RÉGIMENT DE CUISINE ...
SAIBA SENPAI ... HEE HEE HEE ... ♪
AZAMI NAKIRI. WHEN HE GETS EXCITED, HE EMANATES A BLACK AURA...

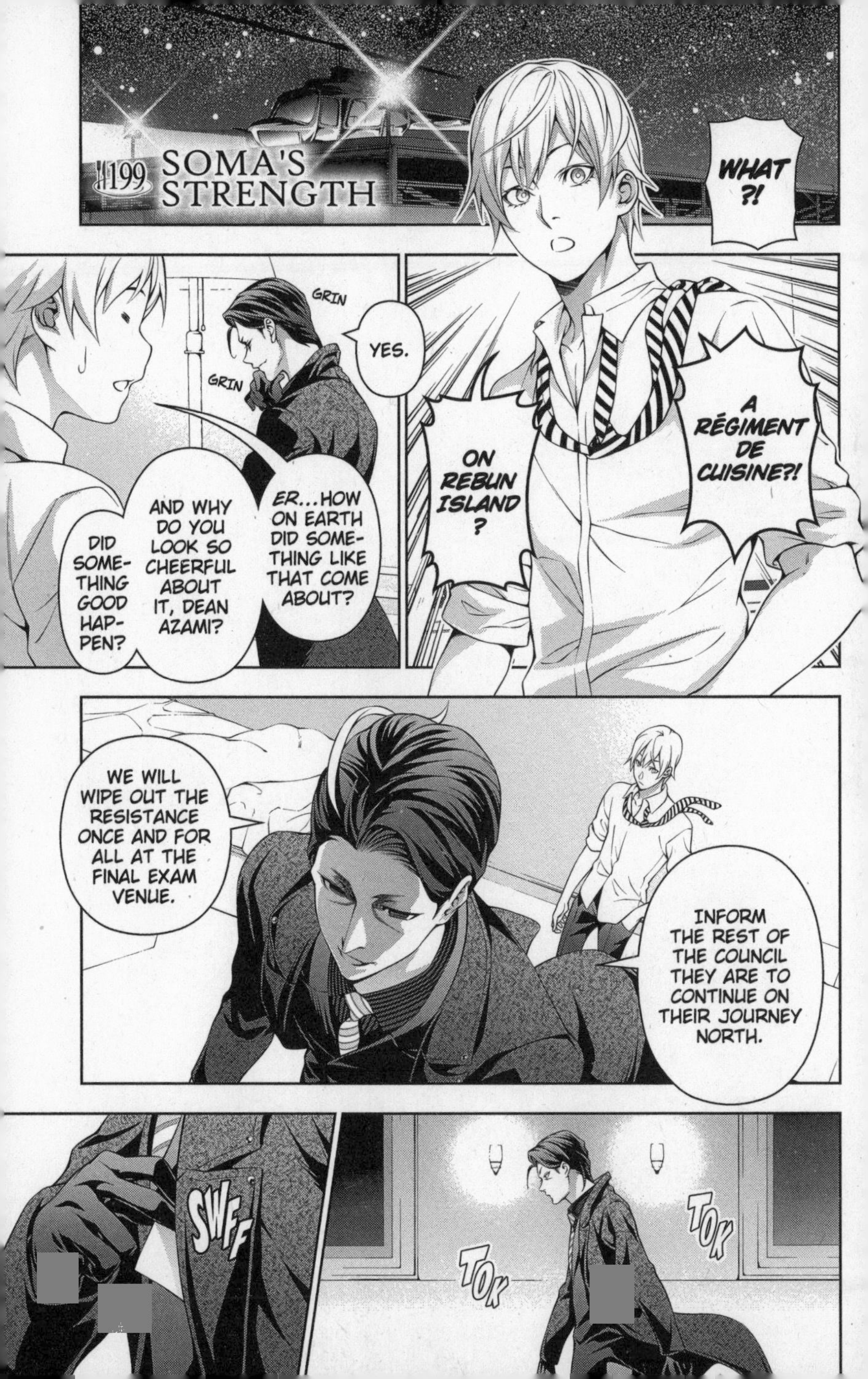
#199 SOMA'S STRENGTH
WHAT ?!
A RÉGIMENT DE CUISINE?!
ON REBUN ISLAND ?
YES.
GRIN
GRIN
ER...HOW ON EARTH DID SOME-THING LIKE THAT COME ABOUT?
AND WHY DO YOU LOOK SO CHEERFUL ABOUT IT, DEAN AZAMI?
DID SOME-THING GOOD HAP-PEN?
WE WILL WIPE OUT THE RESISTANCE ONCE AND FOR ALL AT THE FINAL EXAM VENUE.
INFORM THE REST OF THE COUNCIL THEY ARE TO CONTINUE ON THEIR JOURNEY NORTH.
TOK
TOK
SWFF

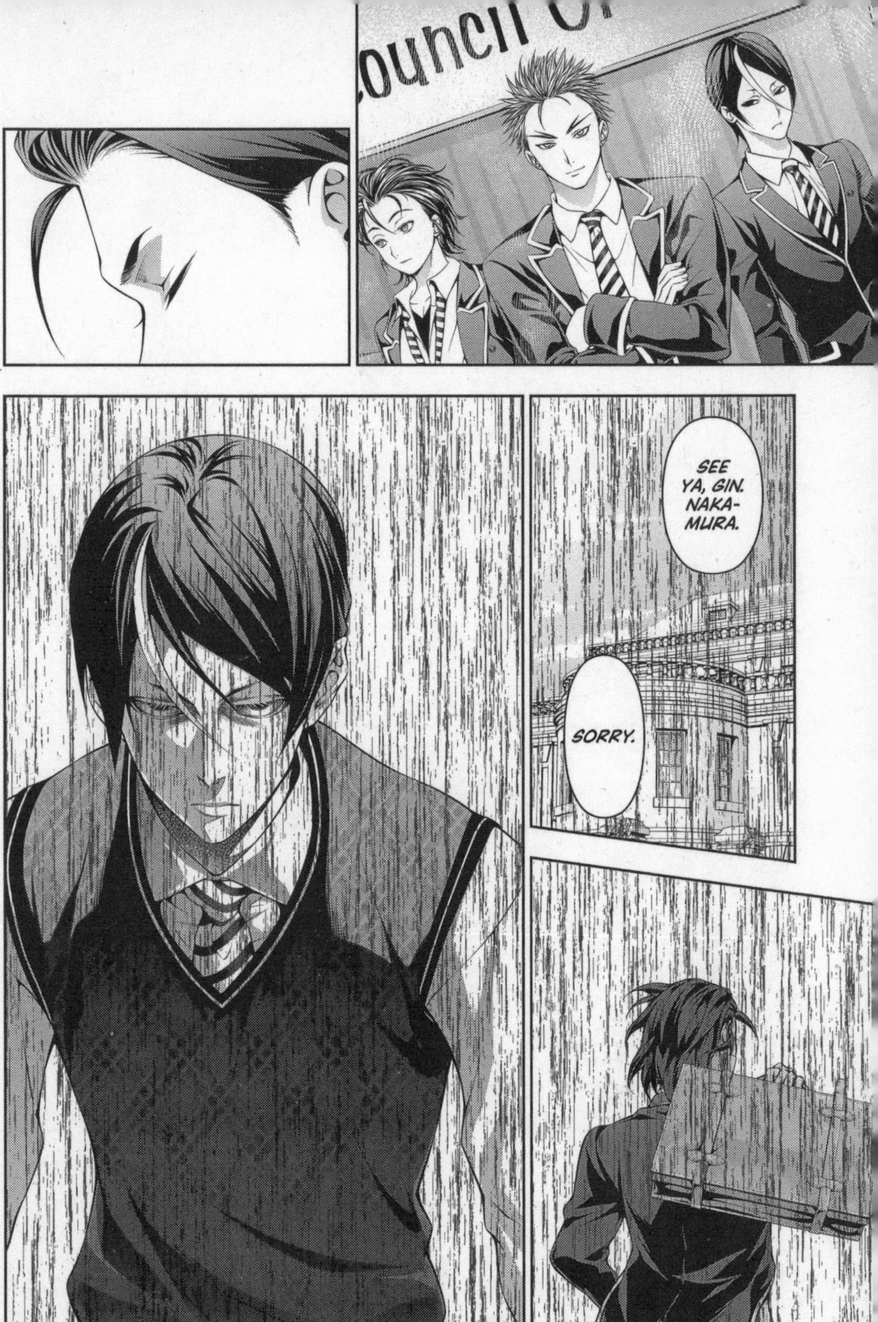
SEE YA, GIN. NAKA-MURA.
SORRY.

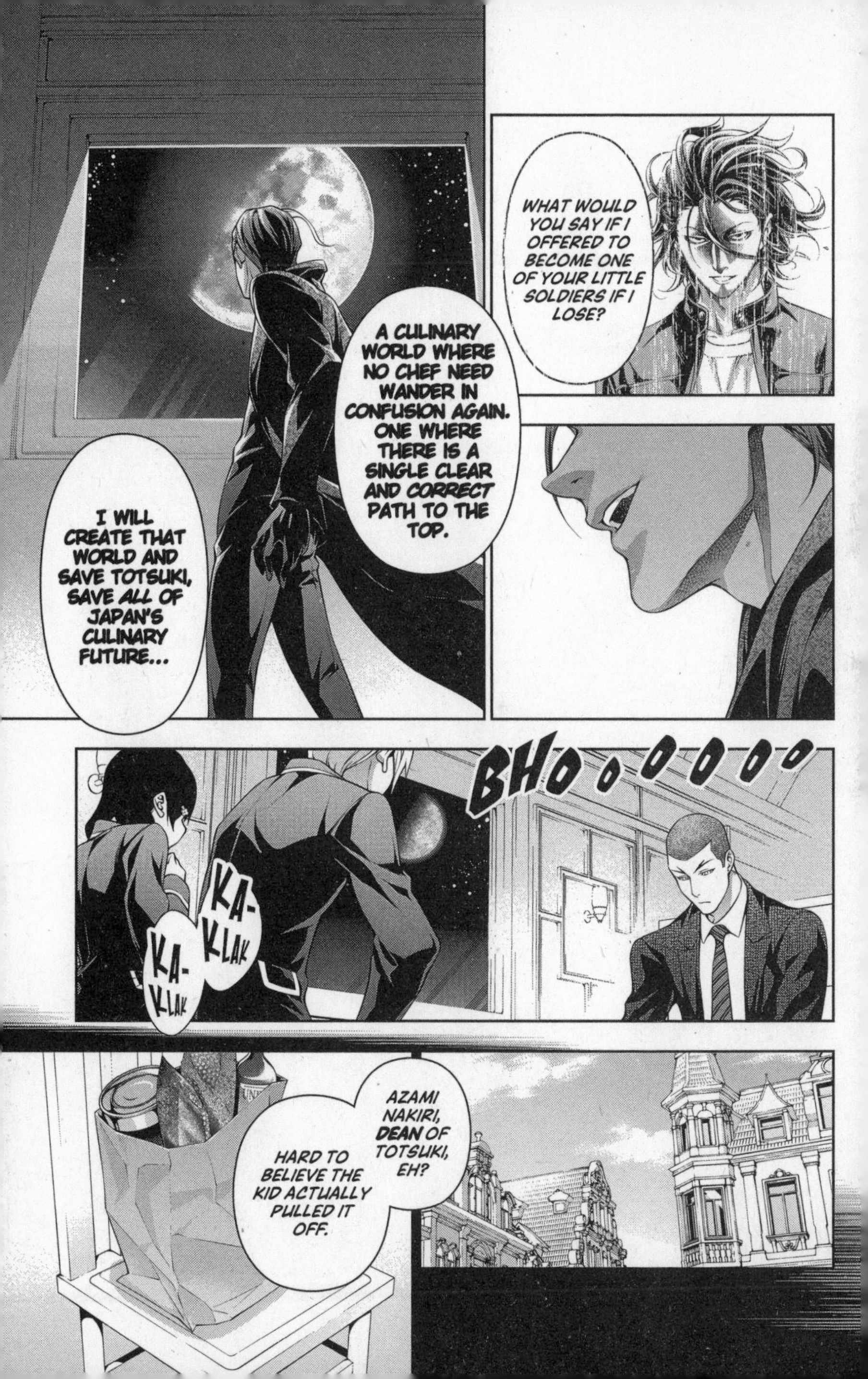
WHAT WOULD YOU SAY IF I OFFERED TO BECOME ONE OF YOUR LITTLE SOLDIERS IF I LOSE?
A CULINARY WORLD WHERE NO CHEF NEED WANDER IN CONFUSION AGAIN. ONE WHERE THERE IS A SINGLE CLEAR AND CORRECT PATH TO THE TOP.
I WILL CREATE THAT WORLD AND SAVE TOTSUKI, SAVE ALL OF JAPAN'S CULINARY FUTURE...
BHOOOOOO
KA-KLAK
KA-KLAK
AZAMI NAKIRI, DEAN OF TOTSUKI, EH?
HARD TO BELIEVE THE KID ACTUALLY PULLED IT OFF.

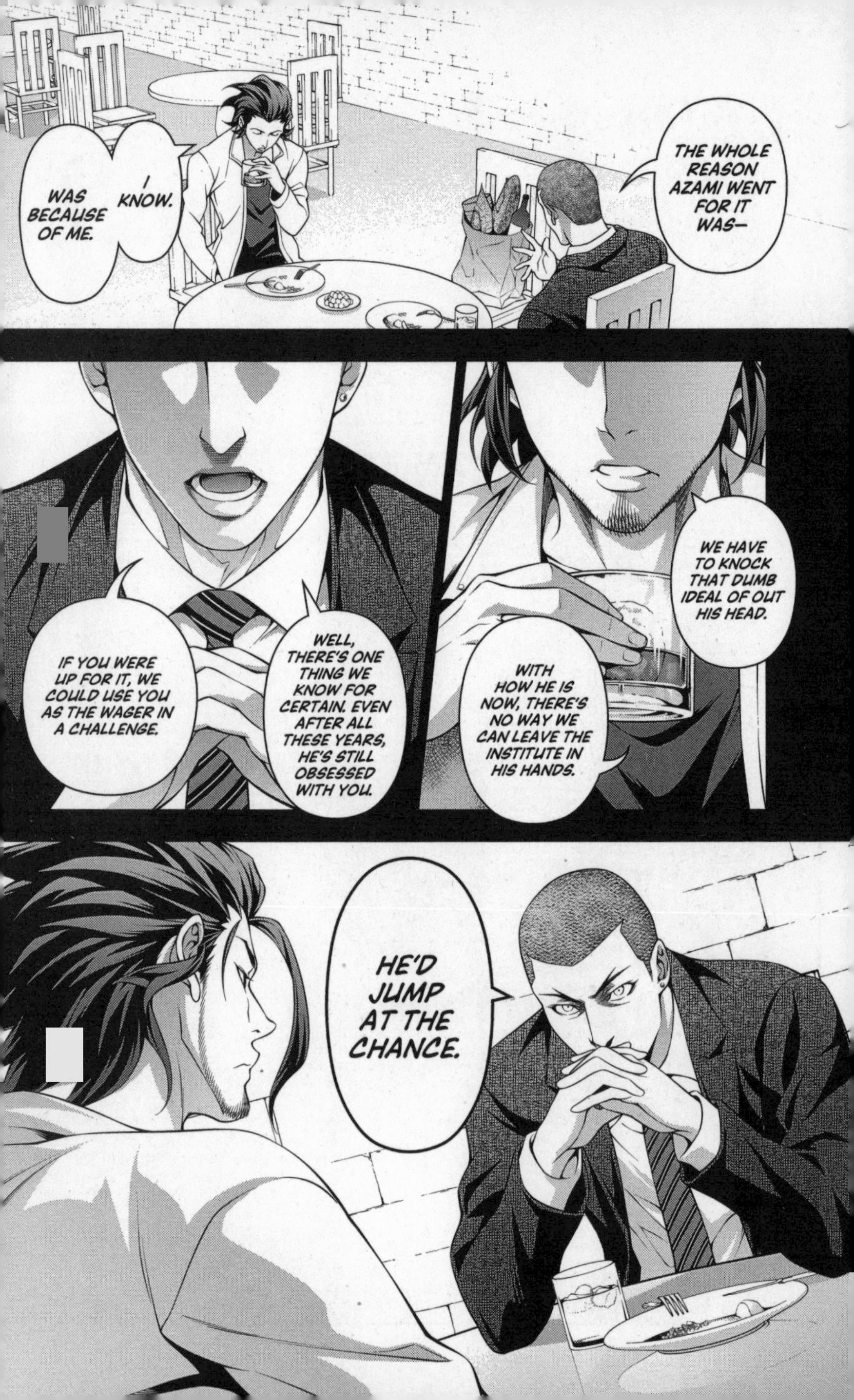
THE WHOLE REASON AZAMI WENT FOR IT WAS—
I KNOW.
WAS BECAUSE OF ME.
WE HAVE TO KNOCK THAT DUMB IDEAL OF OUT HIS HEAD.
WITH HOW HE IS NOW, THERE'S NO WAY WE CAN LEAVE THE INSTITUTE IN HIS HANDS.
WELL, THERE'S ONE THING WE KNOW FOR CERTAIN. EVEN AFTER ALL THESE YEARS, HE'S STILL OBSESSED WITH YOU.
IF YOU WERE UP FOR IT, WE COULD USE YOU AS THE WAGER IN A CHALLENGE.
HE'D JUMP AT THE CHANCE.

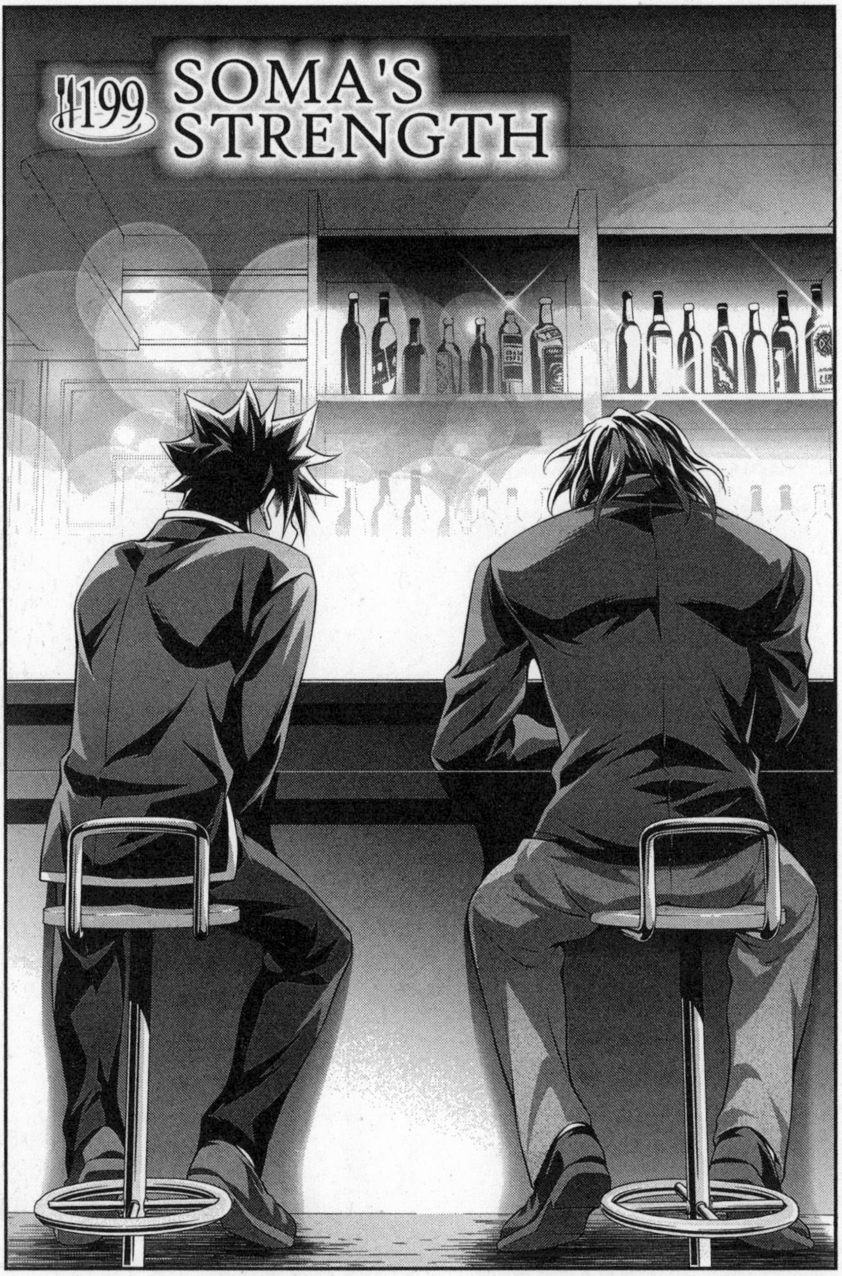
#199 SOMA'S STRENGTH

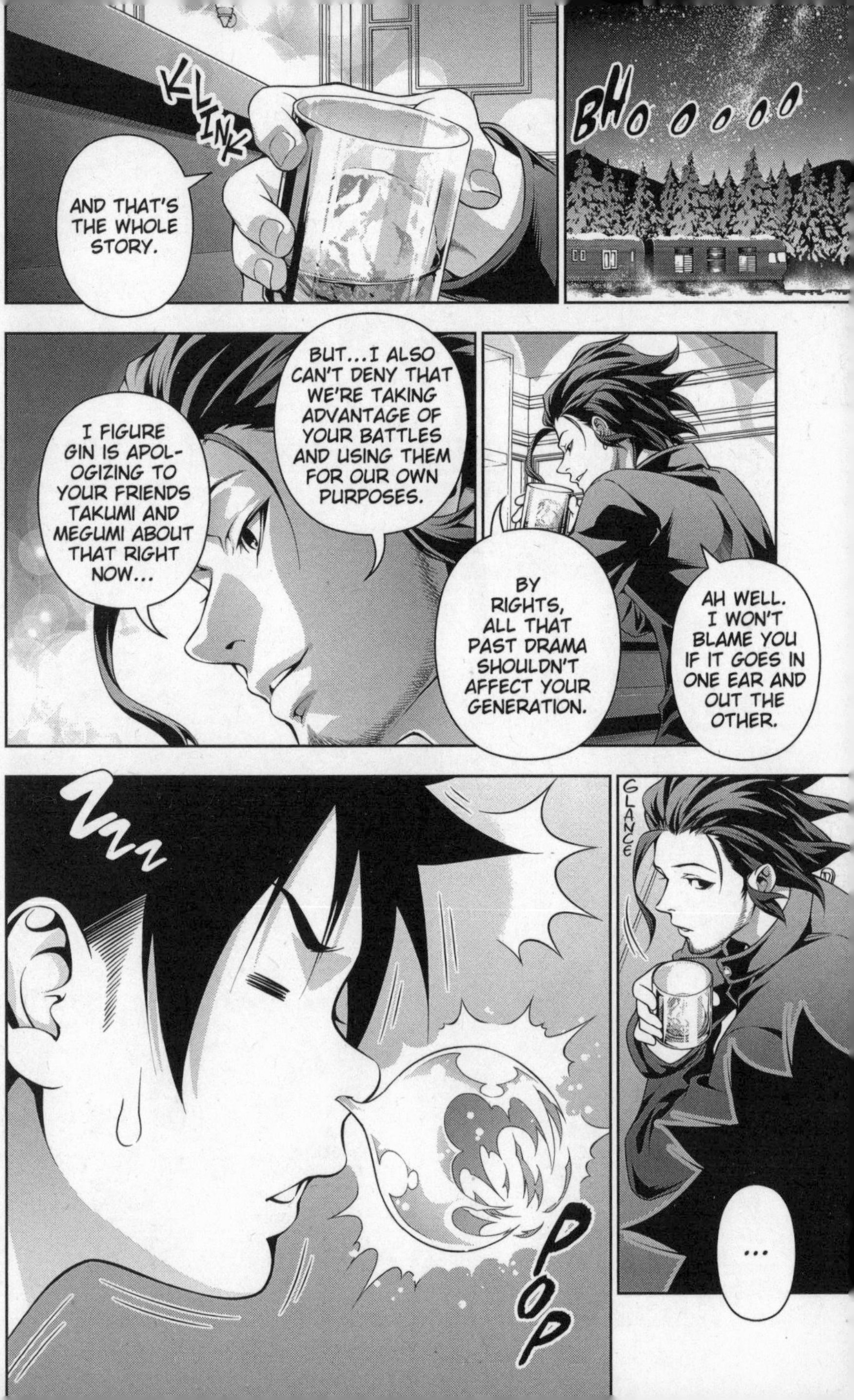
BHOOOOO
KLINK
AND THAT'S THE WHOLE STORY.
BY RIGHTS, ALL THAT PAST DRAMA SHOULDN'T AFFECT YOUR GENERATION.
AH WELL. I WON'T BLAME YOU IF IT GOES IN ONE EAR AND OUT THE OTHER.
BUT...I ALSO CAN'T DENY THAT WE'RE TAKING ADVANTAGE OF YOUR BATTLES AND USING THEM FOR OUR OWN PURPOSES.
I FIGURE GIN IS APOLOGIZING TO YOUR FRIENDS TAKUMI AND MEGUMI ABOUT THAT RIGHT NOW...
GLANCE
...
ZZZ
POP

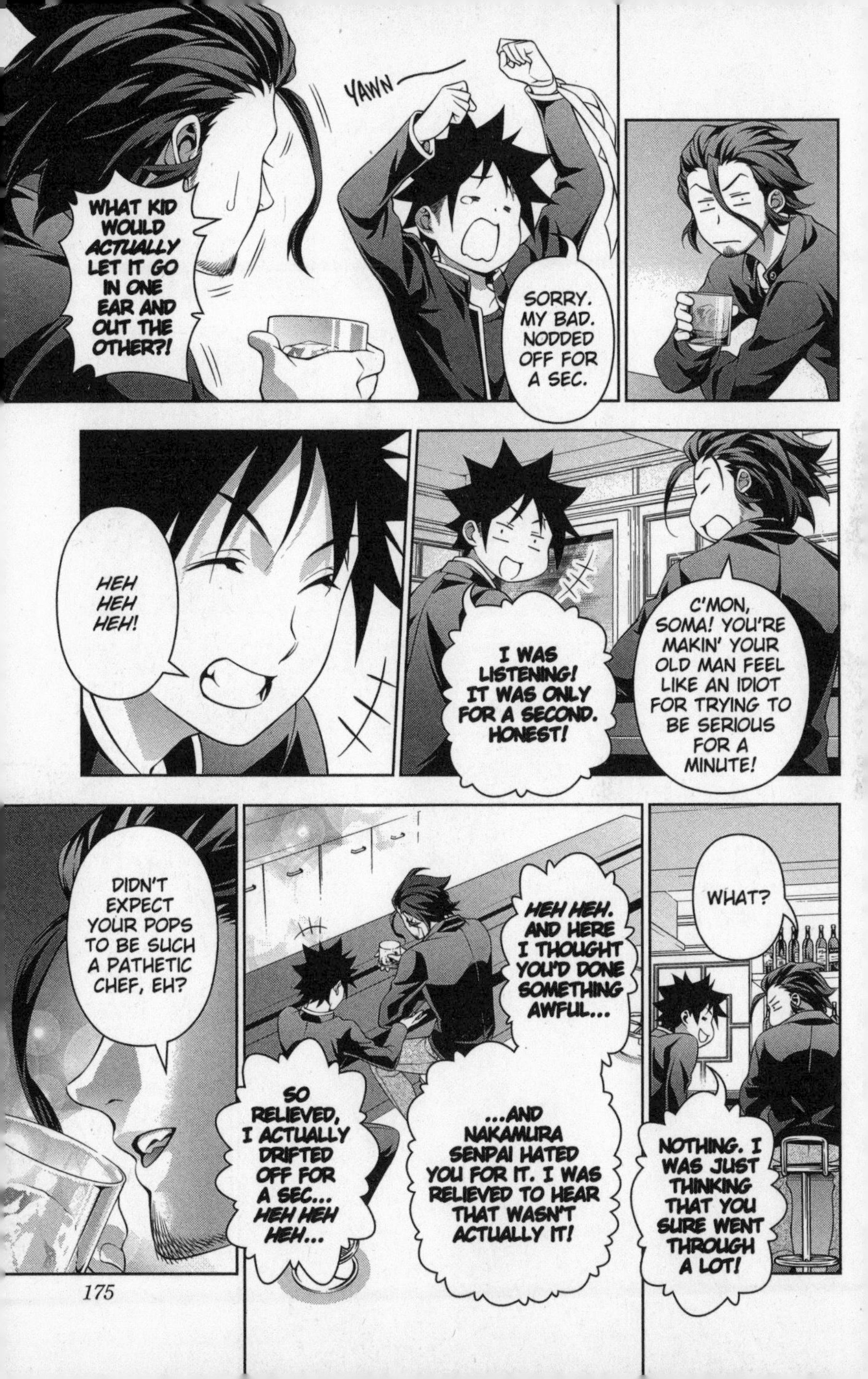
YAWN
SORRY. MY BAD. NODDED OFF FOR A SEC.
WHAT KID WOULD *ACTUALLY* LET IT GO IN ONE EAR AND OUT THE OTHER?!
C'MON, SOMA! YOU'RE MAKIN' YOUR OLD MAN FEEL LIKE AN IDIOT FOR TRYING TO BE SERIOUS FOR A MINUTE!
I WAS LISTENING! IT WAS ONLY FOR A SECOND. HONEST!
HEH HEH HEH!
WHAT?
NOTHING. I WAS JUST THINKING THAT YOU SURE WENT THROUGH A LOT!
HEH HEH. AND HERE I THOUGHT YOU'D DONE SOMETHING AWFUL...
...AND NAKAMURA SENPAI HATED YOU FOR IT. I WAS RELIEVED TO HEAR THAT WASN'T ACTUALLY IT!
SO RELIEVED, I ACTUALLY DRIFTED OFF FOR A SEC... *HEH HEH HEH...*
DIDN'T EXPECT YOUR POPS TO BE SUCH A PATHETIC CHEF, EH?

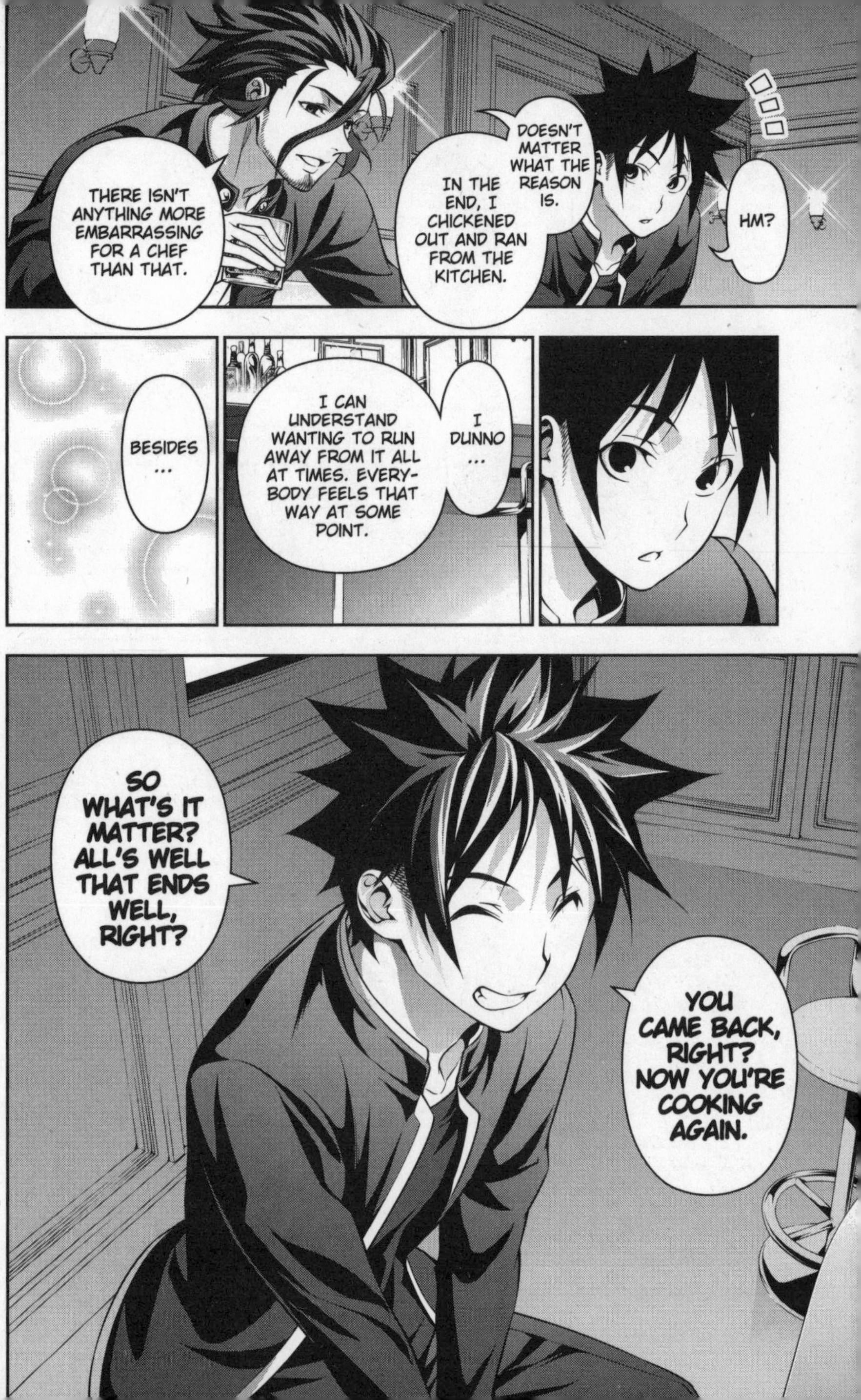
HM?
DOESN'T MATTER WHAT THE REASON IS.
IN THE END, I CHICKENED OUT AND RAN FROM THE KITCHEN.
THERE ISN'T ANYTHING MORE EMBARRASSING FOR A CHEF THAN THAT.
I DUNNO ...
I CAN UNDERSTAND WANTING TO RUN AWAY FROM IT ALL AT TIMES. EVERY-BODY FEELS THAT WAY AT SOME POINT.
BESIDES ...
YOU CAME BACK, RIGHT? NOW YOU'RE COOKING AGAIN.
SO WHAT'S IT MATTER? ALL'S WELL THAT ENDS WELL, RIGHT?

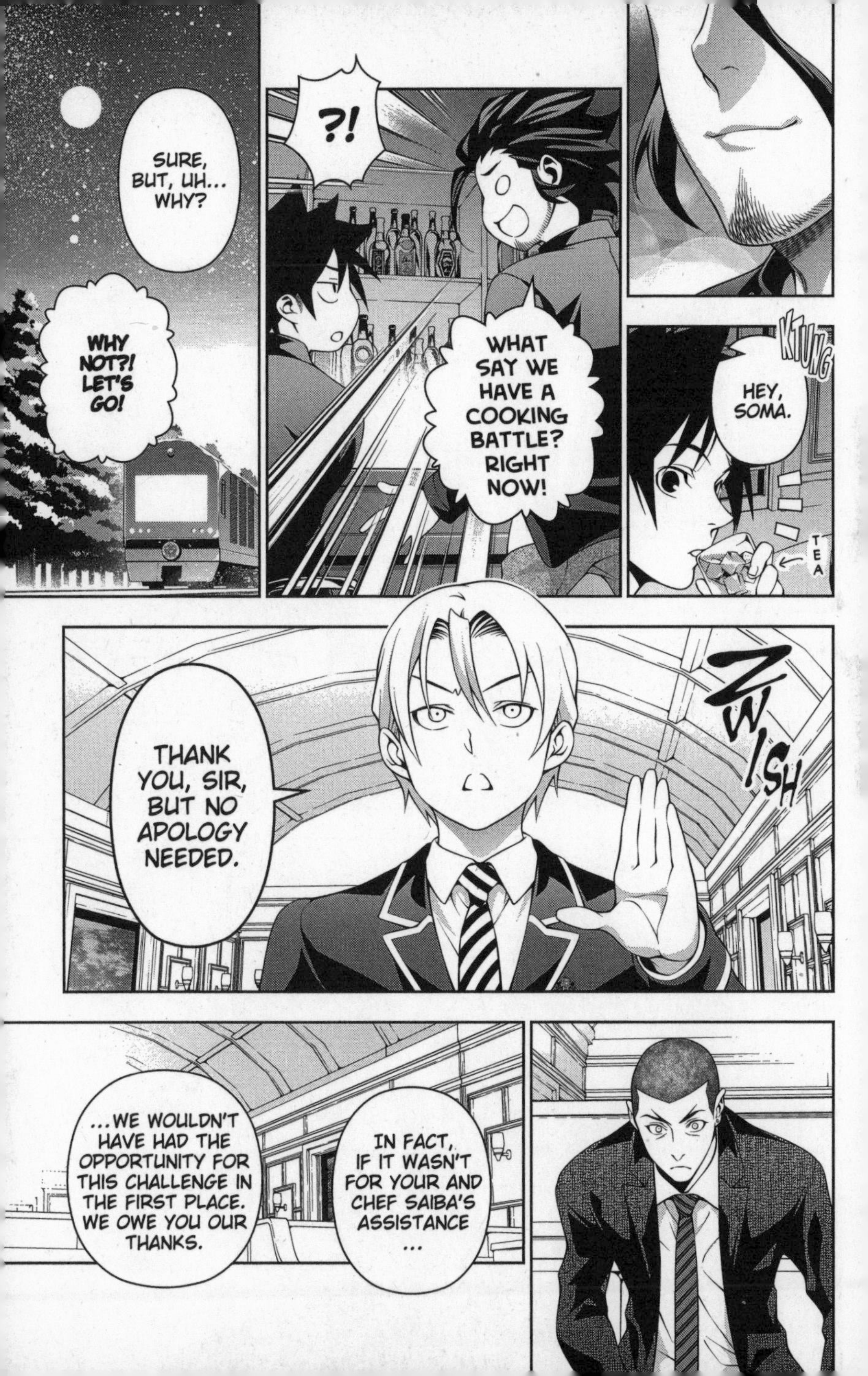
HEY, SOMA.
KTUNG
TEA
?!
WHAT SAY WE HAVE A COOKING BATTLE? RIGHT NOW!
SURE, BUT, UH... WHY?
WHY NOT?! LET'S GO!
ZWISH
THANK YOU, SIR, BUT NO APOLOGY NEEDED.
IN FACT, IF IT WASN'T FOR YOUR AND CHEF SAIBA'S ASSISTANCE ...
...WE WOULDN'T HAVE HAD THE OPPORTUNITY FOR THIS CHALLENGE IN THE FIRST PLACE. WE OWE YOU OUR THANKS.

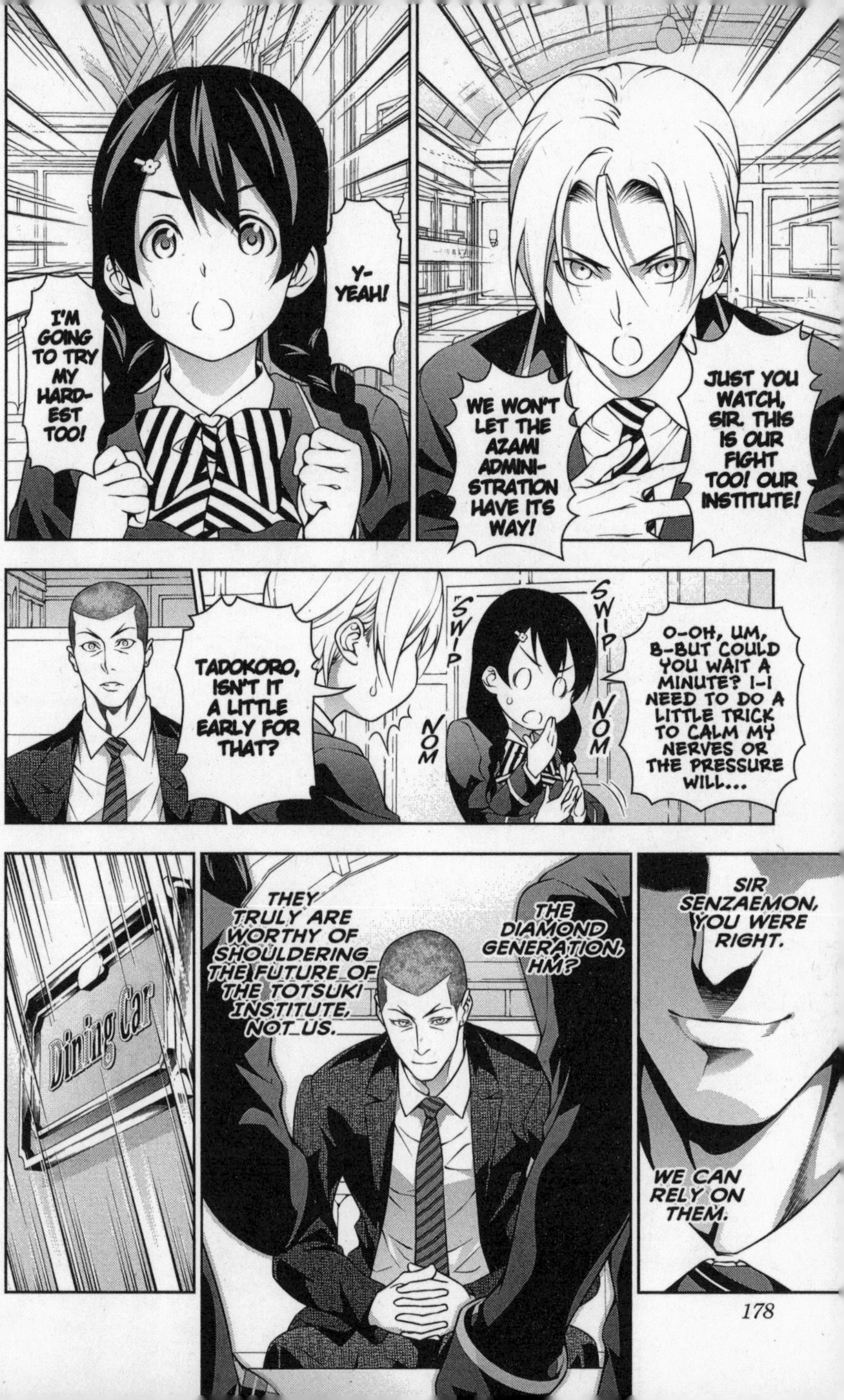
JUST YOU WATCH, SIR. THIS IS OUR FIGHT TOO! OUR INSTITUTE!
WE WON'T LET THE AZAMI ADMINISTRATION HAVE ITS WAY!
Y-YEAH!
I'M GOING TO TRY MY HARDEST TOO!
O-OH, UM, B-BUT COULD YOU WAIT A MINUTE? I-I NEED TO DO A LITTLE TRICK TO CALM MY NERVES OR THE PRESSURE WILL...
SWIP SWIP
NOM NOM
TADOKORO, ISN'T IT A LITTLE EARLY FOR THAT?
SIR SENZAEMON, YOU WERE RIGHT.
WE CAN RELY ON THEM.
THE DIAMOND GENERATION, HM?
THEY TRULY ARE WORTHY OF SHOULDERING THE FUTURE OF THE TOTSUKI INSTITUTE, NOT US.
Dining Car

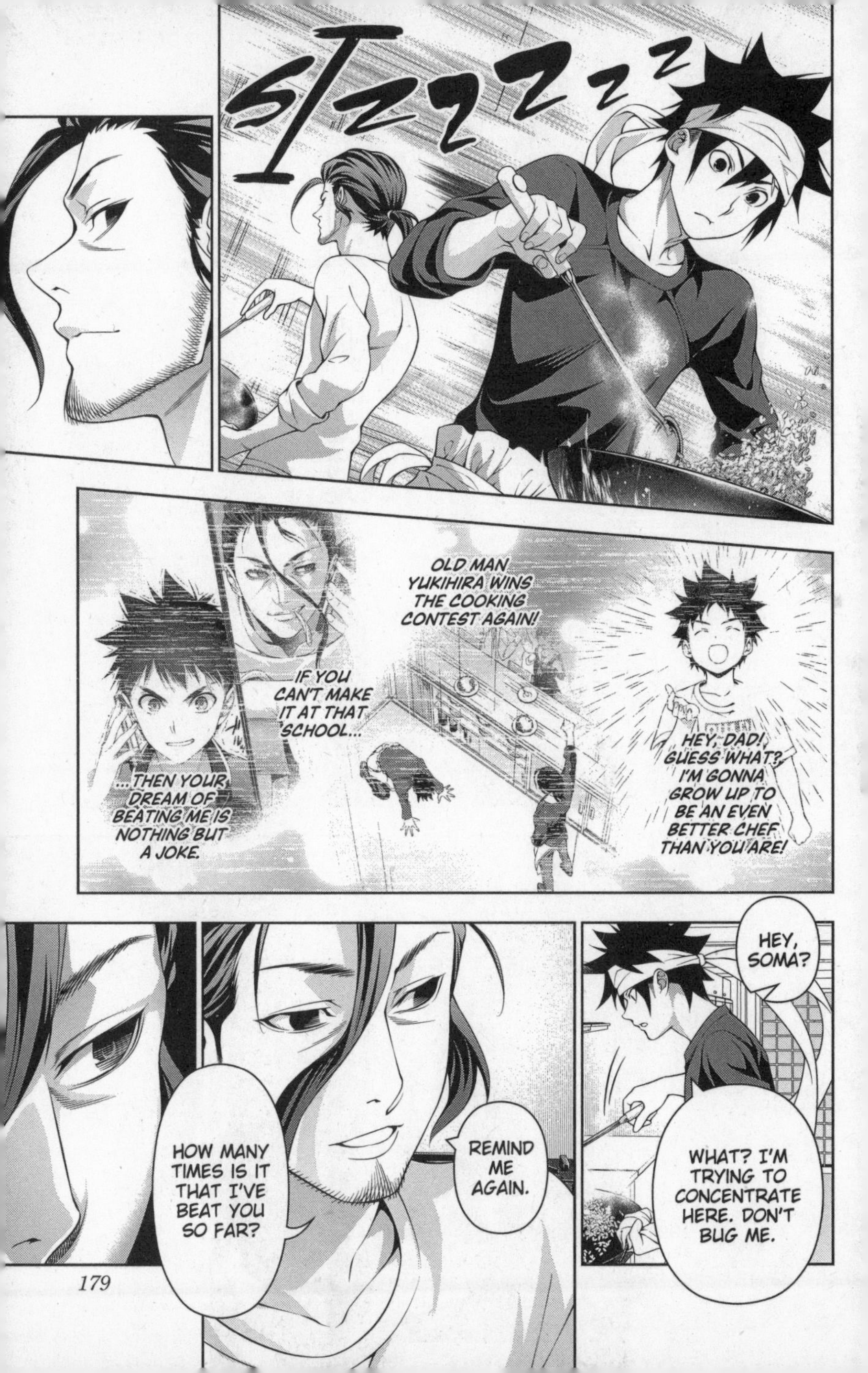
SIZZZZZZ
HEY, DAD! GUESS WHAT? I'M GONNA GROW UP TO BE AN EVEN BETTER CHEF THAN YOU ARE!
OLD MAN YUKIHIRA WINS THE COOKING CONTEST AGAIN!
IF YOU CAN'T MAKE IT AT THAT SCHOOL...
...THEN YOUR DREAM OF BEATING ME IS NOTHING BUT A JOKE.
HEY, SOMA?
WHAT? I'M TRYING TO CONCENTRATE HERE. DON'T BUG ME.
REMIND ME AGAIN.
HOW MANY TIMES IS IT THAT I'VE BEAT YOU SO FAR?

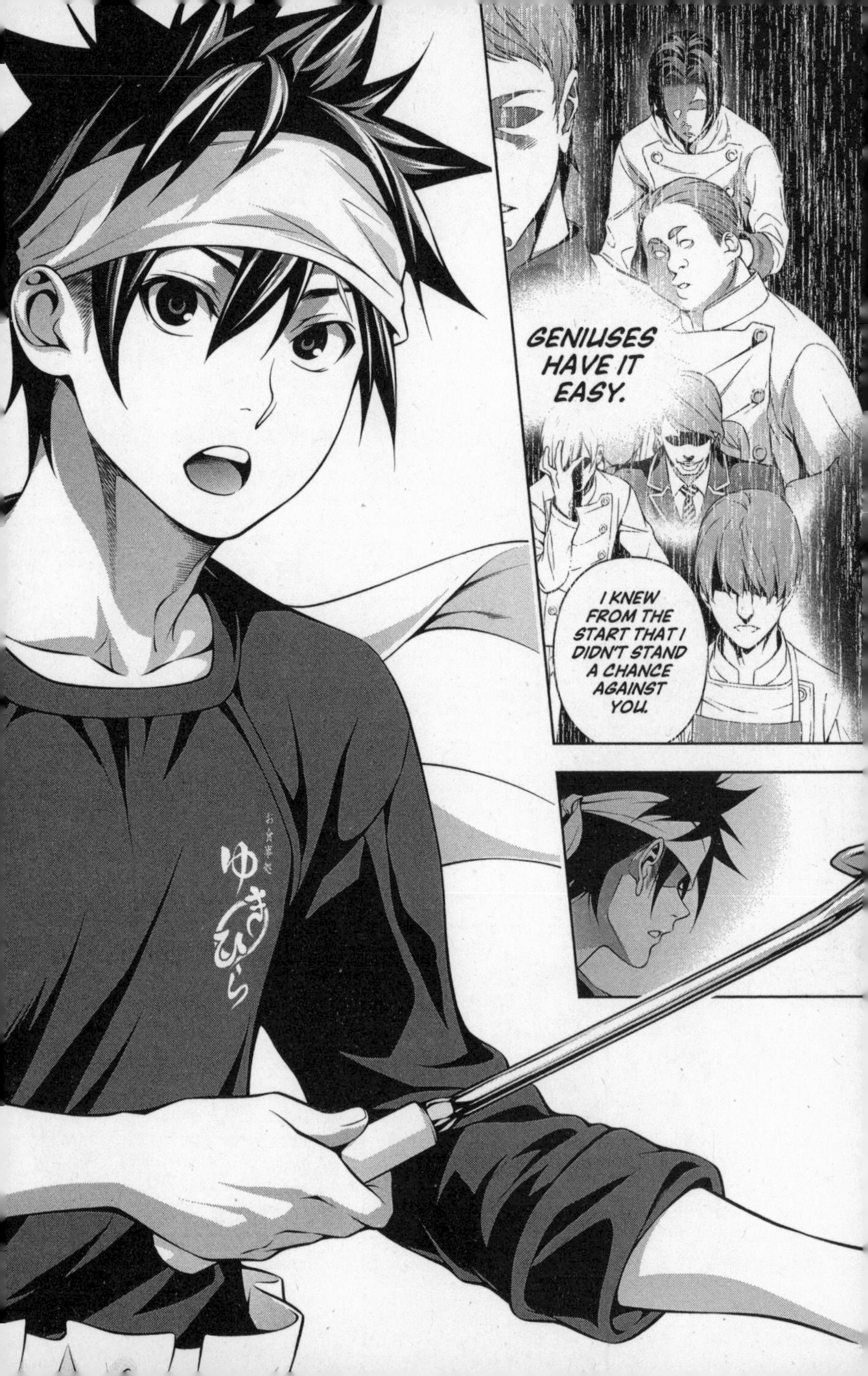
GENIUSES HAVE IT EASY.
I KNEW FROM THE START THAT I DIDN'T STAND A CHANCE AGAINST YOU.
お食事処
ゆきひら

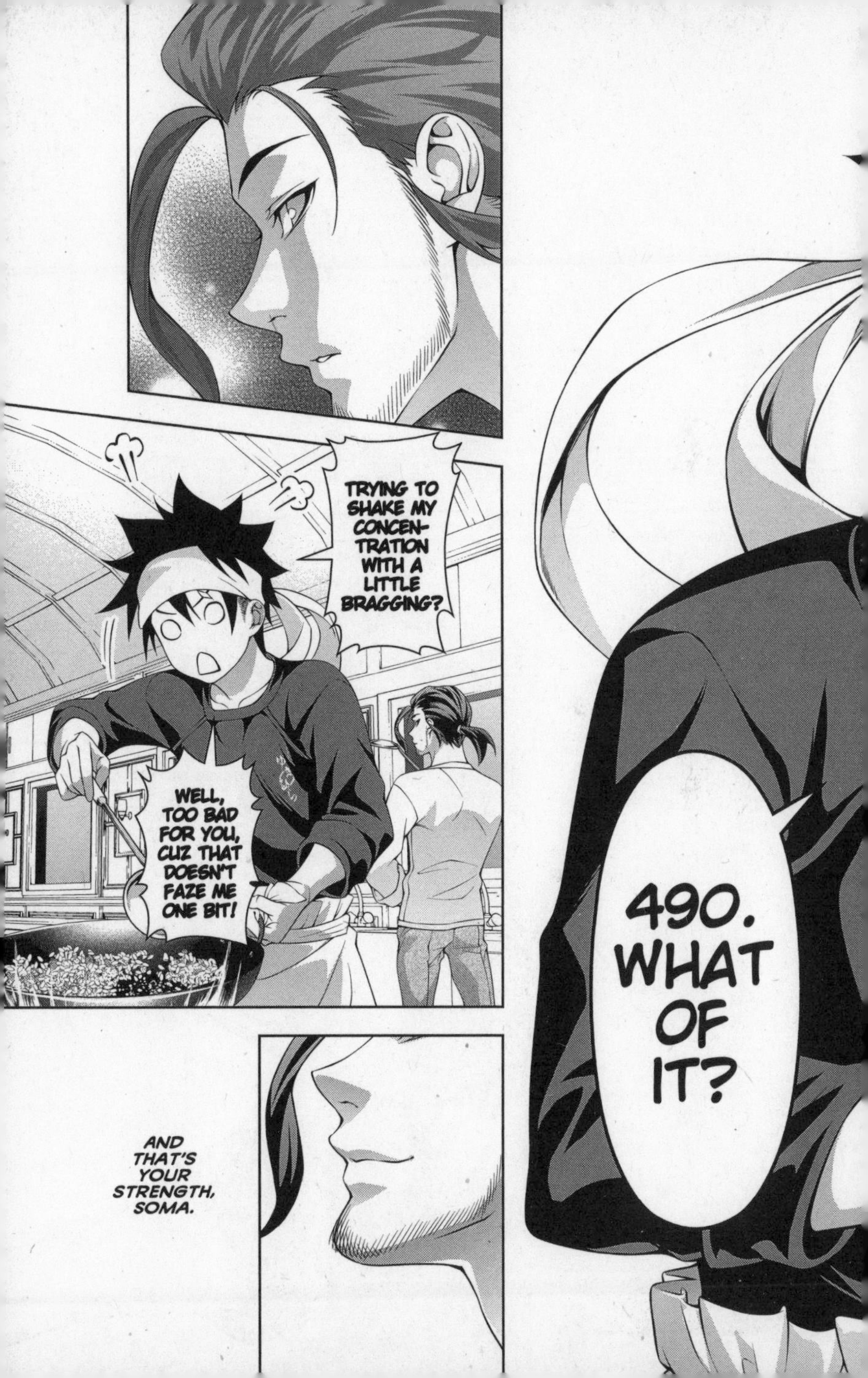
490. WHAT OF IT?
TRYING TO SHAKE MY CONCENTRATION WITH A LITTLE BRAGGING?
WELL, TOO BAD FOR YOU, CUZ THAT DOESN'T FAZE ME ONE BIT!
AND THAT'S YOUR STRENGTH, SOMA.

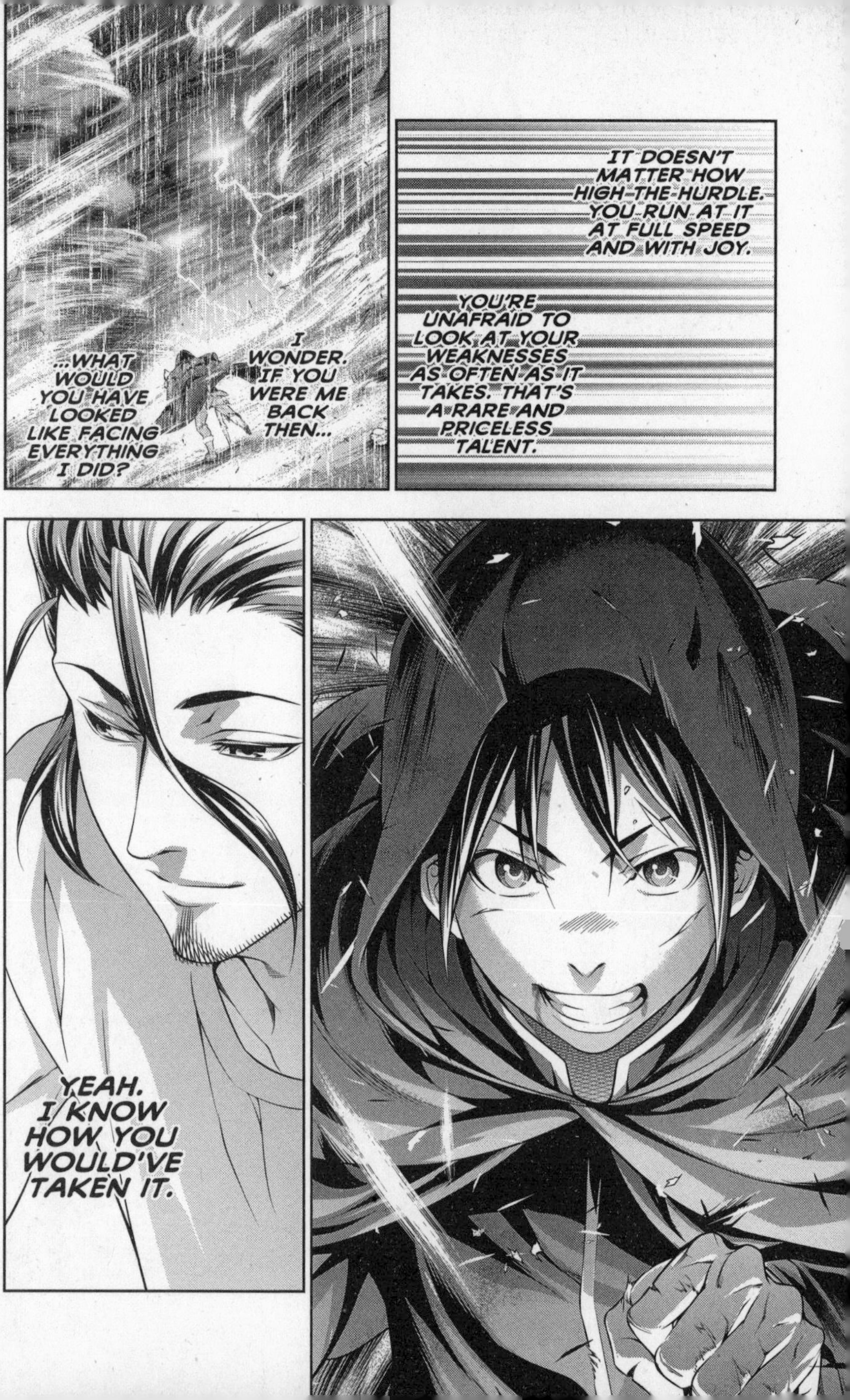
IT DOESN'T MATTER HOW HIGH THE HURDLE. YOU RUN AT IT AT FULL SPEED AND WITH JOY.
YOU'RE UNAFRAID TO LOOK AT YOUR WEAKNESSES AS OFTEN AS IT TAKES. THAT'S A RARE AND PRICELESS TALENT.
I WONDER. IF YOU WERE ME BACK THEN...
...WHAT WOULD YOU HAVE LOOKED LIKE FACING EVERYTHING I DID?
YEAH. I KNOW HOW YOU WOULD'VE TAKEN IT.

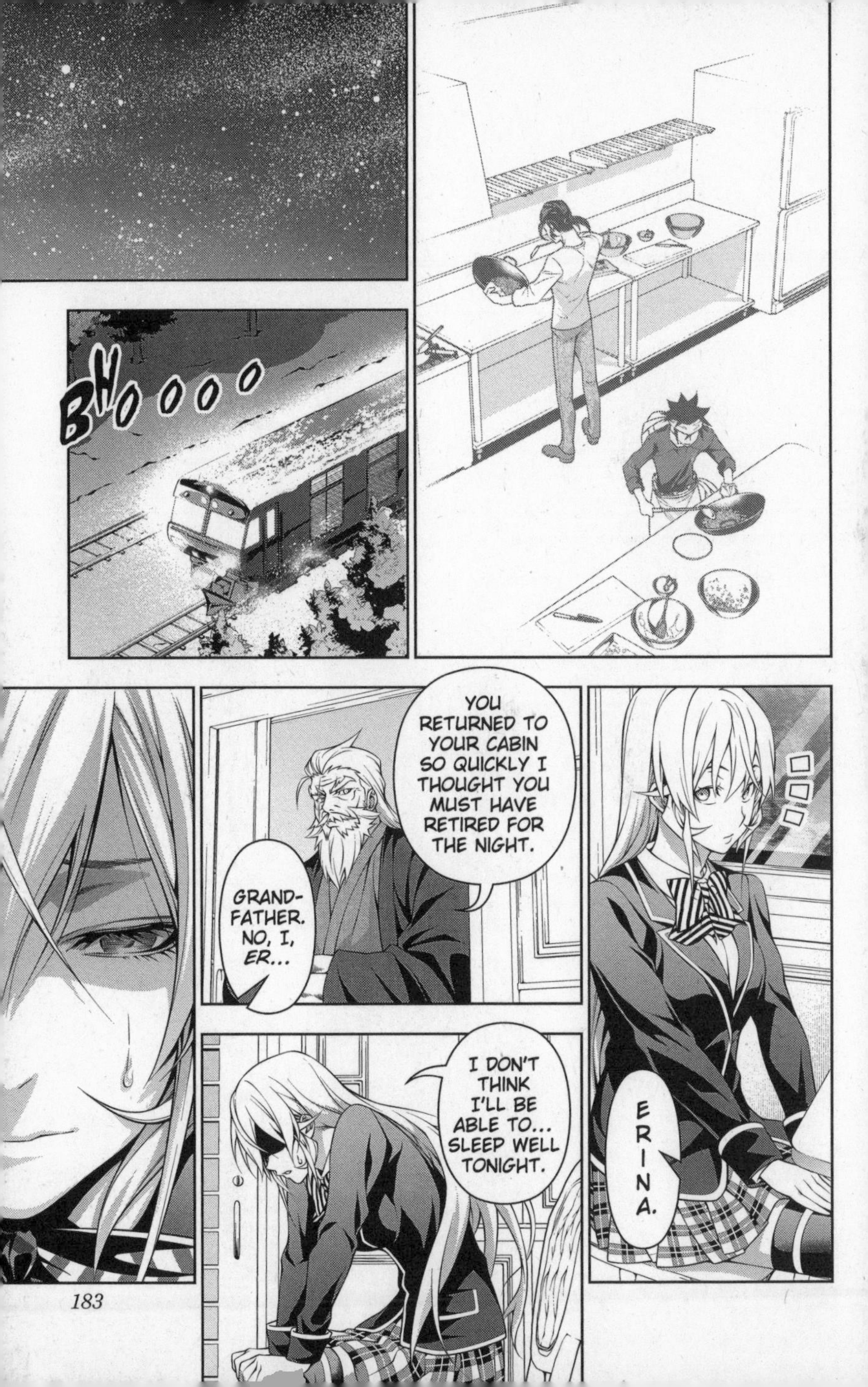
BHOOOO
ERINA.
YOU RETURNED TO YOUR CABIN SO QUICKLY I THOUGHT YOU MUST HAVE RETIRED FOR THE NIGHT.
GRAND-FATHER. NO, I, ER...
I DON'T THINK I'LL BE ABLE TO... SLEEP WELL TONIGHT.

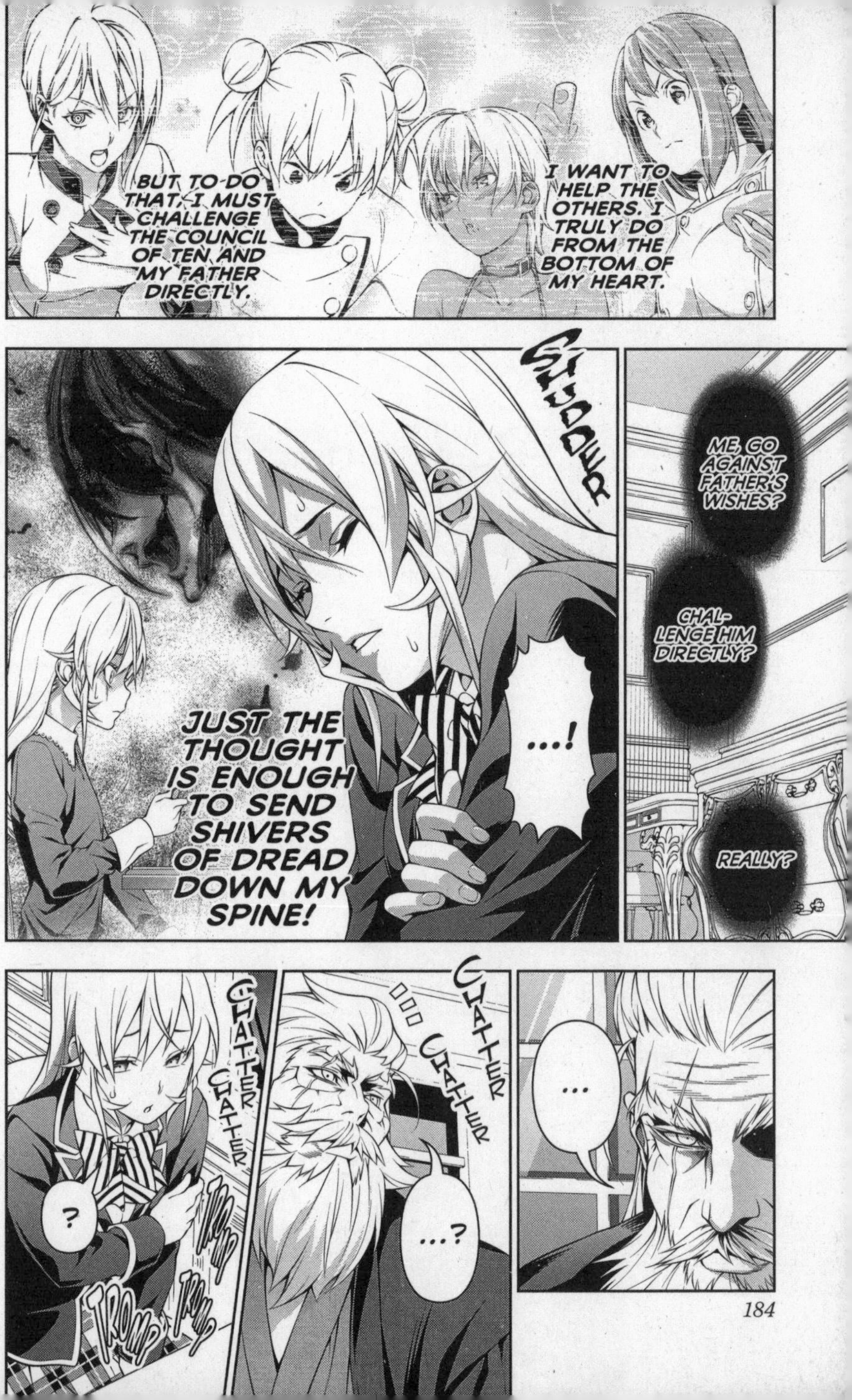

I WANT TO HELP THE OTHERS. I TRULY DO FROM THE BOTTOM OF MY HEART.
BUT TO DO THAT, I MUST CHALLENGE THE COUNCIL OF TEN AND MY FATHER DIRECTLY.
ME, GO AGAINST FATHER'S WISHES?
CHAL-LENGE HIM DIRECTLY?
REALLY?
SHUDDER
...!
JUST THE THOUGHT IS ENOUGH TO SEND SHIVERS OF DREAD DOWN MY SPINE!
...
CHATTER CHATTER
...?
CHATTER CHATTER
?
TREM TREM TREM

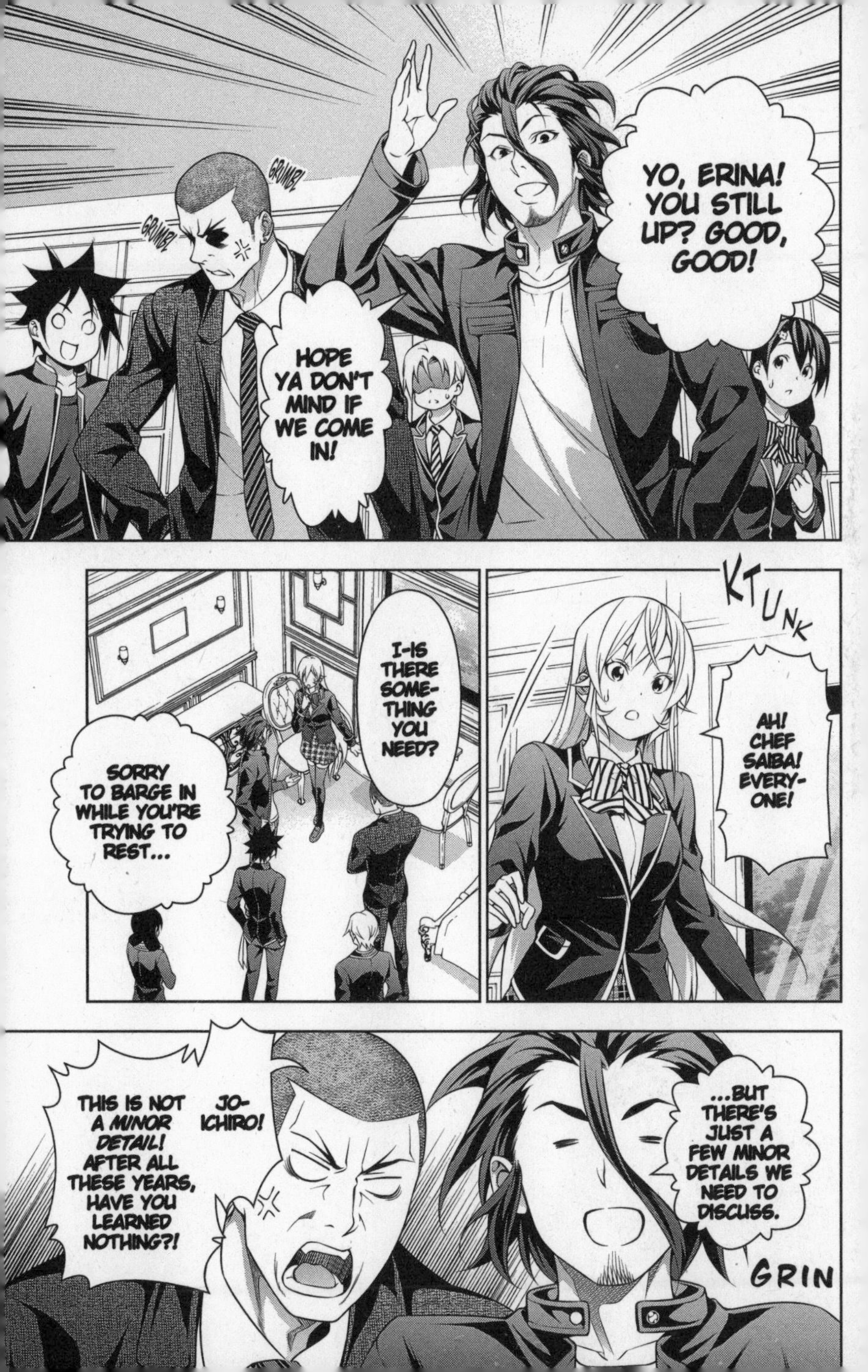
YO, ERINA! YOU STILL UP? GOOD, GOOD!
GRUMBL
GRUMBL
HOPE YA DON'T MIND IF WE COME IN!
KTUNK
AH! CHEF SAIBA! EVERYONE!
I-IS THERE SOMETHING YOU NEED?
SORRY TO BARGE IN WHILE YOU'RE TRYING TO REST...
...BUT THERE'S JUST A FEW MINOR DETAILS WE NEED TO DISCUSS.
GRIN
JO-ICHIRO!
THIS IS NOT A *MINOR DETAIL*! AFTER ALL THESE YEARS, HAVE YOU LEARNED NOTHING?!

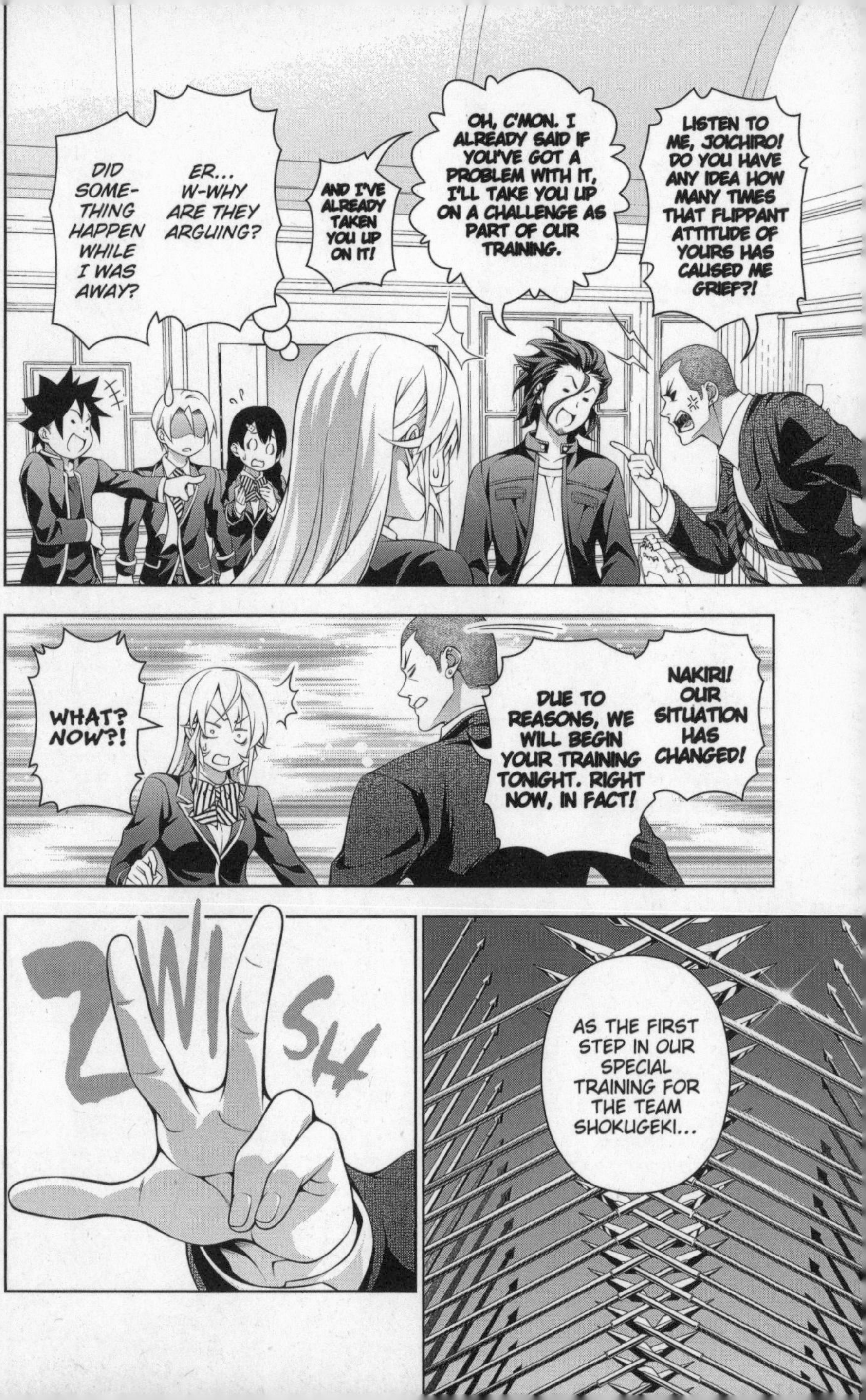
LISTEN TO ME, JOICHIRO! DO YOU HAVE ANY IDEA HOW MANY TIMES THAT FLIPPANT ATTITUDE OF YOURS HAS CAUSED ME GRIEF?!
OH, C'MON. I ALREADY SAID IF YOU'VE GOT A PROBLEM WITH IT, I'LL TAKE YOU UP ON A CHALLENGE AS PART OF OUR TRAINING.
AND I'VE ALREADY TAKEN YOU UP ON IT!
ER... W-WHY ARE THEY ARGUING?
DID SOME-THING HAPPEN WHILE I WAS AWAY?
NAKIRI! OUR SITUATION HAS CHANGED!
DUE TO REASONS, WE WILL BEGIN YOUR TRAINING TONIGHT. RIGHT NOW, IN FACT!
WHAT? NOW?!
AS THE FIRST STEP IN OUR SPECIAL TRAINING FOR THE TEAM SHOKUGEKI...
ZWISH

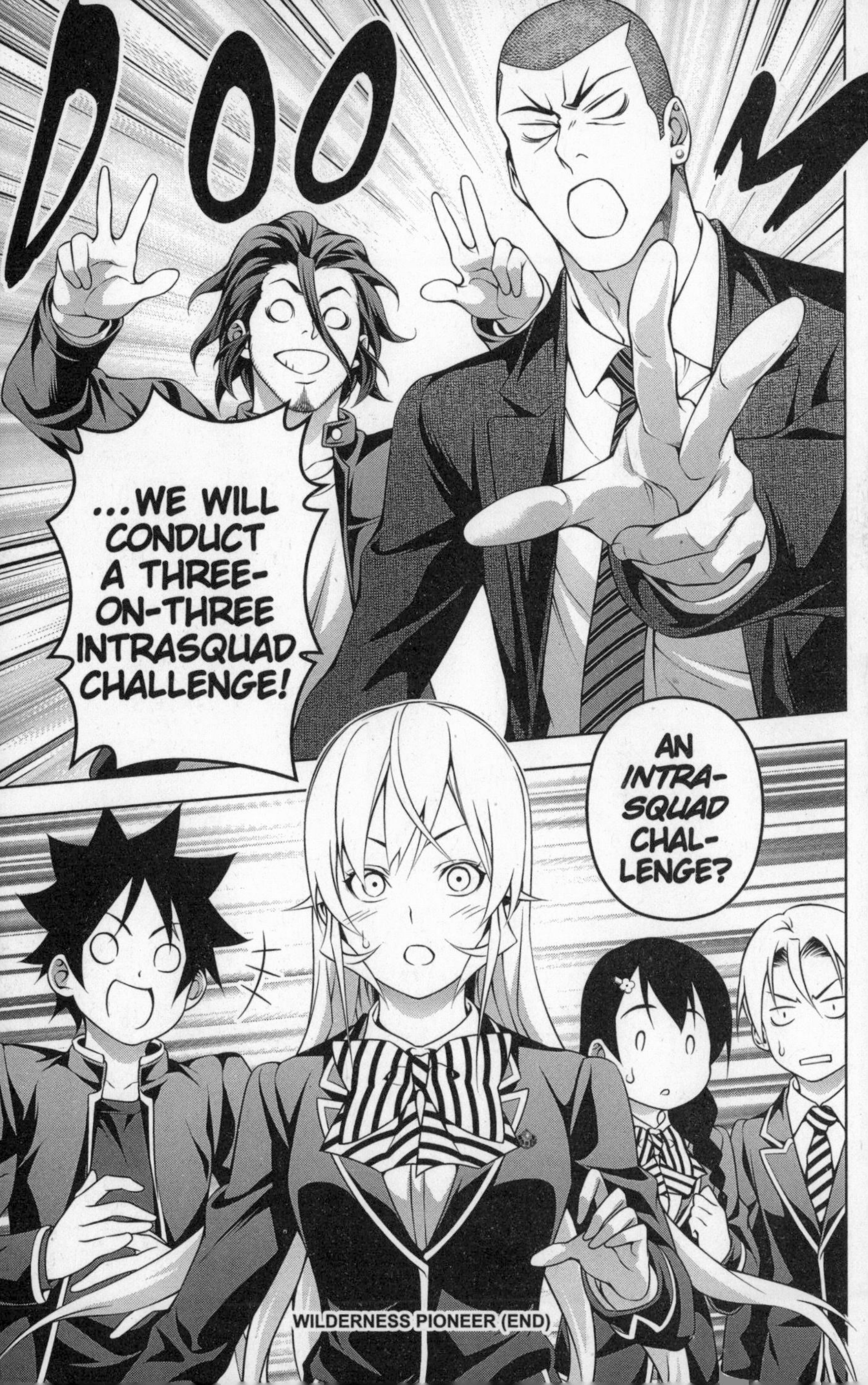
DOOM
...WE WILL CONDUCT A THREE-ON-THREE INTRASQUAD CHALLENGE!
AN INTRA-SQUAD CHAL-LENGE?
WILDERNESS PIONEER (END)

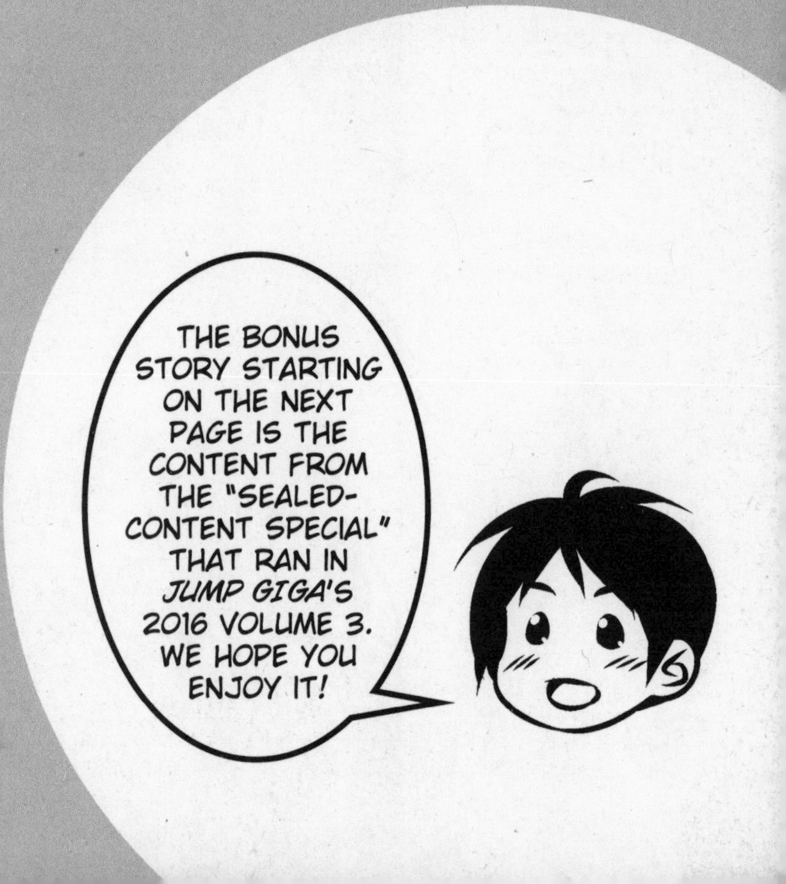
THE BONUS STORY STARTING ON THE NEXT PAGE IS THE CONTENT FROM THE "SEALED-CONTENT SPECIAL" THAT RAN IN *JUMP GIGA*'S 2016 VOLUME 3. WE HOPE YOU ENJOY IT!

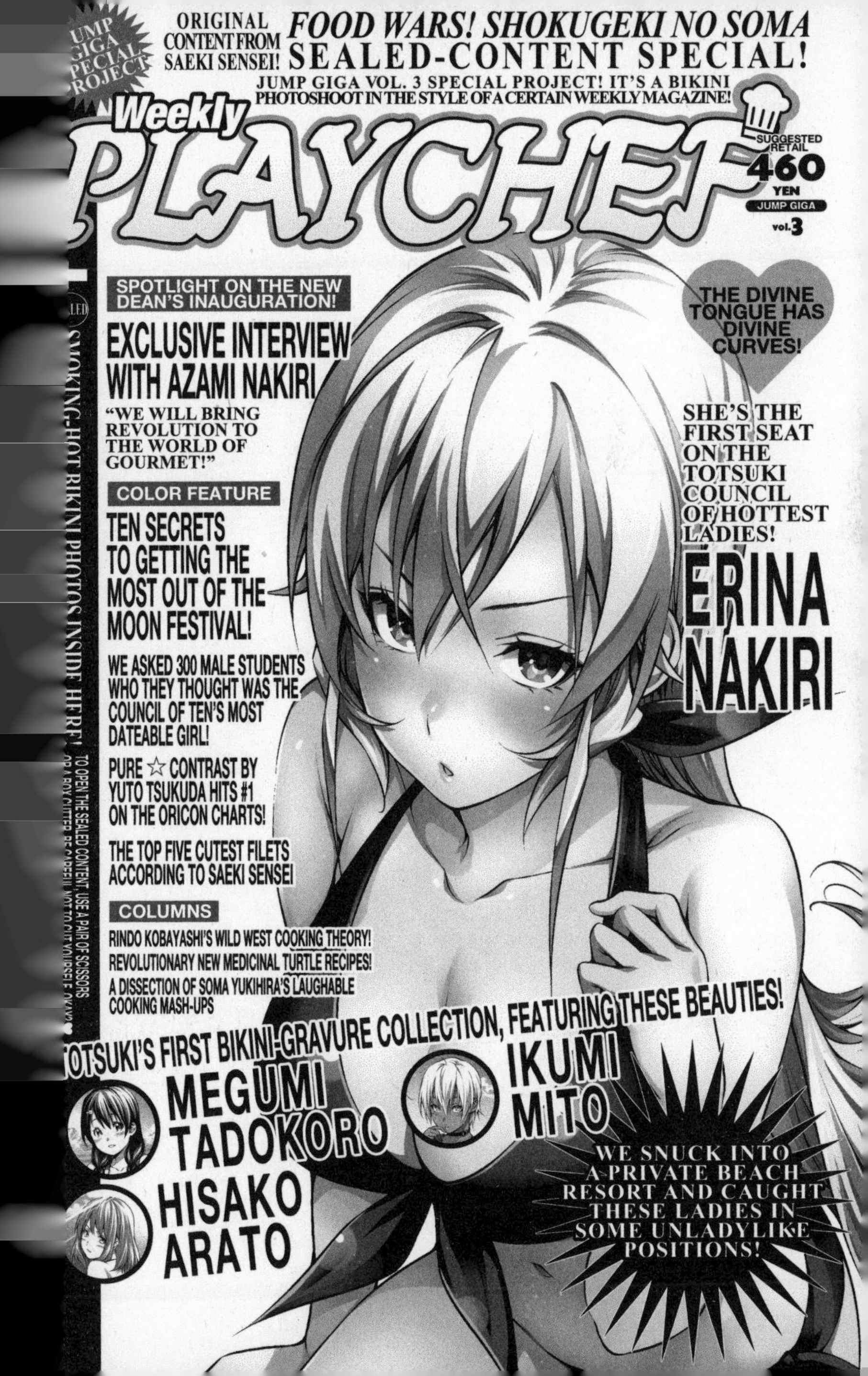

JUMP GIGA
ORIGINAL CONTENT FROM SAEKI SENSEI!
FOOD WARS! SHOKUGEKI NO SOMA
SEALED-CONTENT SPECIAL!
JUMP GIGA VOL. 3 SPECIAL PROJECT! IT'S A BIKINI PHOTOSHOOT IN THE STYLE OF A CERTAIN WEEKLY MAGAZINE!
Weekly PLAYCHEF
SUGGESTED RETAIL 460 YEN
JUMP GIGA vol.3
SMOKING-HOT BIKINI PHOTOS INSIDE HERE!
TO OPEN THE SEALED CONTENT, USE A PAIR OF SCISSORS
SPOTLIGHT ON THE NEW DEAN'S INAUGURATION!
EXCLUSIVE INTERVIEW WITH AZAMI NAKIRI
"WE WILL BRING REVOLUTION TO THE WORLD OF GOURMET!"
COLOR FEATURE
TEN SECRETS TO GETTING THE MOST OUT OF THE MOON FESTIVAL!
WE ASKED 300 MALE STUDENTS WHO THEY THOUGHT WAS THE COUNCIL OF TEN'S MOST DATEABLE GIRL!
PURE ☆ CONTRAST BY YUTO TSUKUDA HITS #1 ON THE ORICON CHARTS!
THE TOP FIVE CUTEST FILETS ACCORDING TO SAEKI SENSEI
COLUMNS
RINDO KOBAYASHI'S WILD WEST COOKING THEORY!
REVOLUTIONARY NEW MEDICINAL TURTLE RECIPES!
A DISSECTION OF SOMA YUKIHIRA'S LAUGHABLE COOKING MASH-UPS
THE DIVINE TONGUE HAS DIVINE CURVES!
SHE'S THE FIRST SEAT ON THE TOTSUKI COUNCIL OF HOTTEST LADIES!
ERINA NAKIRI
TOTSUKI'S FIRST BIKINI-GRAVURE COLLECTION, FEATURING THESE BEAUTIES!
MEGUMI TADOKORO
IKUMI MITO
HISAKO ARATO
WE SNUCK INTO A PRIVATE BEACH RESORT AND CAUGHT THESE LADIES IN SOME UNLADYLIKE POSITIONS!

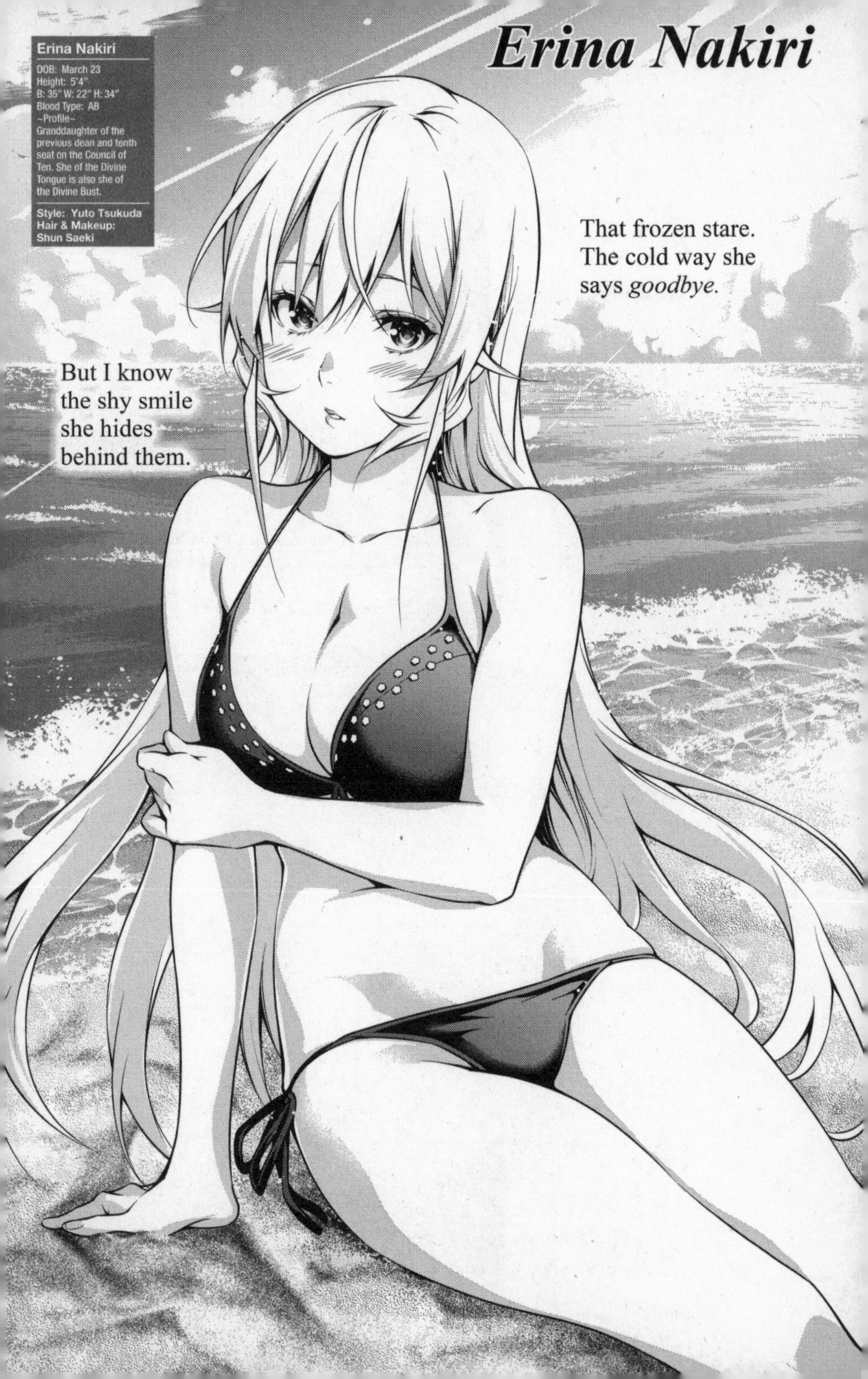
Erina Nakiri
Erina Nakiri
DOB: March 23
Height: 5'4"
B: 35" W: 22" H: 34"
Blood Type: AB
~Profile~
Granddaughter of the previous dean and tenth seat on the Council of Ten. She of the Divine Tongue is also she of the Divine Bust.
Style: Yuto Tsukuda
Hair & Makeup: Shun Saeki
That frozen stare. The cold way she says *goodbye.*
But I know the shy smile she hides behind them.

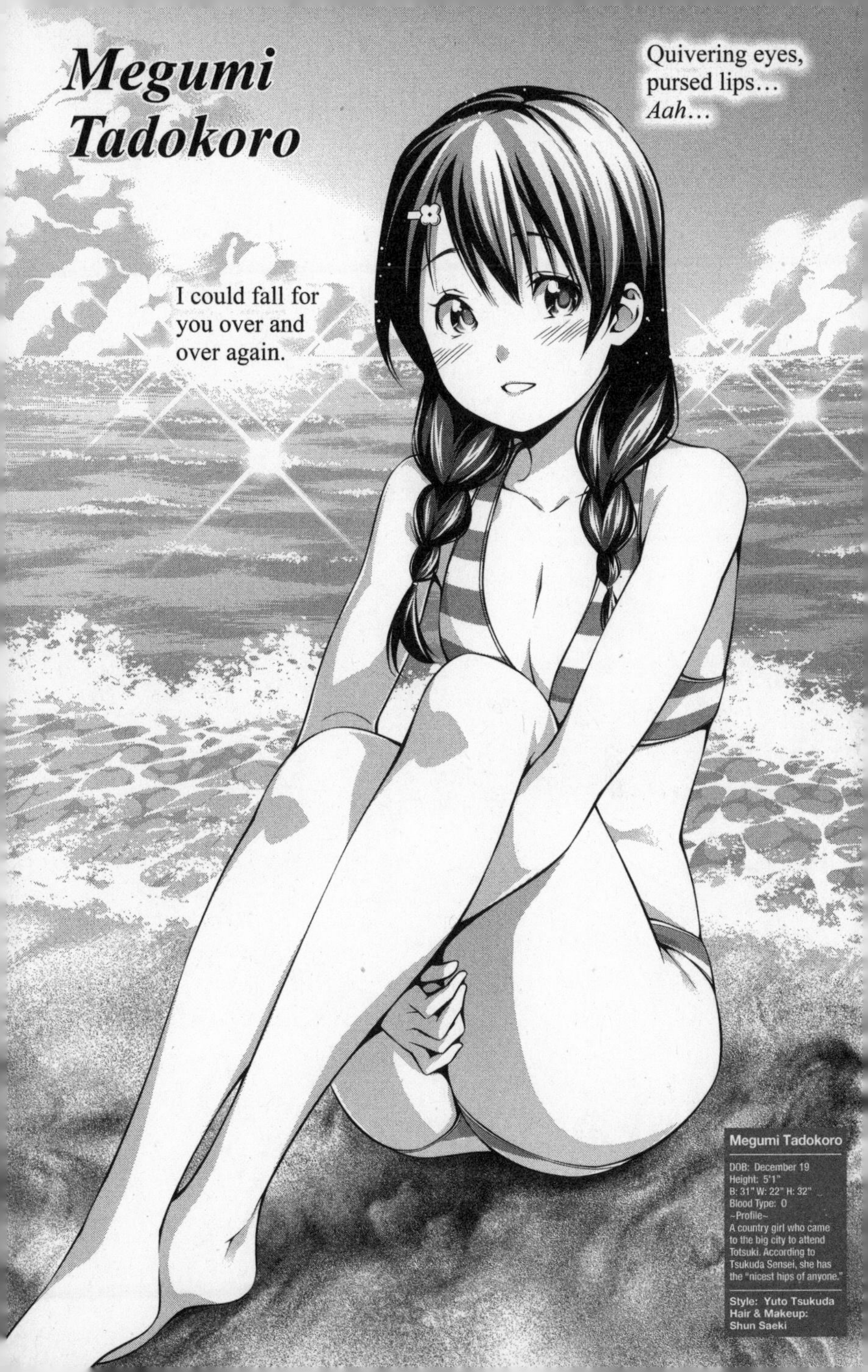

Megumi Tadokoro
Quivering eyes, pursed lips… *Aah*…
I could fall for you over and over again.
Megumi Tadokoro
DOB: December 19
Height: 5'1"
B: 31" W: 22" H: 32"
Blood Type: O
~Profile~
A country girl who came to the big city to attend Totsuki. According to Tsukuda Sensei, she has the "nicest hips of anyone."
Style: Yuto Tsukuda
Hair & Makeup: Shun Saeki

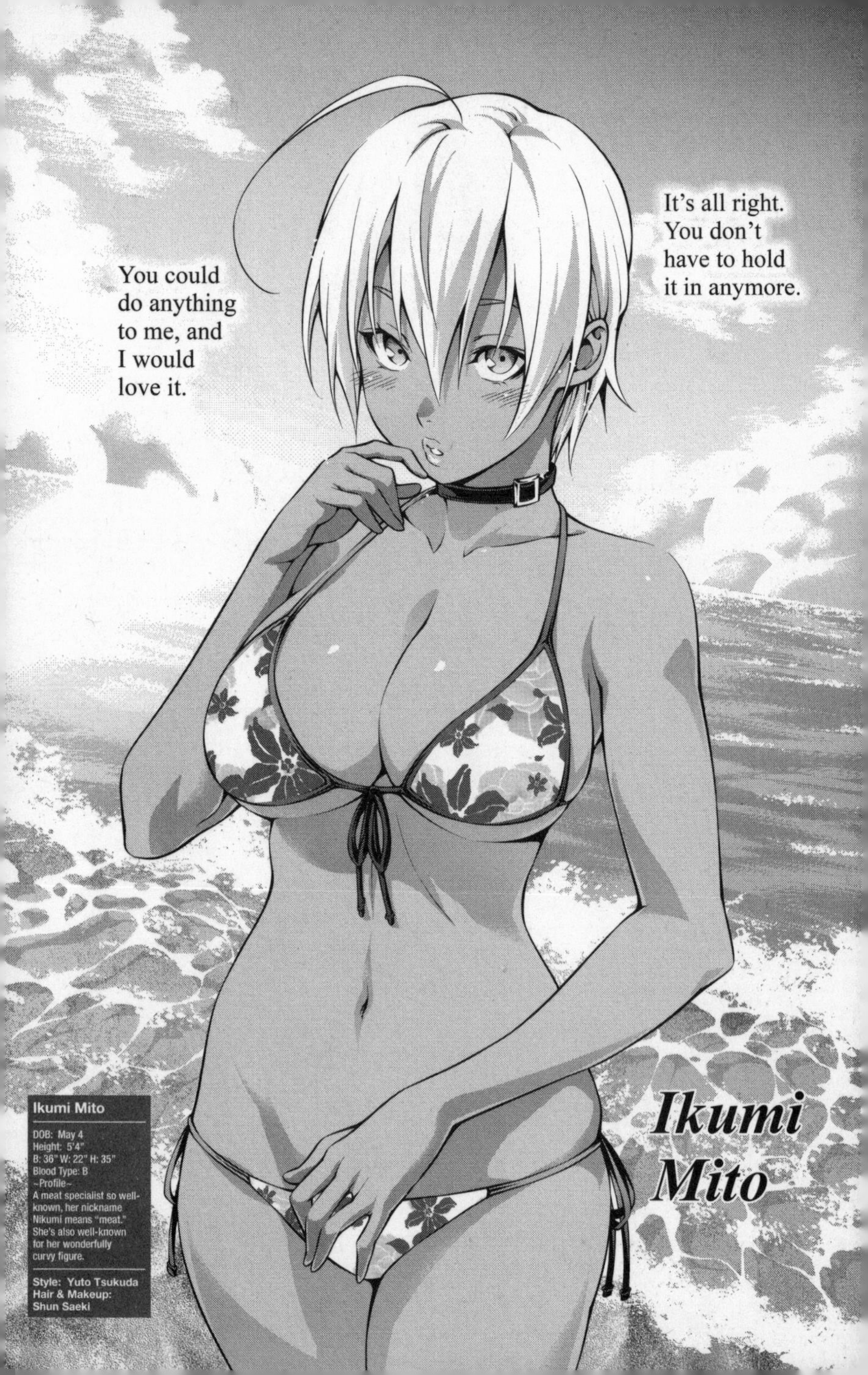
It's all right. You don't have to hold it in anymore.
You could do anything to me, and I would love it.
Ikumi Mito
Ikumi Mito
DOB: May 4
Height: 5'4"
B: 36" W: 22" H: 35"
Blood Type: B
~Profile~
A meat specialist so well-known, her nickname Nikumi means "meat." She's also well-known for her wonderfully curvy figure.
Style: Yuto Tsukuda
Hair & Makeup: Shun Saeki

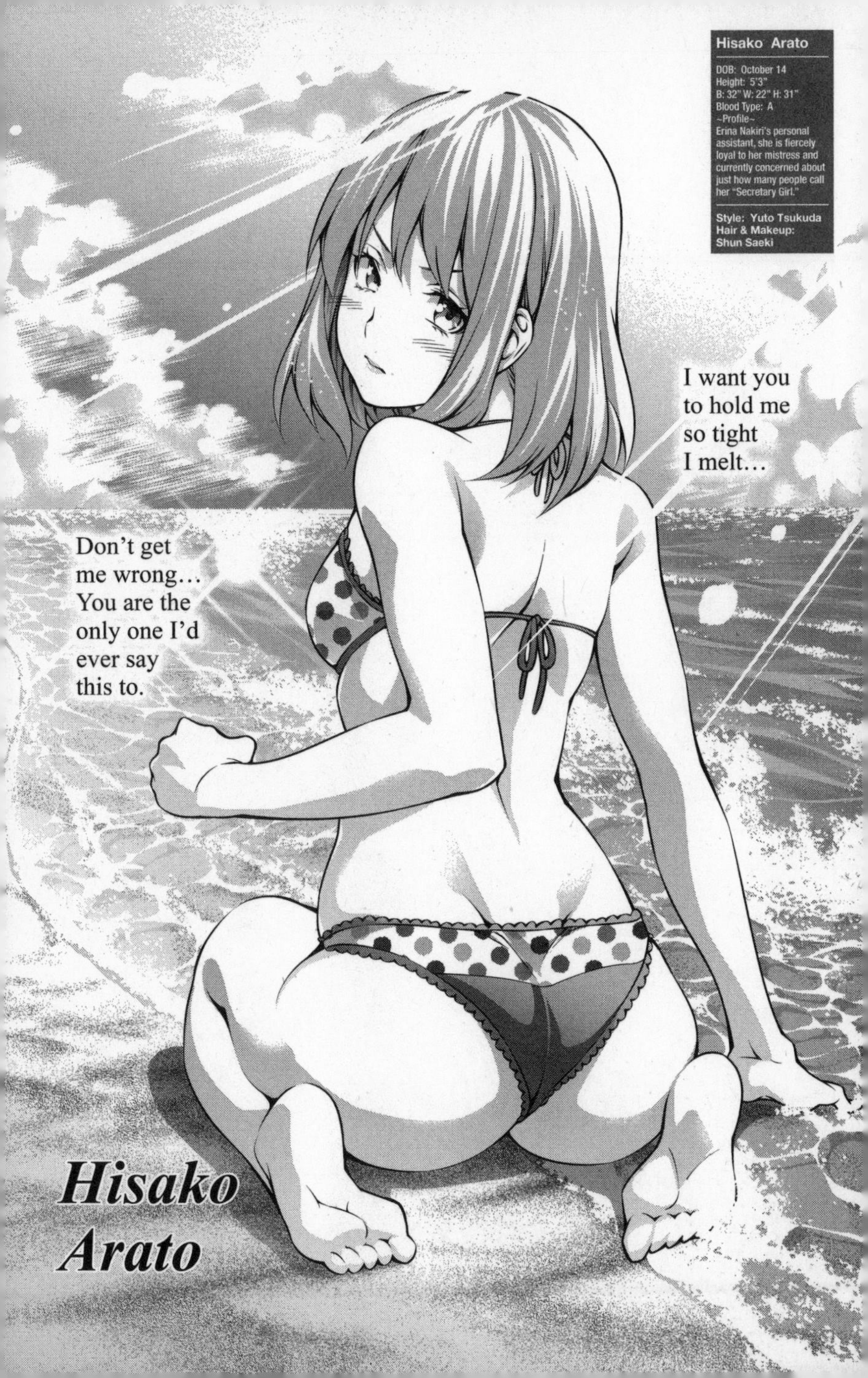
Hisako Arato
DOB: October 14
Height: 5'3"
B: 32" W: 22" H: 31"
Blood Type: A
~Profile~
Erina Nakiri's personal assistant, she is fiercely loyal to her mistress and currently concerned about just how many people call her "Secretary Girl."
Style: Yuto Tsukuda
Hair & Makeup: Shun Saeki
I want you to hold me so tight I melt…
Don't get me wrong… You are the only one I'd ever say this to.
Hisako Arato

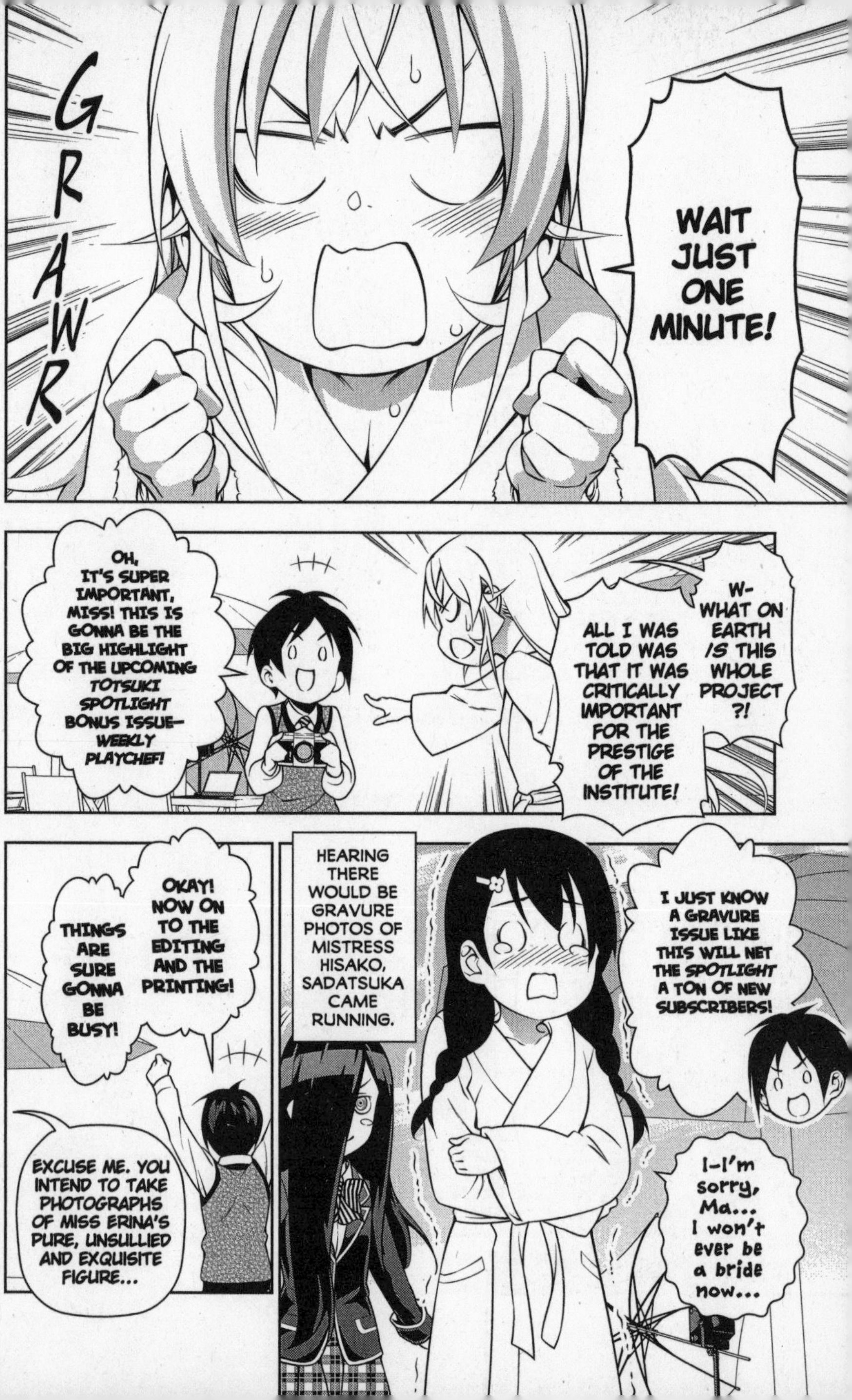
WAIT JUST ONE MINUTE!
GRAWR
W- WHAT ON EARTH IS THIS WHOLE PROJECT?!
ALL I WAS TOLD WAS THAT IT WAS CRITICALLY IMPORTANT FOR THE PRESTIGE OF THE INSTITUTE!
OH, IT'S SUPER IMPORTANT, MISS! THIS IS GONNA BE THE BIG HIGHLIGHT OF THE UPCOMING TOTSUKI SPOTLIGHT BONUS ISSUE—WEEKLY PLAYCHEF!
I JUST KNOW A GRAVURE ISSUE LIKE THIS WILL NET THE SPOTLIGHT A TON OF NEW SUBSCRIBERS!
HEARING THERE WOULD BE GRAVURE PHOTOS OF MISTRESS HISAKO, SADATSUKA CAME RUNNING.
I-I'm sorry, Ma... I won't ever be a bride now...
OKAY! NOW ON TO THE EDITING AND THE PRINTING!
THINGS ARE SURE GONNA BE BUSY!
EXCUSE ME. YOU INTEND TO TAKE PHOTOGRAPHS OF MISS ERINA'S PURE, UNSULLIED AND EXQUISITE FIGURE...

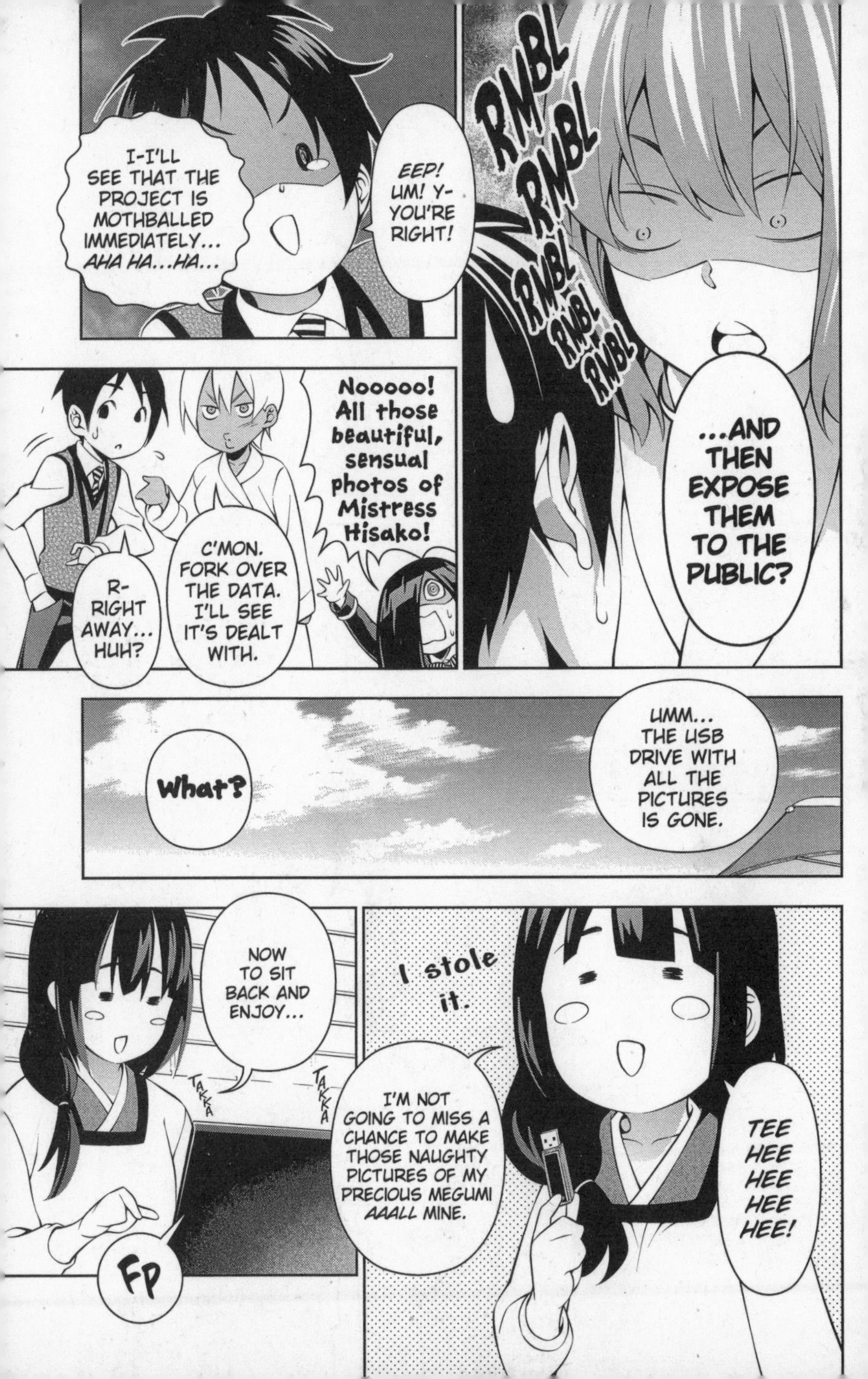
RMBL RMBL RMBL RMBL RMBL RMBL RMBL
...AND THEN EXPOSE THEM TO THE PUBLIC?
EEP! UM! Y-YOU'RE RIGHT!
I-I'LL SEE THAT THE PROJECT IS MOTHBALLED IMMEDIATELY... AHA HA...HA...
Nooooo! All those beautiful, sensual photos of Mistress Hisako!
C'MON. FORK OVER THE DATA. I'LL SEE IT'S DEALT WITH.
R-RIGHT AWAY... HUH?
UMM... THE USB DRIVE WITH ALL THE PICTURES IS GONE.
What?
TEE HEE HEE HEE HEE!
I stole it.
I'M NOT GOING TO MISS A CHANCE TO MAKE THOSE NAUGHTY PICTURES OF MY PRECIOUS MEGUMI AAALL MINE.
NOW TO SIT BACK AND ENJOY...
TAKKA
TAKKA
Fp

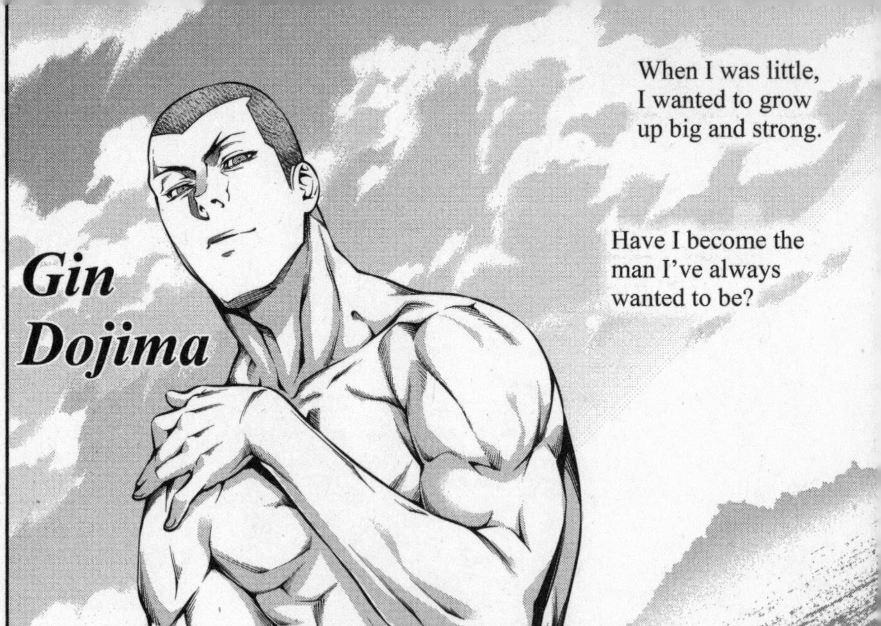
When I was little, I wanted to grow up big and strong.
Have I become the man I've always wanted to be?
Gin Dojima
Gin Dojima
DOB: April 3
Height: 6'2"
B: 50" W: 36" H: 43"
Blood Type: A
~Profile~
Head chef of the entire Totsuki Resort Hotels chain, he's in charge of all cooking done on their premises. He keeps a daily stretching and workout routine.
Style: Yuto Tsukuda
Hair & Makeup:
Shun Saeki

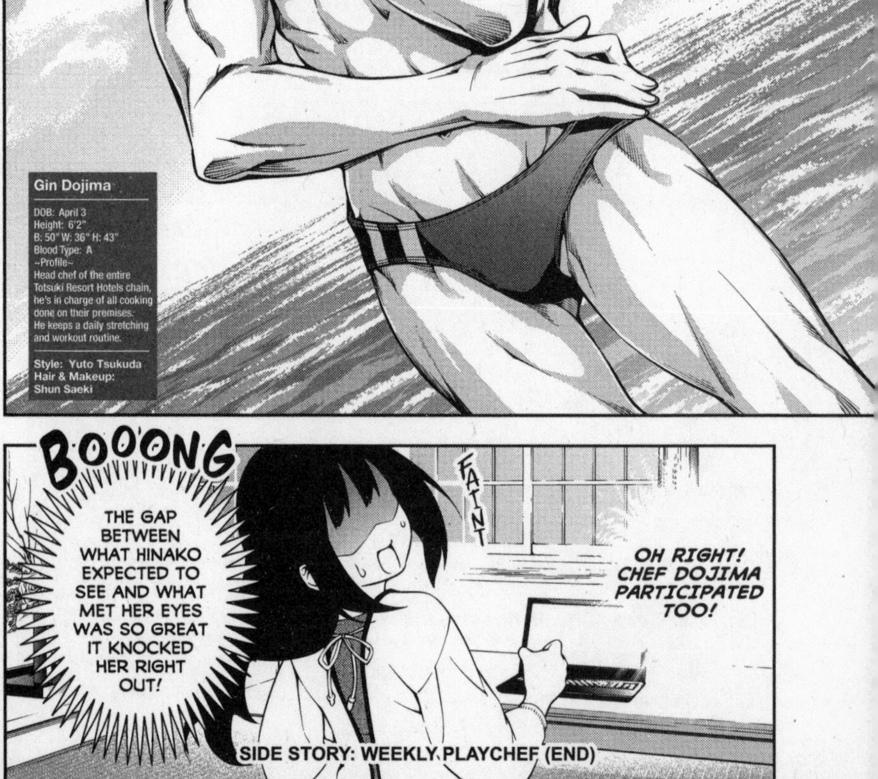
FAINT
OH RIGHT! CHEF DOJIMA PARTICIPATED TOO!
BOOONG
THE GAP BETWEEN WHAT HINAKO EXPECTED TO SEE AND WHAT MET HER EYES WAS SO GREAT IT KNOCKED HER RIGHT OUT!
SIDE STORY: WEEKLY PLAYCHEF (END)

Food Wars! Shokugeki no Soma

FIRST (PROBABLY)

VOLUME 23 SUPER-SPECIAL SUPPLEMENT

CHARACTER PROFILES

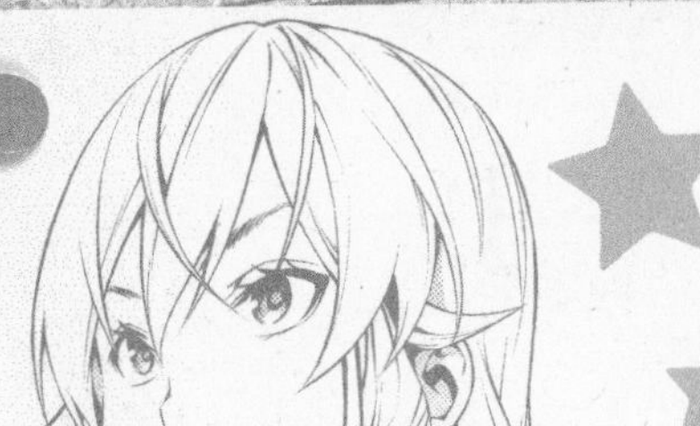

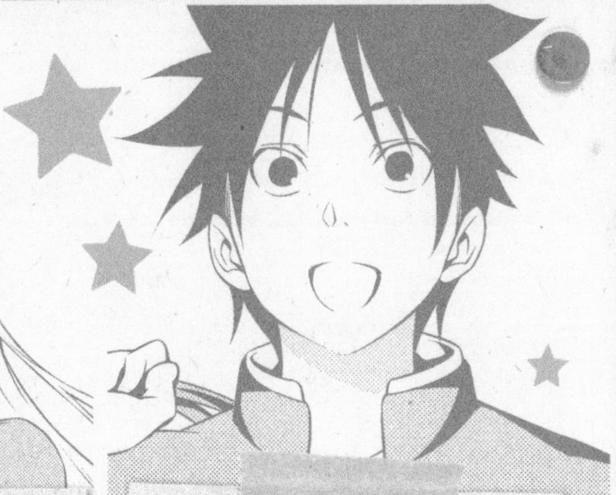

ERINA NAKIRI

BIRTHDAY: MARCH 23

BLOOD TYPE: AB

HEIGHT: 5'4"

FAVORITE SONG: "AMARYLLIS"

FAVORITE GAME: CARDS (ESPECIALLY SEVENS)

SOMA YUKIHIRA

BIRTHDAY: NOVEMBER 6

BLOOD TYPE: B

HEIGHT: 5'7" (AS OF COMMENCEMENT)

FAVORITE HOUSEHOLD CHORE: LAUNDRY

FAVORITE ACCOMMODATION: A BIG BATHTUB

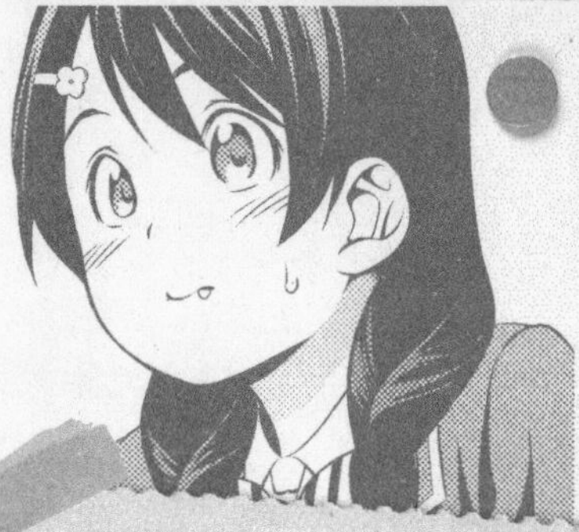

MEGUMI TADOKORO

BIRTHDAY: DECEMBER 19

BLOOD TYPE: O

HEIGHT: 5'1"

FAVORITE BOOK: *RUDOLF THE BLACK CAT*

FAVORITE SPORT: PING-PONG

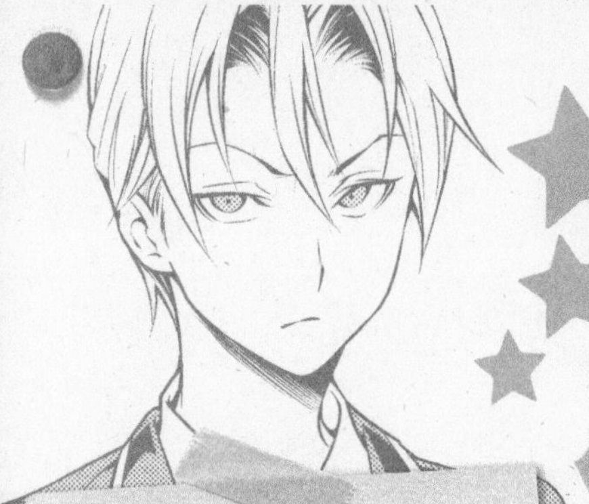

TAKUMI ALDINI

BIRTHDAY: JULY 19

BLOOD TYPE: A

HEIGHT: 5'6" (AS OF COMMENCEMENT)

FAVORITE LEISURE ACTIVITY: VISITING ART MUSEUMS

PREFERRED TYPE: A GRACEFUL, ELEGANT WOMAN

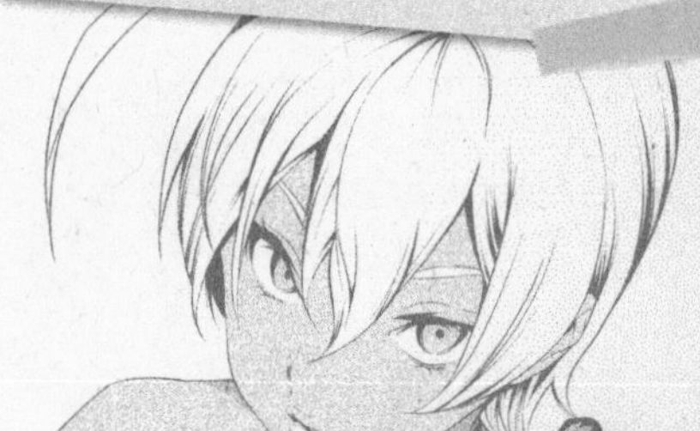

IKUMI MITO

BIRTHDAY: MAY 4

BLOOD TYPE: B

HEIGHT: 5'4"

FAVORITE BOOK: *THE LITTLE PRINCE*

FAVORITE LEISURE ACTIVITY: (BELIEVE IT OR NOT) BAKING SWEETS

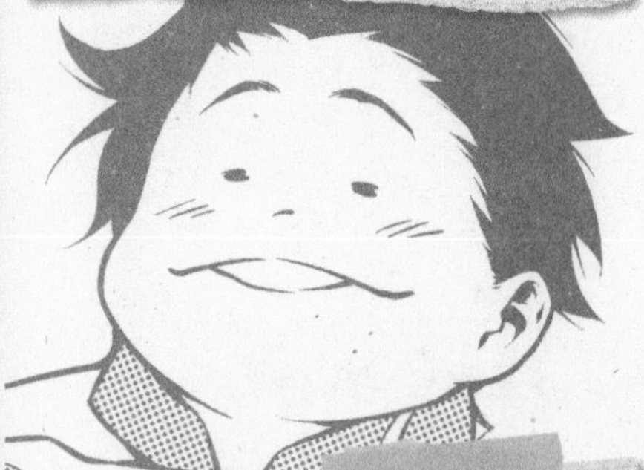

ISAMI ALDINI

BIRTHDAY: JULY 19

BLOOD TYPE: O

HEIGHT: 6'0"

FAVORITE HOBBY: TEASING TAKUMI

PREFERRED TYPE: A GIRL WHO IS RELAXING AND COMFORTABLE TO BE AROUND

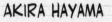

HISAKO ARATO

BIRTHDAY: OCTOBER 14

BLOOD TYPE: A

HEIGHT: 5'3"

FAVORITE MOVIE: *ROMAN HOLIDAY*

FAVORITE LEISURE ACTIVITY: BUYING AND SAMPLING RARE TEAS

AKIRA HAYAMA

BIRTHDAY: UNKNOWN (JUN DECLARED IT'S JULY 7)

BLOOD TYPE: A

HEIGHT: 5'10"

FAVORITE DRINK: COFFEE

FAVORITE LEISURE ACTIVITY: GOING TO THE MARKET ON HIS SCOOTER

ALICE NAKIRI

BIRTHDAY: JANUARY 23

BLOOD TYPE: O

HEIGHT: 5'5"

FAVORITE SPORT: ICE SKATING

FAVORITE DAILY ACTIVITY: WRITING IN HER DIARY

RYO KUROKIBA

BIRTHDAY: AUGUST 20

BLOOD TYPE: O

HEIGHT: 5'10"

FAVORITE DAILY ACTIVITY: WORKING OUT

FAVORITE LEISURE ACTIVITY: FISHING

You're Reading in the Wrong Direction!!

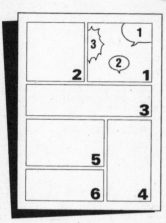

Whoops! Guess what? You're starting at the wrong end of the comic!

...It's true! In keeping with the original Japanese format, **Food Wars!** is meant to be read from right to left, starting in the upper-right corner.

Unlike English, which is read from left to right, Japanese is read from right to left, meaning that action, sound effects and word-balloon order are completely reversed... something which can make readers unfamiliar with Japanese feel pretty backwards themselves. For this reason, manga or Japanese comics published in the U.S. in English have sometimes been published "flopped"—that is, printed in exact reverse order, as though seen from the other side of a mirror.

By flopping pages, U.S. publishers can avoid confusing readers, but the compromise is not without its downside. For one thing, a character in a flopped manga series who once wore in the original Japanese version a T-shirt emblazoned with "M A Y" (as in "the merry month of") now wears one which reads "Y A M"! Additionally, many manga creators in Japan are themselves unhappy with the process, as some feel the mirror-imaging of their art skews their original intentions.

We are proud to bring you Yuto Tsukuda and Shun Saeki's **Food Wars!** in the original unflopped format.

For now, though, turn to the other side of the book and let the adventure begin...!

—Editor